The McGraw-Hill Children's Thesaurus

By the Wordsmyth Collaboratory

The Wordsmyth Reference Series

McGraw-Hill Children's Publishing
A Division of The McGraw-Hill Companies

 Children's Publishing

Columbus, Ohio

 **Children's Publishing**

Library of Congress Cataloging-in-Publication Data on file with the publisher.

Send all inquiries to:
McGraw-Hill Children's Publishing
8787 Orion Place
Columbus, Ohio 43240
www.MHkids.com

ISBN 1-57768-296-3

4 5 6 7 8 9 WAL 08 07 06 05 04

Manufactured in the United States of America.

Table of Contents

Look for special **Graphic Features** at these entry words!
Advertisement • Body • Boat • Building • Celebration • Clothing • Colors
Dance • Dog • Emotion • Entrance • Garden • Insect • Life
Mollusk • Mountain • Music • Sport • Tree • Water

Wordsmyth Collaboratory Staff

Director
Robert Q. Parks, Ph.D.

Editorial Director
Jean V. Callahan, Ph.D.

Information Architect
Aaron Weiss

Art Director
Jen Gage Sage

Senior Editor
Jan Douglas

Editors
Gabriel Tavares, Joan Patrick

Coordinator
Meredith Elaine Wilson

Writers
Michelle Mason, Barth Myers

Book Design
Brian Dudla

Art Team
Christian Wheeler, Keren Cohen

Illustration
Keren Cohen, Jim Houghton, J. M. Barringer,
Robert (Mac) Myers, Chris Jung, Brian Dudla

Photography
Douglas J. Davenport

McGraw-Hill Children's Thesaurus Team

President
Vincent F. Douglas

Publisher
Tracey E. Dils

Editor
Janet D. Sweet

Art Director
Robert Sanford

Designer
Jennifer Bowers

Production Manager
Diane Yarman

Wordsmyth would also like to acknowledge the important contributions of staff members who worked on earlier versions of the Wordsmyth database.

For a listing of staff for the Wordsmyth Educational Dictionary-Thesaurus and our electronic resources, visit our Web site at www.wordsmyth.net.

We wish to acknowledge the assistance of the children who gave their honest and helpful reactions to this thesaurus as it was being written.

Preface

The McGraw-Hill Children's Thesaurus is designed to help the young reader build a vocabulary that is expressive, versatile, and precise. The ample illustration of word usage in lively example sentences will attract young writers to the challenge of saying something well. Usage and writing tips, memorable quotations linked to specific entries, and thoughtful graphic presentation of entries and pictures, work together to enhance the thesaurus content.

The Wordsmyth Word Explorer provides a distinctive point of entry into the content of the thesaurus. Many entry words in the thesaurus have been assigned to topic categories and marked with topic icons. This allows children to search for words connected by a broad category, or to choose one word in a category and explore that word's special subset of related words.

Language is a powerful tool for communication and learning. Enjoy using your McGraw-Hill Children's Thesaurus to embark on an exploration of our language.

What Is a Thesaurus and Why Does a Writer Use One? •••

Next to a dictionary, a thesaurus is the most widely used kind of word book. Most good writers own a dictionary and a thesaurus, or know where to find them in the library. Why is a thesaurus so important to writers and speakers of the English language?

A simple answer to this question is that a thesaurus helps you find the best words for what you are trying to say. People look up a word in a *dictionary* to find information about the word, such as its meaning, spelling, or pronunciation. People look up a word in a *thesaurus* in order to find other words that mean the same, or almost the same, thing. Words that have the same meaning, or almost the same meaning, are called **synonyms**.

The English language is rich in synonyms, in part because of its history. It is full of words that originated in other languages. Often we have three words that mean the same thing because one has come from Latin, one from Greek, and one from Anglo-Saxon (or

entry word	**anger** ⊙
part of speech	*noun*
definition	a strong emotion brought on by a person or thing that causes one great pain or trouble
headword example	*His cruelty filled me with anger.*
synonyms	fury, rage, wrath, outrage, indignance, temper
usage note	Use **fury** or **rage** when referring to *extreme* anger. Use **wrath** if you are writing of a great anger that should be respected or feared.
part of speech	*verb*
	1 to cause anger in; make angry *The speaker's words angered the crowd.*
synonyms	enrage, infuriate, madden, outrage, incense, antagonize, bait, offend, irritate, provoke, incite, make one's blood boil, raise the hackles of
usage note	**Bait, incite,** and **provoke** mean to *try* to make someone angry, as though you were dangling a steak in front of a dog: *Butch Biggs likes to bait me by calling me names, but I just ignore him.*
	2 to become angry *Name-calling angers me.* *He doesn't anger easily.*
synonyms	fume, steam, seethe, explode, bristle, lose one's temper, fly off the handle, blow up
word explorer note	*Some things that angry people do:* argue, bawl out, frown, glare, grimace, growl, roar, scowl, scream, snap, snarl, sputter, stamp, sulk, swear, yell
antonyms	*Antonyms:* appease (1), calm (1)
related entries	*See also:* annoy, upset

Old English). For example, the trio of words **clean** (Old English), **sanitary** (Latin), and **hygienic** (Greek) are synonyms.

You may be wondering why one would want to use a different word to say exactly the same thing. If you reread the definition of synonym above, you will notice that it says synonyms "have the same meaning, or *almost the same* meaning." When it comes to word choice, sometimes a small difference in meaning can make a big difference in how successfully you communicate.

For example, **carry** and **walk** are perfectly correct words to use in this sentence: *Katie carried the sack of dog food up the front steps and walked into the kitchen with it*. But is this really what you saw? Using a synonym for **carry** and a synonym for **walk** can make the image sharper: *Katie lugged the sack of dog food up the front steps and staggered into the kitchen with it*. The word **lug** works better here because it means to carry with great effort, and **stagger** works better because it means to walk unsteadily. Not only can an apt word choice make your writing more vivid to your reader, it can also make writing truer and the writing process more enjoyable.

Let's consider another example. Nancy, an invented character, will illustrate how choosing the wrong synonyms can affect communication. Nancy is excited because her aunt, a famous, prize-winning chemist, has invited Nancy and Nancy's friend Phillip to visit her chemistry laboratory. Nancy knocks on Phillip's door and Phillip's dad answers. Nancy tells him, "My notorious aunt is loitering outside, and wants to take Phillip to her laboratory." Now, it would not be surprising if Phillip's dad, on hearing this, decided that Phillip should not go along. Phillip's dad may know that **notorious** means "famous for doing something bad" and that **loiter** means "to stand around in a suspicious or idle way." Here Nancy's use of synonyms for **famous** and **wait** makes a big difference in how her message is received.

The point of using a thesaurus is not simply to find a different word (or a longer word, or a fancier word), but to choose a better word for what you are trying to say.

Getting to Know This Thesaurus • • •

Navigating the Thesaurus: Finding Entry Words

Each page in the thesaurus has two columns. The words you look up in this thesaurus, the *entry words*, are listed in alphabetical order. They are easy to scan because they are printed in large black type and appear on the lefthand side of each column. To get to the part of the book that has the word you are looking for, use the *guide words* that

palm – party

appear in the blue banner that runs across the top of each page. The guide words tell you what the first and last entry word on a page are.

Parts of a Thesaurus Entry

The entry word is followed by the *entry* itself. The example below shows you what you will see when you look up the word **part.** The synonyms are easy to find; they are the words in bright blue type.

You will notice that there is more information in this entry for **part** than just synonyms.

The word in *red italic type* tells you the ***part of speech*** of the entry word and its synonyms.

After the part of speech comes the ***definition*** (or definitions) of the entry word. Each definition is followed by an ***example sentence*** in *black italic type*, and below that, the synonyms that go with this definition.

The definition and example sentence give you more information about the meaning and use of the entry word. The more you know about the entry word, the more you can be sure you really want a synonym in that neighborhood, and the more likely you are to find the word you want.

This information is especially useful when more than one definition is given for an entry word. When an entry word has more than one definition, each different meaning of the word has its own list of synonyms.

When an entry word has more than one part of speech, definitions, examples, and synonyms are grouped by the part of speech. The entry for **part** has definitions, examples, and synonyms for the noun and for the verb. Notice how different the synonyms can be for two different senses of the same word.

At the very end of an entry, you may notice the phrase *See also*, followed by one or more words. You can look up the entries for these words to find more synonyms related to the entry word you are at now. What related entry is listed at the end of the entry for **part**?

part
noun
   1 a separate piece of a whole
    That store sells car and truck parts.
    I live in an old part of town.
  component, piece, section, portion, member, segment, branch, constituent

   2 an important basic characteristic
    Hard work was a large part of her success.
  feature, element, ingredient, aspect, characteristic, component

   3 share; duty
    Did you have a part in making this mess?
  share, hand, duty, obligation

   Antonym: whole (1)
verb
   to separate one from another
    They shook hands and parted as friends.
  depart, leave, separate, go, split

   See also: piece

Antonyms

Many entries in this thesaurus also give *antonyms*. Antonyms are words which mean the opposite of each other. **Big** and **little** are antonyms, as are **rough** and **smooth**, **gloomy** and **sunny**, **wild** and **tame**, **praise** and **blame**, **noble** and **base**, **hero** and **villain**.

Antonyms for an entry word are listed after the word *Antonyms* (in purple type) at the end of the part of speech to which they are relevant. Some antonyms are followed by a number in parentheses. This number refers to the *definition number*. Look for the word "antonyms" in the entry for **lift**. Try to match each definition of **lift** with the antonym that means its opposite.

lift
verb

1 to bring upward
Mandy lifted her cat off the table.
elevate, raise, boost, hoist, pick up

2 to move higher
The hot air balloon lifted into the sky.
arise, ascend, climb, rise

3 to end, cancel, or take back
The city lifted its ban on skateboarding.
end, revoke, withdraw, call off, cancel

Antonyms: drop (1), enact (3), sink (2)

noun

a machine used for raising or carrying
They rode up the mountain on the ski lift.
crane, derrick, elevator, escalator, hoist

See also: raise, rise

More About Synonyms

Sometimes the synonyms in an entry are listed not in a row but in a column. Next to each synonym is a sentence in *italic type*. This is an example sentence for the synonym. Synonym example sentences illustrate the typical way each synonym is used in a sentence. In this way they can help you choose the best word for your purposes. Try comparing the sentence you are writing with each of the synonym example sentences. The closer the example sentence is to yours, the more likely it is you should choose that synonym.

Imagine that you have written this sentence: *Americans use too much electricity.* You have used the word "use" too often already in your essay and want to find a synonym for it. Which example sentence in the entry for **use** is most like your sentence?

use
verb

to spend
He used his last dollar to buy some bread.
consume *That old car consumes a lot of fuel.*
spend *He spent his energy on the tasks that interested him.*
apply *Jane applied her knowledge of math in solving the problem.*

noun

1 the act or practice of using
We made use of wood for heating this year.
application, employment, usage

2 benefit
There is no use in fighting.
advantage, benefit, profit, usefulness, value, worth, gain, point

3 purpose
This machine has many uses.
function, purpose, application

Special Features • • •

Usage Tips

Some sets of synonyms are followed by a *Usage Tip*. These guide you toward an intelligent choice of synonyms and steer you away from mistakes in word choice. These tips appear against a yellow background within an entry.

Use **notorious** when writing or speaking about a person or thing that is famous only because of something bad: *Jesse James was a notorious outlaw.*

The Usage Tips point out differences in meaning among synonyms, but also other kinds of differences. Even if two words have exactly the same definition, they may not be equally effective choices for a particular occasion. One word may have the right effect if you use it in conversation or e-mail with friends and the wrong effect if you use it in an essay or presentation at school. Like your choice of an outfit, your choice of word has to fit the occasion. The Usage Tips point out synonyms that are considered *informal*, which means they are commonly used in everyday conversation and personal writing but are thought to be out of place in school writing. The White House correspondent for a major newspaper would probably not write in a lead article, *The prez looked beat when he came out of the talks with the prime minister of Mysteria.* **Beat** is considered an informal expression for **tired**. A reporter does not want to sound chatty or personal—or disrespectful. Probably the reporter would write, *The president appeared fatigued when he emerged from negotiations with the prime minister of Mysteria.*

Word Explorer

In certain entries in this thesaurus, you will see boxes with a pale green background. This is the *Word Explorer feature*. Sometimes the word you have in mind when you reach for your thesaurus has no synonyms. It may be a concrete noun like **dog,** or a topic, such as **photography** or **physics** or **electricity.** You may not even need synonyms for these words, but to research or write about them, you still need to know more words that are related. These are some of the situations in which the Word Explorer boxes might be just what you are looking for. The Word Explorer boxes offer sets of words related to the entry word that are neither synonyms nor antonyms.

photography
noun
    the art or practice of taking and making photographs

> *some words related to photography*
>   copy, crop, develop, distort, enlarge,
>   expose, film, filter, focus, mount, pose,
>   print, project, sit
> *some words that describe photographs*
>   action, aerial, close-up, digital, landscape,
>   panoramic, remote, satellite, still,
>   underwater

Each set of words has a heading in *italic type* that explains what the relationship is between the entry word and the word set.

Writing Tips

Writing Tips appear in a box against a light purple background. They offer suggestions for how to use this thesaurus to enliven your writing. Browse through the book to find tips on how to choose adjectives, how to create emphasis in your writing, and more.

> ### Writing Tip: Nouns to Adjectives, Adjectives to Nouns
>
> There are many related nouns and adjectives in English. One common pattern of noun-adjective pairs is shown below. The nouns end in *–ance* or *–ence* and the corresponding adjectives end in *–ant* or *–ent*. The noun names a specific quality, and the adjective is used to describe something that has this quality. For example, *importance* is the quality of having great meaning or value and *important* is used to describe something that has the quality of importance. *The music of Bali has great importance in my life. It is very important to me.* Below are some common noun-adjective pairs that fit this pattern.
>
> importance—important
>
> significance—significant
>
> magnificence—magnificent
>
> independence—independent
>
> resistant—resistance
>
> elegant—elegance
>
> ignorant—ignorance

Quotations

As you leaf through your thesaurus, you will see text with the outline of an orange box around it. These are *quotations*. A quotation is a snippet of something that someone has said or written. Usually a quotation is an especially memorable snippet, because of what was said or how it was said.

Each quotation in this thesaurus uses an entry word or a synonym. The illustrated word is highlighted in **bold type**. Unlike the example sentences found inside an entry, which show you a typical use of a word, the quotations often have been chosen to make you think more about what a word means or show you an imaginative, dramatic, or surprising way of using a word.

Each quotation has an ***attribution*** at the end. The attribution may include the name of the work the quotation is from, the kind of work it is (poem, play, or novel), and who wrote or said it, as well as the birth and death dates of the author.

praise
noun

words that show admiration or respect
The dog received praise for doing a trick.
compliment, acclaim, approval, honor, recognition, applause, flattery, reverence

> We refuse **praise** in order to be praised twice.
> —Francois, Duc De La Rochefoucauld (1613-1680), French author

verb

1 to speak well of
The coach praised the players for their hard work.
commend, compliment, cite, acclaim, congratulate, salute, celebrate, hail, applaud, flatter

2 to honor with words or song
The poet praises human nature in this poem.
glorify, exalt, worship, hymn

Illustrations

The illustrations in this thesaurus will certainly amuse and intrigue you as images. But to get the most out of the illustrations, it is important to know that each appears next to the headword or synonym it illustrates. Furthermore, each picture illustrates a sentence from the entry, either an example sentence or a special caption sentence. Illustrated sentences are in *purple type*. Caption sentences appear in italics just below the list of synonyms. In their own way, the illustrations provide information about word usage, because they show you the picture suggested by a specific sentence.

dramatic
adjective

out of the ordinary
Spring brought a dramatic change in the weather.
impressive, showy, exciting, sensational, conspicuous

The new skyscraper is an impressive building.

Antonyms: everyday, mundane, ordinary

Sometimes one thesaurus entry is accompanied by two illustrations which capture the difference between two synonyms. Can you find the sentences in the entry for **dramatic** which are illustrated here?

Special graphics accompany some of the Word Explorer boxes. For example, the illustrations for **dog** and **emotion** include multiple images, each labelled with a word from the Word Explorer word group. This image of an **advertisement** is labelled with words from the Word Explorer entry for advertisement.

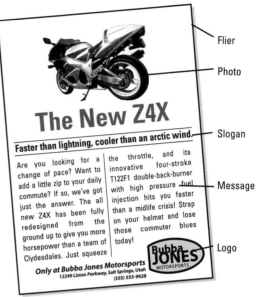

Advertisement

Navigating the Thesaurus • • •

Part Two: Cross-Reference Entries

There are two kinds of entry in this thesaurus: full entries and *cross-reference entries*. We have already looked at several full entries. Think of a full entry as your destination and a cross-reference entry as a crossroads that you come to when you are halfway to your destination.

When you arrive at a cross-reference entry, you find instructions on where to go next to find synonyms. Cross-reference entries point you to the full entry or entries that have synonyms of the word. They tell you to go to or "see" another entry.

For example, try looking up the word **machine**.   You will find an entry that looks like this:

machine See device

The entry word **machine** is followed by the word "*See*" and a cross-reference in blue type that tells you which entry in this thesaurus has synonyms for **machine**.

Some cross-reference entries are longer than the one for **machine**. Think of these as offering several choices of direction. For example, look up the word **project**, and you will find an entry that looks like this:

project See activity, work, photography

From this entry, you know that **activity** and **work** have full entries and that you should look up these words to find more synonyms for **project**. If there is more than one word in blue after the word "*See,*" choose the one closest to the meaning of the word "project" you are thinking of. Or, explore a new avenue, and look up one of the other words. The cross-reference word in green type tells you that the entry word (here, **project**) appears in a Word Explorer box under the entry word **photography**.

To read more about using the Word Explorer and for an *Index of Topics,* please turn the page.

Word Explorer
Index of Topics

Have you ever had an idea that you want to look up, but you don't know where to begin? The Index of Topics is a place where you can find related words on a number of broad topics. Each topic has its own icon, and the related words are marked throughout your thesaurus with the same icons. The Index of Topics is intended to suggest some starting points in your exploration of the English language. You can look up all of these words in your *McGraw-Hill Children's Dictionary* or *Children's Thesaurus* to find their definitions, synonyms, and other information.

The words that appear in **green** in the Index of Topics are entry words that have Word Explorer information in your thesaurus. This means that when you look up a green word, you will find even more related words that you can use to extend your research and improve your writing.

The Human Body

activity, animal, appearance, balance, **body**, breathe, child, **drug**, eat, energy, **exercise**, express, **face**, fat, feel, figure, **first aid**, fit, **foot**, grow, hair, **health**, **hygiene**, **injury**, kid, **life**, listen, look, mature, medicine, move, **nerve**, nose, physical, see, sick, sight, skin, sleep, smell, sport, stress, strong, swallow, taste, **tooth**, touch, wash, weak, wound

 ### The Human Mind

action, affection, afraid, agreement, **anger**, argue, **behavior**, **belief**, brave, **care**, character, clever, consider, courage, crazy, creative, decide, deliberate, desire, **emotion**, examine, exercise, express, **fear**, feel, feeling, grief, **happiness**, **hate**, honest, idea, imagination, interest, jealousy, joy, judge, **knowledge**, **learn**, lie, **love**, mad, matter, mean, memory, merry, **mind**, miserable, mood, mope, **moral**, nature, nerve, opinion, pain, **personality**, persuade, plan, play, reason, religion, remember, **sad**, **sadness**, scare, serious, stress, strong, study, sympathy, teach, temper, think, **thought**, train, trust, understand, upset, value, wise, worry, worship

Everyday Life

air, airplane, boat, building, clothes, community, cook, dress, drink, drive, family, fly, friend, fruit, game, garden, home, house, instrument, jewelry, job, leisure, party, pet, picture, relationship, room, school, sport, store, street, study, train, tree, walk, wash, water, wear

History and Culture

art, belief, celebration, culture, dance, education, event, history, holy, literature, modern, music, parade, party, religion, school, science, story, tradition

Communication

act, answer, art, band, character, color, communication, creative, culture, dance, draw, express, film, instrument, language, literature, music, mystery, note, notice, photography, picture, play, question, read, record, show, sign, song, speak, speech, stage, story, symbol, theater, word, write

The Living World

animal, band, bird, bite, branch, cat, dog, eat, family, fat, foot, fruit, grain, grass, grow, growl, growth, hair, health, insect, kid, leaf, life, mollusk, nature, rodent, root, science, tooth, tree, young

The Physical World

amount, divide, electricity, energy, figure, force, light, measurement, modern, physics, power, research, science, shape, technology, time

Natural Environment

air, **animal**, dirt, environment, **farm**, flood, **forest**, **garden**, ground, land, **mountain**, nature, physical, plain, rain, **river**, rock, **sea**, storm, stream, swamp, territory, tree, valley, **water**, wave, **weather**, wild, wind

 ## The Economy

advertisement, **bank**, business, buy, career, cost, develop, **economy**, goods, job, **money**, office, organization, pay, rich, save, sell, service, store, value, work

Government and Law

army, assembly, battle, charge, control, **country**, enemy, **government**, jail, judge, justice, land, **law**, leader, office, order, peace, **power**, prison, protect, sentence, service, steal, territory, **war**

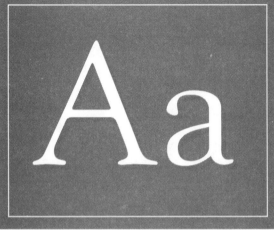

abandon
verb

> to leave behind with no plan to return
> *She abandoned her chores and went fishing.*

desert *The officer deserted his ship.*

forsake *He has forsaken his ideals.*

maroon *The children were marooned on a tropical island.*

turn one's back on *He turned his back on me when I needed help.*

ditch *The pilot ditched his plane and escaped alive.*
> *Forsaking his friends, Ron left the playground.*

> *See also:* leave

abandoned   *See* empty

ability
noun

> 1 the quality of being able
> *Most birds have the ability to fly.*

capability, capacity, faculty, power, potential, strength, resources

Potential is an **ability** that has not been used or developed yet, but could be in the future: *Junior has the potential to be an Olympic champion.*

> 2 skill or talent
> *She has much ability as an ice skater.*

aptitude, flair, gift, knack, talent, facility, adeptness

> *Antonyms:* inability (2), incapacity (2), incompetence (2), weakness (2)

> *See also:* power, skill

able
adjective

> 1 having the skill or power needed to do a thing
> *He is not able to lift heavy objects.*

All of these synonyms for **able** can be used before a noun: *We need capable (or skilled) workers.* Used before a verb, they require prepositions: *capable of driving, skilled at driving.*

---

capable, competent, qualified, skilled

> 2 having special skill or talent
> *She is an able dancer.*

adept, expert, skillful, gifted, masterful, talented

> *Antonyms:* incapable (1), unable (1), weak (2)

abridge   *See* shorten

absence   *See* lack

absent
adjective

> not present; away from where one usually is
> *Don is hardly ever absent from school.*

gone, away, elsewhere, missing, off, out, truant

> *Antonyms:* here, present

absolute   *See* certain, complete, exact, pure, total, power

a
b
c
d
e
f
g
h
i
j
k
l
m
n
o
p
q
r
s
t
u
v
w
x
y
z

absolutely *See* just, quite, stiff, totally

absorb *See* busy, involve, swallow

abundant
adjective
> large in amount or number; more than
> enough
> *The village had abundant stores of grain.*
> ample, bountiful, plentiful, profuse, generous,
> rich, full
> *See also:* great, much, many

abuse *See* insult, wrong

academy *See* school

accept
verb
> 1 to take when given
> *She would not accept the present.*
> *I accepted his apology.*
> take *Don't take orders from him.*
> receive *He received flowers while he was in the hospital.*
> embrace *Nina embraced the chance to go to France.*
> 2 to allow into a group
> *Longbook College accepted my brother in March.*
> admit *The restaurant admitted us after a long wait.*
> receive *They receive guests often.*
> welcome *The townspeople welcomed the refugees into their neighborhoods.*
> *Antonyms:* reject (1), turn down (1), turn up one's nose at (1)
> *See also:* receive, take, believe

acceptable
adjective
> good enough to be accepted or approved of
> *My grades were acceptable to my parents.*
> satisfactory, adequate, fair, respectable, worthy
> *See also:* satisfactory

acceptance *See* approval

access *See* entrance, way

accident *See* chance

accomplish *See* achieve, do, effect

account *See* importance, report, story, worth, bank

accuracy *See* truth

accurate
adjective
> 1 free of mistakes or error
> *The radio gave an accurate report of the fire.*
> *Please make sure your arithmetic is accurate.*
> correct, exact, precise, right, true, perfect,
> truthful, factual, faithful
> 2 careful and precise
> *She was accurate in her measurements.*
> precise, careful, conscientious, particular,
> scrupulous, thorough, strict

When referring to a thing, use the synonyms under definition 1: *a correct answer, a perfect circle, a faithful portrait.* When referring to a person or how a person does something, use the synonyms listed under definition 2.

> *Antonyms:* imprecise (1,2), inaccurate (1,2)

accustomed *See* usual

achieve
verb
> to do or carry out successfully
> *He achieved everything he wanted to as president.*
> accomplish *Lance accomplished his goal.*
> attain *I will attain my goal of becoming a doctor.*
> execute *The inventor had a thousand good ideas but never executed them.*
> fulfill *Good workers fulfill all of their responsibilities.*
> perform *The mayor is not performing his duties.*

> Some are born great, some **achieve** greatness, and some have greatness thrust upon 'em.
> —*From the play TWELFTH NIGHT, by William Shakespeare*

Human Body | Human Mind | Everyday Life | History and Culture | Communication

realize *She realized her wildest dreams.*
reach *It might be dull to have reached perfection.*
carry off *He carried off the tightrope walk.*
carry out *Tomorrow we must carry out our secret plan.*

See also: do

achievement See act, success, work

acknowledge
verb
to admit the truth or existence of
She would not acknowledge her mistake.
accept *My parents accepted my explanation for why I was late.*
admit *Miss Ono refuses to admit that there is both good and evil in everybody.*
allow *Judge Parsons allowed that he might have been too hard on the young thief.*
concede *I concede that he is stronger than me.*
grant *I grant that your idea will probably work better than mine.*
recognize *He recognized his mistake and worked to correct it.*
face up to *You need to face up to the fact that you are lazy.*

See also: admit

acquire See buy, gain, get, learn, receive, win

acres See ground

act ◗ ▭
noun
1 a thing that is done
His act of bravery saved the child from drowning.
action, deed, activity, move, feat, exploit, accomplishment, achievement

2 the process of doing something
He caught the puppy in the act of stealing the hamburger.
action *Dad took a photograph of Mom in action.*
operation *The operation of that large store requires hundreds of workers.*

practice *It seemed like a good idea to shampoo the cat, but in practice it was a mistake.*
process *The process of growing up takes many years.*
performance *The soldier was hurt in the performance of his duties.*

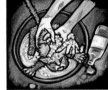

acting ◗ ▭ See stage, theater

action ◗
noun
1 something that is done or is happening
act, activity, deed

> *some words used to describe an action*
> accidental, careful, deft, deliberate, intentional, involuntary, steady

2 the way people act or behave
Her actions are not acceptable.
behavior, conduct, deeds, manner

Some words for the way machines act are **motion**, **mechanism**, **functioning**, **operation**, and **performance**.

---

actions ◗ See behavior

active See busy

activity ◗ ◗
noun
1 the condition of being active or doing something
There was a lot of activity in the streets during the parade.
action, stir, motion, commotion, energy, liveliness, movement, fuss

2 a specific thing that is done
My favorite activity after school is soccer.
pursuit, endeavor, enterprise, project, task, assignment, work, venture

Antonyms: calm (1), inactivity (1), lull (1), quiet (1), stillness (1)

actual See original, present

a
b
c
d
e
f
g
h
i
j
k
l
m
n
o
p
q
r
s
t
u
v
w
x
y
z

actually *See* **really**

acute *See* **serious, severe**

added ❶ *See* **extra**

addition *See* **extra**

additional *See* **extra, more, other**

address *See* **home, speech, talk**

adept *See* **able, clever, expert, fancy**

adequate *See* **acceptable, decent, enough, satisfactory**

adjust
verb
　　1 to bring to a better state or position; make fit
　　I adjusted my seat belt.
　adapt *The church adapted its basement for meetings.*
　align *The mechanic aligned our tires.*
　fit *The tailor will fit the suit for you.*
　right *He righted the vase he had knocked over.*
　set *Francis set the hands on the clock.*
　suit *That actor suited her voice to the role.*
　fix *Let me fix your tie.*
　tune *Please tune your violin!*
　regulate *He regulated all of the clocks in our house.*

　　2 to change in order to fit in; get used to
　　I'm still adjusting to the new school.
　adapt *The former farmer found it hard to adapt to city life.*
　conform *It's not easy for some people to conform to the rules.*
　fit in *Anna fit in well with her new basketball team.*
　　See also: change

adjustment *See* **change**

administration *See* **direction, government**

admit
verb
　　to tell the truth

Did he admit he broke the window?
confess, own up to, acknowledge, reveal, disclose, profess

Confess and **own up to** mean to tell the truth about a bad thing one has done.

Reveal and **disclose** mean to tell something that has been secret or not known before: *The spy did not disclose any information to his captors; Paul revealed his secret to Nan.*

Antonyms: conceal, deny, lie
See also: reveal

adopt *See* **approve, pass**

adore *See* **like, love, prize, worship**

adult ◐ ❶ *See* **grown-up, mature, life**

advance *See* **come, develop, growth, move, offer, pass, propose, suggest**

advanced *See* **physics, technology**

advantage
noun
　　1 a better chance or position
　　He has an advantage in the class election because everyone knows and likes him.
　edge *The Russian team has the edge in this competition.*
　lead *The visiting team had a lead of three points.*
　preference *When deciding who should be hired, the manager gave preference to his nephew.*
　upper hand *Butch Biggs quickly gained the upper hand in the fight.*
　head start *The hard classes you are taking now will give you a head start in high school.*

　　2 the good that is gained from something
　　There are many advantages to having an older brother.
　benefit, gain, good, convenience, profit, positive, plus, asset, use, blessing

　　Antonyms: disadvantage (2), drawback (2), handicap (2), minus (2), negative (2)

　Human Body　　　?　Human Mind　　　Everyday Life　　　History and Culture　　　Communication

See also: good

adventure

noun

an exciting or dangerous activity or journey

Sailing around the world alone would be a marvelous adventure.

enterprise, venture, exploit, expedition, experiment, gamble, risk

advertisement ☻

noun

a public notice that tells people about products, services, or events

some kinds of advertisements
announcement, circular, commercial, display, flier, handout, junk mail, leaflet, notice, poster, spam

some parts of advertisements
caption, cartoon, graphic, jingle, logo, message, photograph, picture, slogan

Advertisement

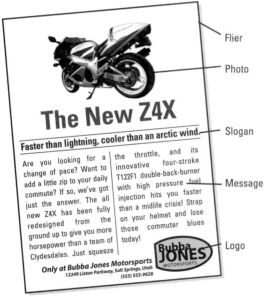

Flier

Photo

The New Z4X

Faster than lightning, cooler than an arctic wind. — Slogan

Are you looking for a change of pace? Want to add a little zip to your daily commute? If so, we've got just the answer. The all new Z4X has been fully redesigned from the ground up to give you more horsepower than a team of Clydesdales. Just squeeze the throttle, and its innovative four-stroke T122F1 double-back-burner with high pressure fuel injection hits you faster than a midlife crisis! Strap on your helmet and lose those commuter blues today! — Message

Only at Bubba Jones Motorsports
12249 Liston Parkway, Salt Springs, Utah
(555) 555-9928 — Logo

affect *See* **influence, move, touch**

affection ⊙

noun

a friendly feeling of liking or loving

I have very strong affection for my grandparents.
warmth, tenderness, friendliness, love, attachment

See also: love

affectionate

adjective

feeling or showing love or affection

Lisa's dad is more affectionate than mine.
loving, tender, fond, warm, caring, friendly

Antonyms: cool, distant

afford *See* **provide**

affront *See* **insult, offense**

afraid ⊙

adjective

feeling fear

Pat is afraid of snakes.

The lights went out, and I was suddenly afraid.
frightened, scared, fearful, terrified, alarmed, apprehensive, worried, uneasy, anxious, aghast

That big dog is making me nervous.

See also: sorry, fear

age ☻ ▢ *See* **develop, time, history**

aged ☻ ▢ *See* **old**

agency ☻ ▢ *See* **company, office, organization**

agent *See* **cause**

agree

verb

1 to have the same opinion or feel the same way (often **agree with**)

I agree with my friend about most things.

concur *The first doctor thought that surgery was needed, and the second doctor concurred.*

sympathize *We sympathize with the mayor's plans for a new library.*

see eye to eye *We see eye to eye on almost everything.*

side with *My father always sides with my brother.*

a
b
c
d
e
f
g
h
i
j
k
l
m
n
o
p
q
r
s
t
u
v
w
x
y
z

2 to say yes
He agreed to do the job for us.
consent, comply, accept, concede, approve, permit

3 to be alike; match
Do our answers agree?
match *Your socks don't match.*
correspond *The two thieves made sure their stories would correspond.*
accord with *This article does not accord with the facts.*
square with *Mike's story does not square with Ike's story.*
conform *In that group you have to conform or you're out.*

Antonyms: differ (1,3), disagree (1), diverge (3), oppose (1,2), refuse (2), resist (2)

agreement ❓

noun

1 the act of coming to a common understanding or of agreeing
We finally reached agreement.
accord, negotiation, settlement, assent, consent, bargaining

2 an understanding between people or groups that states what kind of action is to be taken
My parents asked me to sign an agreement that said I would clean my room at least once a week.
accord, arrangement, bargain, compact, alliance, pact, treaty, contract, deal, understanding
We made a deal to share the money equally.

agricultural ❶ 🌍 *See* technology

ahead *See* first, forward

aid *See* help, prompt, relief, service, support, treat

aim *See* concentrate, design, goal, object, objective, plan, point, purpose, try

air 🏃 👕 ❶ 🌍

noun

1 the mixture of gases that surrounds the earth

some components of air
carbon dioxide, nitrogen, oxygen, ozone
some adjectives used to describe air
clear, damp, foggy, fresh, humid, misty, steamy, stuffy

2 all that is above the ground; sky
The kite flew high up in the air.
heavens, sky, atmosphere, stratosphere, ether

3 movement of the atmosphere; wind
We enjoyed the air coming in through the window.
wind, breeze, breath, current, draft

4 the character or appearance a person or thing has
The magician had an air of mystery.
atmosphere *The restaurant has a lively atmosphere.*
character *This neighborhood has a friendly character.*
cast *Your poem has a somber cast.*
style *I love this dancer's style.*
appearance *His appearance of happiness fooled everyone.*
tone *The movie tried to capture the tone of the 1980s.*
feel *There is a nice feel to this living room.*
expression *An odd expression flitted across his face.*

verb

to speak about, usually in public
He aired his views.
present, broadcast, vent, expose

See also: wind

🏃 Human Body   ❓ Human Mind   👕 Everyday Life   🏳 History and Culture   📞 Communication

airplane ○
noun
>a machine that can fly because of the force of air upon its wings

>*some kinds of airplanes*
>airliner, bomber, jet, seaplane, shuttle, transport
>*some parts of airplanes*
>cabin, coach, cockpit, compartment, control, fin, flap, fuselage, gear, instrument, jet engine, nose, porthole, propeller, rudder, tail, tire, wheel, wing
>*some actions of airplanes*
>ascend, climb, coast, descend, fly, glide, land, pitch, roll, thrust, turn

alarm
noun
>1 sudden fear caused by possible danger
>*The report of a tornado filled us with alarm.*

fear, fright, apprehension, dismay, anxiety, distress

>2 a device that warns of some danger
>*Smoke from the toaster set off the fire alarm.*

warning, alert, bell, horn, signal, siren, whistle

verb
>to make afraid
>*The dog's bark alarmed him.*

frighten, scare, startle, upset, distress, disturb

>*See also:* frighten, scare, fear, worry

alcohol *See* grain

alert
adjective
>watching carefully; quick to notice and act
>*The alert driver avoided a hole in the road.*

attentive, aware, keen, ready, sharp, awake, vigilant, watchful, on guard, on the ball

>*Antonyms:* inattentive, off guard, sleepy
>*See also:* alarm, warn

alike
adjective
>like one another
>*He and his brother are exactly alike.*

equal *The two sisters are of equal height.*
equivalent *Three feet is equivalent to one yard.*
identical *No two snowflakes are identical.*
like *After hearing Kit's story, Nan told of a like experience.*
same *My mother and I have the same nose.*
similar *Lee's handwriting is similar to mine.*
akin *Smiles and laughter are akin.*

>*Antonyms:* different, dissimilar, unlike

alive *See* living

all
adjective
>the whole of or every one of
>*I waited all week for her call.*
>*All men are created equal.*

complete *I have a complete set of kitchen knives.*
entire *The entire house smells like popcorn.*
every *Every seat in the theater was empty.*
full *It took the dentist a full hour to pull the tooth.*
total *I paid the total amount that I owed.*
whole *Lance put together the whole puzzle in half an hour.*

>*Antonym:* none

allow
verb
>to give permission to or for
>*We allowed him to enter.*

let *He let the children pet his dog.*
permit *Will you permit me to go to the dance?*
authorize *This pass authorizes workers to enter the danger zone.*

>*Antonyms:* forbid, keep, prevent, prohibit

The antonyms **prohibit**, **prevent**, and **keep** should be used with "from": *The zoo prohibits visitors from feeding the gorillas;The crossing guard prevented Billy from crossing the road.*

a
b
c
d
e
f
g
h
i
j
k
l
m
n
o
p
q
r
s
t
u
v
w
x
y
z

almost
adverb

not quite all; nearly
The apples are almost gone.
He is almost twelve years old.
just about, mostly, nearly, practically

alone
adverb

without or apart
from anything
or anyone else
She works alone.
separately,
independently,
individually,
solitarily, solo,
apart, by itself, by
oneself

adjective

without or
apart from
everyone or
everything
else
*He was alone
on the island.*
*You alone will
decide your
future.*
individual, lone, separate, single, sole, solitary
Do I really have to water each individual plant?

Unlike **alone**, each of these synonyms must
be used before the noun it describes: *a lone
wolf; each individual plant.*

See also: single

alternative *See* **other, progressive**

altogether *See* **quite, totally**

always
adverb

1 at all times; without stopping
The stars are always in the sky.

I will always remember him.
forever, constantly, continually, continuously,
incessantly, perpetually, endlessly, eternally,
ever

Ever is an old-fashioned and lofty way of
saying **always** or **forever**. Use it only if you
want to sound old-fashioned and lofty. This
usage is common in the Bible: *He is ever
merciful.*

2 every time
He always gets here early.
consistently, constantly, repeatedly, inevitably,
without fail

Antonyms: never (2), rarely (2)

amaze
verb

to surprise greatly or fill with wonder
The girl's musical talent amazed the audience.
astonish, astound, stagger, stun, surprise, awe,
floor

amazing *See* **wonderful**

amount ⬤
noun

1 measure; quantity
This amount of snow isn't enough for skiing.
measure, quantity, sum, volume, portion,
number

2 the sum of two or more quantities
The amount came to eight dollars.
total, sum, count, number

analysis *See* **research, test**

analyze ⓐ *See* **explore, research, study, test**

anchor *See* **fasten, fix, pitch, boat**

ancient ⬤ *See* **old, culture, history, tradition**

anger ⓐ
noun

a strong emotion brought on by a person or
thing that causes one great pain or trouble

 Human Body   Human Mind   Everyday Life History and Culture   Communication

His cruelty filled me with anger.
fury, rage, wrath, outrage, indignance, temper

Use **fury** or **rage** when referring to extreme anger. Use **wrath** if you are writing of a great anger that should be respected or feared.

verb

1 to cause anger in; make angry
The speaker's words angered the crowd.
enrage, infuriate, madden, outrage, incense, antagonize, bait, offend, irritate, provoke, incite, make one's blood boil, raise the hackles of

Bait, incite, and provoke mean to *try* to make someone angry, as though you were dangling a steak in front of a dog: *Butch Biggs likes to bait me by calling me names, but I just ignore him.*

2 to become angry
Name-calling angers me.
He doesn't anger easily.
fume, steam, seethe, explode, bristle, lose one's temper, fly off the handle, blow up

Some things that angry people do:
argue, bawl out, frown, glare, grimace, growl, roar, scowl, scream, snap, snarl, sputter, stamp, sulk, swear, yell

Antonyms: appease (1), calm (1)
See also: annoy, upset

angle *See* **bend, pitch, side, shape**

angry
adjective

1 feeling or showing anger
Liz was angry at George for calling her names.
cross, cranky, sore, irate, indignant, fuming, mad, furious, outraged, livid, sullen, hot under the collar

2 as if showing great force or anger
The ship set sail on the angry sea.

violent, wild, furious, savage, raging

From the bleachers black with people
  there rose a **sullen** roar,
Like the beating of the storm-waves on a
  stern and distant shore,
"Kill him! Kill the Umpire!" shouted
  someone from the stand—
And it's likely they'd have done it had not
  Casey raised his hand.
  —*From "CASEY AT THE BAT,"*
  a poem by Ernest Lawrence Thayer (1863-1940)

animal
noun

one of a large group of living things that can move around by themselves to find food

some examples of animals
  amphibian, arthropod, bird, crustacean, fish, insect, invertebrate, mammal, mollusk, primate, reptile, vertebrate
parts of some animals
  antler, blubber, bristle, claw, flipper, fur, hoof, horn, mane, pad, pouch, quill, snout, tail
groups of some animals
  band, brood, drove, flock, herd, litter, pack, school, swarm, troop
behaviors of some animals
  build, court, crawl, dig, dive, feed, fight, fly, forage, gather, gnaw, hibernate, hide, hop, hunt, mate, migrate, nurse, run, swim, trot, tunnel, walk

annoy
verb

to disturb with irritating behavior
Your loud drumming annoys the neighbors.
irritate, bother, bug, needle, plague, aggravate, rub the wrong way

See also: bother

answer
noun

1 something spoken or done in return
I want an answer to my question.

A B C D E F G H I J K L M N O P Q R S T U V W X Y Z

a
b
c
d
e
f
g
h
i
j
k
l
m
n
o
p
q
r
s
t
u
v
w
x
y
z

reply *Mom's reply was, "Over my dead body!"*
response *Mary wrote to her aunt but got no response.*
acknowledgment *Have you received any acknowledgments since you sent the invitations?*

2 the correct response to a problem
You have to multiply to find the answer.
solution, explanation

Antonyms: invitation (1), question (1)

verb
to speak, write, or act in reply
Tina answered, but no one heard her.
reply *"I love you too," replied Frank.*
respond *The speaker will now respond to questions from the audience.*

Antonym: ask

anxiety ⊘ *See* **alarm, care, fear, worry, emotion**

anxious *See* **afraid, eager, nervous, fear**

anyway
adverb
in any case; no matter what happens
She was ill but went to school anyway.
anyhow, in any event, nevertheless, all the same, regardless

apart *See* **alone**

apartment ⊙ *See* **home**

apparent *See* **obvious, plain, visible**

appeal
noun
1 an earnest request for help
The charity made an appeal for money.
petition, plea, request, prayer

2 the ability to attract interest and attention
Books about magic have great appeal.
attraction, attractiveness, charm, draw

verb
1 to make an earnest request

The mayor appealed for help after the flood.
plead, entreat, petition, beg, pray

2 to have attraction or interest
Adventure movies appeal to me.
attract, engage, interest, invite

See also: ask, attract

appear
verb
1 to come into view; become visible
He appeared out of nowhere.
arise, emerge, show up, come

2 to seem
Jared appears to be smart.
look, seem, come across as

Antonym: disappear (1)

appearance ⊛
noun
1 the act of coming into view or appearing
Everyone welcomed the appearance of the sun after days of rain.
arrival, debut, emergence

2 outward show or aspect; seeming
His appearance of happiness fooled everyone.
look, face, bearing, carriage, facade, guise, image

3 (**appearances**) outward signs
By all appearances, he's an honest man.
signs, aspects, indications, manifestations

4 the way someone is dressed or groomed
Don't judge her by her sloppy appearance.
looks, grooming

application *See* **coat, use**

apply *See* **smear, spread, use, drug**

appointment *See* **office**

appreciate *See* **know, prize, value, welcome**

approach *See* **come, gain, way**

appropriate
adjective
right for the purpose

Human Body   Human Mind   Everyday Life   History and Culture   Communication

Jeans are not appropriate for a formal wedding.
fit, proper, suitable, suited, apt

approval
noun

1 the act of allowing or saying yes to
You need to get approval for that project.
assent, consent, blessing, sanction, OK

2 good opinion; favorable thoughts
The mayor earned the people's approval.
esteem, favor, honor, applause, acceptance

Antonyms: disapproval (2), disfavor (2)

approve
verb

1 to think well of something or someone
He does not approve of people who smoke.
admire, favor, sympathize, agree

2 to accept and allow officially
The council approved a new budget.
authorize, confirm, endorse, ratify, sanction, pass, enact, adopt

Antonyms: ban (2), disapprove (1), oppose (2), outlaw (2), reject (2)

approved *See* **standard**

arc *See* **bend, curve, turn**

arctic ❶ ❻ *See* **weather**

area
noun

1 a place or region
This area of the country is beautiful.
place, region, zone, district, territory

The words **area** and **place** are all-purpose words. They can be used in many different contexts. Use **zone** or **district** for areas that have a particular purpose: *the city's business district, a no-parking zone.*

2 a field of study
The doctor's area of medicine is heart disease.
domain, field, province, sphere, subject

See also: place

argue ❔
verb

1 to express disagreement
The children argued over which DVD to rent.
quarrel, disagree, bicker, dispute, squabble, feud

2 to give reasons for or against something
Some parents argued against school uniforms.
debate, dispute, contend

See also: fight

argument *See* **defense, fight**

arise *See* **appear, happen, lift, rise, stand**

army ◐
noun

1 a large group of soldiers trained to fight on land
troops, militia, infantry, cavalry, artillery

The **infantry** is the part of the army that fights on foot. The **cavalry** fights on horseback or in vehicles such as tanks. The **artillery** uses large weapons such as cannon.

2 a great number of people or things
The movie star has an army of fans.
crowd, horde, host, legion, multitude, throng

3 a large group that works together for a cause
An army of workers cleaned up the park.
battalion, brigade, legion

The fire brigade arrived quickly at the burning building.

See also: group

aroma *See* **scent, smell**

arrange
verb

1 to put in an order
She arranged the papers on her desk.
organize, order, array, position, set up, marshal

2 to make plans for

a
b
c
d
e
f
g
h
i
j
k
l
m
n
o
p
q
r
s
t
u
v
w
x
y
z

They arranged a surprise party for their friend.
plan, prepare, ready, design, line up, set up

3 to change so as to fit a particular type of musical performance
She arranged the violin piece for the piano.
adapt, score, set

Antonyms: disorder (1), mess up (1), scramble (1), shuffle (1)

See also: plan

arrangement *See* **agreement, deal, order**

arrival *See* **appearance**

arrive *See* **come, get**

art
noun
the works produced by artists

some kinds of art
architecture, dance, drawing, film, literature, music, painting, photography, poetry, sculpture, theater, woodworking
some ways people create art
act, carve, compose, dance, design, draw, etch, illustrate, mold, paint, paste, sculpt, sew, sing, sketch, stitch, stroke, weave, weld, write
some people associated with art
actor, architect, artisan, artist, author, composer, craftsman, critic, dancer, dealer, director, illustrator, model, musician, painter, patron, poet, potter, sculptor, writer

article *See* **object, thing**

artificial
adjective
1 made by human beings; not natural
The artificial flowers actually looked real.
manufactured, imitation, synthetic, man-made

2 not true or sincere; pretended
Her apology sounded artificial.
unnatural, insincere, plastic, phony, fake

Antonyms: genuine (2), natural (1),

sincere (2), true (2)
See also: fake, false

artist *See* **art**

ask
verb
1 to put a question to
He asked me about my travels in Nepal.
question, inquire about or of, query, interrogate, quiz

2 to make a request of
The stranger asked him to open the door.
request, bid, beg, beseech, entreat, petition

aspect *See* **part, property, side, way**

aspects *See* **appearance**

assembly
noun
1 a group of people gathered together, usually for a specific purpose
At my school, every student must attend the Monday morning assembly.
meeting, gathering, muster, rally, council, congregation, company

2 (often **Assembly**) a legislative body
The Assembly is the lower branch of the state legislature.
legislature, parliament, congress, council, senate, house

See also: group

assignment *See* **activity, job, task, work**

assist *See* **help, prompt, sport**

assistance *See* **help, relief, service, support**

assistant *See* **help**

associated *See* **related**

association *See* **company, connection, organization, relationship, society, touch**

 Human Body   Human Mind   Everyday Life   History and Culture   Communication

assume *See* bear, imagine, suppose

atmosphere *See* air, environment

atomic *See* energy

atoms *See* physics

atrocious *See* miserable, terrible

attach
verb
   1 to connect or fasten
   She attached the nozzle to the hose.
connect, fasten, fix, join, bind, stick, affix, clip, pin, hitch
   2 to consider as belonging to
   He attached great importance to our talk.
assign, attribute

attack
verb
   1 to begin to cause harm to
   The crow attacked a rabbit.
assault, raid, storm, ambush, charge, strike, besiege

> Use **raid**, **storm**, and **besiege** only when referring to an attack on a building or city.

   2 to speak or write against
   The candidate attacked her opponent.
blast, denounce, criticize, slander, slam, rip into
noun
   1 an act meant to hurt or destroy
   The army carried out a surprise attack.
assault, ambush, raid, siege, charge, aggression, offensive
   2 a sudden beginning of an illness
   He had an attack of appendicitis.
fit, bout, spell
   Antonym: retreat (2)
   See also: beat

attempt *See* chance, effort, seek, try

attend *See* keep, listen, care

attention *See* care, notice, perception, thought

attic *See* home

attitude *See* temper, view

attract
verb
   1 to cause to come near
   The color red attracts hummingbirds.
draw *The star always draws a large crowd.*
lure *They lured the dog back to the house with a bowl of food.*
catch *This hat will catch his eye.*
pull *The magnet pulled the pins towards itself.*
   2 to gain the attention or admiration of
   Her strange clothing attracted us.
draw, intrigue, fascinate, engage, interest
   Antonyms: drive away (2), repel (2), repulse (2)
   See also: tempt, interest

attraction *See* appeal

attractive
adjective
   having qualities that attract people
   He is attractive enough to be a movie star.
charming, winning, magnetic, handsome, pretty, beautiful

> **Handsome** usually refers to the appearance of a boy or man and **pretty** to the appearance of a girl or woman. These words describe physical appearance. A person can be **charming**, **winning**, **magnetic**, or **attractive** without being pretty or handsome.

   See also: beautiful

author *See* produce, write, writer, art

authorities *See* government

authority *See* control, expert, power, reference

 Living World   Physical World   Natural Environment   Economy   Government and Law   13

a
b
c
d
e
f
g
h
i
j
k
l
m
n
o
p
q
r
s
t
u
v
w
x
y
z

available *See* open

avenue *See* street

average
adjective
of the most common or ordinary kind
The average person in this country does not exercise enough.
typical, usual, normal, standard, ordinary, unexceptional

Antonyms: exceptional, extraordinary, inferior, superior, unusual
See also: normal, ordinary

avoid
verb
to keep away from
He avoided the other car by swerving.
escape *Bobby couldn't escape Aunt Sue's wet kiss.*
evade *The fox evaded the hunters.*
miss *The car missed the tree.*
elude *The clever burglar eluded the police*
dodge *The old man dodged the skateboarder.*

See also: escape

awake *See* alert

aware *See* alert, knowledge

awareness *See* care, feeling, knowledge, mind, notice, perception

away *See* absent

awful *See* fierce, terrible

awkward *See* clumsy

Human Body   Human Mind   Everyday Life   History and Culture   Communication

baby See **spoil, young, youngster, care, life**

back See **recommend**

background See **root**

backwater See **country**

bad
adjective

1 not well made or well done
That picture was taken with a bad camera.
I wrote a bad book report and got a D.
poor, deficient, inferior, inadequate, imperfect, terrible, sorry, lousy

2 naughty
Please don't be bad while the guests are here.
disobedient, mischievous, naughty, wicked

3 in pain or poor health
Max stayed home from school because he felt bad.
ill, sick, unhealthy, unwell, lousy

4 terrible or serious
A bad storm is heading our way.
severe, terrible, serious, nasty

5 sorry
Nan felt bad about cheating on the test.
sorry, guilty, sad

6 not healthy
Sugar is bad for your teeth.
harmful, damaging, detrimental, unhealthy

7 wicked

He has done some mean things, but he is not a bad person.
wicked, nasty, wrong, immoral, evil, malicious

Antonyms: good (1,2), healthy (6), mild (4), moral (7), nice (2), obedient (2), proud (5), well (3)
See also: terrible, sick, serious, sorry, naughty, evil, rotten, negative

bag *See* **catch**

balance
noun

1 a state in which opposite forces are equal
Try to have a balance between work and play in your life.
equilibrium

2 the state of being steady in body or mind
Joe kept his balance while standing on one toe.
steadiness, equilibrium, composure

verb

to hold steady
The seal balanced a ball on its nose.
poise, steady

Antonym: upset
See also: steady

ball *See* **party**

balloon *See* **increase, swell**

band[1]
noun

1 a thin strip of material that holds several objects together
She put a rubber band around the pencils.
belt, headband, hoop, ribbon, rope, sash, strip, thong, tie

2 a stripe or strip that contrasts with its surroundings in color or material
That kind of snake is brown with yellow bands.
bar, braid, line, ring, streak, strip, stripe

verb

to tie with a strip of material in order to tell apart or bundle together; put a band on

The scientists banded the birds to learn more about their habits.

belt, bind, bundle, strap, tag, tie

Antonyms: release, unbundle, unstrap, untie

band² ⦿ ⦿

noun

1 a group of people, animals, or objects acting together

There's a band of dogs in the neighborhood.

pack, company, group, tribe, party, assembly

2 a group formed to play popular music

Jo plays guitar in the band.

group, ensemble, combo, trio, quartet, quintet, orchestra, chorus

The first three words in this list can be used instead of **band**. The rest are words for different kinds of musical groups.

verb

to come together into a group

We always band together in emergencies.

ally, gather, league, merge, team up, unite

See also: group, unite

bang

noun

a sudden, loud, explosive sound

The balloon burst with a bang.

clap, boom, blast, crack, explosion, report

bank ⦿

noun

a business for holding, borrowing, or exchanging money

---

words for parts of a bank
ATM, cage, lobby, safe, vault

words for things people do at a bank
borrow, cash, credit, deposit, exchange, finance, invest, lend, loan, pay, repay, save, withdraw

words for things related to banks
account, asset, bill, bond, cash, check, coin, credit, credit card, funds, money, receipt, slip, statement

See also: store

bar ⦿ ⦿ *See* band, barrier, block, except, forbid, line, lock, outlaw

bare

adjective

1 wearing no clothing or covering

It's too cold to go outside with bare legs.

naked, nude, undressed

2 not filled, covered, or decorated

The walls are bare.

blank, empty, vacant, void, stripped

3 plain; simple

Just give me the bare facts.

plain, simple, basic, bald, unadorned

Antonyms: clothed (1), decent (1), dressed (1)

verb

to uncover

Jeffrey bared his chest.

expose, reveal, uncover, show, disclose

Antonyms: conceal, cover, hide

barely *See* just

bark ⦿ *See* dog

barrier

noun

1 something that blocks the way

We built a barrier to keep our dog from running into the street.

wall, fence, bar, obstacle, obstruction, barricade, blockade

The mountains were an obstruction for travelers until airplanes were invented.

Human Body   Human Mind   Everyday Life   History and Culture   Communication

Walls, fences, barricades and **blockades** are **barriers** built by people. An **obstacle** or an **obstruction** can be anything that blocks the way, such as a tree that has blown over or leaves stuck in a drainpipe.

2 anything that gets in the way of action or progress
His youth was a barrier in his search for a job.
bar, obstacle, hindrance, stumbling block, handicap
Rita's height was an obstacle to her becoming a ballerina.
See also: block

base 🔹🔹 *See* bottom, cheap, ground

basic 🔹🔹
adjective
forming or at the basis
The basic idea of bowling is to knock over as many pins as you can.
main, bottom, fundamental, primary, central
noun
(often **basics**) the basic knowledge or skills required to do something
She doesn't even know the basics of cooking.
fundamentals, essentials, ABC's

basically 🔹🔹 *See* generally

basin *See* valley, river

basis *See* bottom, ground

battle 🔹
noun
a fight between two armed persons or forces during a war
The first major battle of the Civil War took place at Bull Run.
clash, combat, engagement, encounter, conflict, fight, struggle, action

verb
1 to take part in a battle or fight
The two skaters battled for the gold medal.
Protesters and police battled for two days.
fight, contend, struggle, duel

Use **duel** for a fight between two people:
The two swordsmen will duel to the finish.

2 to struggle against
I am battling a cold.
fight, combat, engage, encounter
See also: fight, contest

be *See* happen, stand

beam 🔹🔹 *See* shine, smile, stream, happiness

bear
verb
1 to carry or hold up
The servants will bear the gift to the king.
These beams bear the weight of tons of stone.
bring, carry, support, uphold
2 to put up with
Pip could not bear being poor.
tolerate *Very small dogs do not tolerate cold well.*
endure *I have endured your teasing for long enough.*
withstand *He withstood the pressure from his friends to drink and smoke.*
stand *He can't stand it when she is late.*
take *I can't take the cold weather.*
have *I've had all I can take.*
abide *Ms. Grisly cannot abide noisy children.*
suffer *She does not suffer fools gladly.*
3 to give birth to
She bore a son and named him after his father.
deliver, have, produce
4 to produce by growth
Apple trees bear fruit in the fall.
produce *Our chickens produce eggs for market.*
yield *Our garden yielded lots of vegetables this year.*

 Living World Physical World Natural Environment Economy Government and Law

a
b
c
d
e
f
g
h
i
j
k
l
m
n
o
p
q
r
s
t
u
v
w
x
y
z

generate *A worm can generate a new tail but not a new head.*

give *Cows give milk.*

> 5 to have or accept as a duty
> *Who will bear the blame for this?*

accept, assume, shoulder, carry

> *See also:* carry, support

beard *See* **hair**

bearing *See* **appearance, behavior, direction**

beast *See* **monster**

beat 🔵
verb
> 1 to hit again and again
> *She beat the drum with her new drumsticks.*
> *He beats that poor mule when it won't go.*

pound, batter, club, flail, knock, clobber

> 2 to win against
> *Mai beat me at tennis.*

defeat *Mai Lin defeated Nancy Lane in tennis.*

overcome *She overcame all her opponents in the tennis tournament.*

conquer *The Romans conquered enemy tribes.*

best *He bested me in the long jump.*

whip *The Canadians whipped the Americans in hockey.*

lick *"I know when I'm licked," said Nancy.*

> 3 to stir rapidly
> *Beat the eggs.*

blend, whisk, whip, stir, mix, churn

> 4 to pound, as a heart does
> *I was so scared that my heart beat double-time.*

pound, pulse, throb, thump

> These synonyms can also be used as nouns:
> *I could hardly hear the throb of the air-plane's engine over the thump of my own heart.*

> 5 musical rhythm
> *We danced to the beat of the music.*

rhythm, meter, time

6 a person's regular route on the job
Officer Gettem starts his beat at nine o'clock.

route, territory, area, circuit

adjective
> very tired
> *"I'm beat," said Nan, flopping into a chair.*

done in, worn-out, dead, exhausted, drained, fatigued, weary

> **Beat** and **done in** are considered conversational or informal language. In writing essays and reports for school, **exhausted**, **fatigued**, and **tired** are probably better word choices.

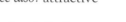

See also: defeat, hit

beautiful
adjective
> lovely to the senses; having beauty
> *The sunset was beautiful.*

gorgeous, exquisite, fair, lovely, divine, attractive, pretty

> *What gorgeous feathers the peacock has!*

> Antonyms: plain, ugly, unattractive

See also: attractive

beauty 🔵 🔵 *See* **grace**

beaver *See* **rodent**

become
verb
> 1 to grow or come to be
> *Liz became ill after eating a poisonous mushroom.*
> *This tadpole will become a frog.*

fall, get, grow, take

> **Fall** only means **become** in certain expressions: *Hannah fell silent; Harry has fallen in love again; David fell ill.* **Take** only means **become** when referring to illness: *The canary took sick.*

🔵 Human Body   ❓ Human Mind   👕 Everyday Life   🏴 History and Culture   ☎ Communication

2 to look good with or on
That jacket becomes you.
flatter, suit, fit
See also: suit

bed ⊙ ⊕ *See* **bottom, patch**

bee *See* **insect**

beef *See* **objection**

beg
verb
to ask in a serious or desperate way
She begged us to forgive her.
appeal to, beseech, entreat, request, plead with

begin *See* **establish, found, open**

beginning *See* **primitive**

behave
verb
1 to act or function in a certain way
The monkeys behave differently in the zoo than in the jungle.
act *He acts like he is the boss of everything.*
function *Mom functions as my nurse when I am sick.*
operate *Paul's computer is not operating properly.*
run *The new car is running well.*

2 to act in a proper manner
Will you please behave?
mind, obey

behavior ⊙
noun
the way a person behaves
Miss Cole's behavior at lunch was shocking.
conduct, actions, manner, bearing, way

some words that can describe behavior
aggressive, apologetic, bad, best, bullying, casual, childish, civil, correct, courteous, crazy, dangerous, discourteous, disturbing, eccentric, formal, good, hysterical, improper, informal, insolent, mischievous, natural, nervous, normal, outrageous, polite, proper, strange, unruly, violent, wicked, wild
some terms for improving one's behavior
clean up one's act, get one's act together, improve, reform, turn over a new leaf

See also: misbehave

being *See* **life**

belief ⊙ ⊙
noun
1 a strong opinion
My teacher has a strong belief that all children can learn.
conviction, opinion, position, viewpoint, view, notion, theory

A **belief** or a **conviction** is stronger than an **opinion**, **view**, or **position**. A **belief** lasts longer, is felt more deeply, and is less likely to change over time.

some kinds of beliefs
lofty, newfangled, obstinate, old-fashioned, open, orthodox, political, religious

2 trust in a person, thing, or idea; confidence
The coach's belief in me helped me to succeed.
confidence, faith, trust

3 an idea accepted as true, even without proof
Some religions hold the belief that the human soul lives on after the body dies.
creed, doctrine, gospel, faith

a
b
c
d
e
f
g
h
i
j
k
l
m
n
o
p
q
r
s
t
u
v
w
x
y
z

beliefs  *See* **value, culture**

believe
verb

1 to accept as honest or true
Please believe what I am about to tell you.
accept, trust, credit, swallow, buy, put stock in

> Use **swallow, put stock in,** and **buy** in informal, everyday speaking and writing. Use **accept, trust,** and **credit** in formal reports and presentations.

2 to have some confidence in; suppose
I believe they will arrive before noon.
guess, suppose, suspect, think, trust, imagine, presume

Antonym: doubt (1)
See also: trust

bell *See* **alarm**

below *See* **down**

belt *See* **band**

bench *See* **sport**

bend
verb

1 to cause to take on a curved or angled form, or a different form
He bent the nail by mistake.
curve, angle, twist, crook, turn, warp

2 to take on a curved or angled form
The fishing rod bent under the weight of the fish.
The arm bends at the elbow.
curve, buckle, crook, double, warp, wind, angle

3 to lean one's upper body from the waist
I bent over to pick up the litter.
lean, bow, double

4 to change direction in a curving or angled way
The road bends sharply just in front of my house.
curve, swerve, turn, veer, wind, zigzag

Antonym: straighten (1)

noun

a curved or bent thing, part, or area
The car hurtled around the bend in the road.
curve, turn, arc, bow, elbow, crook

See also: turn

beneath *See* **down**

benefit *See* **advantage, gain, good, positive, use, worth**

bent
adjective

1 not straight
We hung a swing from the bent branch of the tree.
curved, crooked, twisted, warped, angled, arced, bowed

2 determined or insisting (usually **bent on**)
He is bent on going with us.
set, intent, determined

Antonym: straight (1)

besides *See* **except**

best
adjective

better than all others in quality or ability
Orion was the best hunter.
foremost, superior, super, first, top, finest, excellent, first-class, first-rate, superlative

noun

a thing or person better than all others
Of all the runners, Robin is the best.

number one *We're number one!*
pick *That bright yellow banana is the pick of the bunch.*
cream *The cream of this year's class will go to college.*
fat *The rich man's family is living off the fat of the land.*

Human Body   Human Mind   Everyday Life   History and Culture   Communication

the tops *My grandfather is the tops.*

Antonyms: the pits, worst

bet

verb

to agree to pay if one's guess is wrong
I bet a dollar on the game.
gamble, lay, stake, wager

betray

verb

to help the enemy of; commit treason
The spy betrayed his country.
double-cross, inform on, rat on

better

adjective

1 more excellent; of a higher quality
This is a better restaurant because of its fine service.
finer, greater, superior

2 no longer sick or injured
He is all better now that he has rested.
healthy, well, cured, healed, recuperated

verb

to improve
Abe bettered himself through education.
improve, further, enhance, enrich, upgrade, strengthen

Antonym: worse

big *See* **grand, grown-up, large, measurement**

biggest *See* **main**

bill *See* **charge, peak, bank, bird**

bind *See* **attach, band, fasten, spot, stick, tie, trouble**

biology *See* **science**

bird

noun

an animal with two wings, two feet, and a body covered with feathers

some kinds of birds
fowl, game, nocturnal birds, birds of prey, songbirds, water birds

parts of some birds
beak, bill, comb, crest, crop, feathers, talons, wings

sounds birds make
buzz, caw, chatter, chirp, clatter, cry, gobble, honk, hum, mimic, peep, quack, screech, squawk, squeak, trill, twitter, whistle

bit

noun

1 a small amount
There's only a bit of food left in the cupboard.
crumb, drop, fraction, jot, morsel, particle, piece, pinch, scrap, speck, trace, dab, fragment, touch

2 a very short time
John said he would be home in a bit.
minute, moment, second, flash, instant, spell, wink, jiffy, sec.

bite

verb

to cut or pierce with the teeth
She bit the apple.
nip, nibble, gnaw

noun

that which is bitten off
He took a huge bite of pie.
morsel, mouthful, taste, nibble
The mouse ate a morsel of cheese.

blabber *See* **rattle**

black *See* **dark, hair, sad**

blame

verb

to place responsibility on for a mistake or wrongdoing

Ms. Black blamed Pat for spilling the paint.

accuse *Loretta unfairly accused Pat of stealing her lunch.*

fault *No one faulted Loretta for lying about it.*

charge *The police have charged Lance's father with theft.*

noun

responsibility

I took the blame for the mistake.

fault *"It is not my fault," said Loretta.*

responsibility *Lance's father admitted responsibility for the theft.*

blank *See* **bare, empty**

blanket ⊙ *See* **coat, spread**

blast *See* **attack, bang, blow, burst, party**

blind *See* **mask**

block ⑦ ⊙

noun

a solid piece of hard material, such as wood or concrete, with flat sides

The mason built a wall out of stone blocks.

bar, brick, cube

verb

1 to get in the way of movement or stop progress

The Senator tried to block discussion of the bill.

stop, obstruct, hinder

2 to close off or obstruct by putting something in the way

The stalled truck blocked the road.

clog, jam, obstruct

blow

verb

1 to force air out of the mouth

She blew on the baby's fingers to warm them.

puff, huff, breathe, exhale, expire, pant

2 to make a sound by forcing air through an instrument

The whistle blew.

blare, blast, sound, toot, whistle

Antonyms: inhale (1), suck in (1)

blue *See* **down, heaven, low, unhappy, sad**

board *See* **enter**

boast

verb

to talk with too much pride

She boasts about her musical talent whenever she has a chance.

brag, crow, bluster, blow or toot one's own horn, show off

boat ⊙

noun

a small, open vehicle for traveling on water

some kinds of boats
ark, barge, canoe, catamaran, craft, cruiser, dinghy, dory, ferry, galley, gondola, houseboat, junk, kayak, launch, lifeboat, motorboat, racer, raft, rowboat, sailboat, sloop, steamboat, tugboat, vessel
some parts of boats
anchor, ballast, boom, canvas, deck, engine, fin, galley, hull, jib, mast, motor, oar, outboard motor, outrigger, paddle, prow, rigging, rudder, sail, tiller
some things people do with boats
cruise, launch, moor, paddle, rock, roll, row, sail, swamp, tip, troll

bob *See* **hair**

body ⊙

noun

1 all the physical material that makes up a person or animal

anatomy, physiology

Human Body   Human Mind   Everyday Life   History and Culture   Communication

Boats & Ships

dinghy

frigate · racer

anchor

ceremonial barge

tugboat

aircraft carrier

galleon

cruise ship

canoe

ngè river boat

fishing boats

ferry

a
b
c
d
e
f
g
h
i
j
k
l
m
n
o
p
q
r
s
t
u
v
w
x
y
z

Use **anatomy** and **physiology** only if you are referring to the **body** in a scientific sense. The word **anatomy** refers to the parts of a plant or animal body and how those parts fit together. The word **physiology** refers to the functions and processes of a body's organs, tissues, and cells.

2 the shape, form, or fitness of a person's body
figure, form, frame, physique, build, person

> *some descriptions of the body*
>   burly, muscular, short, stout, strong, sturdy, tall, weak
> *some movements of the body*
>   bend, bow, creep, crouch, curtsy, dance, duck, jump, reach, shake, somersault, squirm, stoop, stroke, twitch, wriggle

bold
adjective
   1 brave; daring

The bold young gentleman walked right up to Mayor Gloryandy.
brave, daring, unafraid, nervy, adventurous

   2 imaginative; creative
Einstein was one of the boldest thinkers of the twentieth century.
imaginative, creative, original

   3 easy to notice; attracting attention
The artist painted a bold design on the wall.
showy, gaudy, striking, colorful

   4 not polite; rude
His bold manner cost him his job.
forward, fresh, impertinent, impudent, insolent, rude

   Antonyms: mousy (1), shy (1), timid (1)

bomb ○ *See* **disaster, fail, failure, war**

bond ◐ ○ *See* **connection, paste, bank**

bone ◉ ◐ *See* **foot**

Body

bending
posing
leaping
gliding
tumbling
reaching
extending
crouching

Human Body   Human Mind   Everyday Life   History and Culture   Communication

book ⊙ ⊘ *See* **charge, register**

boom ⊜ *See* **bang, roar, boat, economy**

border
noun
1 edge; boundary
There is a fence along the border of our yard.
boundary, edge, frontier, limit, margin, verge

We saw a deer at the edge of the forest.
2 the strip around the edge of something
trim, braid, frame, fringe, hem, ruffle

verb
to lie on the edge or boundary of
Canada borders the United States.
neighbor, verge on, touch, skirt, adjoin
See also: edge

borders *See* **confine**

bore *See* **hole**

borrow ⊜ *See* **bank**

boss *See* **leader**

bother
verb
1 to annoy or give trouble to
The loud noise is bothering us.
upset, exasperate, badger, annoy, bug, harass, hassle, irritate, rub the wrong way, nettle, pester, pick on, trouble, worry
2 to make puzzled or worried
It bothers me that he looks so unhappy.
concern, confuse, disturb, puzzle, trouble, worry

noun
a person or thing that annoys or causes trouble
It is a bother to make dinner every day.

She's nothing but a bother to me.
annoyance, headache, inconvenience, nag, nuisance, pest, problem, trouble, worry, hassle

Use **pest** and **nag** only when referring to people. Use **hassle, headache,** and **inconvenience** only when referring to events or situations.

See also: annoy

bottom
noun

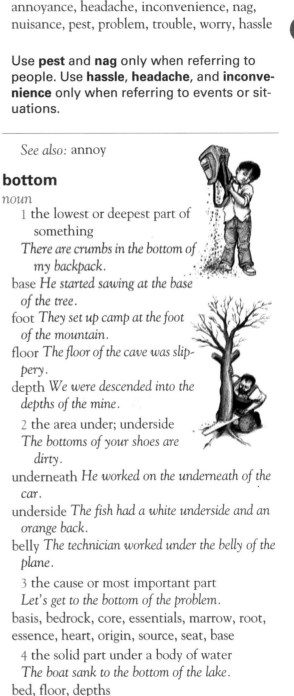

1 the lowest or deepest part of something
There are crumbs in the bottom of my backpack.
base *He started sawing at the base of the tree.*
foot *They set up camp at the foot of the mountain.*
floor *The floor of the cave was slippery.*
depth *We were descended into the depths of the mine.*
2 the area under; underside
The bottoms of your shoes are dirty.
underneath *He worked on the underneath of the car.*
underside *The fish had a white underside and an orange back.*
belly *The technician worked under the belly of the plane.*
3 the cause or most important part
Let's get to the bottom of the problem.
basis, bedrock, core, essentials, marrow, root, essence, heart, origin, source, seat, base
4 the solid part under a body of water
The boat sank to the bottom of the lake.
bed, floor, depths

bound *See* **jump, limit, responsible, spring, sure**

boundaries *See* **confine**

 Living World Physical World Natural Environment ⩗⩗⩗ Economy 📖 Government and Law

a
b
c
d
e
f
g
h
i
j
k
l
m
n
o
p
q
r
s
t
u
v
w
x
y
z

boundary *See* **border, edge, limit, line**

bow ◉ *See* **bend, bent, sag, body, dance, theater**

box *See* **package**

boy *See* **goodness**

brain ◉ ◉ *See* **mind**

branch ◉
noun
   1 a woody part of a tree or bush that grows out from the trunk
   bough, limb, stick, twig, offshoot

   2 a part or division of the main part of something
   We chose a savings bank that has a branch near our house.
   Geometry is an ancient branch of mathematics.
   affiliate, chapter, division, offshoot
verb
   to separate into two or more paths, roads, or directions
   Green Street branches at the third traffic light.
   divide, fork, fan out, part, separate

brand *See* **mark, stain**

brass ◉ *See* **nerve**

brave ◉
adjective
   ready to face pain or danger
   The brave pilot flew alone through the storm.
   bold, courageous, daring, fearless, game
verb
   to face or bear with courage
   The ship's crew braved the rough seas.
   confront, endure, face, meet, weather, bear, suffer, survive, withstand

bread *See* **money, grain**

break ◉
verb
   1 to cause to come apart into pieces
   She broke the nutshell with a hammer.
   shatter, smash, snap, fracture, demolish
   2 to come apart into pieces
   His favorite cup broke into pieces.
   crack, shatter, smash, snap, fragment, fracture
   3 to damage or make no longer usable
   She fell and broke her arm.
   We have no music because you broke the radio.
   ruin, wreck, damage, bust
   4 to fail to obey or be faithful to
   They broke the law.
   He never breaks a promise.
   violate, betray, disobey

Use **betray** when referring to a promise, but not when referring to a law. Use **disobey** when referring to a law, but not when referring to a promise. The word **violate** works in both cases.

---

   5 to go beyond
   She may break the world record.
   beat, top, better, exceed, outdo, surpass
   6 to burst
   Water pipes can break when the temperature drops below freezing.
   burst, rupture, split, explode
noun
   1 the result of breaking into pieces
   There was a break in the dam.
   breach, fracture, crack, fracture, rupture
   2 a period of time when something stops
   We took a break from our work to eat dinner.
   pause, recess, rest, intermission, interruption

breath *See* **air**

breathe ◉
verb
   to draw air into the lungs and let it out
   People breathe faster when they run.
   pant, huff, puff, inhale, exhale, expire, pant, wheeze, respire

 Human Body   Human Mind   Everyday Life   History and Culture   Communication

breathing  See **living**

breeze See **air, float, wind**

brick See **block**

brief See **passing, communication**

brigade See **army, team**

bright
adjective
    1 giving much light; shining
    The sun is bright in the desert.
brilliant, dazzling, glaring, glittering, glowing,
illuminated, incandescent, radiant, shiny
    The radiant sun warmed our backs.

    2 strong or clear in color or shine
    The house is bright yellow.
brilliant, colorful, intense, vivid
    3 quick to learn; smart
    There are bright children in any neighborhood.
clever, intelligent, quick, sharp, smart
    4 lively and cheerful
    His bright face told me he had good news.
cheerful *I love a cheerful fire on a rainy night.*
happy *Tom played a happy song on his tuba.*
merry *Merry laughter came from the living room.*
sparkling *She looked at me with sparkling eyes.*
sunny *He has a sunny smile.*

brilliant See **bright, light, sharp, smart, mind**

bring
verb
    1 to take, lead, or carry from one place to another
    Bring your game over to our house.
fetch, deliver, lead, convey

Use **lead** only when referring to people or animals.

___

    2 to cause to happen or change
    Autumn brings cool weather.
    She thinks a rabbit's foot brings her good luck.
cause, introduce, produce, initiate

broad See **deep, thick, wide**

broke See **poor, money**

broken
adjective
    no longer working
    The television is broken.
out of order, in disrepair, on the blink, out of
commission

brown See **hair**

brush
verb
    to lightly touch or move across
    When I crawled under the house, cobwebs brushed my face.
graze *The cat grazed my leg.*
stroke *My mom stroked my face while I lay sick in bed.*
sweep *Her dress swept the floor.*
touch *I felt something touch my arm.*

buck See **oppose**

buddy See **friend**

build
verb
    1 to make by joining together different parts and materials
construct, assemble, erect, make
    2 to make stronger or larger
    Success built her confidence.
    They are building an excellent team.
develop, fortify, strengthen, reinforce
    3 to grow in size, amount, or intensity
    Listen to the music build.

A
B
C
D
E
F
G
H
I
J
K
L
M
N
O
P
Q
R
S
T
U
V
W
X
Y
Z

a
b
c
d
e
f
g
h
i
j
k
l
m
n
o
p
q
r
s
t
u
v
w
x
y
z

develop, intensify, swell, grow, heighten, increase

noun

a particular type of body
Football players often have a large build.
frame *Mr. George has a large frame.*
figure *My sister has a petite figure.*
physique *The boxers had fine physiques.*

building ⊙

noun

1 a large structure built for people to live in or do things in, such as houses, schools, stores, and offices
construction, house, residence, dwelling, structure, facility

> **Dwelling, residence,** and **house** should only be used when referring to a **building** that people live in.
>
> A **facility** is a building that has been designed to provide a service, such as a gym or hospital.

> *some parts of buildings*
> atrium, balcony, belfry, buttress, cloister, court, dome, eave, elevator, escalator, lobby, loft, steeple, terrace, tower, turret, wing

2 the act or job of making such structures
Building on the new addition will continue until the end of the summer.
construction, architecture

bull See push

bump

verb

to knock against or hit, often by accident
Our car bumped the car parked in front of it.
collide with, hit, jostle, knock into, nudge, thump

noun

a small swelling or raised area
The bump on her arm was a mosquito bite.
lump, bulge, swelling

bunch See circle, concentrate, gather, group, lump

bundle See band, package

burden

noun

something that is carried or difficult to bear
The pack was a heavy burden.
Her ill health is a burden on both of us.
load, hardship, strain, weight

verb

to place a burden on; give a heavy load to
The teacher burdened us with a lot of homework for the weekend.
load, overload, saddle, weigh down, oppress

burn ⊕ ⊙

verb

1 to be in flames; be on fire
The forest burned for three days.
blaze, flame, flare, smolder

2 to cause to be set on fire
He burned his trash in the back yard.
fire, light, spark, ignite, inflame, kindle, set fire to

3 to sting or hurt sharply
This bee sting burns.
smart, sting, hurt, irritate

4 to hurt or damage by too much heat
The pot burned my hand.
broil, blister, scorch, sear, singe

burst

verb

to break or open up suddenly or violently
The balloon burst.
erupt *Lava erupts from a volcano.*
explode *If you blow too much air into a balloon, it will explode.*
rupture *The damn ruptured and caused a flood.*
split *The package split open.*

 Human Body   Human Mind   Everyday Life   History and Culture   Communication

Building

balcony

steeple

buttress

cloister

tower

columns

portico

dome

turret

tower

parapet

façade

spire

onion domes

colonnade

skyline

vault

skyscraper

portal

ornamentation

courtyard

ruins

terrace

plaza

pop *The balloon popped when the dog put his paw on it.*

break *Water pipes can break when the temperature drops below freezing.*

detonate *The police removed the bomb before it detonated.*

bust *The balloon will bust if you squeeze it.*

noun

an act of bursting

I was startled by a loud burst of thunder.

eruption, outbreak, blast, detonation, explosion, outburst, rupture

See also: break, expand

business

noun

1 the work a person does to earn money; job or trade

What business are you in?

occupation *Teaching is the occupation of most members of her family.*

job *Does your job require you to wear a suit every day?*

career *She wants to have a career as a scientist.*

employment *She found employment as an electrical engineer.*

work *She enjoys her work with children.*

trade *He's learning the carpentry trade.*

position *My cousin has a new position as chief of police.*

profession *Marla entered the legal profession after finishing law school.*

line *He chose home repairs as his line of work.*

2 a company or other group that buys and sells goods or services in order to make money

She owns two businesses, a card shop and a restaurant.

company *The company hired ten new workers this year.*

corporation *She is the president of a large corporation.*

establishment *He always gets his hair cut at that establishment.*

firm *Which law firm does Marla work for?*

industry *Most of the people in this town work in the auto industry.*

office *Tom works in a doctor's office.*

shop *Mr. Leonard owns a toy shop.*

store *Please pick up some bread at the grocery store.*

3 a duty or interest

It's my business to see that the work gets done.

affair, concern, problem, responsibility

4 a particular matter, process, or event

His disappearance was a strange business.

affair, happening, matter, event, occurrence, situation, circumstance

busy

adjective

1 doing something or working on something

The mechanic is busy putting the engine back together.

active *My grandmother is retired but still leads an active life.*

engaged *The doctor is engaged with another patient.*

occupied *They are occupied with building their new house.*

working *Are you free for a movie tonight, or are you working?*

involved *Alice is involved in writing another novel.*

2 full of work or activity

Monday was a busy day for you.

active, productive, full

verb

to keep busy or occupied

She busied herself with homework.

absorb *Her new pet lizards absorbed her for weeks.*

engage *A card game engaged the children for hours.*

interest *He interested the baby with a new toy.*

occupy *How do you occupy yourself on weekends?*

work *Cruel overseers worked the slaves in the cotton fields.*

but See **except, only**

butter See **spread**

button See **clothes**

 Human Body   Human Mind   Everyday Life   History and Culture   Communication

buy

verb

to get in return for paying money
She saved her allowance and bought a bicycle.
purchase, acquire, obtain, get, gain

Antonym: sell

noun

something bought
This car was a good buy.
purchase, steal, bargain, deal
The clerk carried my purchases to my car.

Bargain, **steal** and **deal** are all words for something obtained for a low price. They are also informal expressions. When writing something that requires a more formal and less personal tone, use **purchase**.

A
B
C
D
E
F
G
H
I
J
K
L
M
N
O
P
Q
R
S
T
U
V
W
X
Y
Z

a
b
c
d
e
f
g
h
i
j
k
l
m
n
o
p
q
r
s
t
u
v
w
x
y
z

cabin ○ *See* **home, house, airplane**

cage ○ *See* **confine, bank**

call
verb

1 to say in a loud voice or shout out
She called his name, but nobody answered.
shout, cry, roar, scream, yell, bellow, holler, exclaim

All of these words can be used as both nouns and verbs, except for **exclaim**. The noun form of **exclaim** is **exclamation**: *Julie gave an exclamation of surprise.*

2 to tell someone to come
She called us to dinner.
ask, invite, summon, beckon
Dora's friend invited her to spend the night.
The principal summoned the students who had been fighting to his office.

To **beckon** means to tell someone to come by making a motion.

3 to telephone
Call me next week.
phone, telephone, buzz, contact

4 to name
She called her story "The Missing Monkey."
entitle, title, name, term

calm
adjective

not disturbed or excited
A good nurse stays calm at the sight of blood.
cool, peaceful, quiet, serene, still, composed, tranquil

Antonym: excited

noun

freedom from disturbance
There was calm in the house while he was gone.
peace, peacefulness, quiet, restfulness

verb

1 to make less excited or quieter
The speaker calmed the angry crowd.
settle *This music will settle you down.*
quiet *The promise of chocolate pudding quieted little Frieda.*
soothe *The sounds of the sea soothed the sailor.*
compose *Mr. Mello composed himself before he rang the doorbell.*
relax *Having the radio on relaxes Mom.*
pacify *He pacified the watchdog with a juicy bone.*
lull *The song lulled her to sleep.*

2 to become calm
I'll calm down when I know that she is safe.
cool off, settle down, quiet down

Antonyms: excite (1), unsettle (1), upset (1)
See also: still

camp *See* **stay**

can *See* **fire, jail, prison**

cancer *See* **poison**

candle *See* **light**

 Human Body   Human Mind   Everyday Life   History and Culture   Communication

candles *See* celebration

canine *See* tooth

canoe *See* boat

canyon *See* valley

cap *See* close, cover

capable *See* able

capacity *See* ability, power, reach

cape *See* point

capital *See* money, country

captain *See* lead, leader, pilot

capture
verb
    to take hold of by force or the use of tricks
    They captured the escaped tiger by using meat as bait.
seize *The soldiers seized the enemy fort.*
take *The army took the city at dawn.*
catch *Catch me if you can.*
snatch *He snatched my puppy and ran away with it.*
apprehend *The police apprehended the thief.*
    Antonym: release
    See also: catch

care
noun
    1 serious attention
    Do this important job with care.
attention, attentiveness, awareness, watchfulness, notice

The word **notice** is also a verb: *The gardener noticed some hoof prints.* It can also be used as a noun and a synonym for **care**: *The teacher took no notice of their whispering.*

words related to caring
    attend, baby, dote, groom, handle with kid gloves, keep tabs on, maintain, mind, minister, mother, nurse, pamper, protect, support, take care of, tend, keep an eye on, look after, trust, watch

2 worry or concern
Mr. Jones decided to forget all his cares and dance.

When everyone takes **care** of himself, care is taken of all.
—*proverb*

anxiety, concern, worry, trouble
    3 the act of watching over or tending
    The sick man should be under the care of a doctor.
attention, charge, custody, keeping, watch
    Antonyms: carelessness (2), disregard (2), neglect (2)
verb
    to be concerned
    He didn't care what other people said about him.
mind, worry, fret, bother
    See also: like[1], want

career
noun
    the work a person chooses to do through life
    She wants to have a career as a scientist.
occupation *Teaching is the occupation of most members of her family.*
profession *He entered the legal profession after finishing law school.*
vocation *Mel has made acting his vocation.*
livelihood *Dairy farming is his livelihood.*
    See also: business, job

carefree
adjective
    without worries
    We longed for the carefree days of summer.
lighthearted, untroubled, unworried, happy-go-lucky, cheerful
    Antonyms: careworn, concerned, troubled,

A B C D E F G H I J K L M N O P Q R S T U V W X Y Z

 Living World Physical World Natural Environment Economy Government and Law 33

a
b
c
d
e
f
g
h
i
j
k
l
m
n
o
p
q
r
s
t
u
v
w
x
y
z

worried

careful
adjective

1 taking care in one's actions
He is a careful driver.
attentive, cautious, watchful, alert, safe

2 done with care and effort
He did a careful job trimming the bushes.
conscientious, diligent, precise, accurate

See also: careless

carefully   *See* well

careless
adjective

1 not paying close attention; not careful
A careless driver sped through the red light.
negligent, reckless, thoughtless, sloppy

2 showing a lack of planning, thought, or interest
He made some careless mistakes in his essay.
offhand, thoughtless, slipshod, unintentional, casual

Offhand and **thoughtless** mean "done without thinking first": *I made an offhand (or thoughtless) comment that hurt her feelings.* **Slipshod** means "carelessly done or made." **Unintentional** means "done without meaning to."

See also: careful

cargo   *See* load

carriage   *See* appearance

carry
verb

1 to take from one place to another; bear or support while moving
Paul carried his dinner to the table.

bear, bring, cart, cart off, convey, haul, lug, take, tote, transport
She lugged my suitcases up the stairs.
The ferry transports cars across the bay.

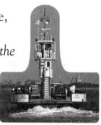

Use **tote** and **lug** only if a person is doing the carrying. **Transport** means to carry by means of a vehicle. **Cart** means to carry in a cart or something like a cart: *They carted him off to jail in a paddywagon.* If you are writing about carrying something heavy or very large, try using **lug** or **haul**.

2 to have in stock; sell
The store carries many different products.
offer, provide, stock, supply, handle

cart   *See* carry

case   *See* example, fact, reason

cash   *See* money, bank

cast   *See* air, pitch, throw, film, theater

cat
noun

1 a small, furry mammal with whiskers, short ears, and a long tail; housecat

some kinds of cats
domestic, purebred, stray, wild
things cats do
arch, feed, hunt, leap, pounce, sleep, stalk
sounds cats make
growl, hiss, meow, mew, purr

 Human Body   Human Mind   Everyday Life   History and Culture   Communication

2 any of the larger wild animals related to the kind of cat kept as a pet

some wild cats
bobcat, cheetah, cougar, jaguar, leopard, lion, lynx, mountain lion, ocelot, panther, puma, tiger

catch
verb

to take hold of something or someone that is moving
Catch me if you can.

capture, seize, nab, bag, corral, nail, snag, trap, snare

Antonyms: fumble, miss, release

noun

1 a thing or the amount that is caught
The hunters brought home their catch.
take, haul, capture, booty

2 a thing that takes hold of something and slows or stops its motion
The catch was broken and the door would not close.
bolt, fastener, latch, hook, lock

3 a hidden trick or flaw in something
When someone offers you a free car, there must be a catch.
hitch, trap, trick, snag, gimmick

See also: capture, stick, surprise

category *See* **class, kind**

cause
noun

1 something or someone that brings about a result or effect
Smoking is one cause of lung cancer.
source *The run-off from farms was found to be the source of the lake's pollution.*
motive *Greed was his motive for robbing the drugstore.*
factor *Poor nutrition is a factor in many diseases.*

stimulus *Sunlight is a stimulus to plant growth.*
agent *People say the new mayor will be an agent of change.*
influence *Jazz music has been an important influence on her piano style.*

2 good reason or enough of a reason
There is no cause for worry.
excuse, reason, grounds, occasion, explanation

Antonym: effect (1)

verb

to make happen; be the cause of
The colony of bats in the attic caused a panic.
bring *She thinks a rabbit's foot brings her good luck.*
lead *New information led to a change in the plan.*
breed *Anger breeds violence.*
determine *The colors you choose will determine the mood of the picture.*
effect *He worked to effect change in local government.*
prompt *Your letter prompted me to call you.*
provoke *The unfair law provoked protest.*
sway *Her speech swayed them to change their vote.*
work *The mechanic worked wonders on our car.*
inspire *The sermon inspired joy in their hearts.*
do *He did no harm.*

cautious
adjective

taking care to avoid danger or trouble
The children were cautious as they entered the haunted house.
careful, wary, watchful, vigilant, on guard, prudent

Antonyms: careless, heedless, rash, reckless

cave *See* **hole**

cavity *See* **hole**

celebrate *See* **observe, praise, religion**

celebration ○
noun

anything done in order to honor something
There will be a celebration on Miss Pigg's birthday.

festival, ceremony, party, festivity, holiday, occasion, gala, feast, merrymaking

> *things found at a celebration*
> balloons, bonfires, candles, champagne, confetti, cornucopias, costumes, crepe paper, decorations, drinks, firecrackers, fireworks, food, garlands, gifts, hats, leis, medals, music, novelties, ornaments, presents, tinsel, trophies

cellar *See* **home**

cement *See* **fix, paste**

center
unknown
1 the middle of something
There is a nut in the center of this candy.
core, middle, midpoint, heart, kernel, marrow, nucleus

A **kernel** is a seed inside a shell. **Marrow** is the soft matter in the center of bones. A **nucleus** is the center of an atom. These words are sometimes used outside their regular meaning: *There is a kernel of truth in what he said; His remarks cut me to the marrow.*

2 a place, person, or thing that is the main object of attention or interest
Mali was a center of commerce and learning in the middle ages.

focus, nucleus, heart, hub
> *See also:* middle

central *See* **basic**

central *See* **main**

century ○ *See* **history**

ceremony ○ *See* **celebration**

certain
adjective
1 having no doubt
I'm certain she is still alive.
sure, positive, confident, convinced
> *He is not yet convinced that he needs to eat vegetables.*
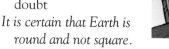
2 known without any doubt
It is certain that Earth is round and not square.
definite, absolute, clear, undeniable, unquestionable
> *Antonyms:* doubtful (2), uncertain (1), unsure (1)
> *See also:* sure, definite, particular

certainly
adverb
yes, indeed; of course
Certainly, you may have some.

Celebration

Human Body   Human Mind   Everyday Life   History and Culture   Communication

all right, by all means, of course, really

chain *See* **line, series, train, jewelry**

challenge
noun
　1 an invitation to enter into a fight or contest of skill
Sir William laid down a challenge to Sir Tom.
dare, provocation
　2 an interesting or difficult problem or task
Getting out of the burning hut was a challenge.
test, venture, obstacle, problem

verb
　1 to question the right of
The Queen challenged Sir John's claim to the throne.
question, dispute, contest, object to, disagree with, deny, protest, oppose
　2 to stir up or make more active
This book will challenge your thinking.
stimulate, arouse, excite, inspire, stretch, try

　See also: protest

chamber *See* **room**

chance
noun
　1 the quality of happening by accident and without being planned or predicted
Chance led me to the only igloo in that part of the Arctic.
accident, fate, coincidence, randomness
　2 luck
It was by chance that the boy found the fossils.
luck, fortune, coincidence, accident
　3 a measure of how likely it is that a thing will happen
What is the chance your hair will turn gray?
likelihood *What is the likelihood that Boris will get up before noon?*
probability *Because you have studied, there is a high probability that you will pass the test.*
prospects *He improved his prospects by going to college.*

possibility *There is a growing possibility that people will someday take vacations on other planets.*
　4 the time when something is possible
Now was his chance to get Missy's attention.
opportunity, time, occasion, break
　5 to take the risk of
The old boat may sink, but we'll have to chance it if we want to escape from this island.
risk, venture, attempt, hazard, try

　Antonyms: design (2), intention (2), plan (2), purpose (2)
adjective
　happening when not expected
He had a chance meeting with a retired robot.
accidental, random, unforeseeable

　Antonyms: deliberate, purposeful

change
verb
　1 to make different
He changed his story when he told it to us.
alter, adjust, modify, rearrange, revise, amend, vary

These are the noun forms of the words listed above: **alteration, adjustment, modification, rearrangement, revision, amendment, variation**.

　2 to become different
You have changed since the last time I saw you.
The leaves change in the fall.
alter, vary, shift, convert
　3 to cause to have a completely different form
The witch changed him into a toad.
turn *The toad turned the wizard into a worm.*
transform *A fresh coat of pink paint transformed the old house.*
transfigure *The fairy's magic transfigured Cinderella.*

A
B
C
D
E
F
G
H
I
J
K
L
M
N
O
P
Q
R
S
T
U
V
W
X
Y
Z

Living World　Physical World　Natural Environment　Economy　Government and Law

convert *We converted the attic into a bedroom.*
revolutionize *The Internet has revolutionized the way people communicate with each other.*

These are the noun forms of the words listed above: **transformation, transfiguration, conversion, revolution.** There is no similar noun form for **turn.**

4 to put another in place of
I change schools next fall.
switch *The two girls switched seats.*
exchange *We exchanged our old car for a new one.*
shift *She shifted seats so that she could see better.*

> If you want to make enemies, try and **change** something.
> —Woodrow Wilson (1856-1924), American president

Antonyms:
freeze (1),
keep (1), retain (1)

noun
the act of changing; the fact of being changed
There are two changes in the class schedule today.
The artist made some changes to his sketch.
difference, shift, adjustment, alteration

Antonyms: changelessness, permanence, stability
See also: adjust, dress, money

channel *See* **passage**

chapter *See* **branch, stage**

character 🔵🔵
noun
1 all those things that make a person, place, or thing different from others
This neighborhood has a friendly character.
He has an honest character.
identity, essence, stamp, disposition, complexion, nature, personality, quality, spirit
2 strong moral qualities
We expect character in our leaders.
integrity, principles, standards, values, backbone

3 someone who is considered odd or peculiar
What a character!
eccentric, oddity, crank, nut, weirdo, oddball

characteristic *See* **part, point, property, typical**

charge 🔵🔵🔵
verb
1 to give a responsibility or duty to
I charged him with the care of my pets while I was away.
assign, entrust, delegate, authorize, saddle with
2 to blame for a crime
She was charged with theft.
accuse *The teacher accused her of cheating.*
blame *Ms. Black blamed me for spilling the paint.*
indict *The grand jury indicted the suspect for stealing.*
book *The police officer booked her on a charge of burglary.*
incriminate *The blood on the man's jacket incriminated him in the assault.*
3 to ask as a price
The cafe charges a dollar for a cup of coffee.
bill, ask, exact, demand, assess
noun
a price asked for
The charge for our meal was more than we expected.
cost, amount, bill, fee, price
See also: attack, charge

charged 🔵🔵🔵 *See* **responsible**

chart
verb
to show on a map, chart, or graph
On this page the author charts changes in temperature.
diagram, graph, plot, map, draw up

charter *See* **hire, law**

chase
verb
1 to follow with the goal of catching

 Human Body   ? Human Mind   👕 Everyday Life   🚩 History and Culture   Communication

The police chased the suspect down the street.
pursue, hunt down, run after, stalk

2 to force to go in a certain direction; drive
   away
Ms. Cohen chased the dog out of the shop.
drive away, run, rout

noun
   the act of chasing
   The car chase is my favorite part of the movie.
pursuit, quest
   See also: follow

cheap
adjective
   1 having a low price
   Vegetables are cheap at the farmer's market.
inexpensive, reasonable, economical

   2 of poor quality
   Cheap clothing wears out quickly.
poor, inferior, base, shabby, shoddy

   3 not willing to spend much money; stingy
   *Andy was too cheap to buy a birthday gift for his
      friend.*
stingy, tight, miserly, penny-pinching
   Antonyms: expensive (1), generous (3)

check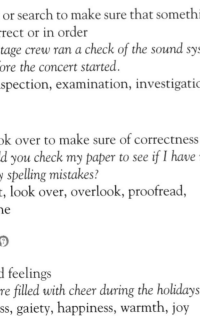
noun
   a test or search to make sure that something is
      correct or in order
   *The stage crew ran a check of the sound system
      before the concert started.*
test, inspection, examination, investigation,
trial
verb
   to look over to make sure of correctness
   *Would you check my paper to see if I have made
      any spelling mistakes?*
inspect, look over, overlook, proofread,
examine

cheer
noun
   1 glad feelings
   We are filled with cheer during the holidays.
gladness, gaiety, happiness, warmth, joy

2 a shout of encouragement, happiness, or
   praise
*The crowd let out a cheer when their favorite team
   scored a goal.*
bravo, hurrah, shout, yell, applause
   Antonyms: boo (2), taunt (2)
verb
   1 to comfort or make happy
   The good news cheered them.
lift, encourage, comfort, console, buoy up

   2 to become happier or less glum
   As the rain stopped, we began to cheer up.
hearten, lighten, revive

   3 to give a cheer to
   They cheered the winners wildly.
hurrah, root for, applaud
   Antonyms: depress (1), boo (3), jeer (3),
      sadden (1)
   See also: encourage

cheerful *See* **bright, carefree, good, merry,
warm**

chemical *See* **energy, technology**

chemistry *See* **science**

chief *See* **first, lead, leader, main**

chiefly *See* **generally, mainly, mostly**

child
noun
   1 a young human
youngster, kid, juvenile, youth, girl, boy, tot,
baby, infant

A **youth** is a teenage boy or young man.

2 a son or daughter
offspring, descendant, issue

choice
noun
   1 the act of picking or choosing
   It was hard to make the right choice.
selection, election, option, pick, decision

a
b
c
d
e
f
g
h
i
j
k
l
m
n
o
p
q
r
s
t
u
v
w
x
y
z

2 the thing or person chosen
Jack was the the drama teacher's choice for the role of king.
pick, selection, preference
See also: choose

choose
verb
to pick one or more from a group
Paul chose three books from the library.
pick *The magician invited me to pick a card.*
select *Maria selected a dress from her mother's closet.*
opt *We finally opted for pizza because we all liked it.*
elect *Reggie elected to stay home rather than go out walking with people he did not like.*
prefer *I would prefer to stay at home.*
single out *The talent scout singled out Erin as the most promising dancer.*
See also: decide

church ⊙ ⊙ *See* religion

circle
noun
1 a closed curve or round shape
We saw a circle of light around the moon.
ring, hoop, halo

2 a group of people who are related by blood or have the same interests
Our family circle comes together for holidays.
clan, crowd, group, society, bunch, crew, brood
verb
to make a circle around
Flowers circle the garden.
encircle, ring, surround, rim, encompass

circuit ⊙ *See* beat

circular *See* round, advertisement, shape

citizens ⊙ *See* country

city ⊙ *See* community, country

civil ⊙ *See* behavior, law

claim
verb

1 to state as true
He was telling the truth when he claimed that his father was seven feet tall.
affirm, assert, maintain, declare, proclaim
2 to need or call for
The children claimed her attention.
call for, demand, require, command, take
noun
a statement of something as true
The king questioned the nobles' claim of loyalty.
profession, declaration

clash *See* battle, difference, fight, war

class ⊙ ⊙ ⊙
noun
a group of people or things that are similar in certain ways
Of all the classes of books, my favorite is fantasy.
category, form, group, kind, sort, type, set

A large group of people met to discuss the plan.
That type of dog has pointed ears.
verb
to group into a class; classify
Our librarian classed the books by author.
classify, designate, group, order, arrange

 Human Body   ? Human Mind   Everyday Life   History and Culture   Communication

clean

adjective

not dirty or stained
I got a clean dish from the shelf.
unsoiled, unstained, sanitary, hygiene

Antonyms: dirty, soiled

verb

to make clean
I clean my face each night before bed.
cleanse, wash, scrub

clear *See* **certain, definite, empty, make, obvious, plain, air, communication, mind, weather**

clearing *See* **space**

clearly *See* **plain**

clever 🄬

adjective

1 having a bright, sharp, and quick mind
She is a clever student who asks interesting questions.
sharp, smart, quick, quick-witted, bright, intelligent, adept

2 showing original thought
His clever invention was successful where many others had failed.
creative, ingenious, inventive, original

Antonyms: dull (1), slow (1)

cliff 🄬 *See* **mountain**

climate 🄬 *See* **environment**

climb

verb

to go up by foot
He climbed the mountain.
ascend, mount, scale, clamber up, shinny up

Scale means to climb up something that is so steep it is almost upright, such as a wall or the face of a cliff. **Clamber** means to climb with effort and using hands and feet: *The chimp clambered up the tree.* **Shinny** means to to climb by gripping with the knees and the hands or arms and pulling oneself up.

Antonym: descend
See also: rise

close

verb

1 to stop up; shut
Close the door.
shut, stop, plug, cap, seal, fasten

2 to block
The police closed the street.
block, choke, obstruct

Antonym: open (1)

adjective

1 near in space or time
It is close to the end of the movie.
We sat close to the screen.
near, next to

2 near in relation or association
She invited her close friends to the wedding.
familiar, special, dear, tight, intimate

Antonyms: distant (1,2), far (1)

closely *See* **well**

cloth

noun

material made by weaving threads or fibers
fabric, material, textile

a
b
c
d
e
f
g
h
i
j
k
l
m
n
o
p
q
r
s
t
u
v
w
x
y
z

clothes ○
plural noun

things worn on the body, such as pants, shirts, and dresses
This store is known for its fine men's clothes.
apparel, clothing, dress, garments, attire, wear, duds, threads

Duds and **threads** are informal, everyday words and are not suited to formal writing or presentations.

---

parts of clothes
button, buttonhole, collar, cuff, drawstring, fly, hem, neck, pocket, seam, seat, sleeve, waist, zipper
words related to clothes
bundle up, change, clothe, design, dress up, iron, launder, mend, press, sew, starch, stitch, strip, try on, undress, wash, wear
some materials that clothes are made of
acrylic, canvas, corduroy, cotton, denim, flannel, hemp, lace, leather, linen, muslin, nylon, rayon, silk, wool

clothing *See* **clothes, dress, wear**

cloud *See* **fog**

cloudy
adjective

covered by or filled with clouds
The skies have been cloudy all day.
gray, overcast, dreary

Antonyms: clear, cloudless, fair

club *See* **beat, hit, organization, society, thump**

clumsy
adjective

1 without physical grace or control
That clumsy child is always dropping things.
awkward, bumbling, hamhanded, klutzy, lumbering

2 difficult to handle or use
It took a long time to set up the large, clumsy tent.
awkward, cumbersome, unwieldy

See also: awkward

cluster *See* **crowd, gather, group, meet**

coach *See* **teach, teacher, train, airplane**

Clothing

monogram, turtleneck, zipper, neck, collar, button, hood, sleeve, snap, belt, drawstring, hem, pocket, seam

Human Body   Human Mind   Everyday Life   History and Culture   Communication

coast ○ 🜨 *See* **fly, slide, airplane**

coat
noun
1 a piece of outer clothing with long sleeves
jacket, overcoat, parka

2 covering or layer
These walls need a new coat of paint.
coating, covering, layer, film, blanket,
application

verb
to cover with a layer
Kiki coated her toast with peanut butter.
cover, spread, blanket, paint, smear

See also: cover

code 🜨 🜨 🜨 *See* **law, rule**

coil *See* **twist**

coin 🜨 *See* **bank, money**

coins 🜨 *See* **money**

cold
adjective
1 without heat or warmth
It's cold outside today, so wear your heavy coat.
chilly, cool, wintry, freezing, frigid, icy

2 feeling cold
*I was so cold last night that I needed an extra
blanket.*
chilled, chilly, chilled to the bone, freezing

Antonyms: balmy (1), hot (2), summery (1),
sweltering (2)

collapse
verb
to fall down; give way
The old house collapsed because of neglect.
buckle, cave in, crumple, sink, tumble

collar *See* **clothes**

collect
verb
1 to gather together

I collected the papers that had fallen on the floor.
assemble, gather, pile up

2 to gather things as a hobby
*He has been collecting stamps since he was five
years old.*
save, accumulate, hoard

3 to make oneself calm
*Kitty collected herself before she answered the
door.*
calm, compose, recover

Antonyms: disperse (1), scatter (1)

collection *See* **group, set**

college *See* **school**

colonial *See* **history**

colony ○ 🜨 *See* **possession, insect**

color 🜨
noun
1 a quality of light as our eyes see it
hue, tint, pigment, shade, tone

> *words that can describe color*
> bold, bright, creamy, dark, dingy, faint,
> gaudy, gay, intense, light, loud, neutral,
> pale, pastel, showy, solid, strong, visible,
> vivid, weak

2 something used to give color
I put color in the cake batter to turn it pink.
coloring, dye, paint, pigment, stain
verb
to give color to
I colored the picture with crayons.
dye, paint, tinge, tint, stain

colorful *See* **bold, bright, personality**

column *See* **train**

combination *See* **cross, mixture**

combine
verb
to bring or join together into a whole
He combined dirt and water to make mud.

Color

cardinal

ruby

cherry

rust

granite

orange

mustard

rose

lilac

canary

lavender

lemon

sky blue

lime

turquoise

pea green

emerald

grass green

olive

raven

charcoal

jet

gold

sand

ivory

lily

snow

mix, blend, join, unite
*If you mix yellow and
blue you will have
green.*
Antonyms: divide,
separate

come
verb

1 to move or travel
toward the speaker
*Some friends are coming
here for dinner tonight.*

advance *The car advanced ten feet.*
approach *The cow approached.*
draw near *We began to wave as the bus drew near.*
near *The train neared the station.*

2 to arrive or enter
Here she comes now!
*I came into the
room when I
heard the
shouts.*
appear *He
appeared out of
nowhere.*
arrive *After
driving all day,
we arrived at the
ocean.*

enter *We entered through the big doors on the side
of the building.*
show up *We waited, but he never showed up.*

comfort
verb

to give relief from a painful or difficult situation
*My mother comforted me when I lost my favorite
toy.*
calm, soothe, console, relieve, ease, support,
cheer

Antonyms: distress, upset, worry
See also: calm

comfortable
adjective

giving ease or comfort
to the body
*When my feet hurt, I wish for
more comfortable shoes.*
cozy, relaxing, snug
*I feel safe when I fall asleep
in my
cozy
bed.*
Antonyms:
ill at
ease, uncomfortable, uneasy

coming See **next**

command See **claim, control, demand,
draw, government, knowledge, lead, order,
power, reach, rule, understanding**

commercial See **advertisement**

commission See **office, permit**

common
adjective

1 belonging equally to all members of a group
*My friends and I have a common interest in foot-
ball.*
joint, shared, public, mutual

2 easily found; happening often
Pigeons are common in our part of the country.
Snow is common in winter.
usual, ordinary, commonplace, everyday,
widespread, familiar, popular, general,
conventional

Antonyms: personal (1), private (1), rare (2),
uncommon (2)
See also: usual, ordinary

communicate See **express, say, language**

communication
noun

the sharing or exchange of messages, information, or ideas

a
b
c
d
e
f
g
h
i
j
k
l
m
n
o
p
q
r
s
t
u
v
w
x
y
z

some kinds of communication
audible, electronic, oral, silent, spoken, written
some words that describe communication
brief, clear, confidential, difficult, direct, indirect, interrupted, long, long distance, mass, mutual, one-sided, precise, rapid, wordy
some uses of communication
advertise, advise, contact, describe, enlighten, express, inform, invite, persuade, promote, reveal, share, speak, talk, teach, tell

community ○
noun
a particular area where a group of people live

examples of communities
borough, city, neighborhood, town, village
kinds of communities
rural, suburban, urban

companion *See* **friend, match**

company
noun
1 a business or organization
The company hired many new workers this year.
business, firm, agency, corporation

2 the presence of another person
I enjoy your company.
companionship, friendship, society, fellowship, association
Their friendship has lasted for many years.

compass *See* **surround**

compete
verb
to try to win or get something that others are also trying to get
The two friends competed for the starring role in the play.

contend, contest, vie, fight

competition ☻ *See* **contest, game, opponent**

complain
verb
to express pain, sadness, or unhappy feelings about something
He complained of a headache.
She complained about the cold weather.
fuss, grumble, moan, whine

complete
adjective
1 having all of the necessary parts
I have a complete set of kitchen knives.
comprehensive, entire, full, perfect, total, whole, intact

2 perfect or thorough
I have complete faith in the weather report.
absolute, total, utter, perfect, thorough

Antonyms: incomplete (1), partial (1)
verb
to finish
He completed the test in one hour.
finish, conclude, wrap up

See also: end

completely *See* **quite, stiff, well, wide**

complex *See* **deep, difficult, hard, structure**

complicated *See* **technology**

composed *See* **calm**

composition *See* **music, piece, structure**

compound *See* **mix, mixture**

concentrate
verb
1 to draw towards or fix on a center
Concentrate your attention on this problem.
center *The movie centered on the adventures of a boy and his dog.*
direct *He directed his attention toward the speaker.*
focus *She focused her energy on reaching her goal.*

 Human Body   ? Human Mind   Everyday Life   History and Culture   Communication

fix *Sara fixed her mind on completing her work in time to go to the dance.*
aim *Why are you aiming your anger at me?*

2 to make stronger or purer
Boiling concentrates thin maple sap into syrup.
boil down, condense, reduce, thicken

See also: gather

concept ⊙ *See* **idea, thought**

concern ⊙ *See* **bother, business, care, matter, subject, worry, emotion**

conclusion *See* **decision, end, finish, judgment, result**

concrete *See* **physical**

condition
noun
1 the state of being of someone or something
He has been in bad condition since his pet died.
situation *The snowstorm put the drivers in a dangerous situation.*
state *The old house was in a bad state.*
shape *The roads are in much better shape now that they have been repaved.*
position *He doesn't understand the homeless man's position.*

2 a state of health or of being fit for use
Her teeth are in good condition from frequent brushing.
The car is in bad condition and needs a new engine.
health *She was in bad health from years of smoking.*
order *If a phone has no dial tone, it is out of order.*
repair *The old shed is still in good repair.*
shape *This old house is in fine shape.*
state *What state are you in?*
trim *Since he exercises, he is in fine trim.*

3 something that must happen before another event or thing can occur
Being over sixteen years old is a condition for getting a driver's license.

circumstance, necessity, provision, requirement, qualification

4 a sickness or an unhealthy state of the body
My mother has a back condition that makes it difficult for her to walk.
ailment, disorder, problem

See also: train

conduct ⊙ ⊙ ⊙ *See* **action, behavior, guide, lead, electricity**

conductor *See* **guide**

conference *See* **meeting**

confidence
noun
a sense of trust or faith in a person or thing, or in oneself
She has confidence in the work I do.
He writes with great confidence.
belief *The coach's belief in me helped me to succeed.*
faith *Linda has faith in herself.*
trust *Your honesty has helped to earn my trust.*

Antonyms: disbelief, doubt, uncertainty

confident
adjective
having trust or faith
We are confident that our team will win.
certain, positive, sure, convinced, secure

Antonyms: uncertain, unsure
See also: certain, sure

confine
verb
to shut in; put in prison
The king confined the thief for thirty days.
enclose, restrict, cage, coop up, imprison, jail, lock up

Antonym: release
noun
border or limit
We kept Rover within the confines of our yard.
boundaries, bounds, borders, limits

a
b
c
d
e
f
g
h
i
j
k
l
m
n
o
p
q
r
s
t
u
v
w
x
y
z

See also: limit

conflict ⊙ ⊚ *See* **battle, difference, war, literature**

confuse
verb
  1 to fail to see the difference between or among
    He was so tired that he confused the sofa with his bed.

mix up *Everyone mixes up my twin brothers.*
mistake *From down the street, I mistook Brian for you.*
confound *He confounds fantasy with reality.*
muddle *Ms. Ambers muddled the names of her students.*

  2 to puzzle or bewilder
    The loud noises and bright lights confused me.
bewilder, daze, baffle, mystify, puzzle
  Antonyms: clarify (2), differentiate (1), distinguish (1), guide (2), orient (2)
  See also: puzzle

congress ⊚ *See* **assembly**

connect
verb
  to join together
    I connected the plug to an extension cord.
join, link, hitch, attach, splice
  Antonyms: cut, disconnect, sever

connected *See* **related**

connection
noun
  the fact of being related, connected, or associated
    There is a connection between drugs and crime.
link, relation, relationship, association, bond, tie
  Antonyms: disconnection, divide, gap, separation

conquer
verb
  to get or overcome by force
    Alexander the Great conquered Persia.
overpower, defeat, overcome

conscious *See* **thought**

consciousness *See* **feeling, mind, perception**

consent *See* **agree, agreement, approval, permission**

conservative *See* **formal, old-fashioned, safe, square, personality**

consider ⊙
verb
  1 to think carefully about; reflect on
    She is considering moving to Alaska.
reflect, think, study, deliberate, contemplate, weigh, ponder

Reflect and **think** are usually followed by "on" or "about": *She reflected on how she would spend her summer vacation; I'm thinking about how to solve this problem.*

  2 to keep in mind; take into account
    My teacher considers test grades, homework, and class participation when she writes report cards.
regard, take into account, take note of
  Antonyms: disregard (2), ignore (2), neglect (2)
  See also: think

considerable *See* **large, much**

considerably *See* **far**

consideration *See* **thought**

considered ⊙ *See* **deliberate, thoughtful**

consistent *See* **regular**

 Human Body   Human Mind   Everyday Life   History and Culture   Communication

constant
adjective
going on without a pause
The child's constant crying annoyed the neighbors.
continual, endless, nonstop, persistent

constantly *See* **always**

constitution ○ *See* **law**

constitutional *See* **walk**

construction *See* **building, structure**

consumption *See* **economy**

contact *See* **call, touch, communication**

contain *See* **control, cover, include, limit, restrict, swallow**

contemporary ○ ● *See* **modern, history, theater**

content *See* **satisfy**

contentment *See* **pleasure**

contest
noun
1 a race or game that people try to win to get a prize
My cousin won first prize in the math contest.
competition, match, game, race, bout, tournament
2 a fight or struggle to win or to be better
A contest among the gods is a theme of ancient tales.
battle, competition, fight, struggle
verb
to argue against
He contested the grade he got on his science project.
challenge, question, dispute, object to, oppose
See also: compete

continually *See* **always**

continue
verb
to keep happening or being; to last for a long time
The snow continued to fall until late at night.
The party continued for an hour after you left.
last, persist, extend, proceed, carry on, go on, keep on
Antonyms: cease, end, lapse, stop

continuous *See* **solid, steady**

contract *See* **agreement, deal, get**

contrary *See* **different, difficult, opposite, stubborn**

contrast *See* **difference**

control ○
verb
1 to use power to manage or command
The king and queen control their country.
command, direct, dominate, lead, manage, regulate, rule, govern
We directed the movers to put the sofa by the window.
2 to hold back or restrain
She tries hard to control her quick temper.
check *The rider checked his galloping horse.*
contain *She couldn't contain her enthusiasm.*
curb *Dan curbed his anger.*
govern *The animal trainer governs his performing tigers with gentle firmness.*
hold *She held her temper even though she was angry at her brother.*
limit *The dam limits the flow of water.*
rein in *We will have to rein in our spending.*
restrain *Try to restrain your dogs.*
restrict *They restricted his free time.*

A B C D E F G H I J K L M N O P Q R S T U V W X Y Z

stop *The police officers were able to stop the crowd and prevent a riot.*

noun

the power or authority to control someone or something

Pirates have control over that island.

Our teacher keeps control over our class.

authority, command, direction, management, power, regulation, rule

convenient *See* **useful, technology**

convention *See* **meeting, practice**

conversation ● *See* **talk**

convince *See* **persuade, knowledge**

convinced *See* **certain, confident, positive**

cook ○

verb

to prepare food for eating by using heat

She cooked the green beans in boiling water.

> *some ways of cooking*
> bake, boil, broil, fry, grill, roast, scramble, simmer, smoke, steam, stew
> *some words associated with cooking*
> beat, chop, dress, glaze, grease, mash, mix, stir, stuff

cool *See* **calm, cold, steady, swell**

copy

verb

1 to do something in the same way as another

Lisa copied her friend's style of dress.

imitate, follow, mimic, mirror, ape, parrot

The chimp mimicked our movements.

2 to make a copy of

I copied the spelling list in my best handwriting.

duplicate, reproduce, trace

noun

something that looks exactly like another

That picture is a copy of the original painting.

duplicate, imitation, reproduction

Antonym: original

cord *See* **line**

core ❶ ❻ *See* **bottom, center, root, fruit**

corn *See* **grain**

corner *See* **turn**

corporation *See* **business, company**

correct *See* **accurate, exact, formal, proper, repair, behavior**

cost ●

noun

the amount of money charged or paid for something

The cost of cereal is higher than it used to be.

charge, price, fee, toll, rate, amount

costly *See* **dear**

cottage ○ *See* **home, house**

cotton *See* **clothes**

council *See* **assembly**

count *See* **amount, depend, total, exercise**

countless *See* **endless, many**

country ◐

noun

1 a large area of land where people live under the same government or have the same culture

Laos is a country in Asia.

Human Body   Human Mind   Everyday Life   History and Culture   Communication

nation, land, state, domain, government, kingdom, commonwealth, power, realm

> *parts of a country*
> capital, city, county, district, province, town, village

2 the land that belongs to a nation or state
That country has many mountains and rivers.
land, possession, territory, soil

3 the people of a state or nation
The whole country speaks the same language.
citizens, nation, people, population, society, public

4 the land a person is born in or is a citizen of
We had to leave our country because of war.
homeland, home, soil, land, nationality, roots

5 the land outside of towns and cities
The Millers live in the country on a farm.
countryside, farmland, land, rural area, outback, boondocks, backwater

Boondocks is an informal word and probably should not be used in formal essays and reports. A **backwater** is a pool of water that is connected to a river but does not flow. When used as a word for the country, it can be insulting, as it suggests that country life is slow and backward.

See also: land

county *See* **country**

courage ⊕
noun
the ability to face fear or danger
It takes courage to stand up for what you believe in.
bravery, daring, heart, guts, nerve

See also: bravery

course *See* **direction, flow, process, run, stream, way**

court ⊜ *See* **animal, building, love**

cover
verb
1 to put, spread, or lie over something, so that it is protected or hidden
Cover your bicycle so it doesn't get rained on.
We covered the cake with whipped cream.
wrap *We wrapped Frieda in a blanket to keep her warm.*
shield *The trees shielded the crops from the wind.*
shade *He shaded his eyes with his hand.*
shelter *This hut will shelter us from the rain.*
envelop *The magician enveloped himself in pink clouds and disappeared.*
cloak *Mist cloaked the hills.*
curtain *Fog curtained the town*
mask *Donny masked his pimple with a bandaid.*
veil *A line of trees veiled the house from view.*
conceal *Conceal the trapdoor with this rug.*
screen *A curtain screened the magician from our view.*
camouflage *When it snows, the soldiers camouflage themselves by wearing white.*
cap *Please cap the bottle so that the liquid won't evaporate.*
clothe *He told her to clothe herself.*
coat *We coated the strawberries with chocolate.*

2 to take into account
The book on magic didn't cover potions.
contain, include, encompass

Antonyms: bare (1), reveal (1), uncloak (1), uncover (1), unveil (1)
noun
something put over or on something else to shelter, protect, or hide
Put the cover back on the can of paint.
cap, covering, lid, screen, shield, top

covering *See* **coat, cover**

cozy *See* **comfortable, warm**

crack
verb
1 to break apart with a snapping sound
The old tree branch cracked under the weight of the child.
snap, burst, pop, break

A B C D E F G H I J K L M N O P Q R S T U V W X Y Z

a
b
c
d
e
f
g
h
i
j
k
l
m
n
o
p
q
r
s
t
u
v
w
x
y
z

2 to break or snap but not into separate pieces
The plate cracked, but it can still be used.
fracture, split, seam, crackle

3 to figure out; find a solution to
They cracked the secret code.
solve, break, decipher, decode

noun

1 a sharp sound
The loud crack of thunder frightened him.
crackle, snap, clap, crash, pop, slam

2 a break in something
There is a crack in the wall.
breach *The soldiers passed through the breach in the wall of the fort.*
break *The break in her leg healed in three weeks.*
cleft *We hid the box in a cleft in the tree.*
fracture *He has a fracture in one of his leg bones.*
gap *Tomorrow I will fix the gap in the fence.*
split *June noticed a split in the seat of Jeff's overalls.*

3 a narrow opening
Daylight came through a crack in the curtains.
chink *Light shone through a chink between two boards in the floor.*
slit *There's a slit in her skirt.*
slot *A nickel stuck in the dime slot.*
aperture *An aperture allows light into the camera.*

See also: break

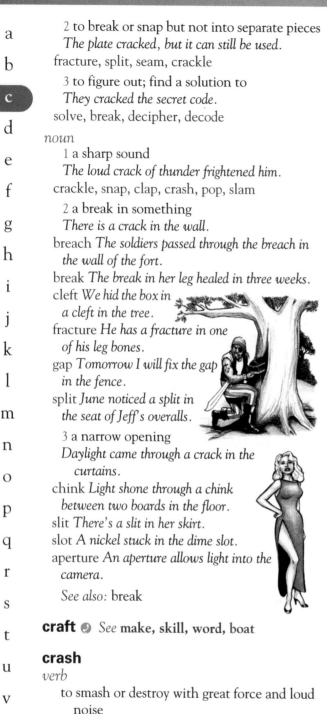

craft See **make, skill, word, boat**

crash
verb
to smash or destroy with great force and loud noise
He crashed his new car.
smash *He smashed the window with a brick.*
dash *Raul dashed the crystal goblet against the bricks.*
shatter *The wrecking ball shattered the side of the building.*

wreck *A tornado wrecked the trailer park.*
noun
1 a loud noise of things breaking or colliding
There was a huge crash when the shelf fell down.
clatter, din, racket, smash

2 a violent collision
Luckily, no one was hurt in the car crash.
collision, wreck, smash-up, pile-up

See also: break

crawl See **drag, edge, animal**

crazy
adjective
1 having a mental illness
The crazy person was being cared for by a doctor.
insane, mad, mentally ill

2 not reasonable or practical
They had a crazy plan to win a million dollars.
foolish *It was foolish to go out in the rain without a coat.*
ridiculous *We had a ridiculous argument about who should take out the trash.*
mad *You must be mad to think you can stay up all night.*
silly *Silly ideas sometimes turn out to be good ideas.*
absurd *It is absurd to think the earth is flat.*

3 very enthusiastic; excited
Jane is crazy about dancing.
wild, nuts, enthusiastic, passionate

Antonyms: practical (2), reasonable (2), sane (1), unexcited (3)

cream See **best, pick**

create See **develop, do, effect, establish, fix, found, make, produce, literature**

creation See **nature, work, world**

creative
adjective
able to make or do something new or with imagination
Lucas always thinks of a creative way to solve problems.

 Human Body   Human Mind   Everyday Life   History and Culture   Communication

That creative inventor designed a new kind of
wheelchair.

imaginative *He told imaginative stories about animals that could read.*

original *He has good
grammar and spelling,
but when it comes to
writing stories, he is
not very original.*

inventive *His
inventive ideas are helping the business to grow.*

Antonyms: uncreative, unimaginative

creature *See* **life, monster**

credit ⚫ *See* **believe, honor, bank**

creek ⚫ *See* **stream**

crew *See* **circle, party, team**

crime ⚫ *See* **offense**

criminal
noun
  a person who is guilty of a crime
  The criminal went to prison for four years.
  lawbreaker, convict, outlaw, crook

  See also: thief

crisis *See* **emergency**

critical *See* **dangerous, serious**

criticism *See* **objection**

crop ⚫ *See* **cut, shorten, bird, photography**

cross
noun
  a mixture of two kinds of animals or plants
    that has characteristics of both parents
  A mule is a cross between a horse and a donkey.
  mix, combination, hybrid, mongrel
verb
  to pass across or intersect

The bridge crosses
    the river.
intersect *This
  road intersects
  the state
  highway.*
meet *Follow Green
  Street until it meets State
  Street, and then turn
  right.*
bisect *The road is bisected
  by the old railroad.*
cut through or across *This path cuts across the
  park.*

adjective
  in a bad mood
  He's very cross today, so don't bother him.
  cranky, disagreeable, grouchy, grumpy

crow *See* **boast, happiness**

crowd
noun
  a large number of people gathered together
  There was a crowd at the baseball game.
  flock, horde, mass, multitude, throng, mob
verb
  1 to gather together in a crowd
  People crowded to see the circus.
  assemble, congregate, gather, herd, throng,
  cluster, pack

  2 to fill up completely
  We crowded the room.
  cram, fill, jam, pack, stuff

crown *See* **honor, top, jewelry**

crude *See* **natural, primitive, raw, savage**

cruel
adjective
  willing to cause pain or suffering
  *The country's cruel leader did nothing to prevent
    the people from starving.*
  vicious, brutal, savage, mean, merciless,
  malicious, ruthless, pitiless, cold-hearted

  Antonyms: kind, merciful

a
b
c
d
e
f
g
h
i
j
k
l
m
n
o
p
q
r
s
t
u
v
w
x
y
z

crush
verb

to cause to lose shape or become flat by pressing or squeezing very hard

Mikey crushed the flowers when he rode his bike on the lawn.

Chris crushed her belongings into the suitcase.

flatten, mash, squash, trample, compress

Use **trample** only when referring to crushing done with the feet (or hooves): *The circus elephants trampled the props and scenery to bits.*

cry
verb

1 to make a loud shout or yell

Cry out if you need help.

He cried out in pain when he twisted his ankle.

call, shout, yell, scream, yowl, howl, shriek, squeal, yelp

I screamed when the lobster pinched my toe.

These words can also be used as nouns:*We heard a shriek (or howl or yowl or scream) from the attic.*

2 to shed tears as the result of pain or strong feelings

The baby cried when he lost his toy.

weep, sob, bawl, blubber, whimper, wail

See also: call, shout, scream

cultural *See* **tradition**

culture
noun

the language, customs, ideas, and art of a particular group of people

> *words that describe cultures*
> ancient, classical, eastern, global, medieval, modern, political, primitive, tribal, urban, western
> *things that are parts of a culture*
> art, beliefs, customs, dialect, folklore, history, ideas, language, legends, literature, music, myth, religion, rituals, values

cure *See* **fix, repair, treatment, drug**

curious
adjective

1 eager to learn or know

She was curious about how stars were formed.

inquiring, inquisitive, nosy

2 interesting because unusual or strange

The curious phone message puzzled us.

strange, peculiar, funny, odd, queer, novel

See also: strange

current *See* **air, modern, present, electricity, knowledge, technology**

curtain *See* **cover, screen**

curve
noun

1 a line that bends smoothly in one direction without any straight parts or angles

arc, arch, bend, bow, turn, wave

2 a bend in a road, path, or river

Drive slowly around the curve.

bend, turn, elbow

verb

1 to cause to curve; give a curve to

The carpenter curved the corners of the table top with a plane.

bend *He bent the nail by mistake.*

turn *The carpenter turned posts for the table legs.*

arch *The cat arched its back.*

 Human Body   Human Mind Everyday Life   History and Culture Communication

bow *Damp weather bowed the planks of wood.*

2 to take the shape of a curve; bend
The river curves around the rocks.
arc *A rainbow arced across the sky.*
wave *His hair waves.*
wind *The trail wound around several small ponds.*
curl *The snake curled around her leg.*
bend *The arm bends at the elbow.*
arch *The batter hit the ball and it arched into the stands.*
bow *His back bowed under the weight of the heavy knapsack.*

Antonym: straighten (2)
See also: bend

curved *See* **bent, round**

custom ⊝ ☋ *See* **practice**

customs ⊝ ☋ *See* **tradition, culture**

cut
verb
1 to pierce, slice, open, or form with a sharp tool such as a knife, ax, saw, or scissors
The barber cut my hair.
She cut her name into the wood with a knife.
carve, clip, nick, split, stab, tear, wound, amputate, chop, crop, hack, lance, mow, notch, pierce, saw, score, shear, slash, slice, slit, snip, trim

2 to divide with something sharp
Cut the cake in half.
section, slice, divide

3 to make shorter or less
He cut his speech to ten minutes.
The store cut its prices during the sale.
shorten, reduce, abbreviate

4 to go quickly from one thing to another
The film cut to another scene.
shift, switch, flit, dart

noun
1 the act or result of cutting

I got a cut on my hand while chopping vegetables.
slash, slice, snip, chop, wound, carving, clipping, incision, piece, cutting

2 a decrease
The toy store is advertising a cut in prices.
decrease, reduction, slash, discount

See also: shorten

cutting *See* **cut, sharp**

a
b
c
d
e
f
g
h
i
j
k
l
m
n
o
p
q
r
s
t
u
v
w
x
y
z

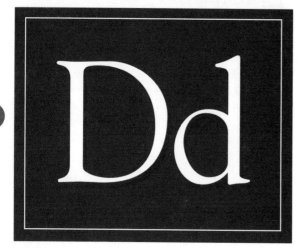

dairy ⊙ ❶ *See* **farm**

damage

noun

harm or loss caused by an injury
We paid for the damage our dog did to his garden.
harm, injury, hurt, destruction

verb

to cause harm or injury to
The movers damaged some furniture.
The fall damaged her knees.
harm, hurt, injure, impair, spoil, ruin, wreck

Use **injure** when referring to a living being: *Your cat injured my dog.* Use **impair** when referring to the physical or mental ability of a living being: *The cold medicine impaired his ability to drive.* **Harm** and **hurt** may be used when referring to both living and non-living things: *Grasshoppers harmed the crops; Poor planning hurt my chances.* Use **spoil**, **ruin**, and **wreck** with objects or things: *The rain ruined (or spoiled or wrecked) my new shoes; The rain spoiled (or ruined or wrecked) our plans for a bike ride.*

---

damp

adjective

slightly wet
His shoes were damp after walking in the puddle.
moist *I used a moist washcloth to clean the bathtub.*

humid *The humid weather made us feel hot and sticky.*
muggy *We wanted to go running, but the weather was too muggy.*
misty *The highlands are known for their cool, misty climate.*
dewy *The dewy grass cooled our feet.*
soggy *He dunks his cookies because he likes them when they're soggy.*
clammy *The sick girl's skin felt cold and clammy.*
dank *She lowered herself into the dark, dank cave.*

noun

moisture in the air or on a surface
Come in out of the damp and cold.
Our basement floor is rotting from the damp.
humidity, moisture, wet, dew, condensation

dance 🏃 ⊙ 🕭

verb

to move the body in a rhythmic way
Everyone danced when the band played.

> *some actions related to dancing*
> bend, bow, clap, glide, hop, jump, kick, leap, prance, rock, skip, stamp, sway, tap, turn, twirl, twist, whirl

noun

a set pattern of movements done to music
The waltz was a popular dance in the 1800s.

> *some examples of dances*
> ballet, belly dance, cancan, cha-cha, conga, contra dance, fandango, flamenco, folk dance, fox trot, hora, hula, jig, jitterbug, limbo, mambo, merengue, minuet, modern dance, polka, reel, rumba, salsa, samba, square dance, sun dance, swing, tango, tap dance, two-step, waltz, zydeco
>
> *some words that describe dances*
> acrobatic, classical, elegant, graceful, lively, popular, rhythmic, traditional

🏃 Human Body   ❓ Human Mind   👕 Everyday Life   🚩 History and Culture   📞 Communication

Dance

fling

prance

undulate

circle

gesture

swirl

dip

twirl

point

shimmy

A B C D E F G H I J K L M N O P Q R S T U V W X Y Z

danger
noun

1 a chance that something bad may happen
The old shed is in danger of falling down.

risk, jeopardy, peril, hazard
A dog crossing this busy road would be in jeopardy.

2 something that causes harm or injury
Firemen face many dangers in their work.

hazard, menace, peril, risk, threat
Antonyms: safe from (1), secure from (1)

dangerous
adjective

likely to cause harm; not safe
The path along the edge of the cliff is dangerous.

hazardous *Smoking is hazardous to your health.*

treacherous *They were warned not to ski the treacherous slope.*

unsafe *Drinking and driving is an unsafe combination.*

critical *She was rushed to the hospital with a critical illness.*

harmful *Be careful when handling this harmful chemical.*

menacing *The menacing dog scared us away from the door.*

Antonyms: benign, harmless, safe, secure

dare *See* **challenge**

dark
adjective
1 having little or no light
It was a dark, moonless night.
black, dim, unlit, shady, overcast, sunless, murky, gloomy, shadowy

2 showing sadness, evil, or mystery
Dan was in a dark mood after his pet died.
Sleeping Beauty fell under a dark spell.
somber, bleak, dismal, grim, gloomy, dreary, sullen, hopeless, evil, wicked, mysterious, ominous, sinister, obscure

Antonyms: bright (1), cheerful (2), light (1), sunny (1,2)

noun
1 lack of light
He lied about his fear of the dark.
blackness, darkness, gloom, murkiness

2 the time of day after sunset
She told him to be home before dark.
night, nighttime, nightfall, evening, dusk, twilight

Antonyms: dawn (2), day (2), daybreak (2), daytime (2), light (1)

darkness *See* **dark**

dart *See* **cut, flash, fly, spring**

dash *See* **crash, drop, escape, flash, fly, run, rush, splash, spring**

data *See* **material**

daylight *See* **light**

dead
adjective
1 no longer alive
The dead tree was gray and leafless.
deceased, done for, expired, lifeless, departed

2 seeming like death
Lara is dead to the world when she sleeps.
numb, insensitive, unconscious

3 without spirit, excitement, or movement
The party was dead at first, but it soon became more fun.
dull, dry, flat, dreary, lifeless

Antonyms: alive (1), lively (3)

deadly
adjective
able to cause death
Rattlesnake bites can be deadly.
fatal, lethal, toxic, poisonous

deal
verb
1 to be concerned or handle
We must deal with this subject carefully.
cope with, handle, treat

2 to act or behave
She is honest in the way she deals with people.
act, behave, function, attend to

3 to do business; trade
My uncle deals in antiques.
trade, traffic

Use **traffic** when writing about an illegal business: *The gangsters trafficked in drugs.*

noun
an agreement or bargain
We made a deal to share the money equally.
agreement, arrangement, bargain, contract, pact, settlement, transaction
See also: sell

dear
adjective
1 much loved
My dear friend Janet is coming to visit.
beloved, cherished, darling, loved, precious, sweet, treasured

2 costing a lot of or too much money
A ring with a real diamond will be dear.
costly, expensive, high, steep

Human Body   Human Mind   Everyday Life   History and Culture   Communication

noun

a person who is liked or loved
What would you like, dear?
darling, honey, sweetheart

See also: expensive

death 🌍⚡ *See* **destruction, doom**

debate ❓💬 *See* **argue, discuss, talk**

decay
verb

1 to rot or become rotted
Leaves decay after they fall to the forest floor.
rot, decompose, spoil, crumble

2 to lose health, strength, or excellence
Her health has decayed over the past year.
decline, ebb, fail, wane, waste, deteriorate

noun

a process of slowly losing quality, strength, or health
The abandoned house is in a state of decay.
deterioration, rot, ruin, collapse

Rust causes the deterioration of metal.

See also: decline, rot

decent
adjective

1 following social standards
In some parts of the world, it is not decent for a woman to show her hair in public.
appropriate, modest, proper, respectable, suitable

2 fairly good
She is a decent cook but will never be a chef.
fair, acceptable, adequate, reasonable, satisfactory, sufficient

3 kind and thoughtful
It was decent of him to help me carry the groceries.
considerate, kind, thoughtful, good

Antonyms: improper (1), indecent (1),

unsuitable (1)
See also: satisfactory

decide ❓
verb

1 to make up one's mind about something
He decided not to run away from home.
Mrs. James decided on the green car.
choose, determine, resolve, settle

2 to reach a decision or solution
In a boxing match, judges decide the winner.
We asked the teacher to decide our dispute.
conclude, determine, resolve, settle, solve, judge, arbitrate

3 to bring to an end
A run in the last inning decided the game.
conclude, determine, end, finish, resolve

decision
noun

the act or result of making up one's mind
I made the decision not to go to camp.
conclusion *I thought long and hard before I came to a conclusion.*
determination *The doctor made the determination that Mo was fit to play football.*
judgment *The court's judgment was in favor of the victim.*
resolution *Their dispute found a speedy resolution.*
settlement *The neighbors reached a settlement about their properties.*
verdict *The jury's verdict was shocking.*

Antonyms: indecision, waffling

deck *See* **boat, home**

declaration *See* **claim**

declare
verb

1 to announce officially
Congress declared a public holiday.
announce, decree, proclaim, pronounce

2 to say strongly or firmly
She declared that she would win first prize.
state, affirm, assert, contend, insist, maintain

3 to make known

a

b

c

d

e

f

g

h

i

j

k

l

m

n

o

p

q

r

s

t

u

v

w

x

y

z

Romeo declared his love for Juliet.
announce, disclose, express, reveal, profess

decline *See* **decay, deny, fall, loss, refuse**

decorate
verb
to make more beautiful by adding
decorations or designs
*We decorated the gym for
the school dance.*
adorn, ornament, trim,
deck out, dress up
*He was decked out in
his best suit.*

decoration ○
noun
1 something used to decorate
Their house was full of holiday decorations.
ornament, trimming, flourish, knickknack

2 something given as a sign of honor
The soldier wore his decorations proudly.
medal, ribbon, laurels, honor, badge

decrease
verb
1 to become less or smaller
The price of snowboards has decreased.
fall, drop, abate, diminish, lessen, shrink,
dwindle, drop off, let up, ease off

2 to cause to become less
Can you decrease the amount of water you use?
lessen, lower, reduce, diminish, cut, pare

Antonyms: increase (1), rise (1)
noun
the act of becoming less or smaller
We are hoping for a decrease in gas prices.
cut, dip, reduction, lessening, lowering

deep ○ ○
adjective
1 reaching far down or back
His cut was deep and needed stitches.
The cave stretched deep inside the mountain.
thick *The ice is three feet thick.*
yawning *She looked across the yawning chasm.*

broad *They crossed the broad river in a canoe.*
wide *There is a wide gap between the mountains.*

2 hard to understand
That poem has deep, hidden meanings.
profound, heavy, complex, obscure

3 intensely felt
I felt deep sorrow when my friend moved away.
intense, heavy, profound, strong

Antonyms: shallow (1,3), superficial (1)

defeat ○
verb
1 to win a victory over in a game or battle
He defeated me in tennis.
beat, best, crush, conquer, overcome, outdo,
overpower, rout, vanquish, lick, clobber,
triumph over.

2 to cause to fail; keep from success
The rainy weather defeated our plans.
frustrate, crush, ruin, overcome
noun
the fact of being defeated
Our team's defeat was hard to bear.
loss, drubbing, failure, overthrow, collapse
See also: beat, lose

defend ○ ○ ○ *See* **explain, protect, sport,
war**

defense
noun
1 something that protects or guards
The castle's defenses withstood the siege.
protection, fortification, shield, safeguard,
guard, security, screen

2 a statement given to support an action
His defense was that he took her socks by mistake.
excuse, explanation, argument, alibi

defiant
adjective
authority
Defiant students will be sent to the office.
The band's defiant songs made them famous.
disobedient, rebellious, bold, insubordinate

Antonyms: compliant, docile, obedient

 Human Body   Human Mind   Everyday Life   History and Culture   Communication

define *See* **mark**

definite
adjective

clearly stated or known
I have a definite plan for my history project.

clear *The clear directions helped with the math assignment.*

explicit *We gave you explicit instructions not to use the computer.*

particular *I only eat that particular brand of ice cream.*

precise *Thanks to the precise map, Bobo was able to find his way home.*

specific *Which specific title are you looking for?*

Antonyms: hazy, unclear, vague

degree 🌐 *See* **level, rank, scale**

delay
verb

1 to put off until a later time
We delayed our vacation until summer.

postpone, defer, suspend, put off

2 to cause to be late
What has delayed him?

detain, slow, hold up, hang up

3 to act slowly so as to cause lateness
If you delay any longer, you'll be late for class.

dawdle, stall, linger, loiter, procrastinate

See also: wait

deliberate ⓘ
adjective

1 said or done on purpose
That was a deliberate insult.

intentional, purposeful, willful, voluntary

2 thought out ahead of time
Mr. Post's apology was deliberate and sincere.

planned, weighed, thoughtful, considered

Antonyms: accidental (1), spontaneous (2), unintentional (1), unplanned (2)

delicate
adjective

1 easy to break or hurt

I gently picked up the delicate cocoon.
My elderly grandmother is in delicate health.

fragile *The fragile chair cracked when he sat on it.*

frail *The frail old man broke his hip.*

tender *Please water these tender plants carefully.*

breakable *Be careful—those crystal glasses are very breakable.*

2 pleasing in a light, soft, or mild way
These flowers have a delicate smell.

exquisite, light, dainty, soft

3 requiring tact and careful handling
Her purple hair is a delicate topic.

sensitive, ticklish, touchy, tricky

Antonyms: rugged (1), sturdy (1), unbreakable (1)

delicious
adjective

having a pleasing taste or smell
The apple pie is delicious.

tasty, appetizing, delectable, scrumptious, heavenly, luscious, mouthwatering, yummy

Antonyms: disgusting, foul, rank

delight
noun

great pleasure or joy
I take great delight in teasing my little brother.

enjoyment, pleasure, amusement, gladness, happiness, joy

Antonyms: grief, sorrow, woe
verb

to give great pleasure or joy to
He delighted us with his wild stories.

charm, enchant, entrance, amuse, please, thrill, cheer, tickle, gratify

Antonyms: burden, grieve, plague, sadden

delighted *See* **happy**

deliver *See* **bear, bring, pass, save**

demand 🔄
verb

1 to ask for forcefully
She demanded he scrub his kneecaps.

democracy – deserve

command *She commanded him to leave the building.*
insist *Ms. Grimly insists on daily homework.*
direct *The crossing guard directed us to wait on the corner.*
order *The sergeant ordered the soldiers to stand at attention.*
urge *I urge you to heed my warning.*

2 to need or require
Babies demand a lot of attention.
claim *The new job claimed more of her time.*
need *Humans need water to live.*
require *Babies require a lot of love.*
want *This coat wants mending.*
take *This assignment took a lot of time.*
exact *The landlord exacted payment from his tenants.*
call for *This situation calls for action.*

noun
something that must be done
There are just too many demands on my time.
claim, requirement, call, drain

democracy *See* government

democratic *See* free

demonstrate *See* display, establish, explain, prove, reveal, show

dense *See* firm

deny
verb
1 to say that something is not true
I denied that I had broken the lamp.
dispute, contradict, refute, rebut, gainsay

2 to refuse to give or provide
My parents denied me a larger allowance.

refuse *I refused him the ten dollars he wanted to borrow.*
reject *The bank rejected his loan application.*
decline *My bank card was declined at the ATM.*
withhold *Her parents withheld permission for her to attend.*
deprive *The tyrant deprived the people of their rights.*

Antonyms: admit (1), affirm (1), confirm (1), grant (2), provide (2), verify (1)
See also: refuse, decline

depend
verb
1 to trust or rely
I'm depending on you to bring the donuts.
count, rely, bank, lean, trust

2 to be decided by or be subject to
Whether I can go to the park depends on how soon I finish my work.
hang, hinge, ride, turn

deposit *See* dump, lay, place, put, bank

depressed *See* sad

depression *See* sadness, economy

depth *See* bottom, shape

depths *See* bottom

describe
verb
to create a picture of in words
This book describes snakes of the desert.
portray, detail, depict, relate, report, illustrate, narrate, tell about

description *See* picture, literature

desert *See* abandon

deserted *See* lonely

deserve
verb
to be worthy of or have a right to

 Human Body Human Mind Everyday Life History and Culture Communication

62

Her accomplishments deserve our respect.
He deserves a reward for saving the child.
merit, rate, earn, warrant, qualify for

design
verb

1 to make or draw plans for
He designed a castle for the queen.
plan *The children helped plan a new playground.*
draft *Maggie drafted a map of the new office.*
sketch *Andy sketched the plot of his new novel.*
diagram *The architect diagrammed the plumbing and heating systems.*
outline *The general outlined a plan of attack.*
devise *He devised a new way to make cookies.*
engineer *She engineered a software solution.*
map out *We mapped out a plan for winning the contest.*

2 to plan for a certain goal or purpose
This playground was designed for younger children.
intend, conceive, target, aim

noun

a plan showing how something is to be built or carried out
The architect presented designs for a new building.
blueprint *Igor's blueprint for the experiment was a success.*
draft *The drafts for the new building are ready.*
plan *The builders studied the plans for the new planetarium.*
program *The library started a fundraising program.*
scheme *We thought of a scheme for making money this summer.*
strategy *What is your strategy for winning the game?*

desirable See good

desire ⓘ
verb

to want or wish for
She desired a new mountain bike.
want, crave, covet, long for, hanker for, wish for

noun

a strong wish or longing
She has a desire to be a commercial pilot.
want, wish, hope, longing, yen, hunger, thirst, appetite, mind, itch

See also: want

desperate See hopeless

destroy
verb

to ruin completely
Fire destroyed the barn.
ruin, wreck, shatter, smash, level, gut, raze, total, trash, demolish, devastate, wipe out

Antonyms: build, construct, create, raise

destroyed See lost

destruction
noun

the process or state of being destroyed
The earth's rain forests are facing destruction.
ruin, death, end, havoc, decay, annihilation, demolition

Antonyms: creation, rebirth, renewal, restoration

detail See describe, picture, point

detect See find, spot

deterioration See decay

determination
noun

the quality of having a firm goal or being determined
People admire his determination to improve at sports.
purpose, resolve, resolution, will, decision

determine
verb

1 to decide or settle finally
We determined our best plan of action.
fix *The club fixed its meeting time for Thursday afternoons.*

set *Have you set a date for your wedding yet?*
appoint *We appointed a time for our meeting.*
resolve *Tom and Jerry resolved their dispute.*
judge *The sheriff judged the pies at the county fair.*
decide *The judge decided the case.*
clinch *The runner's bold move clinched her victory.*

2 to conclude after studying or watching
Scientists determined the age of the shark teeth.
discover, learn, conclude, ascertain, find out

determined
adjective

showing a strong sense of purpose
The determined kids said they would wait in line all night to get tickets to the concert.
ambitious *The ambitious young woman worked two jobs.*
bent *He is bent on going with us.*
decisive *Leaders should be decisive.*
firm *Luke had a firm desire to become a dancer.*
intent *She was intent on winning the contest.*
steady *She tackled the job with steady purpose.*
strong *He gave a strong objection to the court's ruling.*

Antonyms: unsteady, wavering, wishy-washy

develop
verb

1 to bring to a better condition
Try to develop your best qualities.
further, perfect, promote, advance

2 to cause to gain strength or to grow
He tried to develop his muscles by lifting weights.
strengthen, build, grow, enlarge, expand

> Celery, raw,
> **Develops** the jaw...
> —From "CELERY,"
> a poem by Ogden Nash
> (1902-1971), American poet

3 to bring into being or operation
Scientists are developing a new kind of plastic.
create *The chef created a new dessert.*
establish *He established a new club.*
originate *He originated a new dance step.*

evolve *Turtles evolved shells over thousands of years.*
generate *Our discussion generated some great ideas.*
institute *He instituted a way to get the work done more quickly.*
hatch *Marko hatched a plan to earn money.*

4 to grow to or reach a more advanced state
Teenagers develop at a rapid pace.
mature *Malcom has matured as an artist.*
ripen *Apples ripen in the fall.*
age *Grandmother has aged gracefully.*
grow up *My little brother is growing up so quickly.*
evolve *Some scientists believe that birds evolved from dinosaurs.*

Antonyms: ruin (1),
waste away (2),
wither (2),
worsen (1)

development See **growth**

device
noun

1 something used to perform specific tasks
That device removes the pits from cherries.
That device lets a computer respond to speech.
tool, gadget, machine, utensil, instrument, implement, apparatus, contraption

2 a trick or scheme
She used the device of fainting to attract attention.
trick, ploy, ruse, scheme, strategy, maneuver

devil See **personality**

devoted See **loving, loyal**

diagram See **chart, design, plan**

diameter See **shape**

diary See **record**

die
verb

1 to stop living; become dead

 Human Body   Human Mind   Everyday Life   History and Culture   Communication

The plant died because he never watered it.
expire, perish, depart, pass away

2 to lose force or stop working
The car's engine died.
fail, cease, stop, collapse, break down

3 to fade away; gradually disappear
The sounds of the parade died away.
fade, disappear, dwindle, vanish

difference
noun

1 the condition of being not alike
What is the difference between right and wrong?
contrast *What a contrast between your sour mood of yesterday and your good cheer of today!*
diversity *There is great diversity among the schools in our city.*
gap *There is a large gap between what she says and what she does.*
dissimilarity *There is little dissimilarity among the kittens in that litter.*

2 a disagreement or argument
We are friends despite our differences.
conflict, disagreement, clash, quarrel

Antonyms: likeness (1), sameness (1), similarity (1)

different
adjective

1 not the same; not alike
This shop sells several different varieties of cheese.
unlike, diverse, dissimilar, contrary

2 separate; not the same
Three different bus routes go to the library.
distinct, separate, individual, single

Antonyms: identical (1,2), like (1), same (2), similar (1)

difficult
adjective

1 hard to do or understand
The president has to make many difficult decisions.
hard, complex, tough, knotty, challenging, demanding, tricky

2 hard to deal with or please
Mira was being difficult about cleaning her room.
stubborn, obstinate, contrary, demanding

Antonyms: agreeable (2), cooperative (2), easy (1), easy-going (2), pleasant (2), simple (1)

difficulty *See* matter, problem, trouble

dig
verb

1 to make a hole by removing dirt
Pirates dig for buried treasure.
burrow *The rabbit burrowed through the soil.*
delve *Jim was delving in the garden all afternoon.*
tunnel *The miners tunneled through the mountain.*

2 to turn over or remove with a shovel
She dug dirt from the garden for her houseplants.
shovel, mine, excavate, gouge, scoop

3 to shove or poke
He dug his elbow in my side.
poke, jab, shove, thrust

noun

a thrust or poke
He gave me a dig with his finger.
jab, shove, thrust, prod

dignity *See* pride

dim
adjective

1 not well lighted
It's hard to read in that dim corner.
dark, gloomy, murky, shaded, shadowed, sunless, obscure

2 not shining
We noticed her dim, watery eyes.
dull, faint, pale, lackluster, weak, drab

3 not clear to the senses or mind
Only dim shapes could be seen in the fog.
We had only a dim idea of how to build the shed.
blurry, murky, blurred, fuzzy, hazy, unclear, obscure

a
b
c
d
e
f
g
h
i
j
k
l
m
n
o
p
q
r
s
t
u
v
w
x
y
z

Antonyms: bright (1), brilliant (2),
    obvious (3), plain (3), shining (2),
    shiny (2), sunny (1), well-lit (1)

verb
    to make darker
    I dimmed the lights in the room.
    soften, lower, darken, turn down

    Antonyms: brighten, lighten

direct ⟨?⟩ ⟨☎⟩ *See* **concentrate, control, demand,
guide, lead, open, order, point, send, straight,
communication, film, mind, theater**

direction
noun

    1 control or
      guidance
      *He practiced the
      piano under the
      direction of his
      instructor.*
    guidance,
    management,
    control, oversight,
    administration

    *With my grandmother's
    guidance I learned
    how to quilt.*

    2 information on
      which way to go or
      how to do some-
      thing
    A stranger asked us for directions to the fair.
    instruction *The instructions say to unplug the
    toaster before taking it apart.*
    explanation *I did not understand the teacher's
    explanation of the assignment.*
    recipe *If you follow the recipe, your cake will turn
    out fine.*
    guidelines *Ms. Grimly handed us a set of guide-
    lines for writing a report.*
    route *I don't know the route to the beach.*

    3 the way in which one may face or travel
      In which direction did the polar bears go?
    way *Everyone on stage must face this way.*
    bearing *We lost our bearings in the blizzard.*

course *The boat took a dangerous course.*
heading *The submarine set its heading.*

directly *See* **now, soon, straight**

director ⟨☎⟩ *See* **leader, art**

dirt ⟨♪⟩
noun
    1 loose earth or soil
      *The dog is digging a hole in
      the dirt.*
    earth, ground, soil, humus

    2 any dirty material
      such as mud or dust
      *His clothes were covered
      in dirt after the game.*
    filth, grime, mud, muck, slime, slop

> He that flings **dirt** at
> another dirties
> himself most.
> —*Thomas Fuller
> (1608-1661),
> British author*

dirty
adjective
    1 not clean
      We're not allowed to wear dirty clothes to school.
    dingy, soiled, foul, grubby, messy, filthy, muddy,
    stained
      *The office was messy after the
      secretary quit.*

    2 not honest; unfair
      *The press accused the mayor of
      dirty politics.*
    corrupt, foul, crooked,
    dishonest, unfair

    3 not pleasant to do
      Give someone else the dirty work.
    disagreeable, distasteful, unpleasant

    4 showing unfriendliness or contempt
      She gave me a dirty look.
    evil, mean, nasty

    Antonyms: agreeable (3), clean (1), fair (2),
        friendly (4), honest (2), pleasant (3,4),
        pristine (1), truthful (2)
verb
    to make dirty; soil
    Put an apron on so you don't dirty your shirt.
    soil, foul, mess, muddy, stain

    Antonyms: clean, cleanse, wash

 Human Body   ⟨?⟩ Human Mind   ⟨👕⟩ Everyday Life   ⟨⚑⟩ History and Culture   Communication

disappear
verb

to exist or be visible no longer
The plane disappeared into the clouds.
Her smile disappeared.
vanish, dissolve, fade, recede, evaporate, melt away

Antonyms: appear, reappear

disaster
noun

1 a sudden event causing much damage or suffering
The tsunami was a disaster for the island.
calamity, catastrophe, tragedy, blow, misfortune

2 a complete failure
The spaghetti dinner was a disaster.
bust, bomb, dud, flop, fiasco, failure

Antonyms: blessing (1), boon (1), hit (2), sensation (2), smash (2), windfall (1)

discipline ⊘ ⊙ *See* punishment

discourage
verb

1 to cause to lose hope or confidence
His bad test grade discouraged him.
chill, dismay, depress, dampen

2 to try to prevent or persuade not to do
Her parents discouraged her from going skydiving.
hinder, deter, restrain, warn, caution

Antonyms: bolster (1), buoy (1), coax (2), egg on (2), encourage (1,2), persuade (2)

discover *See* determine, find, learn, see

discuss
verb

to consider in writing or speech
This article discusses the alternatives to war.
consider, review, debate, hash out, explore

discussion ⊘ *See* talk

disease ⊙ *See* illness, poison

disgust
verb

to cause strong dislike or illness in
The sight of the dead animal disgusted her.
repel, sicken, offend, revolt, nauseate

Antonyms: attract, delight, please
noun

a strong dislike caused by something that offends
The sight of the maggoty meat filled me with disgust.
distaste, nausea, repulsion, repugnance

Antonyms: delight, pleasure

disgusting
adjective

causing disgust
Rotten fish have a disgusting smell.
vile, sickening, foul, loathsome, obnoxious, offensive, rank, repellent, revolting, horrible, shocking, abominable, ugly

Antonyms: agreeable, delightful, enjoyable, likable, pleasant

dish ⊙ *See* distribute

dishonest
adjective

tending to lie, steal, or cheat
The dishonest student was caught cheating.
crooked, lying, devious, deceitful

Antonyms: candid, honest, plain, straight, truthful

display
verb

1 to cause to be seen
That museum displays modern African art.
show, exhibit, present

2 to make known
He displayed no interest in my new invention.
demonstrate *This painting demonstrates his talent as an artist.*
disclose *Her name tag disclosed her identity.*
reveal *The stage curtain lifted to reveal the actors behind it.*

A
B
C
D
E
F
G
H
I
J
K
L
M
N
O
P
Q
R
S
T
U
V
W
X
Y
Z

show *His yawn showed that he was tired.*
expose *The student exposed a plot to steal the test answers.*

Antonyms: conceal (2), hide (2)

noun

anything brought forth to be seen
We looked over the display of fine jewelry.
show, exhibit, exhibition, exposition, array, presentation

distance

noun

1 the measure of space between things, places, or points in time
The distance from our house to the street is 25 feet.
space, separation, gap, range, opening

2 an amount of space
They walked a distance and then stopped to rest.
way, stretch, length, interval, span

distant See far, outside, remote, family, measurement

distinct See different, independent, particular, plain, single

distinction See honor

distinguished See famous, grand, great, major

distribute

verb

1 to give out to each of several people
The school nurse distributed the vaccine.
allot, dispense, ration, dish, dole, parcel

Dish, dole, and **parcel** are followed by "out."

2 to spread over an area
The farmer distributed the seeds over the field.
broadcast *The news was rapidly broadcast by the neighbors.*
disperse *Birds help trees disperse their seeds.*
scatter *The farmer scattered grain for the chickens.*

spread *Please spread the news that there will be a meeting tonight.*

distribution See spread, economy

district See area, neighborhood, section, territory, country

disturb

verb

1 to interrupt, especially by making noise
The party next door disturbed our sleep.
bother *I'm not supposed to bother my baby brother when he's napping.*
distract *The radio distracted him from his work.*
interrupt *Loud banging on the door interrupted the conversation.*
trouble *May I trouble you to get my coat?*

2 to make nervous or uneasy
It disturbed him to see his mother in the hospital.
bother *It bothers me that he looks so unhappy.*
trouble *It troubles me when you don't do your homework.*
upset *Their complaints upset her.*
worry *He worried his mother by staying out so late.*

disturbance

noun

1 an act or instance of disturbing
The police came to investigate the disturbance.
outburst, storm, upheaval, uproar, ruckus, commotion

2 something that disturbs
The teacher says talking in class is a disturbance.
annoyance, bother, interruption, nuisance

disturbed See upset

dive

verb

to fall downward, usually headfirst
I dived into the pool.
The falcon dove from the sky.
plunge *The swimmer plunged into the cold pool.*
jump *The squirrel jumped to the ground.*
leap *The daredevil leapt from the bridge.*

Human Body　　Human Mind　　Everyday Life　　History and Culture　　Communication

submerge *The seal submerged as the boat came near.*

pitch *He pitched out of his chair in a faint.*

bail out *The paratrooper bailed out of the airplane.*

Dive, plunge, jump, leap, and **pitch** can also be used as nouns.

---

divide
verb

1 to separate into parts
Divide this piece of paper into thirds.
The argument divided the class.
cut, split, partition, portion, section, separate

2 to become separated into parts
The river divides into two smaller streams.
branch, fork, part, split

3 to share in equal parts
Let's divide the pie among all of us.
share, split, apportion, distribute, subdivide

Antonyms: assemble (1), collect (1), combine (1), gather (1), join (2), merge (2)

divine *See* **beautiful, guess, holy, predict**

division *See* **branch, piece, section**

divorce *See* **split**

dizzy
adjective

having a spinning feeling in the head
The carnival ride made him dizzy.
faint, giddy, shaky, unsteady, woozy

Antonyms: balanced, clearheaded, steady

do
verb

1 to carry out
The clown did somersaults.
I have already done my homework.
perform *She performed the lab experiment with care.*
complete *He completed the test in one hour.*
execute *The gymnast executed her routine.*
accomplish *He accomplished his goal.*

fulfill *He fulfilled his obligations on time.*

discharge *Juan discharged his responsibility with great care.*

commit *She committed a crime.*

carry out *Tomorrow we must carry out our secret plan.*

2 to bring into being
He did no harm.
cause *The rain caused flooding.*
create *Her lies created upset at home.*
produce *My class produced a musical show.*
effect *He worked to effect change in local government.*
bring about *The storm brought about damage to the region.*

dock
noun

a raised platform built out into the water
The boats are tied up at the dock.
The boat floated into the dock.
pier, wharf, quay, jetty

doctor *See* **patch, treat**

doctrine *See* **belief**

dog
noun

a furry mammal with four legs, related to wolves

things dogs do
bury, circle, dig, fetch, guard, guide, herd, hunt, lap, lick, pant, play, pull, race, scratch, sniff, stalk, track
sounds dogs make
bark, growl, howl, whimper, whine, yelp

domestic *See* **cat**

don *See* **dress**

A B C D E F G H I J K L M N O P Q R S T U V W X Y Z

a
b
c
d
e
f
g
h
i
j
k
l
m
n
o
p
q
r
s
t
u
v
w
x
y
z

Dogs

circling

doom
noun
an event or end that one cannot escape
The sailors thought the storm would be their doom.
fate, destiny, ruin, death, end, lot

door ○ *See* **entrance**

doorway *See* **entrance**

dot *See* **spot**

double *See* **bend**

doubt
verb
1 to be uncertain about the truth of
He doubts that he passed the exam.
She doubts whether a stork brought her brother.
distrust, question, suspect, wonder

2 to lack trust in
I doubt his ability to complete this task.
question, distrust, mistrust, suspect

 Human Body ? Human Mind Everyday Life History and Culture Communication

Antonyms: bank on (1), believe (1), know (1), rely (2), trust (2)

noun

1 a feeling of being unsure
She has doubts about her future as a chemist.
misgiving, skepticism, uncertainty

2 a feeling of being suspicious
His words filled her with doubt.
distrust, suspicion, mistrust, reservation, qualms

Antonyms: belief (2), certainty (1), confidence (1), faith (2), reliance (2), surety (1), trust (2)

down
adverb

from a higher to a lower position
The rain came down in buckets.
She reached down to pet the cat.
downward *The ball rolled downward into the creek.*
below *Let's go below.*
beneath *The sandwich has jelly on top and peanut butter beneath.*
over *He fell over.*

adjective

1 unhappy
He has been feeling down since he broke his leg.
blue, dejected, low, sad, unhappy, downcast, melancholy

2 sick
The whole family is down with the flu.
ill, sick, unwell

Antonyms: happy (1), joyful (1)

downward *See* down

doze *See* sleep

draft *See* air, design, drawing, plan, wind, write

drag
verb

1 to pull along with effort; haul

We dragged the logs up the hill.
haul, lug, pull, tow, tug

2 to go or do slowly
Traffic often drags at this time of day.
crawl, creep, inch

dragon *See* monster

dramatic
adjective

out of the ordinary
Spring brought a dramatic change in the weather.
impressive, showy, exciting, sensational, conspicuous
The new skyscraper is an impressive building.

Antonyms: everyday, mundane, ordinary

draw
verb

1 to make a picture of with a writing tool
She drew her house on the chalkboard.
sketch, depict, portray, trace, illustrate

2 to move by pulling or dragging
We drew the sleeping dog across the floor.
drag, haul, pull, lug, tow, tug

3 to take out or remove
Who will draw the winning ticket from the bowl?
She drew water from the well.
pick, remove, extract, take, withdraw

4 to cause to come near
This band always draws a large crowd.
attract, lure, pull, command

drawing
noun

a picture made with a writing tool
We attended an exhibit of Rembrandt's drawings.
picture, sketch, design, doodle, draft

dream *See* hope, mind

a
b
c
d
e
f
g
h
i
j
k
l
m
n
o
p
q
r
s
t
u
v
w
x
y
z

dress ○

verb

to put clothing on
He dresses his cat in baby clothes.
clothe, attire, array, costume, outfit, change, don, deck out

noun

clothing in general
The performers wore the traditional dress of their country.
attire, clothing, costume, clothes, outfit, habit

A **habit** is clothing worn for a particular role, such as a nun's habit or a riding habit.

See also: clothes

drift

verb

1 to be carried along by an outside force
The boat drifted in the current.
blow *My cap blew into the water.*
float *The balloon floated in the breeze.*
trail *Smoke trailed from the chimney.*
wash *A strange shell washed up on the beach.*

2 to wander without purpose
He drifted from town to town.
wander, ramble, roam, meander

Antonyms: head for (2), remain (1)

drill *See* **practice, train**

drink ○

verb

to take into the mouth and swallow
I drink orange juice with my breakfast.
She drinks four cups of coffee every day.
swallow, sip, quaff, gulp, guzzle, down, bolt, drain, slurp

drinks ○ *See* **celebration**

drip

verb

to flow downward in drops
Water is dripping from the faucet.

trickle, dribble, leak

drive ○

verb

to operate a car or other vehicle
Tom learned to drive when he was seventeen.
operate, handle, steer

noun

a trip in a car or other vehicle
We took a drive around the lake.
ride *We decided to go for a ride to the lake.*
spin *Let's go for a spin in your new car.*
trip *I made two trips to the store today.*
turn *We took a turn around the village.*
jaunt *Did you enjoy your jaunt in the country?*

See also: trip

drop

noun

a very small amount of anything
I like a drop of milk in my tea.
bit, little, pinch, dash, speck, dab

verb

1 to fall to a lower level
The book will drop off the shelf if you don't move it.
fall, plunge, sink, descend, plummet, tumble

2 to fall in amount, volume, or quality
Their voices dropped when the teacher came in.
The temperature drops after sunset.
fall, sink, decrease, diminish, dwindle, lower, lessen, shrink

drove ○ *See* **animal**

drug ○

noun

a substance used to cure or heal
The doctor gave him a drug to help his digestion.
medicine, medication, remedy, preparation

some kinds of drugs
anesthetic, antibiotic, antiseptic, herb, narcotic, preventive, tonic
some things done with drugs
apply, cure, dispense, give, heal, inhale, prepare, prescribe, swallow, take

 Human Body   ? Human Mind   Everyday Life   History and Culture   Communication

See also: medicine

dry
adjective

> having too little water or moisture
> *It was hard to swallow the dry bread.*
> *The land was dry because of drought.*

parched, arid, stale, bone-dry, thirsty, dehydrated, desiccated

> *Antonyms:* damp, moist, saturated, soaking, wet

duck   *See* body

dull
adjective

> 1 not having a sharp cutting edge
> *You cannot slice a tomato with a dull knife.*

blunt, worn

> 2 lacking in color or brightness
> *They painted their house a dull gray.*

dim, pale, dingy, drab, mousy

> 3 lacking in interest

boring, monotonous, tedious

> *Antonyms:* bright (2), brilliant (2), exciting (3), interesting (3), loud (2), riveting (3), sharp (1)

dump
verb

> 1 to drop in one big load
> *He dumped the newspapers in the recycling can.*

drop, toss, plop, discard, deposit

> 2 to empty or unload by turning over
> *Please dump the spoiled milk down the drain.*

pour, empty, unload, discharge

duty ◉ ◈
noun

> 1 something that should be done because right or fair
> *It is his duty to tell the judge the whole truth.*

responsibility, obligation, burden

> 2 the things to be done in a job or position
> *The duties of chairman include making a speech.*

responsibility, function, job, charge, mission, requirement

A B C D E F G H I J K L M N O P Q R S T U V W X Y Z

 Living World   Physical World   Natural Environment   Economy   Government and Law   73

a
b
c
d
e
f
g
h
i
j
k
l
m
n
o
p
q
r
s
t
u
v
w
x
y
z

Ee

eager
adjective
feeling a strong urge or desire
The admiral was eager for victory.
anxious *He was anxious to return home and see his children.*
avid *Avid for knowledge, Lance spent the whole summer reading in the library.*
greedy *Pat cries a lot because she is greedy for attention.*
thirsty *Aunt Gertrude was thirsty for adventure when she set out on her trip to the rain forest.*

Antonym: reluctant

earliest *See* **first, original**

early *See* **primitive**

earn *See* **deserve, gain, make, receive, win**

earth 🌍 🌐 *See* **dirt, ground, land**

Earth 🌍 🌐 *See* **world**

earthly
adjective
having to do with the earth; of this world
We earthly creatures like to imagine the world of fairies and elves.
terrestrial, worldly, natural, physical

ease *See* **comfort, edge, relax**

eastern *See* **culture**

easy
adjective
1 not hard or difficult
The lazy girl wanted an easy job.
She helped her younger brother find an easy book.
simple *Last year I thought this simple math problem was difficult!*
light *She did some light reading before going to bed.*
effortless *The figure skater made her leaps and spins look effortless.*
soft *Mr. Silver has a soft position at the bank.*

2 without trouble or worry
He leads an easy life.
carefree, untroubled, comfortable, quiet, restful, relaxed

3 not harsh or strict
Many students like the easy teachers best.
gentle, lenient, undemanding, tolerant

Antonyms: challenging (1), demanding (3), difficult (1), hard (1), hard-knock (2), rough (2), stressful (2), strict (3)

eat 🌐 👕
verb
to put into the mouth, chew, and swallow
We will eat soup and sand-wiches for lunch.
consume *He consumed enough food for two people.*
swallow *He swallowed the fish, bones and all.*
wolf *Try not to wolf down your food.*
devour *This dog can devour a steak in seconds.*
gulp *Julio gulped down his breakfast and ran out.*
gobble *It's not polite to gobble your food like that!*

economic *See* **power**

economical
adjective
using only a small amount; without waste
This economical car uses little fuel.

🏃 Human Body   ❓ Human Mind   👕 Everyday Life   🚩 History and Culture   📞 Communication

frugal, thrifty, careful, efficient

Use **frugal**, **thrifty**, and **careful** only when speaking or writing about economical people. Use **efficient** when referring to people or things: *The thrifty man uses both sides of a sheet of paper before recycling it; The efficient flashlight runs for several hours on only one small battery.*

Antonyms: frivolous, wasteful

economy
noun
the way a certain place or region uses and distributes its money or resources
The American economy hasn't been stable this year.

some words associated with economies
consume, distribute, demand, export, import, produce, supply, trade
some words used to describe economies
sound, stable, strong, unstable, weak
some words used to speak of economies
consumption, distribution, employment, goods, production, services, boom, depression, recession

edge
noun
the border or outside line
We saw a deer at the edge of the forest.
border *There is a fence along the border of our yard.*
margin *Wildflowers were growing at the margin of the woods.*
perimeter *The farmers built a fence along the perimeter of the pasture.*
rim *There is a safety fence along the rim of the canyon.*
line *We drove across the state line.*
verge *Karen stood and the verge of the chasm.*

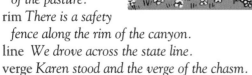

boundary *The fence marks the boundary of our property.*
limits *Our house is just outside the city limits.*
Antonyms: center, middle
verb
to move forward slowly or with care
The children edged away from the snarling wolf.
crawl, creep, inch, ease, sneak, worm

education ○
noun
the act or work of learning or training

some words associated with education
answer, clarify, enlighten, explain, illustrate, instruct, lecture, question, study, teach
some words often used to describe education
basic, elementary, formal, free, higher, practical, well-rounded

effect
noun
1 something produced by a cause
The effect of the snow storm was a day off from school.
consequence, result, impact, outcome

2 the state of being in force
The new rules go into effect tomorrow.
operation, action, force
Antonym: cause (1)
verb
to bring into operation; cause to happen
He worked to effect change in local government.
cause, make, create, produce, accomplish, realize, execute, bring about

effective *See* **practical, successful**

efficient *See* **economical, neat, technology**

effort
noun
1 the action of physical or mental energy
It took a lot of effort to move that furniture.
labor, work, struggle, toil, exertion

2 a hard try

a
b
c
d
e
f
g
h
i
j
k
l
m
n
o
p
q
r
s
t
u
v
w
x
y
z

Please make an effort to finish your book report.
attempt, try, endeavor, push

See also: **work**

elaborate *See* fancy

elbow *See* bend, curve, push

elderly *See* old

election ⊕ *See* choice

electrical *See* energy

electricity ⚡
noun
energy caused by the movement of electrons
through matter

> *some words related to electricity*
> amplify, charge, conduct, discharge,
> disconnect, electrocute, ground,
> magnetize, plug in, power, shock, shut off,
> surge, transform, wire, charge, current,
> frequency, resistance, voltage

electronic ♪ ⚡ *See* communication,
technology

element *See* part, piece

elementary *See* education

elevator *See* lift, building

eliminate *See* kill

elsewhere *See* absent

embarrass
verb
to make uncomfortable or ill at ease
My silly behavior embarrassed my sister.
humiliate, shame, abash

emergency 👟 ⚡
noun
a serious or sudden situation that calls for fast
action
*The flood created an emergency for people living
near the river.*

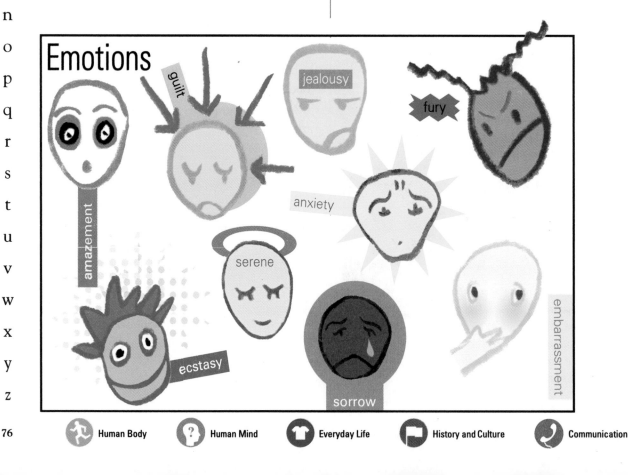

Emotions — guilt, jealousy, fury, amazement, anxiety, serene, embarrassment, ecstasy, sorrow

👟 Human Body   ❓ Human Mind   👕 Everyday Life   🚩 History and Culture   📞 Communication

crisis, extremity, predicament, crunch, pinch

Use **crisis** and **extremity** when speaking or writing about a serious emergency such as one that might involve loss of life or destruction of property. Use **predicament**, **crunch**, and **pinch** when the situation is not as serious, such as forgetting about an important school project until an hour before it is due.

See also: danger

emotion
noun
> a strong feeling

feeling, passion, sentiment, affection

> *some kinds of emotions*
> affection, alarm, amazement, anguish, anxiety, awe, compassion, concern, contempt, desperation, disappointment, disgust, doubt, dread, ecstasy, envy, fright, fury, grief, guilt, hope, jealousy, joy, love, pity, pride, rage, regret, relief, reverence, satisfaction, shame, sorrow, surprise, sympathy, understanding, wonder
> *some words used to describe emotions*
> deep, fiery, fleeting, hot, intense, keen, passionate, profound, shallow, slight, violent, warm

emotional *See* moving, health, injury

emphasis *See* importance, stress, weight

emphasize *See* exaggerate, stress

empire *See* government

employees ⚙ *See* office

employment *See* business, job, practice, use, economy

empty
adjective
> 1 holding or containing nothing

The shelves were empty.
Please recycle your empty bottles.
bare, vacant, blank, void, hollow

> 2 not occupied or used by people
> *The house will be empty while we are on vacation.*

clear, vacant, abandoned, unoccupied

> 3 without purpose, activity, or meaning
> *His life seemed empty after he retired.*

aimless, hollow, insignificant, worthless, barren, trivial, useless, vain

> *Antonyms:*
> full (1),
> in use (2),
> meaningful (3)

> Absence of occupation is not rest,
> A mind quite **vacant** is a mind distress'd.
> —*From "RETIREMENT," a poem by William Cowper (1731-1800), British poet*

verb
> to remove what is inside of; make empty
> *Please empty the garbage can.*

unload *The men unload the truck when it arrives.*
drain *We drained the pool at the end of the summer.*
discharge *The ship discharged its catch of fish.*
clean *We need to clean out the shed to make room for the lawn mower.*
dump *The truck dumped its load of coal.*
hollow *She hollowed out a giant pumpkin.*
evacuate *The police evacuated the building.*

> *Antonyms:* fill, load, stock

enable *See* let, permit

encounter *See* battle, experience, find, meet, meeting

encourage *See* cheer, prompt, support, welcome

encouraged *See* welcome

end
noun
> 1 the point at which anything that has length starts or stops
> *Please tie a knot at the end of the string.*

a
b
c
d
e
f
g
h
i
j
k
l
m
n
o
p
q
r
s
t
u
v
w
x
y
z

There will be a stop sign at the end of the road.

extremity *The extremities of the field were marked by a fence.*

point *The distance of the race is five miles from point to point.*

terminal *Central Station is the terminal of this railway line.*

tip *One tip of this pencil has an eraser.*

2 the last part
I cried at the end of the show.
conclusion, ending, finale, resolution

Antonyms: beginning (2), opening (2)

verb

1 to cause to stop
A knee injury ended her career in hockey.
conclude *We concluded the meeting and went out for lunch.*

finish *Let's take a swim when we finish working.*

abolish *Most countries have abolished capital punishment*

discontinue *Please discontinue this magazine subscription.*

lift *The city finally lifted the ban on skateboarding.*

terminate *We have terminated your membership in our club.*

halt *The umpire halted the game because of rain.*

stop *Please stop your whining!*

2 to reach a conclusion
The class will end around 3:30pm.
cease, conclude, finish, close

Antonyms: begin (1,2), commence (2), start (1)
See also: stop, goal

ending See end, finish, loss

endless
adjective

having or seeming to have no end
We travelled endless highways on our trip last summer.
The possibilities for the future are endless.
countless, infinite, everlasting, immeasurable, vast, boundless

Antonyms: finite, limited
See also: eternal

endure See bear, brave, experience, keep, last, live, receive, stand, take

enemy
noun

1 one who hates or wants to harm another
The wicked king had many enemies in the court.
foe, opponent, adversary, antagonist

2 something likely to cause harm or injury
Hungry grasshoppers are an enemy of our crops.
curse, plague, blight, evil, jinx

Antonyms: ally (1), boon (2), friend (1), partner (1)

energy
noun

1 the power or ability to make something work or be active
Plants use the energy of the sun to grow.
power, force , might, strength, effectiveness

some kinds of energy:
atomic, chemical, electrical, hydroelectric, mechanical, nuclear, solar

2 the amount of such power needed to do something
He did not have enough energy to clean his room.
force *It took force to open the jar.*
go *The old horse still has a lot of go left in her.*
steam *Do you have the steam to climb this hill?*
vigor *He is full of vigor, even at eighty years of age.*
drive *She has the drive to succeed.*
effort *With hardly any effort, the farmer lifted the calf.*
stamina *Exercise will increase your stamina.*

3 eager interest
He spoke with energy on the subject of boat building.
vigor, enthusiasm, liveliness, spirit, pep, zip

Antonyms: apathy (3), lethargy (3)
See also: power

engaged See busy

engine See boat

engineer See design

 Human Body   Human Mind   Everyday Life   History and Culture   Communication

enjoy *See* **have, like, love**

enormous *See* **giant, great, huge, large, vast, measurement**

enough
adjective
as much or as many as needed or required
I have enough money.
adequate *She has adequate funds for a college education.*
sufficient *The amount of food here is sufficient for the camping trip.*
satisfactory *Our supply of fuel is satisfactory.*

Antonyms: inadequate, insufficient, unsatisfactory
adverb
in a way or to a degree that is needed or required
The job doesn't pay enough.
adequately, satisfactorily, sufficiently, acceptably

enter
verb
1 to come or go into
Judge Parsons entered the room.
invade *Ants invaded the kitchen.*
intrude *Please do not intrude while I'm studying.*
infiltrate *A spy infiltrated the enemy's military base.*
board *Bobo boarded the boat.*
break in *A burglar broke into the bakery.*

2 to pass through
The nail entered the wood.
penetrate, pierce, puncture

3 to take part in or compete in
Will you enter this year's spelling bee?
We entered middle school last year.
compete in, engage in, enroll in, participate in, register for

4 to write on a list; type into a computer
I entered my name and address in the hotel guest book.
record, input, register, catalogue

enterprise *See* **activity, adventure**

entertainment *See* **play**

enthrall *See* **fascinate**

enthusiasm *See* **energy, interest, zeal**

enthusiastic
adjective
having or showing great interest
Her book report got an enthusiastic response from the teacher.
keen, avid, hearty, energetic, wild

Antonyms: indifferent, unenthusiastic

entire *See* **all, complete, total, whole**

entirely *See* **quite, totally, wide**

entrance
noun
the place through which one enters
The main entrance to the building faces the street.
entry, door, gate, portal, opening, inlet, access, entranceway, doorway, gateway

Antonyms: escape, exit

entry *See* **entrance**

environment
noun
1 everything that surrounds a living thing and affects its growth and health
Many birds thrive in the environment of a rain forest.
habitat *An animal may suffer when removed from its natural habitat.*
surroundings *They live in poor surroundings.*
setting *A tank is not the natural setting for guppies.*

a b c d **e** f g h i j k l m n o p q r s t u v w x y z

medium *Water is a lobster's medium.*

2 the objects and conditions that make a place what it is
My favorite restaurant is known for its friendly environment.

surroundings, climate, atmosphere, ambience

environmental 🌐 *See* **technology**

envy
noun
a feeling of wanting what someone else has
He looked at her new car with envy.

> Few men have the natural strength to honor a friend's success without **envy**.
> —From AGAMEMNON, a play by Aeschylus (525-456 B.C.), Greek dramatist

jealousy, resentment, covetousness
Antonym: generosity

verb
to look upon with envy
I envied her success.

resent *He resents his brother's happiness.*
covet *The boy coveted his cousins new bicycle.*
grudge *She grudged her sister for winning so many awards.*
begrudge *The Queen begrudged Snow White her beauty.*

See also: jealous

equal
adjective
having the same value, measure, or amount as something else
The two sisters are of equal height.

equivalent, even, identical, like, matching

Entrances

vestibule

hatch

door

access

foyer

doorway

Human Body   Human Mind   Everyday Life   History and Culture   Communication

Antonyms: different, unequal, uneven

noun
> a person or thing that is the same as or equal to another
> *He is my equal at work.*

match, equivalent, peer
> *One dollar is equivalent to one hundred pennies.*

verb
> to be the same as or equal to
> *The load I'm carrying equals yours.*

match, parallel, rival

equilibrium *See* **balance**

equilibrium *See* **balance**

equipment

noun
> anything made or to be used for a particular use
> *Ice skates, footballs, and golf clubs are different kinds of sporting equipment.*

apparatus, gear, implements, paraphernalia

equipped *See* **ready**

equivalent *See* **alike, equal, match, measurement**

era ○ *See* **time, history**

error *See* **fault, mistake**

escape

verb
> to get free
> *The prisoner escaped from jail.*

flee, run, dash, slip away, bolt

noun
> the act or an instance of escaping
> *The prisoner's escape from jail was not successful.*

flight, getaway, runaway, breakout

See also: avoid

especially *See* **most, very**

essential *See* **important, necessary, need, knowledge**

essentially *See* **generally, much**

establish

verb
> 1 to bring into being
> *He established a new club.*

begin, create, form, organize, found, initiate, institute, start

> 2 to prove or show to be true
> *The evidence established the suspect's guilt.*

demonstrate, prove, confirm, verify, uphold

established *See* **tradition**

establishment *See* **business, government, introduction, power**

estate *See* **ground, property**

esteem *See* **approval, favor, honor, prize, value**

eternal

adjective
> seeming to have no end or to go on forever
> *We hoped the twins would stop their eternal fighting.*

endless, everlasting, lasting, perpetual, constant, continual, persistent
> *Antonyms:* brief, fleeting, short-lived, temporary
> *See also:* endless

evade *See* **avoid**

evaluate *See* **grade, judge, test**

evaluation *See* **judgment**

even

adjective
> smooth, level, or flat

a
b
c
d
e
f
g
h
i
j
k
l
m
n
o
p
q
r
s
t
u
v
w
x
y
z

it's best to play ball on an even field.
flat, level, plane, smooth

Antonyms: irregular, lopsided, uneven

verb

to cause to be level, flat, smooth, or regular
We evened the surface of the path by filling in holes.
level, smooth, flatten, grade, plane

evening

noun

the period between late afternoon and night-fall
I like to go out dancing in the evening.
dusk, gloaming, twilight, eventide, nightfall

Antonym: dawn

event ●

noun

anything that happens, often something special or important
Being part of the winning team was the greatest event of my life.
affair *It was a sad affair when the widow Welby's wedding ring was stolen.*
happening *The strange happenings in the old house made us believe in ghosts.*
incident *Several incidents led them to believe she was a thief.*
occasion *He has been late on several occasions.*
occurrence *Jon wanted to report the strange occurrences to the police.*
episode *Leaving home for college was an exciting episode in my life.*

eventually *See* finally

ever *See* always

every *See* all

everyday *See* common, informal, normal, ordinary, regular, standard

evidence

noun

something that gives proof or a reason to believe
Scientists have not found evidence of life on Mars.
proof, demonstration, confirmation

evident *See* obvious, plain

evil

adjective

having a bad or wicked character
The evil queen demanded Snow White's heart.
bad, wicked, immoral, vicious, malicious, malevolent

Antonyms: benevolent, good

noun

anything wrong or bad
Fortunately, there is more good than evil in the world.
wrong, wickedness, harm, immorality, vice, iniquity

Antonyms: good, goodness
See also: bad

exact

adjective

having no mistakes
You may check a dictionary to find the exact spelling of a word.
absolute *The magician asked for absolute silence.*
accurate *The radio gave an accurate report of the fire.*
particular *I'm looking for a particular match to the saucer I broke.*
precise *Thanks to the precise directions, we found our way easily.*
strict *This judge believes in a strict interpretation of the law.*
correct *Bebe raised his hand and gave the correct answer.*

Antonyms: approximate, inexact

exactly *See* just

   Human Body   Human Mind Everyday Life History and Culture   Communication

exaggerate
verb

1 to present as larger, more important, or more valuable

She exaggerated her story about the size of the snake she found.

inflate, magnify, overstate, embellish, blow up

2 to make seem larger or greater

The tall hat exaggerates his height.

emphasize, boost, amplify, inflate

Antonyms: detract from (2), diminish (2), understate (1)

examination   See **check, physical, research, study, test**

examine
verb

to look at closely and carefully

We examined an insect with a magnifying glass.

investigate, probe, scan, scrutinize, study, inspect, observe

The doctor probed my ear.
We scanned the clouds for signs of rain

example
noun

1 something that shows what a group of things is like

An apple is an example of a fruit.

case, instance, representative, specimen, sample

2 a model that should be copied

The examples illustrate how to do this kind of division problem.

Pepe's behavior is an example of thoughtfulness.

model, pattern, ideal, role model, standard

Use **role model** only when speaking or writing about a person.

excel
verb

to do or perform better than others

The Brazilian national team excels at soccer.

tower, shine, lead, dominate

excellent
adjective

very good or much better than others

Ellie is an excellent cellist.

exceptional, fine, outstanding, splendid, super, superior, tremendous, fabulous, fantastic, magnificent, terrific, wonderful, sterling, great, superb, superlative, first-rate, top-notch

Antonyms: awful, horrible, terrible
See also: great, fine, wonderful

except
preposition

apart from; not including

Everyone except Mary went to the seashore.

bar, besides, but, save, excluding

exception   See **objection**

excess
noun

an amount that is more than what is needed

We bought an excess of food for the party, so please take some home with you.

overflow, surplus, abundance, surfeit

Antonyms: deficit, lack, shortage

exchange   See **change, give, sell, switch, bank**

excite
verb

to stir up the feelings of

The first snow of the year always excites children.

A
B
C
D
E
F
G
H
I
J
K
L
M
N
O
P
Q
R
S
T
U
V
W
X
Y
Z

 Living World   Physical World   Natural Environment   Economy   Government and Law

a
b
c
d
e
f
g
h
i
j
k
l
m
n
o
p
q
r
s
t
u
v
w
x
y
z

stir *The orchestra's performance stirred the audience.*

rouse *The mysterious announcement roused the whole class.*

thrill *Skydiving thrills some people.*

stimulate *Professor Ping's lectures stimulate her students.*

inflame *Those hurtful remarks inflamed my anger.*

ignite *That fascinating book ignited my interest in paper clips.*

kindle *Meeting Fluffy kindled my love of racoons.*

agitate *The fiery speaker agitated the crowd.*

> *Antonyms:* bore, tire, weary

excitement *See* **stir**

exciting *See* **dramatic, lively**

excuse
verb
> to forgive or pardon
> *Please excuse me for stepping on your foot.*

forgive, overlook, pardon

> *Antonyms:* blame, grudge, resent

noun
> a reason offered to explain or ask for pardon for a fault
> *My excuse for being late is that I missed the bus.*

defense *His defense was that he had picked up her wallet by mistake.*

explanation *Mrs. Haley didn't want to hear my explanation for not handing in my homework.*

reason *I thought I had a good reason for not doing the assignment.*

plea *She made a plea of hunger as she grabbed the last cookie.*

pretext *Her pretext for missing the bus was that her alarm clock was broken.*

A **pretext** is a false or made-up excuse.

exercise
noun
> activity done to strengthen the body or mind

---

some words related to exercise:
> bend, breathe, count, hold, jog, jump, kick, lift, lower, move, pull, push, raise, run, straighten, stretch, warm up

some words that describe exercise:
> aerobic, anaerobic, gentle, moderate, intense, mental, physical

some words that describe someone exercising:
> breathless, flushed, glowing, hot, perspiring, tired

exhausted *See* **beat**

exhibit *See* **display, reveal, show**

exist *See* **live**

existence *See* **life**

expand
verb
> 1 to make larger or wider
> *The school plans to expand its science program.*

augment, broaden, enlarge, extend, increase
> *I asked my mom to increase my allowance on my birthday.*
> *We extended the ladder so that it would reach the top of the house.*

> 2 to become larger or wider
> *The stomach expands when a person eats.*

enlarge, grow, increase, spread, swell, inflate, stretch

> *Antonyms:* contract (2), shrink (2)

expansion *See* **growth, stretch**

expect
verb
> to hope for or look forward to

 Human Body   Human Mind   Everyday Life   History and Culture   Communication

They expected a letter from their son to arrive soon.

await, anticipate, hope for, wait for

expected *See* **future, natural**

expedition *See* **adventure, travel, trip**

expense ☁ *See* **loss**

expensive *See* **dear**

experience
noun
1 something that a person has done or lived through
The game was a challenging experience.
event, happening, incident, occurrence

2 understanding or skills gained by doing
We need a worker with two years of computer experience.
Captain Black has a lot of experience with that kind of boat.
knowledge, know-how, familiarity, practice

verb
to go through; feel or know
He experienced defeat for the first time.
She experienced joy at the birth of her child.
know, feel, suffer, encounter, endure, undergo, live through

Use **suffer, endure**, and **undergo** when the experience is difficult or painful: *Gigi endured pain after her bike accident.*

See also: event, feel

experienced *See* **expert**

experiment ⚗ *See* **adventure**

experimental *See* **theater**

expert
noun
someone who knows a great deal about a particular thing

He is an expert on the history of the telephone.
ace, authority, master, specialist, whiz

Antonyms: beginner, novice, rookie
adjective
having a great deal of skill or knowledge
Sasha is an expert chess player.
skilled, skillful, adept, experienced, knowledgeable, masterful
My friends and I are adept at skiing.

Antonym: beginning

explain
verb
1 to make clear in speech or writing; show in detail
The carpenter explained how he had made the cabinets.
clarify, demonstrate, show, illustrate, spell out

2 to give reasons for
Please explain why you were not in class this morning.
account for, argue, defend, justify

explanation *See* **answer, cause, defense, direction, excuse, reason**

explore
verb
to try to understand by examining carefully
Let us explore this idea.
examine, investigate, probe, research, analyze

explosion *See* **bang, burst**

express ☁ ⚖ ⚗
verb
1 to make thoughts or feelings known in speech or writing
This author clearly expressed his opinions.
communicate, state, voice, indicate

2 to show thoughts or feelings of
Your frown expresses unhappiness.
convey, reflect, mean, reveal, signify

Antonym: conceal (2)

a

b

c

d

e

f

g

h

i

j

k

l

m

n

o

p

q

r

s

t

u

v

w

x

y

z

expression *See* **air, face, saying**

extend
verb

to make longer in size; make last longer
*We extended the ladder so that it would reach the
top of the tree.*
The teacher extended recess by fifteen minutes.
draw out *Grandmother
drew out the story until we
were asleep.*
lengthen *She lengthened the
rope by tying several pieces
together.*
prolong *One way to pro-
long a pet's life is to feed it
well.*
stretch *Mimi stretched the rubber band until it
broke.*

Antonyms: decrease, shorten

extended *See* **long, family**

extensive *See* **large, long, vast, wide**

extent *See* **length, limit, range, size, stretch**

external *See* **outer, outside, visible**

extra
adjective

more than is expected or usual
I needed extra time to finish the test.
additional, added, more, supplementary
noun

an added and often better thing
*The new house has many extras, including a
swimming pool.*
accessory, addition, bonus, feature, plus
adverb

to a higher degree; more than is usual
Those jeans are made of extra sturdy denim.
remarkably, unusually, exceptionally,
extraordinarily, notably

extraordinary *See* **great, incredible, special,
unusual, wonderful**

extreme
adjective

1 far beyond what is
usual or reasonable
*I do not agree with your
extreme ideas.*
unreasonable, drastic,
outrageous, radical

2 very great; to the
highest degree
She is in extreme pain.
great, intense, supreme, utmost
His guitar playing shows supreme skill.

Antonyms: ordinary (1), usual (1)

extremely *See* **most, very**

eye *See* **look, observe, see**

Human Body   Human Mind   Everyday Life   History and Culture   Communication

face
noun

1 the front part of the head

some actions with faces
blink, wink, frown, grimace, smile, grin
some words used to describe faces
beautiful, cute, fair, haggard, handsome, plain, pleasant, pretty, freckled, rugged, ugly, wrinkled

2 a look or expression on the face that shows feelings
Why do you have such a sad face?
look, appearance, expression, air

3 the outward facing part
The face of the mansion was covered with ivy.
exterior, front, outside, surface, facade

See also: appearance, expression

fact
noun

1 something said or known to be true
It is a fact that water covers most of Earth.
truth, certainty, given

2 something that is real or that happened
It is a fact that it is raining at this very moment.
case, truth, event, reality, phenomenon

factor See cause

facts See information, material

faded See light, pale

fail
verb

1 to be unable to do or complete
Rick failed as a saxophonist.
flop, fizzle, bomb, go down

The synonyms for **fail** are informal. That means they are used in everyday speech and writing but are probably not suited to a formal report or presentation.

2 to lose force or stamina
The runner's strength failed after the fifteenth mile.
fade, dwindle, sink, wane, ebb, deteriorate

3 to stop working
The engine failed, so we walked home.
break, die, stop, quit, break down, conk out

Antonyms: endure (2), last (2), succeed (1), work (3)

failure
noun

a person or thing that does not succeed
He felt like a failure after losing the match.
The new play was a failure.
loser, flop, bomb, bust, fiasco

Use **bomb**, **bust**, and **fiasco** when writing or speaking about things, not people.

Antonyms: success, winner

faint
adjective

likely to become unconscious
She felt faint after standing for hours in the heat.
dizzy, giddy, light-headed, shaky, weak

verb

to become unconscious for a short time
Paul faints at the sight of blood.
collapse, swoon, black out, pass out, keel over

Antonym: revive
See also: dizzy

a
b
c
d
e
f
g
h
i
j
k
l
m
n
o
p
q
r
s
t
u
v
w
x
y
z

fair
adjective
> showing no favor or bias
> *The principal was fair when she punished both kids.*
> even, impartial, just, objective
>> *Antonyms:* biased, unfair, unjust
>> *See also:* just

fairly *See* **quite**

faith ⊙ ⊙ *See* **belief, confidence, religion, trust**

fake
verb
> to make a false copy of
> *She faked her mother's handwriting on the note.*
> counterfeit *The criminal counterfeited ten-dollar bills.*
> falsify *He falsified an important bank document.*
> forge *She forged many checks before her arrest.*

adjective
> not real; made to look like something real
> *We were almost fooled by the fake cockroaches.*
> counterfeit *It is against the law to use counterfeit money.*
> false *George Washington wore false teeth.*
> imitation *Are those diamonds real or imitation?*
> mock *The old lady carried a mock alligator purse.*
> artificial *Those artificial flowers look so real.*
>> *Antonyms:* authentic, genuine, real
>> *See also:* artificial

fall
verb
> 1 to drop downward from a higher place
> *She fell from the top of the tree.*
> *At the end of the play, the curtain fell.*
> drop, plunge, plummet, tumble, topple

> *Niagara Falls drops about one hundred sixty feet.*

> 2 to become less in amount or volume
> *The price of gasoline fell last month.*
> *His voice fell to a whisper.*
> decrease, dip, drop, diminish, lessen, decline
>> *Antonyms:* increase (2), rise (2)

noun
> 1 the act of falling to a lower place
> *The climber had a bad fall.*
> *We watched the fall of the leaves.*
> descent, drop, plunge, tumble, spill

> 2 a sudden drop in a river or stream that causes water to fall
> *We visited Niagara Falls in Canada.*
> cascade, waterfall, cataract

> 3 a defeat or capture by force
> *The fall of King Rufus led to civil war.*
> surrender, defeat, overthrow, capture
>> *Antonyms:* climb (1), rise (1)

false
adjective
> purposely not true or honest
> *That is a false rumor.*
> untrue, dishonest, deceptive, misleading
>> *Antonyms:* honest, true
>> *See also:* fake

familiar *See* **close, common, knowledge**

family ⊙ ⊙
noun
> a group made up of a parent or parents and their children, or of other related people
> *My dad came from a large family.*
> folk *My folks helped me plant a garden.*
> clan *The Smiley clan gathered for Thanksgiving.*
> household *Jack and Jill's grandparents are part of their household.*
> kin *Uncle Hugo invited his kin for a reunion.*

> *some words used to describe families*
> close, distant, extended, nuclear, maternal, paternal, supportive

famous
adjective
> recognized or known by the public

🏃 Human Body   ❓ Human Mind   👕 Everyday Life   🚩 History and Culture   📞 Communication

Do you know any famous people?
well-known, notable, noted, prominent, distinguished, eminent, renowned, notorious

Use **notorious** when writing or speaking about a person or thing that is famous only because of something bad: *Jesse James was a notorious outlaw.*

fancy
adjective

1 splendid; grander than the average
She wore a fancy gown to the ball.
elaborate, extravagant, luxurious, ornate

2 special; showing great skill
The skater did a fancy spin.
skillful, fine, adept, excellent, magnificent

Antonyms: easy (2), plain (1), simple (1,2)

fantastic *See* **excellent, great, imaginary, incredible, legendary, wonderful**

far
adverb

1 at or to a long distance in space or time
We traveled far into the desert.
Far in the past, people lived in caves.
afar, long, deep, well

2 very much
My cold is far worse today.
much, quite, way, considerably

Antonyms: close (1), near (1)
adjective
distant in space or time
Polar bears live in the far north.
distant, faraway, remote

Antonyms: close, nearby

farm
noun

land and the buildings on it used to grow vegetables or raise animals for food or clothing

some kinds of farms
dairy, orchard, plantation, ranch, vineyard

verb

to raise crops or animals

some farming activities
breed, butcher, cultivate, fertilize, grow, harvest, irrigate, mow, plant, plow, prune, raise, reap, shear, slaughter, sow, thresh, till, weed

fascinate
verb

to attract and hold the attention and interest of
The northern lights fascinate me.
bewitch *The many colors of her garden bewitched her guests.*
captivate *The fireworks display captivated everyone last Fourth of July.*
charm *The baby charms everyone with his cute smile.*
enchant *His music enchants us.*
enthrall *That mystery story enthralled me.*
entrance *His magic tricks entranced the audience.*
grip *The children were gripped by the scary movie.*
intrigue *The odd fairy tale intrigued the children.*
mesmerize *I was mesmerized by the beauty of the night sky.*
rivet *The burning building across the street riveted our attention.*
spellbind *We were spellbound by the magician's trick.*

Antonyms: bore, put to sleep, weary
See also: interest

fashion *See* **make, model, shape, style, way**

fast
adjective

moving or operating with speed
He's a fast runner.
She drives a fast car.

quick, rapid, swift, speedy, fleet

Use **swift** and **fleet** only when speaking or writing about a person or other animal: *a swift swimmer; a fleet gazelle.*

Antonyms: plodding, slow

adverb

with speed; quickly
He came fast when his mother called.
quickly, rapidly, swiftly, hastily, speedily, at full tilt, ASAP

The horse galloped rapidly during the race.

ASAP stands for "as soon as possible." You may pronounce it by saying the name of each of its letters a-s-a-p, or as one word: "aysap."

Antonym: slowly
See also: loyal

fasten
verb

1 to join firmly in place or to something
The policeman fastened the badge to his uniform.
affix, attach, connect, join, moor, stick, bind, fix, hitch, nail, secure, anchor

2 to close firmly or cause to stay closed

Ms. Muzzy fastened the suitcase.
Fasten the door when you leave.
latch, lock, secure, buckle, clasp, close

3 to direct at in a fixed or focused way
The dog fastened its eyes on the hamburger.
concentrate, focus, fix, rivet

Antonyms: open (2), undo (2), unlock (2)
See also: fix

fat
adjective

having much extra flesh that is not muscle
That cat is so fat that he can hardly jump.
overweight, heavy, stout, obese, chubby, plump, fleshy, pudgy, rotund, portly

Antonyms: lean, skinny, slender, thin

fate *See* **chance, doom**

father *See* **source**

fault
noun

1 something wrong that causes problems
Nick's fault is talking too much.
That noisy car has a fault in its engine.
deficiency, defect, flaw, shortcoming, vice, weakness, imperfection, failing

2 something done or made incorrectly
Her job at the factory is to find faults in the products.
error, mistake, slip, blunder, bug, glitch, oversight

Bug and **glitch** are often used when speaking or writing about a fault in a computer or computer program.

See also: mistake

favor
noun

1 a kind or helpful act
Would you please do me a favor and set the table?
kindness, courtesy, blessing, boon

2 kind approval shown by a superior

 Human Body   Human Mind Everyday Life History and Culture   Communication

The new player won the favor of the coach.
admiration, approval, esteem, honor, regard, respect, praise

> The winner enjoyed the esteem the medal gave her.

3 a special liking

> That teacher shows favor to the student who gets the highest grades.

bias, preference, partiality, inclination

favorable See **hopeful, positive**

favorite

adjective

liked over all others
> Oranges are my favorite fruit.

pet, select, preferred, choice, ideal

noun

a person or thing treated with favor

> Scary movies are my favorites.

darling, jewel, pet, treasure, preference

fear ❓

noun

a strong feeling when expecting danger or pain

> Falling into the vipers' nest filled her with fear.

apprehension, dread, fright, terror, anxiety, worry, horror, panic, trepidation

> Big, hairy spiders fill her with terror.
> In her fright, she dropped her basket and ran.

some actions related to fear
> cower, cringe, faint, flee, flinch, hide, pale, quail, quake, quiver, recoil, run, scream, shiver, shriek, shrink, shudder, shy, start, startle, sweat, tremble, wail, whimper, whine, wince, yell

without fear
> bold, brave, calm, confident, courageous, daring, fearless, secure, serene

feeling fear
> afraid, aghast, anxious, apprehensive, breathless, frantic, uneasy, nervous, shaky, timid

Antonyms: bravery, courage

fearful See **afraid, nervous, terrible**

feast See **celebration**

feathers ❶ See **bird**

feature See **extra, part, property, film**

fee See **charge, cost**

feed ❶❷ See **animal, cat, grain, grass**

feel ❷❸

verb

1 to find out about by the sense of touch
> Can you feel this bump on my head?

touch, handle, palpate, finger

> She touched the cat's soft fur.

2 to become aware of through the senses
> She felt the cool water dripping down her neck.

perceive, sense, experience, notice, observe

noun

the quality of something to the touch
> I like the feel of this cool, hard stone.

texture, touch, sensation

feeling

noun

1 the condition of being aware

A feeling of hunger came over Jim as he walked past the bakery.

sensation, consciousness, impression, awareness

2 a state of emotion

The tenor sang the aria with feeling.

emotion, passion, sensitivity, sentiment

See also: emotion

fellow *See* **man, match**

fence *See* **barrier**

fever *See* **pitch, zeal**

few *See* **measurement**

fewer *See* **less**

fiction *See* **lie, story, literature**

field *See* **area, spread, world, yard**

fierce

adjective

1 wild and dangerous

Beware! A fierce tiger is on the loose.

ferocious, wild, savage, brutal, bloodthirsty, vicious

There are wild animals in the jungle.

2 extremely strong; causing damage

A fierce storm knocked down many trees last night.

furious, severe, violent, raging, destructive, dreadful, powerful, awful

Antonyms: calm (1), gentle (1,2), mild (2), placid (1), tame (1)

fiery *See* **hot, violent**

fight

noun

the use of weapons, bodies, or words to struggle with someone or something

The fight between the two armies began at dawn.

My brother and I had a fight over whose turn it was to wash the dishes.

battle, clash, combat, engagement, dispute, quarrel, struggle, feud, disagreement, argument, scuffle, scrap, scrape, fisticuffs, row, duel

Two hockey players had a clash on the ice.

Use **combat** and **engagement** for fighting between armed forces.

Use **scrap**, **scuffle**, and **fisticuffs** for physical fights.

Disputes, **disagreements**, **arguments**, **quarrels**, and **rows** are fights that use words.

---

verb

1 to take part in a struggle or conflict

The ducks fought over the bread we tossed to them.

battle, contend, struggle, argue, wrestle, clash, wrangle, come to blows

2 to struggle or use force against

The swimmer fought the strong current to reach the other shore.

struggle against or with, combat, contend against, resist, battle, defy, strive against

See also: battle, argue

figure

noun

1 the shape of something not able to be identified

They saw a figure looming in the distance.

form, shape, outline, silhouette

2 the physical form of a human body

His figure hasn't changed in twenty years.

Human Body   Human Mind   Everyday Life   History and Culture   Communication

build, frame, physique, shape

3 a person of note
The alligator wrestler is a well-known figure.
notable, personality, somebody, celebrity

verb
to believe or conclude
He figured it was safe to enter the dark cave.
believe, conclude, reckon, guess, imagine, suppose, think
See also: amount

file *See* **train**

fill
verb
1 to take up all or most of the space in
Rabbits filled the cage.
clog, consume, cram, crowd, flood, jam, occupy, pack

2 to close up or plug
The dentist filled a cavity in the boy's tooth.
caulk, close, cork, obstruct, plug, seal, stop, stuff

filled *See* **full**

film
noun
a motion picture
What film did you see last night?
movie, picture, flick

> *some kinds of films*
> animated cartoon, documentary, feature
> *some categories of films*
> adventure, comedy, drama, horror, tragedy, romance, science fiction, western
> *some words related to the making of films*
> act, cast, direct, produce, edit, dub, record, splice

final *See* **last**

finally
adverb
at the final moment
After driving for an hour, they finally found the house.

eventually, ultimately, at last, conclusively

find
verb
1 to come upon or meet by accident
I found some money in my pocket.
encounter, bump into, come across, run across, happen upon, stumble upon

> *I encountered a bear in the woods.*

2 to come upon after losing or searching for
Alex found a lost watch under the sink.
discover, locate, recover, regain, retrieve, trace, dig out

3 to discover
The explorers found a pass through the mountains.
detect, discover, locate, spot, uncover, come across, hit upon, stumble upon, search out

Antonyms: lose (2), misplace (2), overlook (3)

finding *See* **judgment**

fine
adjective
of high quality
That was a fine meal.
Hannah is a fine athlete.
good, excellent, wonderful, great, splendid, first-rate, superb, superior

Antonyms: bad, inferior, poor
See also: good, excellent, great

finest *See* **best**

finger *See* **feel**

finish
verb
to reach or cause the end of
You may have dessert after you finish those peas.
Did you finish reading that book?

a
b
c
d
e
f
g
h
i
j
k
l
m
n
o
p
q
r
s
t
u
v
w
x
y
z

stop, cease, end, complete, conclude, quit

Antonyms: begin, start

noun

the end or last part of something

It was a long movie, but we watched it to the finish.

end, close, conclusion, ending, completion, finale

The conclusion of the book was a surprise.

Use **finale** when speaking or writing about the end of a show, concert, or other presentation: *For his finale, the magician made an elephant disappear.*

Antonyms: beginning, onset, start

See also: complete, end, stop

fire ⓞ

verb

to dismiss from a job

The boss fired him for being late to work.

dismiss, discharge, terminate, ax, boot, can, sack, let go

Ax, **boot**, **can**, and **sack** are informal. These words are suited to everyday speech and may not be appropriate for formal writing.

Antonyms: employ, hire

firm

adjective

1 hard or solid when pressed; not soft

I would rather sleep on a firm mattress.

hard, stiff, solid, dense, rigid

2 not easily changed by outside forces

She has firm opinions on government.

set, fixed, fast, frozen, stable, steadfast, steady, inflexible

Antonyms: flexible (2), soft (1)

first

adjective

before all others in time or importance

He was the first person to climb that mountain. She won first prize.

earliest, initial, original, primary, chief, main, eminent, foremost, premier, prime, principal

adverb

in the position before all others

He finished first in the race.

We got to the game first.

foremost, ahead, forward, in advance

See also: main

first aid ⓞ

noun

emergency medical help

> *some conditions that require first aid*
> allergy, asthma, bite, bleeding, blister, burn, choking, convulsion, cut, dehydration, drowning, fainting, fatigue, fracture, frostbite, heart attack, hypothermia, inflammation, injury, nosebleed, poisoning, scrape, scratch, shock, splinter, sprain, sting, stroke, sunburn, trauma, unconsciousness, wound

fish ⓞ *See* **animal, leisure**

fit ⓞ ⓞ

adjective

1 proper or acceptable

This video is fit for children.

appropriate, suitable, proper, right, apt, acceptable, applicable

2 in good bodily condition

Cora is very fit because she exercises daily.

healthy, trim, sound, hale, hardy, robust

Antonyms: unfit (1), unsuitable (1)

 Human Body   ⓠ Human Mind   Everyday Life   History and Culture   Communication

verb

to be proper for

I like the song, but it doesn't fit the occasion.

suit, match, become, agree with, conform to

fix
verb

1 to make steady or fasten firmly

He fixed the wooden sign to his tree house.

fasten, affix, attach, secure, pin, rivet, cement, anchor

2 to bring back to working order or good condition

Do you think you can fix my bike chain?

mend *The carpenter mended the hole in the fence.*

repair *I took my broken bicycle to the shop to be repaired.*

cure *The plumber replaced a washer and cured the dripping faucet.*

remedy *Whenever she makes a mistake, she tries to remedy it.*

patch *My mother patched the elbow of my torn sweater.*

renew *They renewed the old house with a fresh coat of paint.*

restore *Hans restored the finish on the scratched table.*

3 to get or make ready

The chef fixed a delicious meal.

make, prepare, create, produce, assemble

Antonyms: break (2), damage (2), loosen (1), unfasten (1)

See also: fasten, adjust

fixed See **firm**

flag See **standard, tire**

flame ❶ See **burn, light, love**

flash
noun

1 a sudden light that quickly disappears

The flash of lightning was followed by a clap of thunder.

blaze, flare, flicker, spark, streak, glimmer

2 a sudden show of feelings, talent, or understanding

A flash of disappointment crossed the coach's face when Paul missed the catch.

display *We had never seen such a display of anger from him.*

outburst *There was an outburst of laughter in the audience when a barking dog ran across the stage.*

show *Many people joined the picket as a show of support for the workers.*

glimmer *There was a glimmer of hope in her eyes before the judge announced the winner.*

spark *A spark of confidence set the tone for our fantastic performance.*

3 a very short amount of time

I'll be there in a flash.

instant, minute, moment, second, twinkle, jiffy

He disappeared in an instant.

verb

1 to shine brightly

The diamond ring flashed in the sun.

gleam, glimmer, glint, glitter, sparkle

2 to come, move, or happen suddenly

An image of her flashed into his mind.

dart *The lizard darted out of sight.*

shoot *The speeding car shot by us.*

streak *The runners streaked down the road.*

bolt *The deer bolted across the field.*

dash *Did you just see something dash through the woods?*

tear *The thief tore through the crowd and disappeared.*

See also: instant

flat See **dead, even**

flavor
verb

to give a flavor to

The chef flavored the stew with garlic and onion.

season *The cook seasoned the dish with garlic and pepper.*

A B C D E F G H I J K L M N O P Q R S T U V W X Y Z

Living World   Physical World   Natural Environment   Economy   Government and Law

spice *We spiced the soup with a bit of pepper.*
accent *The chef accented the meat with a dash of sage.*
lace *A baba is a rich cake laced with rum.*
imbue *The rich sauce was imbued with cream.*

flaw
noun

a fault or defect
His worst flaw is his short temper.
The flaw in the car's finish was caused by a paint bubble.
defect, blemish, fault, imperfection, shortcoming, weakness

Antonym: strength
See also: fault

fleet *See* fast, quick

flesh ⊕ ● *See* fruit

flexible
adjective

1 easily bent without breaking
Give the baby some flexible toys.
Most dancers are quite flexible.
bendable, elastic, pliable, pliant, supple, lithe

Use **supple** and **lithe** when speaking or writing about people or other animals. Use the other synonyms when referring to things.

2 able to change or meet new situations
They had a flexible plan for the day's activities.
adaptable, adjustable, accommodating

Antonyms: fixed (2), inflexible (1,2), rigid (1), set (2), stiff (1)

flight ○ ● *See* escape

float
verb

1 to rest on the surface of a liquid or drift in a gas without sinking
The girl floated on her back in the water.
The balloon floated in the breeze.
drift, hang, suspend, waft, hover

2 to move in a light and airy way
The dancer floated across the stage.
breeze, flit, flow, flutter, glide, waft

flock ● *See* crowd, animal

flood ●
noun

an overflow of water onto land
Many homes were damaged in the flood.
deluge, inundation, surge, torrent
verb

1 to cover or fill with a flow of water
A heavy rain flooded the fields.
deluge, inundate, engulf, submerge

2 to fill with too much of something
Angry phone calls flooded the radio station.
deluge, inundate, overwhelm, swamp

3 to overflow as if in a flood
Water flooded into the basement.
Students flooded into the hallways.
gush, pour, overflow, stream, surge

floor *See* amaze, bottom, surprise

flour ○ *See* grain

flow
verb

1 to move in a smooth, steady stream
The river flows to the sea.
Sand flowed through her fingers.
stream, run, glide, course, pour, roll

2 to move in a smooth and easy way

 Human Body   ? Human Mind   Everyday Life   History and Culture   Communication

Thoughts flowed through his mind as he listened to the music.

drift, float, glide, roll, waft

noun
a series of things that continues steadily
The car moved with the flow of traffic.
stream, progression, procession, parade

See also: run

fluid ⚙ ⚪ *See* **graceful**

fly ⚪
verb
1 to move through the air by means of wings
The birds flew over the house.
wing, soar, coast, flap, flit, float, flutter, hover, sail, skim, soar, swoop

2 to pass by or move quickly
She flew from the room when she heard her mother calling.
bolt, dart, dash, hurry, run, rush, scurry, shoot, speed, tear, spring, race

3 to wave or float in the air
The kite flew high on the windy March day.
flutter, hang, wave, float, flap
The flag waves at the top of the pole.

focus *See* **center, concentrate, fasten, point, photography**

fog
noun
1 a cloud of water droplets near the ground
cloud, mist, murk, vapor
There was a mist on the mountain.

2 a condition of mental confusion
He was in a fog all day and couldn't get any work done.

daze, haze, muddle, bewilderment, trance
verb
to cover with or as if with a fog
The child fogged the window with her breath.
The politician fogged the issue with too many facts and figures.
cloud, mist, blur, veil, obscure

fold
verb
1 to bend over upon itself so that one part lies on the other
She folded the letter before putting it in the envelope.
crease, lap, pleat, tuck, double over

2 to bring in toward the body from a stretched position
The hawk landed on a branch and folded its wings.
retract, tuck, pull in

Antonyms: open (2), unfold (1)
noun
a line made by folding
She cut the paper along the fold.
bend, crease, furrow, ridge, wrinkle

folk ⚪ ⚫ *See* **family, people**

folks ⚪ ⚫ *See* **people**

follow
verb
to go or come after
The detective followed the suspect.
chase, shadow, tail, trail, hound, pursue, stalk

following *See* **next**

fond
adjective
having or showing loving feelings
He has fond memories of his grandparents.
affectionate, loving, tender, adoring, warm
My affectionate mom always

a
b
c
d
e
f
g
h
i
j
k
l
m
n
o
p
q
r
s
t
u
v
w
x
y
z

gives me a kiss before she leaves.

food 🔲 ❶ *See* **celebration, grain**

fool
noun
1 a person who has poor sense or judgment
Max was a fool to think he could get up late and make it to school on time.
idiot, dolt, imbecile, knucklehead, nitwit, numskull

2 a person whose job was to entertain by acting in a funny way for a king or noble
buffoon, clown, jester
verb
to trick into believing something false
He fooled his mother with a card trick.
deceive, trick, dupe, mislead, hoodwink, bamboozle

See also: idiot

foolish
adjective
having or showing poor sense
It was foolish to go out in the rain without a coat.
silly, ludicrous, stupid, inane, asinine

Antonyms: rational, sensible, thoughtful, wise

foot 🔲
noun
the end part of the leg of animals

some parts of feet
arch, bone, claw, digit, heel, instep, ligament, muscle, nail, pad, sole, tendon, toe, web

forbid
verb
to give orders that prevent or prohibit
They have forbidden swimming here.
ban *The law bans drunk driving.*
bar *The police barred anyone from entering.*
outlaw *The mayor outlawed skateboarding on city streets.*
prohibit *State law prohibits smoking on buses.*

proscribe *The principal proscribed loitering between classes.*

Antonyms: encourage, promote

force 🔲
noun
power, energy, or physical strength
The force of the wind knocked down the trees.
energy, power, strength, vigor, might
verb
to cause to do by using strength or power
Ivan forced her to tell the truth.
compel, make, pressure, oblige, press, push

See also: power

force 🔲 *See* **energy**

ford *See* **river**

foreign *See* **new, strange**

forest 🔲
noun
a large area of land covered with trees
All kinds of animals live in the forest.
woodland, woods, wilderness

some kinds of forests
jungle, rain forest, deciduous forest

forever *See* **always**

fork *See* **branch, divide, split, river**

form *See* **body, class, establish, figure, found, kind, make, model, shape, structure**

formal
adjective
1 following accepted rules of behavior
He made a formal request for help with his project.
conventional, correct, official, proper, legal

2 proper to the point of being cold
Her parents were so formal that they made their guests feel uncomfortable.
stiff, proper, prim, stuffy, conservative

Antonyms: casual (2), informal (1)

🐾 Human Body   ❓ Human Mind   👕 Everyday Life   🚩 History and Culture   📞 Communication

former   *See* old

forsake   *See* abandon, quit

forth   *See* forward

fortune   *See* chance, success

forward
adverb
1 toward a place or time that is further on
She looked forward to a long vacation.
The line for tickets finally moved forward.
ahead, on, onward, hence

Hence should only be used when referring to time: *From this day hence, peace will reign in the land.* **Hence** is rather formal. You will find it used mostly in literature of the past.

2 closer or into view
If you want to help, please step forward.
forth, up, out, to the
fore

The wolf came forth from its den.
Antonyms:
back (2),
backward (1)

foul
adjective
very unpleasant to taste, smell, or look at
What is that foul odor?
offensive, rank, rotten, loathsome, nasty, disgusting
Antonym: pleasant

found
verb
to set up or create; establish
In 1857, Dr. Elizabeth Blackwell founded a hospital run by women.
start *She started the discussion by asking for questions on her book.*

create *They created an organization for young writers.*
form *He formed a band in high school.*
begin *She began her business after college.*
establish *He established a new club.*
organize *I organized a meeting of herpetologists.*
originate *Who originated the idea of cake mixes?*
institute *He instituted a new procedure at work.*
initiate *Our teacher initiated a rule of no eating in the classroom.*
Antonyms: dissolve, end, terminate
See also: establish

foundation   *See* ground, reason

frame   *See* body, border, build, figure, lay, put

frank   *See* honest, open, straight

free
adjective
1 not held back, enslaved, or in prison
The prisoner forgot what it was like to be free.
emancipated, liberated, unrestricted, at liberty

2 having a type of government that is controlled by and gives rights to all the people
The people of Canada live in a free nation.
democratic, independent, self-governing

3 without cost
That store gives a free balloon to every child.
complimentary, on the house, gratis
Antonyms: enslaved (1), imprisoned (1), totalitarian (2)

freedom
noun
1 the condition of being free or freed
After years of being forced to work for no pay, the slaves at last gained their freedom.
liberty, liberation, emancipation

2 the state of being free to act or move as one wishes
The children enjoy the freedom they have at recess.
liberty, license, independence

3 a specific right

A B C D E F G H I J K L M N O P Q R S T U V W X Y Z

Freedom of speech is a right enjoyed by all Americans.

liberty, right, entitlement, privilege

Antonym: bondage (1)

freezing *See* **cold**

frequency ⓔ *See* **electricity**

fresh *See* **bold, late, new, original, sweet, air, grass**

friction *See* **physics**

friend ⊙

noun

a person whom you like and who likes you
Sheila and I have been friends since kindergarten.
buddy, chum, pal, comrade, amigo, companion
He and his buddies go fishing together every other weekend.

Amigo is the Spanish word for **friend**.

---

friendly

adjective

1 welcoming and pleasant toward others
Our town is a friendly place.
pleasant, warm, amicable, amiable, genial, neighborly

2 kind and helpful
The friendly waiter made our meal enjoyable.
kind, helpful, kindly, cordial, affable, sympathetic

Antonyms: hostile (1), rude (2),
unfriendly (1), unkind (2), unpleasant (1)

friendship *See* **company**

fright ⓔ *See* **alarm, fear, jolt, panic**

frighten

verb

to cause fear in
The growling dog frightened the children.
scare, panic, terrify, alarm, horrify, petrify, chill, startle, threaten, terrorize, agitate, spook

Antonyms: comfort, reassure
See also: afraid, fear

frightened *See* **afraid, nervous**

frightening *See* **terrible**

front

noun

the place at the head or beginning
He went to the front of the line.
lead, top, head

Antonyms: back, rear

adjective

having to do with or located in the front
The story was on the front page of the newspaper.
foremost, forward, head

verb

to face or look out on
The hotel fronts the ocean.
face, overlook, view

frontier *See* **border, limit**

frown ⓑ ⓔ

verb

1 to wrinkle the forehead to show anger, unhappiness, or confusion
Why are you frowning?
gloom, scowl, grimace, sneer, glower

2 to disapprove
She frowned upon his rude behavior.
object to, disapprove of

Antonym: smile (1)

frozen *See* **firm**

fruit ⊙ ⓔ

noun

the part of a plant that has seeds and flesh

Human Body   Human Mind   Everyday Life   History and Culture   Communication

some parts of fruits
core, flesh, hull, husk, juice, kernel, meat, peel, pit, pulp, rind, seed, skin, stone

fuel ○ ● *See* **power**

full
adjective

1 not able to hold or contain any more
The trunk is full, so put your suitcase in the back seat.
brimming, filled, packed, stuffed, replete

2 having a large number or amount
Your spelling test was full of mistakes.
rich, thick, flush, rife, riddled, teeming

Thick, **flush**, **rife**, **riddled**, and **teeming** are followed by "with": *The pond is teeming with fish.* **Rich** is followed by "in": *Spinach is rich in iron.*

3 whole; complete
Grandpa has a full life these days.
complete, whole, rich, satisfying

Antonym: empty (1)

fully *See* **quite, totally, well, wide**

fun ○ ● *See* **play, pleasure**

function *See* **behave, deal, duty, party, place, serve, use, work**

fundamental *See* **basic, knowledge, physics**

funds *See* **money, bank**

funny
adjective

1 causing laughter or amusement
My uncle's jokes are funnier than my father's.
comical, humorous, hilarious, hysterical

2 strange or odd
There was a funny smell in the attic.
odd, peculiar, curious, strange, weird

Antonyms: normal (2), ordinary (2), serious (1), solemn (1)

fur ● ● *See* **animal**

furious
adjective

1 full of anger
She was furious at him for insulting her mother.
mad, angry, enraged, incensed, infuriated, irate, livid, fuming

2 very violent
There was a furious storm last night.
fierce, raging, wild, brutal, violent

See also: angry, fierce

further *See* **better, develop, more, other**

future
noun

time that is yet to come
He hopes to become a teacher in the future.
tomorrow, hereafter, offing

adjective

of or taking place in the time yet to come
All future e-mails should be sent to our new address.
anticipated, expected, imminent, succeeding

Antonym: past

A B C D E F G H I J K L M N O P Q R S T U V W X Y Z

a
b
c
d
e
f
g
h
i
j
k
l
m
n
o
p
q
r
s
t
u
v
w
x
y
z

gag *See* **joke, trick**

gain
verb
> 1 to get
> *He worked hard to gain respect.*
> acquire, get, obtain, secure, earn

> 2 to get closer or move nearer (usually **gain on**)
> *"Faster, he's gaining on us!" panted Billy.*
> approach, close in on, catch up to or with
>
> *Antonyms:* give (1), lose (1)

noun
> something gained
> *Where is the gain in hurting your brother?*
> advantage, benefit, profit, good, use
>
> *Antonyms:* detriment, disadvantage, loss
> *See also:* advantage, get

game ○ ◐
noun
> 1 a form of play or sport having certain rules and equipment for play

We enjoyed a game of chess.
My whole family went to the football game.
competition, event, match, sport, contest, match

> 2 something done for fun or amusement
> *He always acts silly and thinks life is a game.*
> pastime, play, amusement, diversion
>
> *Antonym:* work (2)
> *See also:* sport

gang *See* **party**

gap *See* **crack, difference, distance, space**

garage ○ *See* **home**

garbage ○ *See* **junk**

garden ○ ◉
noun
> an area of land used for growing vegetables, flowers, or other plants
>
> > *some words related to gardening*
> > cultivate, dig, graft, grub, harvest, hoe, irrigate, pick, pluck, plant, plow, prune, rake, reap, sow, transplant, weed

gate *See* **entrance**

gather
verb
> 1 to bring together into one place or collection
> *The boy gathered his marbles and put them in a bag.*
> collect, assemble, compile
>
> 2 to come together
> *The crowd gathered to hear the poetry reading.*
> assemble, collect, congregate, convene, group, bunch, cluster, band together, crowd, mass, meet, rally, swarm, concentrate
>
> *Antonyms:* break up (2), disperse (1,2), scatter (1,2), separate (2), spread (1)
> *See also:* collect

gathering *See* **assembly, meeting, party**

   Human Body   Human Mind  Everyday Life   History and Culture Communication

Garden

blossoms blossoms

blossoms

cultivation

herbs

transplant

greenery

hedge pick

cultivate

hoe

wagon

landscape

avenue arboretum

landscape symmetry

topiary

formal formal

a
b
c
d
e
f
g
h
i
j
k
l
m
n
o
p
q
r
s
t
u
v
w
x
y
z

gear *See* **equipment, airplane**

general *See* **common, open, regular**

generally
adverb
1 for the most part
The doctor said my grandmother was generally healthy but needed to keep up her weight.
basically, chiefly, essentially, fundamentally, mainly, mostly, for the most part, on the whole, overall
2 usually
Professor Dewey's lectures are generally boring.
conventionally, habitually, ordinarily, usually, mostly, on the average
Antonyms: barely (1), hardly (1), rarely (2), scarcely (1), seldom (2)
See also: mainly, mostly

generation *See* **production, history**

gentle
adjective
1 having a kindly character
We love him for his gentle ways.
mild, tender, sweet, humane, kind
2 not harsh or violent
A gentle breeze rustled the leaves.
moderate, soft, light, mellow, mild
Antonyms: ferocious (2), harsh (2), violent (2)
See also: mild

gentleman *See* **man**

get
verb
1 to receive
I got a new bicycle for my birthday.
acquire *He is acquiring some bad habits from his friends.*
attain *I will attain my goal of becoming a doctor.*
gain *He worked hard to gain respect.*

obtain *He obtained his college degree in just three years.*
receive *He received many gifts while he was in the hospital.*
secure *Vincent secured a good job.*
achieve *She achieved a good grade on her math test.*
win *The slaves won their freedom after years of pain and struggle.*
2 to go after and bring back
Get your coat.
fetch, retrieve, bring, snatch
3 to come under the power of
She is getting a cold.
catch, contract, take

In this sense, take is used only with the word "ill," as in *She took ill.*

4 to understand
Do you get the meaning of this story?
catch, comprehend, follow, grasp, perceive, realize, see, seize, sense, understand, fathom
Now do you realize how big a redwood tree is?

5 to arrive
You will get home one way or another.
arrive, come, show up
6 to become
She is getting mad.
become, grow
Antonym: give (1)
See also: gain

ghost *See* **spirit**

giant
adjective
very great in size, strength, or importance
She took a giant leap across the brook.

 Human Body   Human Mind   Everyday Life   History and Culture   Communication

enormous, huge, great, immense, jumbo, mammoth, monstrous, tremendous, massive, gigantic, mountainous, colossal

We ate a monstrous sundae that had thirty scoops of ice cream.

Antonyms: baby, little, small, tiny
See also: huge, great

gift
noun

1 something given freely
She gave me a gift on our anniversary.
present *She received presents on her birthday.*
donation *He gave the charity a donation.*
grant *The scientist received a grant of ten thousand dollars.*

2 a special quality or capacity
He has a gift for painting.
ability, aptitude, faculty, knack, talent, flair

gifts *See* celebration

girl *See* child

give
verb

1 to put into someone's possession
The teacher gave the students their report cards.
bestow *The president bestowed an award on the famous scientist.*
present *The judge presented a blue ribbon to the winner.*
render *He rendered aid to the accident victim.*
accord *The council accorded her its highest honor.*
award *The college awarded her a scholarship.*
donate *Many people donate money to charity.*
confer *The university conferred degrees on the graduates.*
furnish *She furnished me with the needed information.*

2 to hand over in return for something
I gave him a dollar for the ticket.
exchange, pay, trade, dish out

Antonyms: get (1), receive (1), take (1)

given *See* fact, truth

glad *See* happy, joyful

glance
verb

to take a quick look
He glanced at the clock to see if he was late.
glimpse, look, peek, peep

Antonym: stare

noun

a quick look
One glance at her told me she was angry.
glimpse, look, peek, peep

Antonym: stare
See also: look

glare
verb

1 to give off a very bright light
The sunlight glared off the desert sand.
gleam, blaze, dazzle, glisten, radiate

2 to look at steadily or angrily
The teacher glared at the noisy students.
scowl, glower, stare, frown

gleam *See* flash, glare, glow, shine

globe *See* world

gloomy
adjective

1 cheerlessly dark
The sky looks gloomy today.
dismal, dim, dreary, dark, murky

2 showing sadness or hopelessness
Why does Lucy look so gloomy today?
glum, melancholy, sad, somber, grim, bleak

Antonyms: bright (1), cheerful (1), merry (2)

glory *See* honor

glow
noun

a warm, steady light

glowing – goodness

a
b
c
d
e
f
g
h
i
j
k
l
m
n
o
p
q
r
s
t
u
v
w
x
y
z

The lantern's glow lit the path.
gleam, shine, luster, radiance

verb
to shine with warm, bright light
The flames died down, but the coals still glowed.
shine, glimmer, radiate, gleam

See also: shine

glowing *See* **bright, exercise**

glue ○ *See* **paste**

go
verb
to move or travel
I go to school by bus.
We went to the beach on Saturday.
move, travel, pass, advance, proceed, ride

to move away from a place
We will miss her when she goes
leave, depart, exit, flee

to reach from one point to another
The driveway goes from the house to the road.
reach, run, stretch, extend

to be moving or working properly
My electric train will not go.
work, run, function, operate, perform

to belong with something else
This blouse goes with that skirt.
match, harmonize, fit, belong, relate

to pass
How fast the days go by!
pass, elapse, fly, flow, run

to become
The milk has gone sour.
grow, become, get, turn

goal
noun
a result that a person wants and works for

Her goal is to become an animal doctor.
aim, ambition, aspiration, end, intention, purpose, target, intent, object, objective

golden *See* **hair**

gone *See* **absent**

good
adjective
1 having desirable qualities
That was a good movie.
She came up with a good idea.
beneficial, desirable, positive, fine, first-rate, satisfactory

> It is **good** to love the unknown.
> —From VALENTINE'S DAY, by Charles Lamb (1775-1834), British essayist

2 doing what is right
A good person helps others.
just, moral, upright, decent, honorable

3 pleasant
We had a good time at the park.
agreeable, enjoyable, nice, pleasant, cheerful

4 behaving in the proper way
Spot is a good dog.
obedient, well-behaved, well-mannered, dutiful

Antonyms: bad (1,2,3), detrimental (1), disagreeable (3), dishonorable (2), disobedient (4)

noun
benefit
The new law was for the good of the people.
benefit, interest, sake, success, welfare, advantage

Antonyms: disadvantage, hindrance, impediment
See also: positive, moral, obedient

good-hearted *See* **kind**

goodness
noun
the quality or condition of being good

106   Human Body   Human Mind   Everyday Life   History and Culture   Communication

The goodness of his heart was never in doubt.
virtue, integrity, merit, worth, excellence

Antonyms: evil, harm, wickedness

interjection
a word used to express surprise or alarm

Goodness! You've had all your hair shaved off!
gracious, heavens, wow, my, boy, jeepers

Wow! look at the size of that elephant!

See also: worth

goods
plural noun
1 things that belong to someone
Lulu saved her household goods from the fire.
belongings, possessions, property, stuff, things

2 things that are sold
That shop is known for its baked goods.
merchandise, stock, wares, commodities

See also: possessions, property

gorgeous See beautiful

govern See control, lead, rule

government
noun
1 the political direction and control of people living in a community, state, or nation
Government is complex in a country where the people speak different languages.
administration, management, command, control, rule

2 the group of people that give this direction and have this control
The government decided to build a public park.

administration, authorities, establishment

> *some kinds of governments*
> commonwealth, confederacy, democracy, empire, federation, monarchy, republic, tyranny

grab
verb
to take hold of suddenly or with force

The man grabbed his hat and rushed out.
clutch, grasp, seize, snatch, clasp, grip, take

He snatched the book from my hands.

Antonyms: drop, let go

grace
noun
1 beauty in form, style, or motion
She ran with the grace of a cheetah.
charm, loveliness, beauty, coordination

2 the tendency to be kind or polite
Marcus had the grace to ignore her error.
tact, courtesy, goodness, taste

See also: charm

graceful
adjective
marked by grace or beauty of movement or manner
Fred is a graceful dancer.
elegant, charming, lovely, fluid, smooth, beautiful

Antonyms: awkward, clumsy, oafish, tactless

grade
noun
1 a level, degree, or rank in a scale
These are the top grade of eggs.

A B C D E F **G** H I J K L M N O P Q R S T U V W X Y Z

level, notch, position, quality, rank, status, league, scale, class, tier

2 a number or letter given on schoolwork to show quality or correctness
What grade did you get on your book report?
mark, score, rating

3 the slope of a road or railroad
The locomotive chugged up the steep grade.
rise, slope, pitch, hill, inclination, incline, upgrade

verb

1 to give a grade to
The teacher graded the papers.
evaluate, mark, rate, score

2 to organize or sort by steps or degrees
Beef is graded by the amount of fat it contains.
rate, rank, class, sort, classify, value, graduate, group, type

See also: rank

graduate *See* **grade**

grain
noun

1 the small hard seeds of cereal plants such as wheat or rice

> *some examples of grain*
> barley, buckwheat, corn, oats, rice, rye, wheat
> *some things made from grain*
> alcohol, bread, broth, cereal, feed, flour, fodder, food, graham, granola, meal, oatmeal, oil, porridge

2 any tiny, hard piece of something
The ant carried away a grain of sugar.
There is a grain of truth to what she says.
particle *There's a particle of dirt on your glasses.*
speck *There is a speck of dust in my eye.*

grand
adjective

1 splendid in size or appearance
Rich people often live in grand houses.

majestic, big, lofty, mighty, great, impressive, magnificent
The Taj Mahal is a majestic building.

2 of the highest rank
Shakespeare was a grand writer.
great, supreme, distinguished, eminent, important

Antonyms: lowly (2), ordinary (2), plain (1), simple (1)

See also: great

grant *See* **acknowledge, gift, permit**

graph 🎵 👤 *See* **chart**

grasp *See* **get, grab, hold, know, knowledge, learn, possession, reach, read, see, take, understand, understanding**

grass ⬤
noun

a green plant with narrow pointed leaves and stems with joints

> *some words used to describe grass*
> fresh, green, lush, short, tall, thick
> *some things people do to grass*
> cut, edge, feed, fertilize, landscape, mow, plant, rake, seed, store, water, weed

grate
verb

to make a sharp grinding noise
The rusty gate grated on its hinges as it swung open.
rasp, creak, scrape, screech

See also: scrape

grateful
adjective

feeling thankful or showing thanks for kindness or something pleasing
We were grateful for your help fixing the tire.
thankful, indebted, obliged

Antonyms: thankless, ungrateful

grave *See* **serious**

Human Body   **?** Human Mind   Everyday Life   History and Culture   Communication

gravity ❶ *See* **importance, weight, physics**

gray *See* **cloudy, hair**

great
adjective

1 very large in size or number
A great crowd came to see the parade.
enormous, huge, immense, tremendous, vast, gigantic, giant, grand

2 unusual in degree or amount
He showed great courage in saving the drowning child.
exceptional, extraordinary, extreme, intense, vast, immense, terrific, outstanding, remarkable

3 very important or distinguished
Shakespeare was a great writer who lived hundreds of years ago.
distinguished, eminent, first-rate, major, notable, prominent, grand, esteemed, important

4 (informal) very good
This is great ice cream.
excellent, exceptional, fabulous, fantastic, first-rate, outstanding, splendid, super, superb, superior, swell, terrific, tremendous, wonderful

Antonyms: awful (4), common (2),
horrible (4), horrid (4), insignificant (3),
minuscule (1), normal (2), ordinary (3),
small (1), terrible (4), tiny (1), typical (2),
undistinguished (3), usual (2)

adverb
(informal) very well
He is doing great at work.
excellently, fine, exceptionally, well, splendidly

Antonyms: badly, poorly, terribly
See also: excellent, huge

greater *See* **better**

green *See* **grass**

greet
verb

1 to speak to with friendly or polite words upon meeting or when starting a letter
The Porters greeted their dinner guests at the door.
hail, meet, receive, welcome

2 to respond to or receive in a certain way
He greeted the news with a smile.
meet, welcome, receive, accept

Antonyms: avoid (1), ignore (1), shun (1)
See also: welcome, meet

grief ❷
noun

great sadness
Her grief over her friend's death lasted many months.
sorrow, woe, anguish, mourning, pain

Antonyms: bliss, delight, ecstasy, gladness, happiness, joy
See also: sorrow, pain

grip *See* **fascinate, grab, handle, hold, understanding**

ground ❷ ❸
noun

1 the earth's solid surface
earth, land, soil, turf
When the wind stopped, the kite fell to the earth.

2 (often **grounds**) a piece of land that has a special purpose
There are several gardens on the campus grounds.
acres, property, estate, land, tract

3 (sometimes **grounds**) the reason or basis for saying or doing something
What are the grounds for failing Jimmy?
basis, foundation, reason, root, premise, base
Trust is the basis of friendship.

a
b
c
d
e
f
g
h
i
j
k
l
m
n
o
p
q
r
s
t
u
v
w
x
y
z

verb

to make the basis for

He grounded his argument in facts.

base, establish, found, institute, predicate

See also: earth, land, property

grounds ? 🌐 *See* **cause, reason, yard**

group

noun

a collection of people, things, or ideas that are in one place or are related by characteristics

A large group of people met to discuss the plan.

assortment, body, bunch, cluster, collection, congregation, set, assembly, community, company, knot

We saw a coin collection at the museum.

verb

1 to put with other items that are similar

The librarian grouped the books by topic.

sort, class, classify, bracket, grade, rank, organize

Boxers are classed by their weight.

2 to bring together into a group; gather

The teacher grouped the students in a circle.

assemble, bunch, cluster, collect, combine, gather, marshal, round up

Antonyms: disassemble (2), disperse (2), jumble (1), mix up (1), scatter (2), shuffle (1)

See also: assembly, band

grow ⊗ ▲

verb

1 to become larger

She grew an inch over the summer.

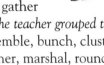

enlarge, expand, increase, wax, bud

The stomach expands when a person eats.

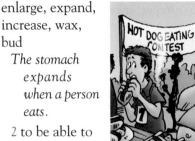

2 to be able to live

This plant doesn't grow in the shade.

bloom, blossom, flourish, prosper, thrive, progress

3 to become

The weather grew warmer.

become, get, wax

4 to make grow

The farmer grows corn and beans.

cultivate, produce, raise

Antonyms: decrease (1), die (2), diminish (1), ebb (1), hamper (4), hinder (4), perish (2), shrink (1), succumb (2), thwart (4), wane (1), waste away (2), wither away (2)

growl ▲

verb

1 to make a deep, rumbling sound to express anger or hostility

The dog will growl if you try to take away its bone.

snarl

2 to make a deep rumbling sound like a growl

His stomach is growling.

rumble, grumble, murmur

See also: murmur

grown ⊗ ▲ *See* **grown-up, mature**

grown-up

adjective

having become an adult

My grown-up sister has an apartment of her own.

grown, mature, big, adult

See also: mature

 Human Body   Human Mind   Everyday Life   History and Culture   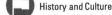 Communication

growth

noun

1 the process of growing
Teenagers experience rapid growth.
That town had a large growth in population during the 1990s.
enlargement, expansion, increase, raise, rise, development, advance

2 that which has grown
A growth of weeds is taking over the garden.
cultivation, expansion, development, extension, multiplication

Antonyms: decrease (1), fall (1), shrinkage (1)
See also: increase, raise, rise

guarantee

noun

a promise to make sure that some duty or responsibility will be met
The babysitter gave us her guarantee that she would be here every afternoon at three o'clock.
assurance, pledge, promise

verb

to make certain or promise
The salesman guaranteed my satisfaction on the new van.
assure, promise, ensure

guard

verb

1 to watch over to prevent escape or intrusion
The soldiers guarded the prisoners.
watch, patrol, restrain

2 (**guard against**) to do what is necessary to prevent
The farmers in the valley need to guard against floods in the rainy season.
provide, prepare

Antonyms: invite (2), welcome (2)

noun

1 a person who watches out for danger or protects property
The museum had guards at every exit.
defender, preserver, shield, watchdog, watchman, security

2 A person who watches over another person to prevent escape
There are guards in the prison day and night.
escort, lookout, watchdog, warden

See also: watch

guess

verb

to form an opinion without enough information to be certain
He tried to guess the reason for her laughter.
reckon, infer, figure, divine

See also: figure

guidance   See direction

guide

verb

1 to direct or lead along a way that is not familiar
The librarian guided us to the books about Asian snakes.
conduct, direct, lead, pilot, show

2 to offer advice to
My father guided me through the job application.
advise, steer, tutor, counsel, instruct

Antonym:
follow (1)

noun

a person who points out the way or leads others
The guide led us on our hike.
adviser, conductor, counselor, leader, instructor

Antonym: follower
See also: lead, show

guilt

noun

a feeling of being sorry or responsible for having done something wrong

a
b
c
d
e
f
g
h
i
j
k
l
m
n
o
p
q
r
s
t
u
v
w
x
y
z

He felt a deep sense of guilt over the expensive dish he'd broken.

regret, remorse, responsibility

Antonym: pride

See also: responsibility

guilty *See* bad

gulf *See* swallow

guy *See* man

112

 Human Body   Human Mind   Everyday Life   History and Culture   Communication

habit 🔊 *See* **dress, practice**

hair 🔊 🔊

noun

a thin, thread-like strand that grows from the skin of humans and other mammals

some words used to describe hair
brittle, coarse, curly, fine, fuzzy, long, oily, shaggy, shiny, short, soft, straight, thick, thin, unruly, parted, layered, frizzy

some hair colors
auburn, black, blond, brown, golden, gray, red, white

some hairstyles
bangs, bob, braid, bun, dreadlocks, permanent, pigtail, ponytail

some kinds of hair growth
beard, eyebrow, eyelash, mane, mustache, sideburns, whiskers

without hair
bald

halfway *See* **middle**

hall 🔊 *See* **passage**

halt *See* **end, pause, quit, stop**

hand 🔊 *See* **part, pass**

handle

noun

the part of an object made to be held in order to lift, grasp, or hold the object
Use the handles to open the drawer.

grip *The tool has a rubber grip.*

hilt *The hilt of the sword was etched with fancy designs*

hold *He gripped the hold of the chainsaw.*

shaft *The shaft of the hoe was made of wood.*

knob *We couldn't open the door because the knob fell off.*

verb

1 to deal with; manage
He handled the extra guests well.

cope with, deal with, hack, manage

2 to touch or examine with the hands
Please handle the flowers gently.

hold, touch, feel

handsome *See* **attractive, face**

hang

verb

to attach to a point above without support from below
She hung a pair of curtains.

suspend, dangle, drape, hook

happen

verb

to take place
The wedding will happen next summer.

occur *While we were exploring the old house, something occurred that I shall never forget.*

fall *Night fell and the children got ready for bed.*

pass *It came to pass that the king and queen had twin sons.*

take place *The picnic took place at the lake.*

befall *We were afraid of what might befall during our walk through the dark forest.*

come *Dessert usually comes after dinner.*

be *Do you think we have control over what will be in the future?*

arise *Problems may arise if you don't come on time.*

A
B
C
D
E
F
G
H
I
J
K
L
M
N
O
P
Q
R
S
T
U
V
W
X
Y
Z

a
b
c
d
e
f
g
h
i
j
k
l
m
n
o
p
q
r
s
t
u
v
w
x
y
z

happening *See* **business, event, experience, thing**

happiness 🔵
noun
the fact or condition of being happy or glad
Your friendship has brought a lot of happiness to my life.
gladness, cheer, delight, joy, bliss

> some things people do out of happiness
> beam, chuckle, crow, frolic, glow, kick up one's heels, laugh, prance, radiate, rejoice, romp, smile, twinkle

Antonyms: sadness, unhappiness
See also: cheer, delight, joy

happy
adjective
feeling joy or pleasure; being glad or content
She was very happy with her birthday gifts.
glad, pleased, joyful, blissful, jubilant, delighted
See also: joyful

harbor 🔵 🔵 *See* **hide, shelter**

hard
adjective
1 not soft
It hurt when I fell on the hard ground.
firm, rigid, solid, tough, stony, steely
2 difficult
Learning to ice skate is hard for some people.
difficult, tough, tricky, complex, rough
Math is really tough for me.
3 asking for a great effort
We think she is a hard teacher because she gives so much home-work.

demanding, harsh, severe, strict, exacting
Antonyms: easy (3), soft (3)
See also: firm, difficult, harsh

hardly *See* **just**

harm
noun
1 injury or hurt
Although he fell a long way, no harm came to the child.
injury, hurt, ill, damage, trauma
2 wrong or evil
He did great harm by lying to us.
evil, wrong, ill
Antonyms: good (2), help (1)
verb
to hurt or damage
Too much sun can harm the skin.
damage, hurt, injure, impair, wound
Antonyms: ameliorate, help, improve
See also: hurt, damage, good

harmful *See* **bad, dangerous, unhealthy**

harsh
adjective
1 rough or not pleasing to the eyes, ears, or other senses
The harsh music hurt my ears.
rough, abrasive, grating, hard, gruff, jarring
2 rough and not pleasing in action or result
She had a harsh manner.
abrasive, hard, rough, rude, rugged, stiff, tough, unpleasant, severe
3 severe
The mayor wants harsher punishments for drug dealers.
severe, strict, hard, tough, demanding, stern
Antonyms: easy (3), light (3), pleasant (1,2)
See also: rough, hard, severe

harvest 🔵 🔵 *See* **farm, garden**

hatch *See* **develop, lay, produce**

 Human Body   ❓ Human Mind   👕 Everyday Life   🚩 History and Culture   📞 Communication

A
B
C
D
E
F
G
H
I
J
K
L
M
N
O
P
Q
R
S
T
U
V
W
X
Y
Z

hate

verb

to dislike very strongly; detest
The people hated the cruel king for allowing their children to die of starvation.
abhor, detest, loathe, despise

> We **hate** some persons because we do not know them, and will not know them because we hate them.
> —Charles Caleb Colton (1780-1832), British author

some things people do out of hate
glare, growl, scorn, scowl, sneer
some words that describe someone who hates
abominable, callous, evil, hateful, hostile, loathsome, malignant, nasty, vicious, wicked

Antonyms: adore, love, relish

hats ○ *See* **celebration**

have

verb

1 to own
I have five dollars.
keep *Ms. Hall keeps the keys to the office.*
occupy *We occupy two booths at the farmers' market.*
own *We own our house and the two acres of land around it.*
possess *I now possess a new bicycle.*

2 to experience
We always have a good time at recess.
experience *Ms. Norris experienced some discomfort in her neck after the accident.*
feel *At the first sign of sun in a week, I felt hope.*
take *I take pleasure in helping you.*
enjoy *The students enjoyed the library's large choice of books.*

head ○ ○ *See* **front, lead, leader, main, rule**

heading ○ ○ *See* **direction**

health ○ ○

noun

the condition of one's body or mind

some kinds of health
emotional, mental, physical
words for someone in good health
energetic, fit, flourishing, hardy, healthy, hearty, lively, right, robust, sane, sound, strong, thriving, trim, well
words for someone in poor health
diseased, failing, ill, run-down, sick, sickly, unhealthy, unwell, weak
healthful
beneficial, nourishing, nutritious, wholesome
harmful
detrimental, hazardous

healthy

adjective

1 being free from sickness
Will you be healthy enough to play in the game tomorrow?
healthful, sound, well, robust, fit

2 showing good mental or physical condition
She has a healthy appetite for fruits and vegetables.
healthful, wholesome, right

Antonyms: sickly (1), unhealthy (1,2), unwholesome (2)
See also: well, fit

hear ○ *See* **learn**

heart ○ *See* **bottom, center, courage, root, spirit, sympathy**

heat ○ ○ ○ *See* **pressure, warm, physics**

heaven

noun

1 the sky, including the stars, sun, moon, and planets as seen from the earth
It was a perfect night for gazing at the heavens.
skies, stars, blue

a

b

c

d

e

f

g

h

i

j

k

l

m

n

o

p

q

r

s

t

u

v

w

x

y

z

2 a state or condition of great happiness
It is heaven to see you again.
Eden, bliss, paradise, rapture, ecstasy

Antonym: hell (2)

heavy
adjective
having much weight or hard to lift
We tried to lift the heavy box.
weighty, hefty, cumbersome, ponderous

Antonyms: light, lightweight, weightless

height
noun
1 the distance from the bottom to the top
The height of that pine tree is fifteen feet.
elevation, altitude, tallness

2 the highest point or degree
She's at the height of her success.
At the height of the sale, there were hundreds of people shopping.
apex, crest, peak, summit, zenith, climax, top

Antonyms: bottom (1), base (1), low (2)

help
verb
to aid or assist
I helped my mother set the table.
aid, assist, support

Antonyms: hinder, harm, impede
noun
1 the act of giving assistance
When they had a lot of planting to do, she offered her help.
aid, assistance, service, support

The old lady was glad to have the aid of her neighbor.

2 one who gives assistance
She is a big help to her mother.
aide, assistant, attendant, auxiliary

Antonyms: burden (2), hindrance (1),

deterrent (1), obstacle (1)

helpful
adjective
giving help or aid
I wish you would be more helpful around the house.
useful, constructive, advantageous, beneficial, profitable, valuable

Antonyms: unhelpful, burdensome, useless
See also: useful

hence See forward

herd ❶ See crowd, animal, dog

hero See ideal

heroic
adjective
1 of or having to do with a hero or heroes
The firefighter had a heroic life.
legendary, noble, courageous, daring

2 like a hero
Jumping into the river to save the boy was a heroic deed.
brave, courageous, daring, bold, noble, gallant

3 having to do with literature about a hero
He liked to read heroic poems.
epic, legendary

Antonym: cowardly (1,2)
See also: brave

hidden See secret

hide
verb
to put or hold out of sight; keep from view
Did you hide the present under the bed?
conceal, veil, disguise, harbor, mask

Antonyms: reveal, expose, uncover

high
adjective
reaching up a great distance
We had a great view from the top of the high cliff.
lofty, tall, elevated, towering

 Human Body   Human Mind   Everyday Life   History and Culture   Communication

Antonyms: low, short

higher *See* education

highly *See* quite

highway ⊙ *See* street

hill *See* grade, rise

hire
verb
  1 to take on as a worker for money or other
    reward
  We hired a crew to paint the house.
employ, engage, enlist
  2 to have the use of in return for a payment of
    money
  We hired the concert hall for the evening.
charter, engage, lease, retain, rent, reserve
  Antonyms: dismiss (1), fire (1)

historical *See* literature

history ⊙
noun
  everything that has happened in the past to
  someone or something

> *some descriptions of periods in history*
> ancient, colonial, contemporary, modern,
> classical
> *units for measuring history*
> age, century, eon, epoch, era, generation,
> millennium, period

hit
verb
  1 to give a blow or stroke to
  He hit the ground with a stick.
strike, beat, punch, club, rap, knock, bang, cuff,
slap, smack, whack, pound
  2 to come in contact with
  The stone hit the window.
strike, bump, knock, collide, crash

Collide is followed by **with** in this sense. *I collided with Mr. Moody in the hall.*

Crash is followed by **into** or **against**. *That car crashed into a tree.*

  Antonym: caress (1)
noun
  1 a blow or stroke
  The boxer took three hits to the stomach.
bang, blow, stroke, clip, punch, strike, cuff
  2 someone or something that is very popular
  The young piano player was a hit with the audience.
  The movie was a big hit.
sensation *Everyone is talking about what a sensation your performance was.*
success *She's going to keep writing, since her first novel was such a huge success.*
smash *Their latest song is a real smash.*
  Antonym: caress (1)
  See also: beat

hold
verb
  1 to have or
  contain
  within one's
  hand
  *He picked up the
  cricket and
  held it gently.*

clasp, clutch, grasp, grip, take
  2 to keep for a certain time
  Hold this letter until I return.
keep, retain, save, preserve, reserve, take care
of, watch

hole
noun
  1 an opening or hollow cavity in something
  We dug a small hole for the seeds.
cavity, hollow, opening, pit, bore, aperture,
cave, crater, pocket
  2 an animal's burrow
  Some snakes live in holes in the ground.

A B C D E F G H I J K L M N O P Q R S T U V W X Y Z

a
b
c
d
e
f
g
h
i
j
k
l
m
n
o
p
q
r
s
t
u
v
w
x
y
z

burrow, tunnel, den

> The mouse that hath but one **hole** is quickly taken.
> —From JACULA PRUDENTUM, by George Herbert (1593-1633), British poet

holiday ○ *See* **celebration**

hollow *See* **empty, hole, valley**

holy ○ ○
adjective

1 sacred according to a particular religion
We read from the holy scriptures each night.
divine, sacred, religious, hallowed

2 devoted to the church, to God, or to religion
The priest is a holy man.
devout, pious, religious, dedicated, faithful, reverent

Antonyms: irreverent (2), unholy (1), sacrilegious (1), unfaithful (2)

home ○
noun

1 the place where a person or animal lives
The forest is home to many animals.
dwelling *This tiny cottage has been their dwelling for years.*
place *Let's meet at your place tomorrow.*
residence *His family lives in a grand old residence up on the hill.*
habitat *This jungle is the habitat of many creatures.*
house *Their house was built in 1870.*
address *There are four people living at my address.*
homestead *He built a homestead for his family out on the plains.*
lodging *A beaver uses a dam as its lodging.*

2 the house, apartment, or other building in which a person lives
Her home has three rooms.

apartment, cabin, condominium, house, mansion, mobile home, palace, bungalow, cottage

> *some words associated with homes*
> build, clean, construct, decorate, dwell, garden, landscape, live, paint, reside
> *some parts of homes*
> attic, balcony, cellar, deck, garage, hallway, patio, porch, roof, room, yard

honest ○
adjective

1 truthful, real, or sincere
She made an honest attempt to answer their questions.
truthful, sincere, earnest, genuine, frank

2 not lying or cheating in one's friendships or business relations
I trust her because she has always been honest with me.
straight *She has always been straight with me.*
upright *The upright boy refused to cheat on the exam.*
decent *I trust him because he's always been a decent person*
respectable *Sam is a respectable man who would not lie to anyone.*
honorable *She got the job because she proved that she was honorable.*
moral *My older brother is a very moral person.*

3 not meant to trick or mislead
I assure you, I'm telling the honest truth.
authentic, frank, sincere, true, truthful, valid, earnest, genuine, legitimate
I've always wanted to own a true diamond.

4 earned in a fair way
He makes an honest wage as a carpenter.
fair, just, even, right, square

Antonyms: insincere (1), crooked (2), devious (2), dishonest (2)

honey *See* **dear**

Human Body   Human Mind   Everyday Life   History and Culture   Communication

honor
noun

1 high public value or respect
The mayor holds a place of honor in our community.
distinction, esteem, respect, credit, estimation, favor, glory, laurel, prestige, note

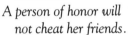

My grandparents enjoy the respect and love of our entire family.

2 the state of having a good character and honest behavior
A person of honor will not cheat her friends.
honesty, integrity, truthfulness, uprightness, principle, conscientiousness, virtue

> *Antonyms:* dishonor (1), disrepute (2), disgrace (1), notoriety (2)

verb

to give a special award or recognition to
The world champions were honored by the President.
crown, reward, decorate, salute, acclaim, commend, praise, recognize

> *Antonyms:* dishonor, defame, discredit, shame

hook *See* **catch, hang, stick**

hope
noun

a wish for something that one thinks could come true
It is my hope to play on the high school baseball team someday.
desire, wish, ambition, aspiration, dream

verb

to look ahead to with a good feeling, with confidence
I hope to get a good score on the test.
anticipate, count on, think, trust, believe

hopeful
adjective

1 showing or feeling hope
She was hopeful about passing the test.
optimistic, confident, positive

2 showing that something hoped for will happen
Melting snow is a hopeful sign of spring coming soon.
bright, favorable, reassuring, positive, promising

> *Antonyms:* despairing (1), discouraging (2), disheartening (2), hopeless (1)

hopeless
adjective

without hope
The hurricane left many people in a hopeless situation.
despairing, desolate, dejected, desperate, discouraged, sick at heart

> *Antonyms:* encouraged, hopeful

horn *See* **alarm, animal**

horror *See* **fear, panic, film**

host *See* **army, lot**

hot
adjective

1 causing the physical feeling of great heat
It's a hot summer day.
warm, torrid, blistering, sweltering, sultry

2 causing a burning feeling in the mouth
I like to put hot pepper on my spaghetti.
fiery, spicy, pungent
That restaurant serves a fiery chili.

> *Antonyms:* bland (2), cold (1), freezing (1), mild (2)

a
b
c
d
e
f
g
h
i
j
k
l
m
n
o
p
q
r
s
t
u
v
w
x
y
z

house ⊙ ▣
noun
> a building in which people live
> *This neighborhood has houses and shops.*
dwelling, home, residence, mansion, villa, cottage, lodge, cabin, shack, bungalow

The synonyms for **house** name different kinds of buildings in which people live. They range from a **shack**, which is poor and small, to a **mansion**, which is large and splendid.

See also: home

household *See* family

however *See* still

hug
verb
> to hold with the arms in a loving way
embrace *The two friends embraced.*
squeeze *She squeezed him close.*
wrap *He wrapped her in his arms.*
fold *Mamma folded the infant in her arms.*
cuddle *Fiona cuddled her pet ferret.*

huge
adjective
> of very large weight, size, or amount
> *The hippopotamus is a huge animal.*
> *I can't believe you ate such a huge sundae!*
enormous, gigantic, immense, mammoth, great,

giant, jumbo, massive, tremendous, vast
> *The Empire State building is an enormous building.*

Antonyms: little, minuscule, minute, small, tiny
See also: giant, large

human ✦ ❓ *See* person

hunger *See* desire

hunt
verb
> 1 to set out to find and kill for food or sport
> *Tom and his father hunt deer every November.*
chase, pursue, stalk, track

> 2 to try to find
> *He hunted for the lost gloves.*
search, seek, look, forage, rummage

noun
> a search to find something
> *The hunt for the lost ring took six hours.*
search, pursuit, quest
See also: chase, search

hurry
verb
> to move or act with speed
> *If we don't hurry we'll miss the train.*
hasten, rush, speed up, hustle, hotfoot it, step on it, make tracks, hop to it

Antonym: slow down
See also: rush

hurt ✦ ❓
verb
> to cause pain or suffering to
> *Did you hurt yourself when you fell off the bike?*
injure *He injured his leg in the car accident.*
wound *The bomb wounded many civilians.*
kill *This toothache is killing me.*

 Human Body   ❓ Human Mind   Everyday Life   History and Culture   Communication

damage *Years of smoking damaged her lungs.*

Kill is informal. It is used in everyday speech and writing but is usually not suitable for a formal report or presentation.

Antonyms: help, cure, relieve

noun

a pain or injury
Did the hurt go away when you took aspirin?
The child had a hurt on her knee.
injury, pain, ache, wound, affliction

See also: injury

hygiene

noun

the practice of keeping clean to stay healthy and prevent disease

some actions of good hygiene
bathe, brush, clean, cleanse, comb, cut, disinfect, dry-clean, floss, flush, freshen up, gargle, groom, pick up, purify, rinse, scrub, shampoo, shower, sponge, spruce, steam, trim, wash, wipe

some descriptions of someone with good hygiene
clean, healthy, immaculate, sterile, tidy

some descriptions of someone with bad hygiene
dingy, dirty, disheveled, disorderly, messy, soiled

A
B
C
D
E
F
G
H
I
J
K
L
M
N
O
P
Q
R
S
T
U
V
W
X
Y
Z

Living World   Physical World   Natural Environment   Economy   Government and Law

a
b
c
d
e
f
g
h
i
j
k
l
m
n
o
p
q
r
s
t
u
v
w
x
y
z

ice  *See* **water**

icy *See* **cold**

idea
noun
> 1 a thought or image formed in the mind
> *What ideas do you have for your next painting?*
image, concept, thought, notion, conception

> 2 an opinion, and held as true
> *He has bizarre ideas about education.*
belief, opinion, view, point of view, judgment, conviction, theory

ideal
noun
> 1 an idea of something in its perfect form
> *A community without violence is our ideal.*
model, exemplar, paradigm

> 2 a belief or aim considered to be worthy of
>   honor or respect
> *He has high ideals.*
standard, value, aspiration, conviction

> 3 something or someone seen as perfect
> *The famous singer was her ideal.*
role model, heroine, hero, idol, paragon
adjective
> seen or understood as the best of its kind or
>   the best under certain conditions
> *That is the ideal restaurant for a party.*
best, perfect, exemplary, consummate
> *See also:* model

ideas *See* **culture**

identical *See* **alike, equal**

identification *See* **mark**

identify *See* **label, name**

identity *See* **character**

idiot
noun
> a stupid person
dummy, moron, dunce, fool, dope
> *Antonyms:* genius, intellect, prodigy

ignorant
adjective
> without knowledge or education
> *Some people are ignorant because they do not
>   know how to read.*
illiterate, uneducated, unschooled
> *Antonyms:* educated, knowledgable, literate

ignore
verb
> to fail to take notice of or pay attention to
> *She ignored me at the dance.*
discount *I discounted the rumors about my best
>   friend.*
disregard *He disregarded his mother's advice and
>   now he's in jail.*
neglect *Claude was so busy with work that he
>   neglected his friends.*
overlook *I overlooked Jennifer's lies because I
>   wanted to be her friend.*
snub *She snubbed me after I tattled on her.*
> *Antonyms:* heed, note, notice, regard

ill *See* **bad, down, harm, sick, unfortunate, unhealthy, health**

illegal
adjective
> against the law or rules; not lawful
> *Stealing is illegal.*
outlawed, unlawful, banned, prohibited

 Human Body   Human Mind   Everyday Life   History and Culture   Communication

Antonyms: lawful, legal, licit

illness
noun

an instance of being ill
He has a serious illness.
ailment, disease,
sickness, disorder,
affliction
Measles is a sickness.

illustrate *See*
**describe, draw,
explain, picture,
show, art,
education**

illustration ⊘ *See* picture

image ⊘ ⊘ *See* appearance, idea, picture

imaginary
adjective

existing only in the imagination
An imaginary monster lives under your bed.
make-believe, made-up, fantastic, mythical

Antonyms: actual, real, tangible

imagination ⊘
noun

the power of the mind to form a thought or
image of something that is not present to
the senses
Imogen's stories are full of imagination.
Tim's pet unicorn exists only in his imagination.
artistry, inventiveness, fantasy, originality,
fancy, make-believe

Antonyms: actuality, reality

imagine
verb

1 to form a thought or image of in the mind
Can you imagine living on Mars?
picture *It's hard to picture your parents as children.*
dream up *I spent the day dreaming up where I
might spend my vacation.*
envision *Can you envision world peace?*

fancy *What do you fancy your life will be like in ten
years?*
visualize *He visualized the sculpture before he
began working.*
invent *While walking
in the woods, she
invented a story
about a girl who
lived in the trees.*
fantasize *I fantasized
that I would be a
pilot someday.*

2 to suppose to be
true
I imagine Mr. Lagworth will be late again.
assume, believe, fancy, guess, reckon, think,
suppose, presume, suspect

> One of the advantages
> of being very young
> is that you don't let
> the facts get in the
> way of your **imagina-
> tion**.
> —Sam Levenson,
> American humorist

immediate *See* **instant, present, prompt**

immediately
adverb

right away; at once
You must leave the country immediately!
instantly, on the double, right away, soon,
pronto, now, forthwith, promptly

Pronto is informal. It is used in everyday
speech and writing but may not be suitable
for a formal report or presentation. **Pronto** is
a Spanish word.

---

immense *See* **giant, great, huge, large, vast**

impact *See* effect, influence, shock

implement *See* device, instrument

importance
noun

the quality or condition of being important
Doctor Winkel is a person of great importance.
account, consequence, emphasis, gravity,
import, magnitude, moment, significance

Antonyms: insignificance, unimportance

A B C D E F G H I J K L M N O P Q R S T U V W X Y Z

important – incredible

a b c d e f g h **i** j k l m n o p q r s t u v w x y z

important
adjective

1 having great meaning or value
Buddha's teachings have been important to many people.
great *She was expected to do great things as the next President.*
serious *Keeping the air and water clean is a serious matter.*
vital *She had vital things to say to the audience.*
essential *What is most essential to you?*

2 powerful or having great influence
The mayor of our city is an important woman.
eminent *She is an eminent scientist.*
influential *He is a very influential person in this town.*
major *Robert Frost is considered a major poet in American literature.*
notable *She has written some notable books.*
prominent *He was a prominent judge before he retired.*

impression ⑦ See feeling

impressive *See dramatic, grand, moving, noble*

improve
verb

to make better
Adding salt and pepper improved the sauce.
better *Abe bettered himself through a university education.*
enrich *The teacher enriched our understanding of the poem.*
enhance *The flowers in the park enhanced my enjoyment of the day.*
ameliorate *Coco tried to ameliorate her employment situation.*
upgrade *If I upgrade my computer, it will run faster.*

Antonyms: degrade, worsen

inch *See drag, edge*

incident *See event, experience, thing*

incline *See grade, pitch, rise, slope*

include
verb

to have or contain as a part
The tea set includes cups and saucers.
Your report includes some odd statements.
contain *Does your toy chest contain any stuffed animals?*
incorporate *Can you incorporate chocolate cake into tonight's meal?*
embrace *This book doesn't embrace all the information I need for my report.*
comprise *The United States was once comprised of thirteen states.*

Antonyms: bar, exclude, keep out

increase
verb

to become greater in quantity or size
The population of Smallburg has increased.
enlarge, expand, grow, augment, mount, multiply, swell, rise, balloon, mushroom

Antonyms: decrease, diminish, lessen

incredible
adjective

1 difficult or impossible to believe
Did you hear that incredible story?
unbelievable, inconceivable, implausible, improbable, flimsy
Sharon's story about an alligator being in the swimming pool is unbelievable.

2 amazing; astonishing
What incredible luck!
marvelous, astounding, awesome, fabulous, tremendous, extraordinary, fantastic

Antonyms: believable (1), credible (1), plausible (1)

124   Human Body   ? Human Mind   Everyday Life   History and Culture   Communication

indeed *See* **really**

independence *See* **freedom**

independent
adjective
   1 not ruled by another
   France is an independent nation.
sovereign, autonomous, free, liberated
   2 without connection to another
   Our school encourages independent study.
distinct, individual, separate, single
   3 not needing the support of another
   She earns enough money to be independent.
self-sufficient, self-reliant, self-supporting
   Antonyms: dependent (3), needy (3)

indicate *See* **express, mention, point, register, represent**

indirect *See* **communication**

individual *See* **alone, different, independent, own, particular, person, personal, single, special**

industrial *See* **technology**

industry ⬣ *See* **business**

infant ◉ *See* **child, young, youngster, life**

inflate ⬣ *See* **exaggerate, expand**

influence
noun
   the ability of one thing or person to affect
     another
   Professor Hyde has a lot of influence on campus.
pull, sway, impact, effect, leverage, clout
verb
   to have influence on
   Your ideas have influenced my thinking.
affect, sway, color, guide, bias, prejudice

informal
adjective
   1 not formal; without ceremony

*They would not allow him into the ball in informal
   dress.*
casual, everyday, ordinary, common, simple,
plain
   2 used often and correctly in everyday conver-
     sation or casual writing
   *He told the class not to use informal language in
     their essays.*
everyday, common, colloquial
   Antonyms: customary (2), formal (2)

information ◉ ◉
noun
   an item of knowledge given or learned
   The report gave a lot of information about snakes.
   Here is the information you asked for.
knowledge, intelligence, material, facts, news

initial *See* **first, original**

injury ◉
noun
   any damage or wrong that causes pain or diffi-
     culty

> *some examples of injuries*
>   break, bruise, burn, concussion, cut,
>   fracture, scrape, sore, sprain, strain,
>   trauma, wound
> *some kinds of injuries*
>   emotional, fatal, minor, physical, serious
> *some reactions to injuries*
>   clench, cry, gasp, grimace, gulp, pout,
>   scream, squirm, wince
> *some words used to describe injuries*
>   painful, sensitive, sore, tender

   See also: hurt

innocent *See* **pure**

input *See* **enter**

insect ◉
noun
   a small animal with a hard covering over its
     body

A B C D E F G H I J K L M N O P Q R S T U V W X Y Z

some examples of insects
ant, aphid, bee, beetle, bookworm, butterfly, cicada, cockroach, cricket, dragonfly, firefly, flea, fly, glowworm, gnat, grasshopper, hornet, housefly, Japanese beetle, katydid, ladybug, locust, louse, mayfly, mosquito, moth, praying mantis, termite, wasp
parts of some insects
abdomen, antenna, feeler, stinger, thorax, wing
some sounds of insects
buzz, chirp, hum, trill

inside See secret

instance See example, moment, time

instant
noun
a very short space of time; moment
He disappeared in an instant.
moment, second, flash, twinkle, jiffy, minute

Jiffy is informal. It is used in everyday speech and writing but is probably not suitable for a formal report or presentation.

Antonyms: age, eon, eternity
adjective
1 happening right away; without delay
The teacher gave me an instant answer to my question.
immediate, prompt, quick, swift, rapid, fast
2 needing only water, milk, or the like to be ready to eat or drink; capable of being prepared quickly
Sometimes I eat instant oatmeal in the morning because it does not take long to make.
prepared, powdered, dehydrated
See also: moment, point

instantly See immediately, now

institute See develop, establish, found, ground, school

institution See introduction, school

instruction See direction, order

instrument
noun
a tool or mechanical device used for special work
The dentist has a special instrument for cleaning teeth.
device, implement, tool, apparatus, utensil
A pen is a writing implement.

insult
verb
to speak to or treat without respect or in a way that hurts feelings
She insulted the family by not attending her sister's wedding.
offend, affront, cut, abuse, slight, put down
The boy affronted the girl by pulling her hair.
Antonyms: compliment, honor, praise
noun
a rude statement or action that hurts someone's feelings
His comment about her clothes was an insult.
offense, affront, barb, slight
See also: attack

intellectual See mental

intelligence See information, mind, understanding

intelligent See bright, clever, sharp, smart, learn

intense See bright, deep, extreme, great, severe, strong, violent, color, emotion, exercise

126 Human Body Human Mind Everyday Life History and Culture Communication

nsects

cetonid beetle

mosquito

locust

yellow jacket

tick

housefly

bumble bee

praying mantis

katydid

mite

cicada

pepsis wasp

stag beetles

butterfly

silkworm

damselfly

ladybug

intention *See* **goal, objective, plan, purpose, spirit**

interest ⦿ ☻
noun
  the desire to learn, know, or take part in something
  The professor had an interest in his student's work.
enthusiasm, stake, involvement
  Antonym: disinterest
verb
  to cause to have the desire to learn or know about something
  Math has interested me for many years.
engage, involve, appeal, engross
  Antonym: repel

international ⊙ *See* **universal**

interpret ⦿ ☻ *See* **language, theater**

interrupted *See* **communication**

intimate
adjective
  very personal or private
  In the story, he revealed intimate information about his family.
confidential, personal, private, secret
  Antonyms: public, well-known
  See also: personal

introduce *See* **bring, offer, propose**

introduction ☻
noun
  1 the act or process of introducing
  The introduction of the factory started the industrial revolution.
establishment, inauguration, institution, presentation
  2 the preface to a book or other work
  He read the introduction to see if the book interested him.
foreword, overture, preface, opening

investigate ⦿ ⊙ *See* **examine, explore, research, study, test**

investigation *See* **check, research, study**

invite *See* **appeal, call, welcome**

invited *See* **welcome**

involve
verb
  1 to have as a necessary part or result
  Police work involves some danger.
include *His job includes answering the phone and making appointments.*
mean *Picking blackberries means getting scratched by the thorns.*
imply *Working on a police force implies some danger.*
entail *Learning to play a musical instrument entails a lot of practice.*
  2 to bring into a situation
  He involved me in a fight with his friend.
include, entangle, enmesh
  3 to give full attention to or be busy with
  She was involved in learning her part for the school play.
bury *Naomi is buried in her homework.*
engross *He's restless and can't find anything that engrosses him.*
absorb *They are absorbed with a new card game.*
engage *She engaged him in the conversation.*
busy *The committee is busy making plans for the art fair.*
immerse *She immersed herself in a book of Indonesian poetry.*
occupy *He's occupied with repairing the car.*
wrap up in *I was so wrapped up in the book, I didn't hear the phone.*
  Antonyms: inattentive (3), preoccupied (3)

involved *See* **busy**

involvement *See* **interest**

iron ⦿ ⬤ *See* **set, clothes**

Human Body   ❓ Human Mind   👕 Everyday Life   🚩 History and Culture   📞 Communication

irregular
adjective

1 uneven in how often or for how long something happens
There was an irregular beep coming from the smoke detector.
erratic, random, variable, uneven

2 not fitting into a standard law, method, or custom
In our country, it is highly irregular to serve dessert before dinner.
unorthodox, abnormal, odd, deviate

Antonyms: customary (2), regular (1)
See also: rough

irritable
adjective

easily bothered or angered
He is irritable without his morning coffee.
grumpy, touchy, out of sorts, cranky, edgy, grouchy, impatient, sensitive

Tim is touchy about the size of his ears.

Antonyms: composed, even-tempered

isolated *See* **remote**

issue *See* **child, problem, produce, question, shoot, stream, subject**

item *See* **object, piece, thing**

A
B
C
D
E
F
G
H
I
J
K
L
M
N
O
P
Q
R
S
T
U
V
W
X
Y
Z

a
b
c
d
e
f
g
h
i
j
k
l
m
n
o
p
q
r
s
t
u
v
w
x
y
z

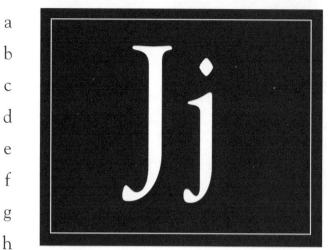

jacket ⊙ *See* **coat**

jail ⊙
noun
a building where people are held while awaiting trial or after having been convicted of a crime
prison, penitentiary, lockup, slammer, can

Slammer and **can** are informal words and are not suited to formal writing and presentations.

verb
to place in a jail
The judge jailed the man for thirty days.
imprison, confine, incarcerate, detain, lock up
See also: prison

jar *See* **jolt, shock**

jealous
adjective
feeling envy of what another person has or can do
He was jealous of his friend's new bike.
envious, resentful, covetous, begrudging

jealousy ⓘ
noun
a feeling of envy towards another person and what he or she has or can do

He couldn't hide his jealousy when his friend won first prize.
envy *The stepsister was filled with envy when Cinderella put on the glass slipper.*
spite *The Queen tried to poison Snow White out of spite.*
See also: envy

jeopardy *See* **danger**

jet ⊙ *See* **shoot, airplane**

jewelry ⊙
noun
rings, watches, necklaces, or other ornaments

some kinds of jewelry
anklet, band, bracelet, brooch, chain, crown, earrings, necklace, pendant, pin, ring, stone, watch
some words associated with jewelry
dazzle, flash, gleam, glint, glisten, glitter, shine, sparkle, twinkle

jingle
verb
to make a sound like light metal objects hitting against each other again and again
The sleigh bells jingled.
tinkle, ring, clink, chink

job ⊙ ⊚
noun
1 a regular position for which a person is paid to do particular duties
Does your job require you to wear a suit every day?
employment, work, position, occupation, labor, livelihood

2 a specific task
It's his job to mow the lawn.
task *Jon's task was to deliver the package safely to Mr. Martin.*
assignment *The newspaper reporter received a dangerous assignment.*
chore *Pat looked forward to her Sunday chores.*
duty *One of a nurse's duties is to give patients their medicine.*

Human Body ● Human Mind ● Everyday Life ● History and Culture ● Communication

See also: work, duty, career, business

join
verb

to become a member of
Will you join the Girl Scouts this year?
enter, enroll in, enlist in, sign up

Antonyms: leave, quit
See also: enter

joint ● *See* common

joke
noun

something said or done to make people laugh
gag *As a gag, they gave him a rubber chicken for his birthday.*
jest *He added a jest or two to his speech.*
pun *I didn't get the pun the first time I heard it.*
wisecrack *It was wrong of you to make a wisecrack about the principal's new haircut.*

verb

to talk or act so as to make people laugh
Please don't joke around in class.
clown, fool, jest, kid, rib, wisecrack

jolt
verb

1 to shake up or cause to move with a jerk
The clap of thunder jolted her out of her chair.
jar, rock, shake, shock, stun

2 to move in a rough, jerky way
The wagon jolted along the dirt road.
bump *The wheelbarrow bumped along across the field.*
jog *The men jogged the heavy piano slowly down the stairs.*
jump *Tom jumped when he heard the thunder.*
lurch *He lost his balance when the boat lurched.*

noun

a sudden shock
The news of the attack gave us a jolt.
blow, fright, jar, shock, start

See also: rock, shake, shock

journal ● *See* record, register

journey *See* travel, trip

joy ●
noun

1 a great feeling of happiness or pleasure
Knowing you has given me joy.
bliss, delight, happiness, ecstasy, elation, glee, jubilation, pleasure, rapture

2 something that causes good feelings or happiness
The baby is a joy to its parents.
bliss, cheer, delight, pleasure, treat

Antonyms: grief (1), sadness (1), sorrow (1), woe (2)
See also: happiness, pleasure, delight

joyful
adjective

showing or causing great happiness
She laughed when she heard the joyful news.
blissful, delightful, joyous, jubilant, glad, rapturous, happy

Antonyms: crestfallen, downhearted, sad
See also: happy

judge ● ●
noun

1 a person trained to hear and decide cases brought before a court of law
justice, magistrate

2 a person who decides the winner in a contest or competition
arbiter, arbitrator, juror, referee, umpire

verb

to form an opinion of or about
Don't judge a book by its cover.
appraise, assess, evaluate, gauge, reckon, value, weigh

judgment
noun

1 a carefully formed opinion
The mayor's judgment is that a new city hall is needed.
conclusion, decision, estimation, evaluation, opinion, position, assessment, view, viewpoint

2 a decision made by someone in power
The court handed down a judgment in favor of the person who was hurt by a drunk driver.
decision, finding, opinion, ruling, verdict

Antonyms: notion (1), whim (1)
See also: decision

juice ○ See fruit

jump
verb
1 to leap into the air
The horse jumped over the hurdle.
bound, leap, spring, hop, vault

2 to move or jerk suddenly
Grover jumped when he heard the scream.
jolt, skip, start, startle, twitch

3 to increase suddenly in amount
The price of a new car jumped last year.
surge, skyrocket, soar

Antonyms: plummet (3), plunge (3)
noun
the act of jumping
Her jump was measured at twelve feet.
bound, leap, spring, hop, vault

See also: spring, surge

jungle ○ See forest

junk
noun
things having little or no worth
The garage is filled with junk.
garbage, refuse, rubbish, trash, waste, scrap

Antonym: treasure
verb
to throw away
Tim junked his rusty old bicycle.
discard, dispose of, scrap, dump, chuck

Antonym: salvage
See also: garbage, refuse, scrap

just
adjective
1 having a fair and honest character
The just judge was known for making good decisions.
fair, impartial, evenhanded, honest, principled, scrupulous, upright, equitable

2 deserved or earned
Punishment was the criminal's just reward.
deserved, justified, merited, warranted

Antonyms: biased (1), dishonest (1), undeserved (2), unfair (1)
adverb
1 by a very small margin
Casey just missed the bus.
barely, hardly, scarcely

2 exactly
That's just the point I meant to make.
precisely, exactly, absolutely, expressly

See also: fair, honest, only

justice ○
noun
1 the upholding of what is fair and right
Max was admired for his keen sense of justice.
fairness, honesty, impartiality, virtue

2 the giving out of something deserved
The victim finally received justice.
punishment, penalty, compensation, reward, reparations, restitution

Human Body   Human Mind   Everyday Life   History and Culture   Communication

This sense of **justice** can be either desirable or undesirable depending on what one has done to deserve it. **Punishment** and **penalty** are received for having done something wrong. **Compensation**, **reward**, **reparations**, and **restitution** often refer to money given to make up for a wrong or injury.

Antonym: injustice (1)
See also: judge, punishment, reward

 Living World    Physical World   Natural Environment   Economy   Government and Law

a
b
c
d
e
f
g
h
i
j
k
l
m
n
o
p
q
r
s
t
u
v
w
x
y
z

keen ⊙ *See* **alert, enthusiastic, quick, sharp, emotion, mind**

keep
verb
1 to manage, attend to, or take care of
He keeps tropical fish.
care for *She cares for stray cats.*
look after *Will you look after my dogs while I'm away?*
manage *He manages a farm as well as a business in town.*
protect *The trees protect the flowers from too much sun.*
attend *Nurses attend sick people.*
maintain *That farmer maintains a herd of cattle.*
mind *Mind the store while I go to lunch.*
support *He supported his sick brother while he was ill.*
sustain *The sun sustains all living things.*
tend *Alice will tend the garden when I'm on vacation.*

2 to put or store
She keeps her notes in a locked drawer.
bank, collect, hoard, put, store

3 to continue being responsible for; be faithful to
Peter kept his promise to Wendy.
abide by, comply with, conform to, mind, obey, observe

4 to continue; persist

Keep going along this road until you get to Main Street.
continue, endure, persevere, persist, remain

5 to stop or hold back
He can't keep from lying.
cease *Cease that noise!*
refrain *Will you refrain from telling any more tall tales?*
restrain *She was restrained by the police officer.*
stop *The child was stopped from running into the street.*
withhold *He withheld his anger.*

See also: hold

keeping *See* care

kick *See* dance, exercise, sport

kid ⊙ ⬤
noun
a child or young person
child *The winner of the pie-eating contest was a child from my neighborhood.*
juvenile *As a juvenile, he was not allowed to see certain movies.*
minor *Minors are not allowed to see this film.*
youngster *The playground is full of youngsters every Saturday morning.*
youth *A youth from the neighborhood offered to help the old couple.*

Kid is informal. That means it is used in everyday speech and writing but is probably not suitable for a formal report or presentation.

Antonyms: adult, grownup

kill ⊙ ⬤
verb
to cause to die
The hunter killed a deer.
execute, exterminate, murder, do away with, slay, assassinate, eliminate, finish, end, dispatch, wipe out

Human Body   Human Mind   Everyday Life   History and Culture   Communication

kind[1]

noun

1 a group of things, people, or animals that are thought of together because of like characteristics

The people here are not familiar with our kind.

class, type, sort, set, species, category, breed

2 type; sort

There's a different kind of rock on the moon.

type *Whole wheat is the only type of bread that she will eat.*

sort *What sort of dog is that?*

variety *What variety of apple is this?*

manner *One finds all manner of wildlife in the forest.*

nature *He likes action films, adventure books, and things of that nature.*

form *This is a rare form of plant life.*

kind[2]

adjective

1 helpful; friendly; good

You were so kind to help that old woman up the stairs.

considerate, decent, good-hearted, helpful, generous, good, obliging, friendly, kindly, warm-hearted

Our good-hearted neighbor takes care of stray animals.

2 showing understanding or sympathy

Your kind words made him feel better.

compassionate, considerate, thoughtful, empathetic, gracious, sympathetic, understanding

Antonyms: cruel (1,2), harsh (2), inconsiderate (2), mean (1), unkind (1)

kingdom

noun

a country that is ruled by a king or queen

domain *This is the sovereign domain of the king.*

dominion *The British monarachy once ruled a vast dominion.*

realm *Have you read about King Arthur's realm?*

kit *See* set

knock *See* beat, hit

know

verb

1 to understand, perceive, or experience directly

Do you know what I'm doing?

appreciate, comprehend, experience, understand, fathom, get, grasp, perceive, realize, recognize

2 to be acquainted with

She knows some famous people.

He knows the plays of Shakespeare.

recognize, recall, recollect, remember

knowledge ⊕

noun

1 understanding; awareness

Alice left home without her parents' knowledge.

awareness, comprehension, grasp, memory, recollection, sense, understanding

2 a particular form of understanding or skill

Working in a restaurant gave Jim a good knowledge of cooking.

command *He has a good command of Spanish.*

experience *We need a worker with two years of computer experience.*

> **Knowledge** is a wild thing and must be hunted before it can be tamed.
> —Persian proverb

expertise *My mother has expertise in architecture.*

know-how *He has the know-how to run a successful business.*

understanding *She has a good understanding of math.*

3 learning; education

A B C D E F G H I J K L M N O P Q R S T U V W X Y Z

knowledge

a
b
c
d
e
f
g
h
i
j
k
l
m
n
o
p
q
r
s
t
u
v
w
x
y
z

Reading is a good way to gain knowledge.
education, learning, teaching, schooling, training, wisdom

some words used to describe knowledge
abstract, basic, certain, current, definite, essential, familiar, fundamental, obscure, trivial, useful, useless

having knowledge
aware, certain, current, familiar, learned, literate, smart, streetwise, well-read, worldly

 Human Body    Human Mind   Everyday Life   History and Culture   Communication

label – land

label

noun

a piece of paper or cloth that is attached to an object and gives information about it

tag *The price tag shows that this shirt is on sale.*

sticker *I read the sticker on my orange and learned that it was grown in Florida.*

verb

to put a label on

My father labels his suitcase before he travels.

tag, mark, designate, identify

labor

noun

hard work or effort

The workers put in hours of labor to finish the building.

work, toil, travail, exertion, effort, drudgery

Antonyms: leisure (1), recreation (1), relaxation (1), repose (1), rest (1)

verb

to do hard work

They labored on the house until it was done.

toil, slave, travail, drudge, strain

Antonyms: play (1), relax (1), repose (1), rest (1)

See also: work

lack

noun

the condition of being without

She had to cancel her vacation because of a lack of money.

absence, need, deficiency, want, shortage

Antonyms: abundance, surplus

verb

to be without

He lacked the strength to climb the rope.

need, want

Antonyms: contain, have

See also: need, want

lamp ○ See light

land

noun

1 the solid part of the earth's surface

Fish live in the sea, and tigers live on land.

earth, ground, terra firma

2 a country or nation

We visited many lands on our vacation.

country *Laos is a country in Asia.*

domain *During the Second World War, Germany tried to increase its domain by invading Russia.*

dominion *Canada's dominion now extends from coast to coast.*

homeland *I was born in Paris, the capital of my homeland, France.*

nation *Mexico is a nation in North America.*

a
b
c
d
e
f
g
h
i
j
k
l
m
n
o
p
q
r
s
t
u
v
w
x
y
z

realm *He dreamed of the day that he would be king of his realm.*

Antonyms: air (1), sea (1)
See also: earth, ground, country

landscape 🌐 🏠 *See* **view, grass, home, photography**

language 🌐
noun
1 the system of spoken or written words with which people communicate thoughts, ideas, or feelings
Language is a way of sharing our ideas with one another.

> *some verbs associated with language*
> babble, chatter, communicate, decipher, decode, gesture, gossip, interpret, mumble, mutter, program, sign, speak, swear, taunt, translate
> *some forms of language*
> formal, informal, spoken, written

2 a particular system used by people of the same nation, region, or group to communicate with one another
The English language is hard for some people to learn.
dialect *Since I didn't understand the tourist's dialect, I couldn't give him the directions he requested.*
idiom *Speaking with a drawl is considered part of the idiom of the southern United States.*
speech *Have you heard the musical speech of the elves of Fantabula?*
tongue *She spoke in a foreign tongue.*
vernacular *Are you able to understand the vernacular of that region?*

See also: speech

lap *See* **fold, splash, wash, dog**

large
adjective
of a size, or amount bigger than normal or average

We will need to buy a large pizza for this many people.
big, ample, great, giant, enormous, jumbo, huge, considerable, copious, extensive, immense, vast, voluminous

Antonyms: little, small
See also: great

largely *See* **mainly, mostly, quite**

last¹
verb
to go on through time
The movie lasted for two hours.
carry on, continue, endure, go on, hold out, linger, persist, remain, abide
Boats don't last, but the oceans endure.

See also: continue

last²
adjective
coming after or finishing behind all others
Ours is the last house on our block.
final *The mystery was not solved until the final chapter of the book.*
terminal *Vancouver was the terminal destination of the ferry.*
ultimate *The obstacle course was the ultimate test for the competitors.*

Antonym: first

lasting
adjective
continuing for a long time, not ending
We all hoped for a lasting peace.
everlasting, enduring, persistent, perpetual

Antonyms: brief, fleeting

late
adjective
1 happening after the usual or expected time
I was late because I missed the bus.
belated, delayed, overdue, tardy

🧍 Human Body   ❓ Human Mind   👕 Everyday Life   🚩 History and Culture   ☎ Communication

2 happening not long ago
Did you hear the latest news?
fresh, new, recent, up-to-date

3 having recently died
We all loved the late Mr. Smith.
departed, perished, deceased, expired, dead

This sense of **late** has a certain polite sensitivity. Its synonyms have been ordered from most to least sensitive.

Antonyms: early (1), old (2), punctual (1)
adverb
after the usual or expected time
The bus arrived late.
belatedly, tardily

latest *See* **modern, new**

laugh ❓ *See* **happiness**

law 📖
noun
1 the set of rules that people in a society must follow
Each country has its own system of law.
charter, code, constitution, regulations, rules

Some kinds of law:
civil, criminal, military, religious

2 a rule that people in a society must follow
According to this law, you must be eighteen years of age to vote.
act, commandment, decree, edict, mandate, order, ordinance, regulation, rule, statute

See also: rule

lawn *See* **yard**

lay
verb
1 to cause to lie down
He laid the pencil on the table.
place, put, rest, set, position, deposit

2 to put forward or offer as a reason
He laid the blame for the accident on me.
put, attribute, assign, allot

3 to think of or come up with
The generals laid their plans for the next attack.
devise, conceive, frame, hatch, plan, contrive

Antonyms: lift (1), pick up (1), take (2)
See also: place, put

layer *See* **coat**

lazy
adjective
not willing to give much effort or to work
Lazy Laura never finishes cleaning her room.
sluggish, slack, slothful, indolent, idle

Antonyms: active, energetic

lead ❶
verb
1 to give direction to
He led us through the woods.
guide, direct, conduct, steer, escort, marshal, pilot, shepherd, show, usher, walk, blaze the trail or way for

You might know **marshal**, **pilot**, **shepherd**, and **usher** as names for occupations. But these words can also be used as verbs.

---

2 to direct
The president led the nation during a difficult time.
direct, command, captain, conduct, control, rule, govern, head, moderate, preside over, reign over

Antonym: follow (1,2)
adjective
first or most important
The lead story in today's paper was about the election.
main, principal, chief, premier, primary, prime, paramount, uppermost

See also: guide

lead ❷ *See* **main**

A
B
C
D
E
F
G
H
I
J
K
L
M
N
O
P
Q
R
S
T
U
V
W
X
Y
Z

🌲 Living World   🔬 Physical World   ⛰ Natural Environment   〽 Economy   📖 Government and Law

a
b
c
d
e
f
g
h
i
j
k
l
m
n
o
p
q
r
s
t
u
v
w
x
y
z

leader ⊙
noun

a person who leads or guides
Who will be the leader on this project?
chief, head, captain, guide, boss, director

Antonym: follower
See also: chief, guide

leaf ⊙
noun

a sheet of paper, usually bound in a book
He cut his finger on a leaf of paper.
sheet, page
Each side of a leaf is a page.

verb

to quickly turn the pages of a book or magazine (usually **leaf through**)
She had time to leaf through the book, but not to read it.
browse, flip, scan, skim, thumb

league *See* **band, grade, organization, society, union**

lean *See* **bend, depend, skinny, slope, thin**

leap *See* **dive, jump, spring, cat, dance**

learn ⊙
verb

1 to get to know or gain knowledge of through study or experience
She learned the craft of weaving from her grandmother.
acquire, assimilate, catch, comprehend, get, grasp, master, pick up

some descriptions of someone learning
apt, bright, curious, inquisitive, intelligent, quick, slow, smart, stupid
some aspects of learning
comprehension, memory, perception

2 to find out about; become aware or informed of
Did you ever learn how the accident happened?
ascertain, discover, determine, find out, hear

3 to fix in the mind
I learned the poem for my English class.
ingrain *He ingrained the spelling rule in his mind*
memorize *She memorized the alphabet.*
commit to memory *He committed the speech to memory.*

Antonym: forget (3)

learned ⊙ *See* **knowledge**

learning ⊙ *See* **knowledge**

leather ⊙ *See* **clothes**

leave
verb

1 to go away from
I'll leave the city soon.
depart, exit, quit, shove off, clear out, split

Shove off, **clear out**, and **split** are informal terms.

2 to give into the care or possession of as a result of one's death
He left his money to his sons.
bequeath, hand down, pass on, will

Antonyms: arrive (1), come (1), enter (1), inherit (2)

leaving *See* **outgoing**

legal
adjective

allowed by law
I am the legal owner of the car.
lawful *Driving faster than the speed limit is not lawful.*
legitimate *We checked to make sure it was a legitimate business.*
valid *She has a valid license to drive.*
sanctioned *Smoking is not sanctioned here.*

 Human Body ⊙ Human Mind ⊙ Everyday Life ⊡ History and Culture Communication

Antonyms: banned, illegal, prohibited, unlawful

legend

noun

a story that has been handed down from an earlier time. Many people know these stories, but they cannot be proven true

The coyote is a central figure in Native American legend.

fable, folk tale, myth

legendary

adjective

having to do with or like a legend
John Henry is a legendary figure.
mythical, fabulous, fantastic

See also: fantastic

legislature ○ *See* assembly

leisure ○

noun

freedom from work or other duties that take time and effort; free time

some words associated with leisure
amble, fish, garden, idle, lounge, muse, picnic, play, putter, read, relax, stroll, unwind, calm, lazy, peaceful, quiet, serene

lend *See* bank

length

noun

1 the entire amount of a distance from beginning to end
We walked the length of the street.
distance, span, extent, measure, range

2 a part of the entire extent of something
Tie the dog to the tree with this length of rope.
measure, piece, section, segment, portion

3 an amount of time

The baby slept for the entire length of the film.
duration, span, extent, term, time

See also: distance, measure

let

verb

to allow
He let the children pet his dog.
allow, permit, authorize, sanction, approve, enable

Will you permit me to go inside?

Antonyms: ban, bar, prohibit
See also: allow, permit

letter ○ *See* line

level

noun

1 position in height, stage, or rank
People have different levels of ability at math.
The level of the water in the river was high after the flood.
stage, position, rank, status, degree

2 a flat surface

liberal *See* progressive

liberty *See* freedom

license *See* freedom, permission, permit

lid *See* cover

lie[1] ○

noun

an untrue statement made on purpose
I told Mom a lie because I was afraid to tell her the truth.
deceit, falsehood, fabrication, fib, fiction, pretense, story, tale

Antonym: truth

verb

to make a false statement on purpose
Misha lied when he said the dog ate his homework.
deceive, falsify, fib, fool, prevaricate

a
b
c
d
e
f
g
h
i
j
k
l
m
n
o
p
q
r
s
t
u
v
w
x
y
z

lie²
verb

to be in or place oneself in a flat or resting position
I spent all morning lying in bed.
recline *The man reclined in his hammock for a nap.*
lounge *He lounged at the pool all day.*
stretch *The woman stretched out on the couch for a nap.*
rest *He rested in bed while he was sick.*
loll *She lolled on the sofa and watched television.*

life ⓘ
noun

1 the state of being that sets animals and plants apart from rocks, minerals, and other things. Things that have life grow, reproduce, and use energy
being, existence, mortality

> some stages of human life
> adolescent, adult, baby, child, elder, embryo, fetus, infant, juvenile, newborn, senior citizen, teen-ager, toddler, tot, youngster, youth

2 something that is alive, or all living things
Ten lives were lost at sea yesterday.
Pollution has affected the plant life in the area.
being, creature, organism

3 the time between birth and death
He has had a long life.
life expectancy, life span, lifetime

4 energy, movement, or spirit
He spoke with life on the subject of political reform.
energy, liveliness, pep, vigor, vitality, zip

Antonym: death (1)
See also: energy

> My **life** is like a stroll upon the beach, As near the ocean's edge as I can go.
> —From "THE FISHER," a poem by Henry David Thoreau (1817-1862)

lifetime See **life**

lift
verb

1 to bring upward
Mandy lifted her cat off the table.
elevate, raise, boost, hoist, pick up

2 to move higher
The hot air balloon lifted into the sky.
arise, ascend, climb, rise

3 to end, cancel, or take back
The city lifted its ban on skateboarding.
end, revoke, withdraw, call off, cancel

Antonyms: drop (1), enact (3), sink (2)
noun

a machine used for raising or carrying
They rode up the mountain on the ski lift.
crane, derrick, elevator, escalator, hoist

See also: raise, rise

light¹ ⓘ
noun

1 the form of energy that makes it possible for the eye to see
The sun produces light.
daylight, illumination, moonlight, starlight, sunlight, sunshine

> some verbs associated with light
> dazzle, fade, flash, flicker, glare, gleam, glimmer, glow, shine, sparkle, twinkle
> some adjectives used to describe light
> aglow, bright, dim, fluorescent, incandescent, luminous, radiant, shiny, solar, sunny

2 something that gives off light
Turn off the light when you go to bed.
beacon, candle, flame, flare, flashlight, lamp, lantern, match, torch

Antonym: darkness (1)
adjective

1 being bright or illuminated
This room isn't light enough to read in.
aglow, alight, bright, brilliant, sunny, shining
The stars were luminous in the night sky.

2 pale in color

 Human Body　　?　Human Mind　　👕 Everyday Life　　🚩 History and Culture　　 Communication

Life

<table>
<tr><td>

He has very light hair.
faded, fair, pale, pallid, white

Antonym: dark (1,2)

verb
to catch fire
The wet logs would not light.
catch, catch fire, ignite, kindle

light²

adjective
not heavy, full, intense, or powerful
My backpack was light enough to carry all day.
He woke up from a light sleep.
delicate, slight, airy, soft, mild, moderate
She enjoyed the delicate color of the flower.

Antonym: heavy
See also: delicate

like

verb
1 to find pleasure in
Annette likes going to the movies.
enjoy *I enjoy skating.*
love *I love fishing and swimming.*
relish *I would relish the chance to meet him.*
delight in *He delights in a good book.*

2 to have affection or regard for
I really like her a lot.
adore *I adore that new song, don't you?*
fancy *I fancy your red hair.*
favor *I favor the rule about wearing bicycle helmets.*
love *She loves her friends.*
worship *The new parents worship their baby.*

3 to feel a desire or want
We can go swimming if you like.
want, desire, wish, prefer, please, care

Antonym: dislike (1,2)

noun
(usually **likes**) the things a person enjoys or prefers
What are his likes and dislikes?
love *He has a great love for music.*
preference *What are his musical preferences?*

</td><td>

liking *My mother has a liking for chocolate.*
fondness *I have a fondness for poetry.*
taste *She has a taste for flying.*

See also: love, want

likely *See* **possible**

limit

noun
the point at which something ends; a boundary or border
The limit of our yard is that line of trees.
border, boundary, end, extent, frontier, line, margin

verb
to put boundaries on or around
We limited our game to two hours.
bound, confine, contain, curb, delimit, demarcate, restrict

Antonym: extend
See also: border, confine

limits *See* **confine, edge**

line

noun
1 a long, thin mark
I drew a line in the dust with a stick.
stripe *My favorite shirt has red and blue stripes on the sleeves.*
band *That kind of snake is brown with yellow bands.*
bar *The owl has bars on its chest.*

2 a boundary or limit; point at which something must stop
Jamie, your behavior has crossed the line!
border, edge, limit, boundary

3 a string, rope, or wire
Put the wet clothes out on the line to dry.
rope, cord, cable, wire, string, twine

4 a row of people or things
The line for tickets went all the way around the block.
row, string, chain, series, queue, file

5 a very short written message

</td></tr>
</table>

 Human Body   Human Mind   Everyday Life   History and Culture   Communication

Drop me a line and let me know when you will be in town.

note, memo, letter, memorandum, notation

See also: rope

line   *See* **edge**

linen   *See* **clothes**

link   *See* **connect, connection**

linked   *See* **related**

lion   *See* **cat**

liquid ⓔ   *See* **water**

listen ⓢ

verb

to pay attention to the sound of
Listen to the wind in the trees.

attend, heed, mind, tune in, mark

Antonym: ignore

literature ⓔ ⓢ

noun

writings that have lasting value. Literature includes stories, poems, plays, and essays

some kinds of literature
fiction, nonfiction, poetry, prose
some words used to describe literature
aesthetic, classic, comic, controversial, dramatic, heroic, historical, humorous, imaginative, juvenile, lyric, romantic, tragic
some words associated with literature
characterize, compose, create, critique, depict, describe, entertain, examine, explain, expose, express, imagine, influence, inspire, portray, read, relate, rhyme, tell, write
some elements of literature
allegory, alliteration, character, climax, conflict, description, dialogue, humor, idiom, irony, metaphor, meter, plot, rhyme, setting, simile, symbol, theme, title, tone

little

adjective

small in size
The kittens are still little, but they are growing fast.

small, tiny, teeny, wee, diminutive

Antonyms: big, large
See also: tiny

live

verb

1 to have life; be in an active state
People need food and water to live.

breathe, exist, survive

2 to support oneself in life
I can live on very little money.

exist *He existed on berries and insects until he was rescued.*

get along *He can barely get along on the money he makes.*

make ends meet *She works hard just to make ends meet.*

manage *She managed just fine on her own.*

subsist on *They subsisted on roots and berries.*

3 to stay or reside (often **live in** or **live at**)
He lives in a cabin in the mountains.

abide, dwell, lodge, reside, stay, settle, sojourn

4 to continue to be in existence or be present to the memory
Even though she's gone, her memory lives on in her children.

abide, endure, hold out, last, linger, persist, remain, survive

Antonyms: die (4), end (4)

livelihood   *See* **career, job, living**

lively

adjective

1 full of life or energy
She is a very lively person.

animated, brisk, energetic, peppy, vigorous, vital, zippy

2 gay or exciting
This is a lively party.

A
B
C
D
E
F
G
H
I
J
K
L
M
N
O
P
Q
R
S
T
U
V
W
X
Y
Z

airy, blithe, exciting, festive, gay, lighthearted, merry, playful, spirited

3 striking
The painter Vincent van Gogh used colors to create a lively effect.
stirring, striking, vivid

Antonyms: boring (2), dull (2), sluggish (1)

adverb
with quick movements or lots of energy
The gym teacher told us to move lively.
briskly, energetically, nimbly, quickly

living

adjective
having life
All living things need water.
alive *Animals need air to stay alive.*
animate *Rocks are not animate objects.*
breathing *As long as I am breathing, you will have a home with me.*
live *We saw live baby chicks at the farm.*
vital *The nurse checked the patient's heartbeat and other vital signs.*

Antonyms: dead, inanimate

noun
the way in which a person earns money
She has a comfortable living as an artist.
livelihood, career, profession, vocation
Farming is his livelihood.

See also: live

load

noun
an amount of something carried
The truck carried a load of logs.
burden, cargo, freight, shipment
Luke showed me the contents of his pockets.

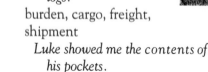

verb
to put on or in something in order to carry
Every morning, I load my books in my backpack and walk to school.
fill, heap, pack, pile, sack, stow, stuff

Antonyms: remove, unload
See also: burden, fill

loan ☻ *See* bank

locate *See* find, place, station

location

noun
place or position
I marked the location of my house on the map.
place, position, site, situation, spot

See also: place

lock ⊙

verb
to keep closed by means of a lock
We locked all of the doors and windows of our house when we left for vacation.
bolt, secure, latch, bar, padlock, fasten

Antonym: unlock

log *See* record, register

logical *See* reasonable, thought

lonely

adjective
1 without company
There was a lonely hill on the horizon.
She is content with her lonely life.
solitary, secluded, lonesome, hermitic

2 empty of humans
He walked for miles through lonely woods.
desolate, uninhabited, deserted

Antonym: crowded (2)

long

adjective
having greater than usual length in distance or time
There is a long driveway leading to our house.

Human Body Human Mind Everyday Life History and Culture Communication

The runners were very tired after the long race.
drawn out, extended, extensive, prolonged, protracted, stretched

> *Antonym:* short

long *See* **want**

look 🌐
verb

1 to use the eyes to see
I feel happy when I look at my puppy.
eye, gaze, glance, observe, peek, peep, peer, see, sight, squint, stare, watch

> *Rick's grandmother peered down at him from her big chair.*

2 to seem or appear
My new haircut looks awful.
appear *Jared appears to be smart.*
come across *He comes across as a shy person.*
seem *He seems like a nice man.*

3 to try to find (usually **look for**)
She looked for the lost keys.
hunt, search, seek, scout, scour

> *See also:* air, search, appearance

looks 🌐 *See* **appearance**

loop *See* **twist**

loose
adjective

not held back
Cora's loose hair fell over her shoulders.
The loose tiger ravaged the village.
untied, free, unrestrained

> *Antonyms:* enclosed, restrained, snug, tight

verb

1 to set free
The children loosed the dog at the park.
free, release, untie, liberate, emancipate

2 to make less tight
He loosened the knots in his bootlaces.
loosen, release, undo, unfasten, untie

> *Antonyms:* capture (1), restrain (1), tighten (2), trap (1)

See also: free

lose
verb

1 to no longer have; be unable to find
I lost my shoe.
mislay, misplace

2 to fail to win
She lost the contest.
They lost the war.
fall, surrender, yield, forfeit

> *Antonyms:* find (1), recover (1), win (2)
> *See also:* defeat

loss
noun

1 a failure to keep or continue
The loss of his friendship made me very sad.
failure, ending

2 a decrease in size or amount
The loss of ten pounds made him look very thin.
decrease, reduction, diminishment, decline

3 that which is lost; someone or something that can not be found or is taken away
After the fire, the business was a loss.
expense, waste, sacrifice

4 a defeat or failure to win
The team was unhappy about their loss.
defeat, failure, surrender

> *Antonyms:* gain (1), increase (2), triumph (4), victory (4), win (4)
> *See also:* decline, failure, defeat

lost
adjective

1 no longer possessed; not able to be found
Percy never found the lost treasure.
mislaid, misplaced, missing

2 not aware of where one is
The lost children wandered in the woods.
astray, bewildered, stray, off the track

3 ruined or destroyed
Their possessions were lost in the fire.
destroyed, ruined, done for, wrecked

> *Antonyms:* found (1), recovered (3)

A B C D E F G H I J K **L** M N O P Q R S T U V W X Y Z

🌳 Living World   🔬 Physical World   ⛰ Natural Environment   〰 Economy   📖 Government and Law

a
b
c
d
e
f
g
h
i
j
k
l
m
n
o
p
q
r
s
t
u
v
w
x
y
z

lot

noun

a large amount or number
We bought a lot of food for the party.

quantity *This factory makes a great quantity of pencils.*

mass *A mass of people walked into the hall.*

horde *There was a horde of flies in the barn.*

host *There was a host of people at the funeral.*

heap *There's a heap of laundry to do.*

multitude *A multitude of people attended the wedding.*

throng *She made a stew large enough to feed a throng of guests.*

ton *They have a ton of work to do on the house.*

army *An army of children filed into the cafeteria.*

mountain *There was a mountain of dishes in the sink.*

pile *He received a pile of gifts.*

deal *She tended her plants with a great deal of care.*

Note that **deal** and **quantity** mean **a lot** only when used with an adjective such as "great."

Horde, host, and **army** are used only when referring to people.

Antonym: few
See also: mass

lots *See* many

loud

adjective

having a large amount of sound
The dish made a loud noise when it fell to the floor.

noisy, crashing, deafening, harsh, roaring

Antonyms: low, soft
See also: harsh

lovable

adjective

having a nature that attracts love
Mary is so lovable!

adorable, sweet, charming, cuddly, cute, darling, dear

Antonyms: abhorrent, hateful, loathsome
See also: nice

love ?

noun

1 strong feelings of affection for another person
She has a deep love for her childhood friend.

affection, devotion, passion

some words associated with love
adore, care, caress, cherish, court, cuddle, dote, elope, embrace, fancy, flirt, hug, kiss, like, marry, melt, pat, propose, treasure, worship

some words used to describe love
ardent, crazy, deep, devout, everlasting, faithful, intimate, lasting, lifelong, mad, passing, passionate, pious, precious, romantic, true, warm

some words that describe someone who loves
affectionate, close, demonstrative, fond, loving, tender

2 strong interest in or liking for something
He has a great love of music.

devotion, passion, dedication, like

3 a person, activity, or object for which one has great affection or strong liking
She was his first love.
Sailing is one of her loves.

passion *Painting is his passion.*

devotion *She is his one devotion.*

flame *She could not get over an old flame.*

desire *She was my one desire.*

boyfriend *She bought a gift for her boyfriend.*

girlfriend *He held his girlfriend's hand.*

dear *She gave a kiss to her dear.*

fancy *Chocolates are a fancy of mine.*

sweet *He brought flowers to his sweet.*

Antonyms: disdain (1), hatred (1),

Human Body   Human Mind   Everyday Life   History and Culture   Communication

loathing (1)

verb

1 to have strong and tender affection for
He loves his family.
adore, care for, cherish, worship

2 to enjoy or have a strong interest in
I love fishing and swimming.
adore, enjoy, like, relish, delight in, fancy

Antonyms: despise (1,2), hate (1,2), loath (1)

loved See **dear**

lovely See **beautiful, graceful, sweet**

loving

adjective

feeling or showing love
He is a loving father.
She has a loving smile.
affectionate, fond, tender, caring, devoted

Antonyms: hateful, malevolent
See also: affectionate, fond

low

adjective

1 close to the ground or bottom
The wall is low enough for us to step over it.
short, small, squat

2 unhappy or weak
She was in a low mood because of her poor grade in math.
blue, dejected, down, unhappy, downcast, sad, glum, gloomy, melancholy

3 not loud
I heard the low sound of a train in the distance.
soft, faint, hushed, quiet, muted

4 below average in quality
His history grade is low.
poor, inferior, inadequate

5 nearly used up or empty
We have to go shopping, because our food supply is low.
diminished, reduced, meager, scarce

Antonyms: happy (2), high (4), loud (3), plentiful (5), superior (4), tall (1)

lower

verb

1 to come down, grow less, or descend
The price of milk lowered during the sale.
decrease, descend, drop, lessen, diminish, dwindle, fall, abate

2 to make less in amount or quantity
The shop lowered the price of flowers before Mother's Day.
decrease, lessen, reduce, cut

3 to make less loud
Please lower your voice in the library.
mute, decrease, soften, dampen, quiet, hush, tone down

Antonyms: increase (1,2), lift (3), raise (3)
See also: drop, decrease

loyal

adjective

showing devotion and faithfulness to someone or something
She was a loyal friend.
dedicated, faithful, steadfast, true, devoted, constant, fast

Antonyms: disloyal, unfaithful

loyalty

noun

the condition of being faithful or loyal
The soldiers showed great loyalty to their country during the war.
allegiance, faithfulness, steadfastness, devotion

Antonym: betrayal

luck See **chance**

lucky

adjective

resulting from or having good fortune
My father is a lucky man to have a job that he loves.
fortunate *You are fortunate to receive such a good education.*
happy *It was a happy coincidence that we were both there at the same time.*

Antonyms: unfortunate, unlucky

Living World   Physical World   Natural Environment   Economy   Government and Law   149

a
b
c
d
e
f
g
h
i
j
k
l
m
n
o
p
q
r
s
t
u
v
w
x
y
z

lug *See* **carry, drag, draw**

lump
noun
1 a small mass or pile with no special shape
He took a lump of clay and made it into a vase.
clod, clump, chunk, mass

2 a bump or swelling
I had a lump on my forehead from running into a tree.
bump *The bump on her arm was a mosquito bite.*
swelling *She has a large swelling where the bee stung her arm.*
bulge *There was a bulge on his knee after he fell of his bike.*
growth *You should see a doctor about the growth on your forehead.*
tumor *She had an operation to remove the tumor from her breast.*
verb
1 to gather into or consider as a single whole (often **lump together**)
He lumps all types of fish together as if they were all the same.
combine, bunch, group

2 to come to have or be formed into a lump or lumps
If you don't stir the oatmeal while you cook it, it will lump.
clump, congeal, clot

Antonyms: differentiate (1), distinguish (1)
See also: mass, bump

luxurious
adjective
giving great comfort or pleasure
They drive a big, luxurious car.
plush, fancy, lavish, lush, luxuriant

Antonyms: basic, plain, simple
See also: fancy

lying
noun
the telling of lies
He was punished for his lying.
falsehood, deception, fibbing

Antonyms: honesty, truthfulness
adjective
not telling the truth on purpose
Don't believe that lying man.
dishonest, devious, crooked, false

Antonyms: honest, truthful
See also: dishonest

 Human Body Human Mind Everyday Life History and Culture Communication

machine ⚙ 🔬 *See* **device**

machinery *See* **process**

mad ❓
adjective
    angry
    My brother gets mad when I pinch him.
  angry, enraged, fuming, furious, incensed,
  infuriated, irate, sore, indignant, raging

    See also: angry

magic
noun
    1 mysterious control of physical forces
    Some say that witches use magic to turn people
      into frogs.
  spells, bewitchment, sorcery, witchcraft,
  wizardry

    2 tricks used to entertain by suggesting such
      mysterious control
    He entertained the children with magic.
  tricks, sleight of hand, hocus-pocus
adjective
    produced by magic or as if by magic
    The fairy put her to sleep with a magic potion.
  bewitched, charmed, enchanted

magnetic *See* **attractive, personality**

magnificent *See* **excellent, fancy, grand, noble**

main
adjective
    most important; first
    What are the main ingredients in your pizza?
    The main entrance to the building is on the other
      side.
  biggest *Her biggest worry right now is how she will*
    pay the rent.
  cardinal *It is a cardinal rule that everyone be quiet*
    in the library.
  chief *Potatoes are the chief crop of Idaho.*
  paramount *The doctor's paramount concern was*
    for his patients' health.
  primary *He played a primary role in our success.*
  principal *The principal job of the police is to keep*
    the peace.
  premier *That chocolate company claims to make*
    the premier candy in the world.
  central *Harry is the central character in the book.*
  prime *Sugar was the prime export of Hawaii for*
    many years.
  supreme *His case went all the way to the Supreme*
    Court.
  lead *The lead story in today's paper was about our*
    school.
  head *The head surgeon led the operation.*
  foremost *He is the foremost expert in his field.*
  uppermost *She has the uppermost authority in this*
    department.

    Antonyms: incidental, secondary,
      unimportant
    See also: first

mainly
adverb
    for the most part; mostly
    The movie was mainly about monkeys that had
      escaped from a zoo.
  chiefly *The yard is chiefly grass.*
  for the most part *For the most part he is a good*
    worker.
  generally *The doctor said my grandmother was*
    generally healthy but needed to keep up her
    weight.
  largely *The delicious dessert was largely made of*
    sugar.

A
B
C
D
E
F
G
H
I
J
K
L
M
N
O
P
Q
R
S
T
U
V
W
X
Y
Z

 Living World   Physical World   Natural Environment   Economy   Government and Law

mostly *The weather report said that today will be mostly sunny.*

practically *She is practically done feeding her pet bats.*

maintain *See* **claim, declare, keep, say, support,** care

majestic *See* **grand, noble**

major
adjective

great in importance, position, or reputation
Robert Frost is considered a major poet in American literature.

important, great, significant, prominent, outstanding, principal, distinguished, reputable, eminent, notable, momentous

Antonyms: insignificant, minor, small

make
verb

1 to bring into being by building from separate parts
Tammy made a model airplane.

build, construct, assemble, form, prepare, craft, fashion

2 to create or produce
Stop making so much noise!

create, produce, form, manufacture, generate

3 to force to
The teacher made him stop pulling the girl's hair.

force, compel, require, get, pressure, persuade

Use the preposition **to** with **force, compel, require, get, pressure, persuade.** *She forced him to stop bullying the younger children.*

4 to put in order; prepare
I will make the bed if you'll do the dishes.
He makes dinner for us every night.

prepare, fix, arrange

5 to earn
Mr. Marks makes a lot of money.

earn, clear, receive, get, net

6 to arrive at or in time for
Did you make the bus?

catch, intercept, nab

Antonyms: demolish (2), destroy (2), miss (6), prevent (3), tear down (1)

male *See* **man**

man
noun

1 an adult male human being
This man is one of the best friends I've ever had.

gentleman, guy, fellow, chap, male

2 human beings in general
Man cannot live without air and water.

people, humanity, humankind, mankind

manage *See* **control, handle, keep, live**

management *See* **control, direction, government, office**

mankind *See* **man, world**

manner *See* **action, behavior, kind, style, way**

manufacture *See* **make, produce, production**

manufactured *See* **artificial**

many
adjective

a large number of
At the animal shelter, there were many kittens that needed homes.

numerous, various, countless, abundant

Antonyms: few, scant, scarce

noun

a large number of persons or things
Many in the group could not go on the trip because they became ill.

lots, plenty, tons, heaps, gobs, oodles, scads

Antonyms: few, handful

map ◉ *See* **chart**

march
verb
> to walk in a way that shows strength and
> determination
> *I marched into his office and demanded some
> answers.*
stride, stomp, strut, walk

noun
> the act or an instance of marching
> *Thousands of people took part in a march for civil
> rights.*
parade, procession, walk

> *See also:* walk

margin *See* border, edge, limit

marine *See* sea

mark
noun
> 1 something, such as a spot or scar, that can be
> seen on a surface
> *He has a mark on his chin from a nasty fall.*
spot, scratch, scar, blemish, blot, trace

> 2 a symbol or sign
> *The cows have a mark on their coats to identify
> them.*
badge, emblem, identification, signature,
brand, symbol, sign

> *The spy had to show
> her identification
> before the guards
> would let her into
> the secret cave.*

verb
> 1 to put a mark on
> *The table had been
> heavily marked
> with a knife.*
scratch, score, spot, scar,
blemish, sign

> 2 to show limits
> *This line marks off our property.*
define, outline, denote, rope

The preposition **off** is often used with **mark**
and **rope**. *An area was roped off for
dancing.*

> *See also:* goal

market *See* sell, store, worth

marriage ○ *See* union

marry *See* love

marsh *See* swamp

marvelous *See* incredible, wonderful

mash
noun
> any soft, mushy mixture
> *She crushed the turnips into a mash.*
mush, paste, pulp
verb
> 1 to crush or smash
> *The closing door mashed her finger.*
jam, smash, crush, crunch

> 2 to make into a soft mass by grinding or
> crushing
> *This tool will mash potatoes.*
pulp, squash, crush

mask
noun
> anything that hides or covers up
> *He hid his sad feelings behind the mask of a smile.*
cover, veil, cloak, masquerade, disguise, blind,
camouflage, screen

> *See also:* cover

mass *See* crowd, gather, lump, sea, weight,
communication

mass *See* lot

massive *See* giant, huge, vast, measurement

master *See* expert, learn, teacher, winner

 Living World　 Physical World　Natural Environment　Economy　Government and Law

match ⊙
noun

1 a person or thing that is like another
This chair is a match of the one in your living room.

twin, equivalent, likeness, mate, companion, counterpart, fellow

This vase is a twin of the lamp.

2 a person able to equal another in a contest or other activity
He was no match for her in the spelling bee.

equal, rival, peer, equivalent

verb

1 to be the same as or equal to
His skill as a baseball player does not match hers.

equal, compare with, rival, parallel

2 to be similar in size, color, or other qualities
Your socks don't match.

coordinate *His shirt coordinated with his pants and tie.*

go *Those red sneakers go well with your purple gown.*

correspond *Your story corresponds with his.*

coincide *His choice of a movie coincides with mine.*

agree *Do our answers agree?*

Antonyms: clash (2), differ (2)

See also: equal

mate See **match, animal**

material
noun

1 cloth or fabric
Karin wears clothes made only of cotton material.

cloth, fabric, textile

2 any group of ideas or information that can be used to create a larger work
The reporter interviewed people to collect material for her article.

data, information, facts, statistics, fodder

See also: information

matter ⊙ ⓐ
noun

difficulty or trouble
What's the matter?

problem, trouble, difficulty, concern, dilemma, distress, predicament

See also: trouble

mature ⊙ ⓐ
adjective

1 fully grown
A mature dog needs more food than a puppy.

adult, grown, grown-up

2 fully developed in mental or physical qualities
Her experience at the newspaper helped her become a mature writer.

adult, grown-up, seasoned

Antonyms: green (2), immature (2), undeveloped (1)

verb

1 to cause to become ripe or developed
Plenty of sun and water matured the apples.

ripen, season, develop

2 to come to full physical development
He matured more rapidly than his friends.

grow up, evolve, develop

maybe See **perhaps**

meal ⊙ See **grain**

mean ⊙
adjective

not nice; nasty
The mean sorcerer in the fairy tale turned the children into pigs.

malicious, nasty, lousy, cruel, vicious, wicked, ornery

Antonyms: agreeable, nice

meaning ⊙ See **point, value**

a
b
c
d
e
f
g
h
i
j
k
l
m
n
o
p
q
r
s
t
u
v
w
x
y
z

 Human Body   Human Mind   Everyday Life   History and Culture   Communication

measure ⦿⦿ *See* **amount, length, measurement, register, size**

measurement ⦿
noun
the specific size of something that is determined by measuring
The measurements of the room are ten feet by twenty feet.
dimension, size, measure, magnitude, expanse

> *some words used in describing measurements*
> big, bright, close, cold, deep, dim, distant, empty, enormous, equal, equivalent, fast, few, heavy, high, hot, large, light, long, loud, low, many, massive, minute, narrow, quiet, scant, shallow, short, slender, slim, slow, small, tall, thick, thin, vast, wide

meat ⦿⦿ *See* **point, fruit**

mechanical *See* **energy**

mechanism *See* **process**

medical *See* **technology**

medicine ⦿
noun
a drug or other substance used to treat a disease, injury, pain, or other symptoms
She took medicine every day for her cough.
drug, preparation, antidote, prescription, remedy

medium
adjective
middle or average in size or amount
He has a medium build.
intermediate, moderate, average
See also: middle

meet
verb
1 to come face to face with
Mel met Ann while he was waiting for the bus.
encounter *I encountered him at the zoo.*

hit *I hit some bad traffic on the highway.*
bump into *I bumped into him at the party.*
happen upon *Did you happen upon any of your old friends in the city?*
run across *We ran across several bears in the woods.*
face *What sort of obstacles did you face on your treasure hunt?*
2 to gather together for a meeting
The chess club will meet next Tuesday.
assemble, gather, convene, congregate, cluster
See also: gather, connect

meeting
noun
1 the act of coming face to face
Our meeting at the library was a pleasant surprise.
encounter, brush, rendezvous
2 an assembly of persons for a particular purpose
The Acme tool company has weekly staff meetings.
assembly, conference, convention, gathering, get-together
3 a coming together or joining
A large rock marked the meeting of two paths.
conjunction, connection, intersection, junction, union

melodious
adjective
having a pleasant melody
I was awakened by the melodious song of birds.
musical, sweet, lyric, melodic, tuneful
Antonyms: discordant, jarring

melt
verb
1 to change from a solid to a liquid state through heat or pressure
The wax melted as the candle burned.
dissolve, liquefy, thaw, soften
2 to fade or mix, as from one state to another (often **melt away**, **melt in**, or **melt into**)
Our fortune is melting away.

A B C D E F G H I J K L M N O P Q R S T U V W X Y Z

Living World　Physical World　Natural Environment　Economy　Government and Law

He melted into the crowd.

dissolve *The clouds dissolved, leaving a clear blue sky.*

fade *The sound of the train faded away into the distance.*

disappear *His money problems disappeared when he got the job.*

vanish *Her worries vanished after a talk with her sister.*

blend *The thief blended into the crowd.*

merge *I could no longer see her as she merged with the commuters in the station.*

Antonyms: freeze (1), solidify (1)

member *See* part, piece

memory

noun

the ability to remember an experience
My memory is very good when it comes to the events in my childhood.

mind, recall, recollection

mental

adjective

of or having to do with the operation of the mind
The very old man still had all his mental powers.

intellectual, reasoning, psychological

mention

verb

to speak of briefly or in passing
Sam mentioned that he is going away for the weekend.

remark, note, refer to, indicate, allude to

noun

a brief, casual statement, said in passing
She made a mention of next week's concert.

reference, comment, remark, note

merchandise *See* goods

mercy

noun

kind treatment by someone who has some power over another

The principal showed mercy to the students who broke the window.

compassion, forgiveness, humanity, kindness

mere *See* pure

merry

adjective

cheerful and happy, or likely to be so
She is always such a merry person.

gay, jolly, jovial, cheerful, happy, joyful, happy-go-lucky, lighthearted, sunny

Antonyms: glum, heavy-hearted, sad

mess *See* dirty

message

noun

1 spoken or written information, sent from one person or group to another
There are three messages on the answering machine.

communication *The President received a communication from the Speaker of the House.*

note *She left a note for the plumber to fix the drain.*

word *They sent word that they had arrived.*

2 a public speech or other official communication
The mayor gave his yearly message in front of City Hall.

communication, statement, announcement, bulletin

messy *See* dirty

meter *See* beat, literature

method *See* process, way

middle

adjective

halfway between two things, places, or points
The two boats met at the middle point of the river.

halfway *The runners turn around at the halfway mark.*

midway *The city of Columbia lies midway between Baltimore and Washington, D.C.*

Human Body   Human Mind   Everyday Life   History and Culture   Communication

intermediate *He finished the intermediate level and moved on to the advanced level.*
medium *I'll have a medium fries, please.*

Use medium only when referring to the size of something or the degree of something. To put it another way, medium is the right word for halfway between small and large or halfway between low and high: *Set the stove at medium heat.*

noun
the central or middle location, point, or position
The boat is in the middle of the lake.
center *There is a nut in the center of this candy.*
median *He calculated the median between the numbers.*
medium *There must be a happy medium between what you want and what your sister wants.*
midst *In the midst of the confusion, he lost his wallet.*

midst *See* **middle**

might *See* **energy, force, power**

mighty *See* **grand, strong, sturdy, violent**

mighty *See* **powerful**

mild
adjective
1 gentle or calm
She is a mild girl compared to her wild sister.
gentle, calm, moderate, quiet, placid, tranquil, temperate

2 not harsh; not extreme
We had a mild winter.
moderate, temperate, fair, genial, placid, soft, gentle, calm

3 not harsh in taste
These are mild peppers.
bland, mellow, weak

Antonyms: excitable (1), harsh (2,3), strong (3)

military ⬤ *See* **service, law, power, technology**

mind ❓
noun
1 the part of a person that thinks, understands, remembers, directs, and feels
What is your mind occupied with right now?
intellect, intelligence, reason, thought, brain, consciousness, wit

> The growth of the human **mind** is still high adventure, in many ways the highest adventure on earth.
> —Norman Cousins, American author

some actions of the mind
associate, choose, decide, desire, direct, dream, experience, fancy, feel, imagine, imprint, judge, learn, note, notice, perceive, picture, recall, regard, remember, sense, think, understand, visualize, want
some words related to the mind
brilliant, clear, clever, insane, keen, mad, rational, sane, sharp, smart, sound, strong

2 memory or awareness
Please keep Arnie's request in mind.
awareness, consciousness, memory

mine *See* **dig**

miniature
noun
1 a very small copy or model of something
He bought a miniature of his favorite car.
model, mock-up, mini, replica

2 something that is smaller than other members of the same class
That poodle is a miniature.
midget, toy, dwarf, runt
adjective
on a very small scale
She has a miniature goblet for her doll.
tiny, midget, toy, little, small, wee

A B C D E F G H I J K L **M** N O P Q R S T U V W X Y Z

Antonyms: enormous, gigantic, huge

minister *See* care

minor
adjective
> less important or serious than others of the
> same kind
> *My problem is a minor one compared to yours.*
unimportant, insignificant, small, lesser,
secondary, petty, trivial
> *Antonyms:* important, major

minute *See* bit, flash, instant, spell, tiny, measurement

mirror *See* copy, reproduce

misbehave
verb
> to act or behave badly
> *The children misbehaved in the restaurant.*
act up, carry on, disobey, roughhouse, make a
spectacle of oneself
> *Antonyms:* behave, mind, obey
> *See also:* behavior

mischief
noun
> 1 behavior such as teasing that is playful but
> can be annoying or dangerous to others
> *He yelled at the children for their mischief on the
> playground.*
naughtiness, playfulness, misconduct, monkey
business, high jinks
> 2 the quality that leads to such behavior
> *Those boys have mischief in them.*
naughtiness, playfulness, impishness, friskiness

miserable
adjective
> 1 very unhappy
> *He's feeling miserable about losing his job.*
wretched, dejected, desolate, glum
> 2 having or causing discomfort or unhappi-
> ness
> *She suffered through a miserable illness.*

dreadful, lousy, terrible, wretched, atrocious,
rotten
> 3 having little value
> *He did a miserable job of cleaning his room.*
poor, pitiful, pathetic, sorry, wretched
> *Antonyms:* exuberant (1), happy (1),
> joyful (1)
> *See also:* unhappy

misery
noun
> 1 a condition in which one is very unhappy or
> suffers very much
> *She was in misery when her house burned down.*
anguish, woe, wretchedness, agony, torment,
distress
> 2 a state of need and suffering caused by being
> poor, sick, or in trouble
> *Times were bad, and the people were in misery.*
distress, need, poverty, want, adversity, trouble,
misfortune, hardship, pain, sorrow
> *Antonyms:* exuberance (1), happiness (1),
> joy (1)

missing *See* absent, lost

mission *See* duty, task

mist *See* fog, rain, spray, weather

mistake
noun
> a thought or action that is not correct
> *The teacher noticed his mistake on the test.*
error, fault, slip, blunder, miscalculation,
oversight
> *See also:* fault

mix
verb
> 1 to put different things together so that the
> parts become one
> *If you mix yellow and blue you will have green.*
combine, blend, merge, mingle, compound,
stir, unite, weld
> 2 to put together in a confused way

Human Body   Human Mind   Everyday Life   History and Culture   Communication

Their hats and coats were all mixed up.
confuse, jumble, scramble, garble, muddle

Antonyms: divide (2), separate (2), sift (2)
See also: combine

mixture
noun

something that is made by two or more things
that are mixed together
A mixture of flour and water made a paste.
combination, compound, composite, blend,
amalgam, medley, assortment, solution

mock
verb

1 to make fun of in a mean way
*The other kids mocked him when he fell off his
scooter.*
make fun of, tease, poke fun at, taunt, ridicule,
scorn

2 to make fun of by
imitation
*She mocked her
mother's way of speaking.*

mimic, imitate, ape, impersonate, parody,
spoof, travesty

model ✏
noun

1 an example that should be copied or an ideal
that others are compared to
*Mr. Magnus, the millionaire, is my model of suc-
cess.*
archetype, guide, ideal, mold, paragon, pattern,
prototype, standard, precedent

2 a particular type or style of a product
*The salesman showed us a newer model of the
car.*
kind, make, pattern, sort, style, type, variety

adjective

serving as an example or ideal that should be
copied

*Carmen has always been a model citizen who
works to help the community.*
classic, exemplary, ideal

verb

1 to plan or form according
to a model
*She modelled herself after
her mother.*
copy, pattern, emulate,
mold, duplicate,
fashion, form,
reproduce

2 to form or shape
He modeled the clay.
fashion, form, mold, shape

See also: ideal, miniature

modern ◐ ❸
adjective

1 having to do with the present or current
times
We live in the modern age.
present, current, contemporary, present-day

2 of or having to do with the latest styles or
ideas
Our school just bought a modern sound system.
up-to-date, state-of-the-art, latest,
contemporary, new, trendy, newfangled

modest
adjective

1 not thinking too highly of oneself
*Ann was modest about getting the highest grade
on the test.*
humble, meek

2 simple or humble in appearance
*They found a modest little house to buy in the
country.*
humble, simple, plain, austere

3 moderate in amount, size, or value
The boat cost a modest amount of money.
medium, moderate, small, slight

See also: plain

moist See **damp, wet**

A B C D E F G H I J K L **M** N O P Q R S T U V W X Y Z

moisture *See* damp, wet

mold ❶ *See* model, shape, art

mollusk ❶
noun

an animal in a large group of invertebrates or animals without backbones. Most kinds of mollusks live in the ocean and have soft bodies covered by a shell

some examples of mollusks
abalone, clam, cockle, conch, mussel, octopus, oyster, quahog, scallop, slug, snail, squid

moment
noun

1 a very short amount of time
May I talk with you for a moment after class?
bit *John said he would be home in a bit.*
flash *I'll be there in a flash.*
instant *He disappeared in an instant.*
jiffy *I'll be done in a jiffy.*
second *Can you wait a second before going out-side?*
twinkling *The hummingbird seemed to come and go in a twinkling.*

2 a particular point in time
The moment he got home, the phone rang.
instant, occasion, point, instance, time

See also: bit, point, instant

money 〰
noun

the coins or paper notes used to buy things or pay for services
cash, coins, capital, currency, change, funds, finances, legal tender, dough, bread

mussel

scallop

murex

cockle

clams

conch

sea slug

snail

sea slug

whelk

Human Body   Human Mind   Everyday Life   History and Culture   Communication

Dough and **bread** are informal. They are used in everyday speech and writing but are probably not suitable for a formal report or presentation.

---

some words associated with money
buy, coin, donate, pay, pay off, pay the piper, pick up the tab, purchase, save, sell, spend
some descriptions of people and their money
affluent, bankrupt, broke, frugal, greedy, middle class, pauper, penniless, poor, rich, stingy, wealthy

monster
noun

1 a large, frightening, imaginary creature
He likes books about monsters.
creature, dragon, ogre, troll

2 anything that is large enough to be shocking
That twenty-pound trout is a real monster.
giant, mammoth, colossus, behemoth, whopper

3 a person who is mean or cruel
Only a monster would beat his dog.
brute, demon, beast, fiend, ogre, savage, barbarian

monstrous *See* **giant, vast**

mood
noun

the way a person feels at a certain time
Overwork has put him in a bad mood.
humor *I'm in a bad humor today, so leave me alone.*
spirits *He was in low spirits from the bad news.*
state *She is in a happy state.*
temper *I decided to stay because she was in a good temper for once.*

moody
adjective

1 having moods that change often or without a pattern
That moody Sam was laughing one minute and crying the next.

unstable, skittish, changeable

2 usually feeling angry or sad
Alice is so moody, she never wants to play with us.
sullen, irritable, downcast, gloomy, melancholy

mope
verb

to act dull and sad
Kai always mopes when it's time to do homework.
sulk *He sulked when his mother told him to stop riding his bike.*
pout *Madeline pouted when she couldn't have more candy.*
grouch *He grouched about having to stay inside on a rainy day.*
grump *Stewart grumped about having to go to bed.*

moral
adjective

following rules of right or fair behavior

some words for a person who is moral
decent, ethical, good, honest, honorable, just, proper, noble, responsible, scrupulous, steadfast, upright
some descriptions of a person who is not moral
criminal, dishonest, disreputable, evil, immoral, misguided, shady, wicked, wrong

noun

(**morals**) ideas or habits of behavior that relate to what is right and what is wrong
A person with morals will not cheat or steal.
principles, values, standards, ideals

more
adjective

extra; additional
I'd like more spaghetti, please.
additional *I will need additional furniture for the living room.*
extra *I asked for extra time to finish the test.*
further *The judge asked if there were further comments to be made.*
other *The saleslady showed us some other necklaces.*

A B C D E F G H I J K L **M** N O P Q R S T U V W X Y Z

a
b
c
d
e
f
g
h
i
j
k
l
m
n
o
p
q
r
s
t
u
v
w
x
y
z

morsel *See* **bit, bite**

most
adverb
in the greatest extent or degree
He behaved in the most foolish way at the party.
especially, extremely, exceedingly, terribly, extraordinarily, severely, quite, very

mostly
adverb
for the most part
The weather report said that today will be mostly sunny.
mainly, primarily, chiefly, generally, on the whole, by and large, largely, principally
See also: mainly

mother *See* **source, care**

motion
noun
the act or particular way of changing place; movement
With one jumping motion, the rabbit was gone.
The car's motion made me sick.
movement, action, activity, play, travel
verb
to signal by a movement of the body
The crossing guard motioned the children to wait at the corner.
beckon *Our host beckoned us into the dining room.*
gesture *He gestured wildly with his arms.*
wave *He waved them off the stage.*
See also: action

motor ⭕👤 *See* **boat**

mount *See* **climb, increase, rise, photography**

mountain 🌍
noun
a land mass with great height and steep sides that is higher than a hill

> *some parts of mountains*
> cliff, crest, foothill, ledge, peak, ridge, spine, summit, tip, top, zenith
> *some verbs associated with mountains*
> ascend, clamber, climb, descend, hike, scale, ski

mouse 👤👥 *See* **rodent**

mouth 🌍👤🔵 *See* **river**

move 🌍⭕
verb
1 to change position or place
Let's move to better seats up front.
budge *The horse was tired and would not budge an inch.*
relocate *She relocated to another country.*
migrate *Geeese migrate to the south when the weather gets cold.*
shift *The boy shifted in his chair.*
stir *She did not stir when I called.*
transfer *I transferred my books from my locker to my backpack.*
2 to go ahead or progress
Work on the new bridge is moving slowly.
go, progress, proceed, advance, climb, march, travel, pass
3 to change the position or location of
I moved my bed to the other side of the room.
relocate, remove, shift, switch, displace, transfer, dislodge, transport, transpose
4 to put or keep in motion
The wind moved the sailboat.
push, propel, drive, launch, convey, impel, carry, roll, stir, send
5 to cause to have tender or powerful feelings
We were moved by his story.
affect, stir, provoke, touch, inspire, impress, imbue
Antonyms: keep (3), regress (2), remain (1), stay (1)
noun
the act or an instance of moving
The dog made a move toward the cat.
motion, movement

🏃 Human Body ❓ Human Mind 👕 Everyday Life 🚩 History and Culture   Communication

See also: motion, step

movement
noun

1 the act or manner of moving
There was hurried movement toward the door when the bell rang.
activity, motion, action, locomotion, passage

2 a group or groups of people acting as one
Many people joined the peace movement because they wanted the war to end.
alliance, cause, coalition

Antonyms: inactivity (1), stillness (1)

movie ⊘ *See* film, picture

moving
adjective

causing a strong feeling
He read some moving poems.
emotional *It was an emotional film.*
powerful *That is a powerful piece of music.*
touching *The letter he wrote you is so touching.*
impressive *His writing is impressive.*

much
adjective

great in degree, number, or amount
There is much work to do in the yard.
plentiful, considerable, abundant, ample, copious, profuse, bounteous

Antonym: little

noun

a great amount or number
There was much for him to fix in that old house.
plenty, lot, abundance, heaps, stacks, tons

Antonym: few

adverb

nearly
She and I are much the same.

A
B
C
D
E
F
G
H
I
J
K
L
M
N
O
P
Q
R
S
T
U
V
W
X
Y
Z

Mountain

range

monticule

cliff

saddle

foothills

ridge

peaks

Living World   Physical World   Natural Environment   Economy   Government and Law

essentially, nearly, almost, practically, virtually

mud 🔵 *See* **dirt**

muddy *See* **dirty**

murder ⚪ *See* **kill**

murmur
noun
> a sound that is soft, muffled, and ongoing, like the sound made by quiet conversation
> *There was a murmer coming from down the hall.*
> mumble, mutter, whisper, buzz, babble

verb
> to make a soft, muffled, continuous sound
> *Do you hear the children murmering in their bedroom?*
> whisper, mutter, buzz, mumble, babble

muscle ⚪ *See* **squeeze, foot**

muscular
adjective
> having muscles that are large or strong
> *Tennis players have muscular arms.*
> husky, powerful, brawny, burly, strong, robust, solid, rugged, Herculean
>
> *Antonyms:* skinny, weak

music 🔵 🔵
noun
> 1 a work of art that can be played or sung
> *Do you like this music by my favorite composer?*
> piece, composition, song, melody, tune, work
>
> 2 the written or printed signs for a musical composition
> *I bought the music for some of my favorite songs so I could play them on the piano.*
> score, notation, accompaniment

musical *See* **melodious, theater**

mutter
verb
> to speak in a low tone that is hard to understand

> *Casey muttered to herself when she failed to catch the ball.*

mumble *If you mumble, I won't be able to hear you.*

murmur *Mrs. Parsons murmured something in her sleep.*

whisper *She whispered to me so that no one else would hear.*

grumble *He grumbled under his breath about not being able to play with his friend.*

Mutter, mumble, murmur, grumble, and **whisper** can also be used as nouns. *There were grumbles from the students who had to stay after school. The shy boy spoke in such a whisper that the teacher had to lean over to hear him.*

---

mutual *See* **common, communication, relationship**

my *See* **goodness**

mysterious
adjective
> not known and not able to be explained
> *Astronomers became interested in the mysterious flashes of light in the sky.*

baffling *Her behavior in class was baffling.*

elusive *The instructions she gave for tonight's homework were elusive.*

mystifying *The treasure map was mystifying.*

obscure *The archaeologist couldn't make out the meaning of the obscure symbols on the walls of the cave.*

puzzling *The book's puzzling ending was the topic of conversation.*

> *Antonyms:* obvious, plain

mystery 🔵 ⚪
noun
> a matter that is secret or that cannot be known or explained
> *Nobody fully understands the mystery of how the human brain works.*

a b c d e f g h i j k l **m** n o p q r s t u v w x y z

Human Body   Human Mind   Everyday Life   History and Culture   Communication

enigma *Although the effect of gravity is understood, what causes it remains an enigma.*

puzzle *Car engines are a puzzle to some people.*

riddle *How our dog found us hundreds of miles from home is a riddle.*

secret *Scientists try to discover the secrets of nature.*

A
B
C
D
E
F
G
H
I
J
K
L
M
N
O
P
Q
R
S
T
U
V
W
X
Y
Z

Writing Tip:

Verb Phrases: Two Words for One

Here are some common verb phrases that use **make**, with their synonyms.

make believe: pretend
Pip pretended he was a pirate.

make good: succeed
If you try hard, you will succeed.

make like: imitate
Gigi imitated a monkey.

make up: reconcile
Jack and Jill reconciled after the accident.

make up: constitute
What constitutes a good book report?

a b c d e f g h i j k l m n o p q r s t u v w x y z

nail ⊕ ○ *See* **catch, fasten, foot**

naked *See* **bare**

name
noun
  a word or words by which someone is known
  My name is Millicent Marbury.
  What is the name of that kind of car?
term *The term for that kind of dog is "Welsh Terrier."*
nickname *Some common nicknames for "William" are "Bill," "Billy," "Will," and "Willie."*
tag *His tag is "Shorty."*
epithet *Thomas Edison was known by the epithet "Wizard of Menlo Park."*
verb
  1 to give a name to
  I named my kitten Fluffy because she has fluffy fur.
call *She called her room "The Cave."*
designate *He was designated "King of the Hill" when he reached the top.*
christen *He christened the sailboat "Sea Swan."*
entitle *He entitled his poem "Worm Trip."*
title *She titled the story before sending it to the publisher.*
  2 to call or mention by name
  The teacher named those who had to stay after school.
call, mention, identify, designate

3 to choose for a particular office or duty
The mayor named him chief of police.
appoint, assign, make, designate, nominate

narrow
adjective
  1 not wide or broad
  Our bus got stuck in the narrow alley.
close, slim, tight, thin, constricted
  2 being fixed in ideas or opinions
  That narrow man talks only to people from his church.
  People with narrow minds find it hard to try new things.
small-minded, narrow-minded, intolerant, bigoted, rigid, set, inflexible, intractable
  Antonyms: broad-minded (2), wide (1)

verb
  to become narrower
  The road narrows here, so drive carefully.
taper, thin, constrict, squeeze
  Antonym: open
  See also: close

nation ○ *See* **country, land, people**

national *See* **power, tradition**

native
adjective
  belonging to or originating in a specific place
  There are many native Alaskan languages.
  Potatoes are native to South America.
indigenous, aboriginal, original
  Antonyms: alien, foreign
  See also: natural

natural
adjective
  1 of or produced by nature, not by humans
  She uses only natural ingredients in her cooking.

 Human Body   ? Human Mind   Everyday Life   History and Culture   Communication

That sweater is made out of natural fibers.
organic, untreated, unadulterated, crude

2 according to human nature
Human beings have a natural desire for love.
inborn, instinctive, innate, native

3 expected; ordinary
It is natural for teenagers to be confused about life.
normal, regular, typical, usual, common, customary, expected, ordinary

4 not pretended or forced
Your smile in this photo doesn't look natural.
authentic, genuine, real, sincere, spontaneous, true

Antonyms: artificial (1), man-made (1), unnatural (4)

nature ⓘ ⓐ
noun

1 the basic qualities of a person or thing
It's not in his nature to be mean.
He doesn't understand the nature of our business.
character, quality, spirit, essence

2 the physical world and living things in their natural state
A camping trip is a good way to experience nature.
wild, wilderness, outdoors, creation

Use **the** before **wild, wilderness,** and **outdoors**: *We camped in the wilderness. They love hiking in the great outdoors.*

---

3 kind; variety
She likes action films, adventure books, and things of that nature.
kind, type, sort, variety, stripe, ilk

naughty
adjective

not behaving or obeying
That naughty child pulled the cat's tail.
bad, misbehaving, disobedient, mischievous, unruly, obstreperous, wicked

Antonyms: good, nice, obedient

See also: bad

near *See* **close, come**

nearest *See* **next**

nearly *See* **almost, much**

neat
adjective

1 clean and in proper order, or liking to keep things that way
I keep my room neat.
tidy *It's hard for some people to keep their desk tidy.*
orderly *It was easy to find the book I wanted on the orderly shelf.*
shipshape *Lulu keeps her locker in shipshape condition.*
trim *I keep my work clothes pressed and trim.*

2 organized and exact
Sharif found a neat way to solve that math problem.
efficient, simple, organized, elegant

3 clever
He came up with the neat idea of shoveling sidewalks to earn money.
artful, clever, ingenious, slick

Antonyms: disorderly (1), messy (1), sloppy (1)

necessary
adjective

not able to be put aside
My brother does not have the cash necessary to buy a car.
A strong goalie is a necessary part of a soccer team.
needed, essential, indispensable, required

Antonyms: optional, unnecessary

> Patience is a **necessary** ingredient of genius.
> —Benjamin, Earl of Beaconsfield Disraeli (1804-1881), British statesman and author

necessity *See* **condition, need**

 Living World   Physical World   Natural Environment   Economy   Government and Law

a
b
c
d
e
f
g
h
i
j
k
l
m
n
o
p
q
r
s
t
u
v
w
x
y
z

neck ⊕ *See* **clothes**

need
noun
1 something that one must have
I have a need to be with my family.
essential, necessity, requirement
2 the lack of something needed
The crops are in need of rain. There is a need for skilled workers.
lack, dearth, shortage, want

Use **of** after **lack, dearth, shortage**, and **want**: *lack of hope; dearth of food; shortage of water; want of money.*

3 a state of want; poverty
It is a shame that many people live in need.
poverty, hardship, misery, want, destitution
verb
to have a requirement for
Do you need anything from the store?
require *I require colored pencils for this assignment.*
must have *Animals must have water to live.*
demand *This situation demands my attention.*
call for *This cookie recipe calls for a pound of butter.*

needed *See* **necessary**

needle ⊕ ○ *See* **annoy, tease**

neglect
verb
to pay too little or no attention to
Don't neglect your friends!
disregard, ignore, overlook, slight
Antonym: attend to
noun
an act or result of neglecting

The starving cats were victims of neglect.
carelessness, oversight, negligence
Antonyms: attentiveness, care, regard
See also: ignore

neighbor *See* **border, touch**

neighborhood
noun
1 a small area or district in a city or town that is set off from other areas because it is a community or has a special character
Most of the people are friendly in my neighborhood.
block, locality, precinct, quarter, district
2 the entire group of people who live in such an area
Our neighborhood gets together for a Labor Day picnic every year.
community, street, neighbors

neighboring *See* **next**

neighbors *See* **neighborhood**

nerve ⊕ ⊕
noun
1 any of the fibers that carry messages to and from the brain and other parts of the body
The injured nerves in his hand made it difficult for him to feel heat or cold.

some kinds of nerves
auditory (hearing), motor (movement), optic (sight), olfactory (smell), spinal, facial, motor (movement)

2 courage, strength, or patience
It took a lot of nerve for him to jump off the high diving board.
backbone, courage, guts, pluck, bravery, grit
3 (informal) boldness without shame or respect
She has a lot of nerve to say mean things about me.
boldness, brass, guts

 Human Body   ? Human Mind   Everyday Life   History and Culture   Communication

nervous
adjective

1 having a very anxious or fearful nature
Kathy fidgets and bites her nails because she's a nervous person.
edgy, high-strung, jittery, jumpy, on edge, panicky, skittish, tense, uneasy

2 being fearful or anxious in a specific situation
That big dog is making me nervous.
aflutter, afraid, agitated, anxious, apprehensive, fearful, frightened, scared

net *See* **make**

neutral *See* **objective, color**

nevertheless *See* **anyway, still**

new
adjective

1 having recently arrived, or come into being
The band's new CD is now in the stores.
latest *Did you hear the latest news?*
recent *I enjoy looking at magazines to see the recent fashions.*
hot *The newspaper is hot off the press.*
up-to-date *We listened to the most up-to-date news report.*

2 not known
He had a desire to see new places.
alien, foreign, novel, strange, unfamiliar
The inventor found a novel use for old tires.

THE FLULA FLOOP
THE FLOPPY HULA HOOP
ALPHA TESTING IN PROGRESS

3 not used
Start your essay on a new sheet of paper.
brand-new, fresh, mint, original, pristine

Antonyms: familiar (2), old (1), outdated (1)

news *See* **information, word**

next
adjective

1 coming immediately after; following
I'll see you next week.
The first question on the test was easy, but the next one was hard.
following, coming, subsequent, succeeding

2 closest in position
My best friend lives in the next house.
adjacent, adjoining, neighboring, nearest

Antonym: previous (1)

nice
adjective

1 pleasing or attractive
He has a nice face.
She has a nice way of talking.
pleasant, agreeable, sweet, charming, pretty, attractive

2 having good manners
Theo has some nice friends.
polite, courteous, considerate, gracious, decent, well-mannered

Antonyms: mean (2), rude (2), unpleasant (1)
See also: fine

nick *See* **cut, scratch**

night
noun

the hours of darkness between sunset and dawn
Snow had fallen during the night.
dark, nightime, nightfall, after dark

Antonym: day
See also: dark, evening

nitrogen ⚬ ⚬ *See* **air**

no *See* **zero**

A
B
C
D
E
F
G
H
I
J
K
L
M
N
O
P
Q
R
S
T
U
V
W
X
Y
Z

a
b
c
d
e
f
g
h
i
j
k
l
m
n
o
p
q
r
s
t
u
v
w
x
y
z

noble
adjective

1 of or showing a strong or excellent mind or character
Putting yourself at risk to help another is a noble act.
honorable, selfless, righteous, virtuous

2 strong or powerful in apperance
A noble statue of Lincoln stands in the park.
grand, impressive, lofty, majestic, splendid, magnificent, imposing

Antonym: ignoble (1)

noise
noun

an unwanted or unpleasant sound
There is too much noise in the house for me to sleep.
din, racket, clamor, roar, tumult

Antonym: silence
See also: racket

noisy *See* loud

none *See* zero

nonsense
noun

1 words or actions that make no sense
Stop talking nonsense!
rubbish, gibberish, hogwash, balderdash, bunk, poppycock

2 rude or silly behavior
The student's nonsense angered the teacher.
mischief, foolishness, silliness, tomfoolery

Antonyms: common sense (1), sense (1)

normal
adjective

1 close to what is usual or standard
This rainy weather is normal for this time of year.
average, everyday, ordinary, typical, regular, conventional, customary, standard, usual

2 having a healthy mind
A normal person does not enjoy making animals suffer.
sane, rational, right-minded, reasonable

3 physically healthy
My height is normal for my age.
fit, healthy, sound, right

Antonyms: abnormal (1), atypical (1), unusual (1)

nose
verb

to meddle; snoop (often followed by **about**, **around**, or **into**)
He's always nosing into someone else's business.
meddle, mess in, poke into, pry, root, snoop

note
noun

a short letter or other piece of writing
I sent him a note about my coming visit.
line, memo, memorandum, notation
verb

to write down
I noted the homework for tomorrow's class.
record, scribble, pencil in, jot down

notebook *See* pad

noted *See* famous

nothing *See* zero

notice
noun

1 a statement or warning, usually printed
There is a notice on wine bottles about the dangers of alcohol.
statement, warning, bulletin, advisory

2 an instance of observing
The new building escaped my notice.

 Human Body   Human Mind   Everyday Life   History and Culture   Communication

attention, awareness, observation, perception

Antonym:
oversight (2)

verb
to be aware of
Henry didn't notice the monster in his closet because he was fast asleep.

see, note, mark, observe, perceive

Antonyms: ignore, miss

notion *See* **belief, idea, thought, view**

novel *See* **curious, new, original, special**

now
noun
the present moment or time
It was easy until now.
nowadays, the present, today

adverb
1 at this time or in these times
If we leave now, we won't be late for school.
at present, currently, presently

2 at the present moment
Come here now!
immediately, instantly, right away, straightaway, directly, forthwith, at once

nuclear *See* **energy, family, physics, technology**

nucleus *See* **center**

number *See* **amount**

numerous *See* **many**

nurse *See* **treat, animal, care**

nuts *See* **crazy**

A
B
C
D
E
F
G
H
I
J
K
L
M
N
O
P
Q
R
S
T
U
V
W
X
Y
Z

a
b
c
d
e
f
g
h
i
j
k
l
m
n
o
p
q
r
s
t
u
v
w
x
y
z

oath
noun
a serious promise
He made an oath to tell the truth in court.
pledge, promise, vow

obedient
adjective
likely or willing to obey rules or orders
He isn't obedient when his father is away.
dutiful, compliant, governable

Antonyms: disobedient, unruly

obey   See **behave, keep, observe**

object
verb
to present reasons against something
I object to your use of your room as a dump.
oppose, dispute, dissent, protest, disapprove
noun
1 anything that can be seen or touched
The only object in the room was a chair.
thing, article, item
2 anything intended to be done or achieved
The object of the game is to get the most cards.
aim, goal, intent, objective, purpose, point
3 a thing or person to which a thought or action is directed
I sent a valentine to the object of my affection.
subject *Miss Grackle's voyage was the subject of a magazine article.*

target *Judge Kruk is the target of an investigation.*
butt *Why am I always the butt of your jokes?*
See also: thing, goal

objection
noun
1 a statement of not liking or not agreeing with something
Ling's objections to the law were printed in today's paper.
dissent, protest, exception, challenge
2 a cause or reason for not liking or agreeing with something
She didn't understand her mother's objection to her wearing makeup.
criticism, exception, beef, complaint
Antonyms: accord (1), approval (2), consent (1)
See also: protest

objective
noun
a goal or purpose that a person works to achieve
My objective is to become a teacher.
aim, goal, intent, intention, purpose, target
adjective
not influenced by personal feelings or opinions
The teacher thought about her student's problem in an objective way.
fair, impartial, disinterested, just, neutral
Antonyms: biased, unfair
See also: goal, fair

observation   See **notice, study**

observe
verb
1 to notice or see
Ms. Lear observed her child playing.
behold, eye, note, notice, perceive, see, view
We beheld the beautiful sunset.

 Human Body   Human Mind   Everyday Life   History and Culture   Communication

2 to make a close observation of
The cat observed the bird with hungry interest.
watch, monitor, follow

3 to say in a casual way
Uncle Earl observed that we had grown.
remark, note, comment, mention, notice

4 to act in keeping with
She observed all the rules of the game.
obey, follow, abide by, adhere to, comply with, conform to

5 to celebrate
The nation observes several holidays.
celebrate, keep, mark, recognize, respect

Antonyms: buck (4), deviate from (4), ignore (2,4,5), miss (1), overlook (1,2,5)
See also: watch, comment, obey, celebrate

obstacle *See* barrier, challenge

obstruction *See* barrier

obtain *See* buy, gain, get, receive, take, win

obvious
adjective
easily seen or understood
He has an obvious dislike of mushrooms.
apparent, clear, evident, plain, visible, conspicuous, plain

Antonyms: concealed, hidden
See also: plain

occasion *See* cause, celebration, chance, event, moment, thing, time

occupation ◎ *See* business, career, job, practice, work

occupation ◎ *See* possession

occupied *See* busy

occur *See* happen

ocean 🌐 *See* sea

odd *See* curious, funny, irregular, single, strange, unusual, weird

odor *See* scent, smell

off *See* absent

offense
noun
1 the act of breaking a law or rule or doing something wrong
After the drunk driver's third offense, the judge sent him to jail.
crime, sin, trespass, breach

2 something that causes anger or a feeling of not being respected
The five rusty cars on his front lawn are an offense to the neighborhood.
insult, affront, outrage, slap

Antonym: compliment (2)

offer
verb
1 to present to be accepted or refused
I offered a toy to the baby.
submit, present, extend

2 to present for discussion
She offered ideas about how we could save money.
advance, present, propose, pose, submit, suggest, introduce, volunteer

Antonyms: retract (2), take (1), withdraw (2)
noun
that which is offered
We made an offer of nine hundred dollars for the boat.
bid, proposal, proposition, suggestion

See also: extend, propose

office ◎ ◯
noun
1 a place where business or professional work is done
Tom works in an office with twenty other people.
workplace, agency, firm, company

2 the people who work in such a place

A
B
C
D
E
F
G
H
I
J
K
L
M
N
O
P
Q
R
S
T
U
V
W
X
Y
Z

a
b
c
d
e
f
g
h
i
j
k
l
m
n
o
p
q
r
s
t
u
v
w
x
y
z

The office gathered for a meeting.
staff, employees, workers, businessmen, businesswomen, management, professionals

3 a position of trust or responsibility
Ms. Gold holds the office of treasurer.
position, post, appointment, commission

official *See* **formal**

offspring *See* **child, young**

oil 🜂 🜄 *See* **grain**

oily
adjective
of or like oil
I don't like this oily potato salad.
greasy, slick, unctuous, lubricious

old
adjective
1 having lived for many years
My grandparents are old, but they are healthy.
elderly, aged, senescent, long-lived

2 having existed for many years
There is a lot of old furniture in our house.
aged, antique, ancient, age-old, old-time

3 of a time past
My mother showed me her old neighborhood.
former, past, previous, bygone

Antonyms: current (3), new (2), young (1)

old-fashioned
adjective
1 looking or being like past styles
We have an old-fashioned rotary telephone.
dated, outdated, out-of-date, obsolete

2 having the values or manners of the past
My old-fashioned teacher does not let us wear hats in class.
quaint *Grandfather taught us about the quaint customs of his native village.*
conservative *The conservative chef refuses to use a microwave oven.*
classic *"The Secret Garden" is a classic work of fiction.*

Antonyms: contemporary (1), current (1), new (1,2), new-fangled (2), trendy (2)

on *See* **forward**

one *See* **single**

only
adverb
at the least
If he'd only studied, he'd have passed the test.
at least, just, but, simply

adjective
being without others
Marva is the only person who knows the code.
sole, lone, single, solitary, exclusive

See also: just, single

open
adjective
1 that may be attended or taken part in by all
Our town held an open meeting to introduce the new mayor.
free, public, general

2 available
My school has open positions for two teachers.
unfilled, vacant, available

3 behaving or speaking in an honest or direct way
Maria is open about her problems in school.
direct, frank, outspoken, sincere

Antonyms: guarded (3), indirect (3), private (1), restricted (1), unavailable (2)

verb
1 to start or begin
The play opens with a speech by a young girl.
begin, commence, start

 Human Body   Human Mind   Everyday Life   History and Culture Communication

2 to become spread out (often **open out**)
My umbrella opens out when I push the button on its handle.
spread, unfold, expand

Antonyms: close (1), close up (2), end (1)
See also: free

opening *See* **distance, entrance, hole, introduction, passage, space, way**

operate *See* **behave, drive, work**

operation ⊛ *See* **act, effect, order, process**

opinion ⊙
noun
what one thinks about something or somebody
Do you have an opinion on school uniforms?
What is your opinion of the new art teacher?
view, idea, position, viewpoint, feeling

Opinion can be used with "on" or "of."
When **position** and **feeling** mean opinion, they can be used with "on" but never "of."

Antonym: fact

opponent
noun
one who fights, plays, or takes a position against another
I never win at tennis when she is my opponent.
Sir Lionhart slew his opponent in combat.
foe, enemy, competitor, adversary, rival, competition, antagonist

Antonyms: ally, partner, teammate
See also: enemy

opportunity *See* **chance**

oppose
verb
to think, act, or be against
Students who opposed the plan for a longer school day spoke at the school board meeting.

fight, combat, resist, buck, contest, dispute, object to, protest, defy, challenge, strive against

Antonyms: advocate, support
See also: fight, resist

opposite
adjective
as different as possible
Tom and Jerry have opposite tastes in food.
differing, contrary, contradictory, conflicting, contrasting
You and I hold contrary opinions.

Antonyms: alike, identical, same

opposition *See* **resistance**

oral *See* **communication, tradition**

order ⊙ ◑ ⊚
noun
1 a direction or command
The recruit was punished for not following the order.
command, direction, instruction, charge, decree, demand, mandate
2 the way something is set up or arranged in space or time
Please write your spelling words in alphabetical order.
sequence, arrangement, organization, succession
3 the working condition of something
An electrician restored our stove to proper working order.
condition, repair, operation

A B C D E F G H I J K L M N O P Q R S T U V W X Y Z

a
b
c
d
e
f
g
h
i
j
k
l
m
o
p
q
r
s
t
u
v
w
x
y
z

verb

1 to tell to do in a firm way; give a command to

The lifeguard ordered everyone to get out of the pool.

command, direct, instruct

2 to put in order

He ordered the books on the shelf by topic.

arrange, array, organize, classify, sort

Antonym: shuffle (2)

See also: direction

orderly *See* **neat**

ordinarily *See* **generally**

ordinary

adjective

without special qualities; common

He was a wonderful athlete but had just an ordinary mind.

common, everyday, typical, standard, commonplace, pedestrian

Antonyms: extraordinary, special

noun

the usual or common degree or condition

Her singing is out of the ordinary.

average, routine, standard, usual, norm

See also: usual

organic *See* **natural**

organism ◑ *See* **life**

organization ◠

noun

a body of persons acting together

That organization helps during emergencies.

club, group, agency, alliance, association, fellowship, guild, league, society, team

See also: group

organize *See* **arrange, establish, found, group, order, produce, rank, rate**

organized *See* **neat**

origin *See* **bottom, root, source**

original

adjective

1 first

The original owner of our car had it for ten years.

earliest, first, initial

2 new or fresh

She has an original idea for a book.

creative, fresh, new, novel, unique

3 able to think of new ideas

When it comes to writing stories, he is not very original.

creative, inventive, imaginative, inspired, clever, ingenious

4 not a copy

Our library has an original letter signed by Abraham Lincoln.

authentic, real, actual, genuine

Antonyms: final (1), humdrum (2), last (1), stale (2), unimaginative (3), uninspired (3)

other

adjective

1 the one remaining out of two or more

I like the other hat more than this one.

remaining, alternate, alternative

2 being an addition

Are there other people interested in coffee?

additional *Sophie bought additional furniture for the living room.*

further *The judge asked if there were further questions.*

more *Are there more people who would like to try out for the play?*

extra *He bought some food for himself and extra things for the kids.*

out *See* **absent, forward**

outdoors *See* **nature**

 Human Body   ? Human Mind   Everyday Life   History and Culture   Communication

outer
adjective

of or having to do with the part most distant from the center
Many families choose to live in the outer areas of the city.
The rain drenched our outer clothes.
exterior *The exterior walls of our house are painted green.*
external *Insects have an external skeleton.*
outside *The cake has an outside layer of chocolate.*
outward *Brian showed no outward sign of fear.*
outlying *The Bushes live in an outlying suburb.*

Antonyms: closest, innermost, interior, internal, nearest
See also: outside

outgoing
adjective

1 going out or leaving
The outgoing ship was held up by the storm.
The outgoing governor made one last speech.
departing, exiting, leaving

2 liking to talk to and interested in others
Holly has an outgoing manner.
friendly, extroverted, social, warm

Antonyms: aloof (2), incoming (1), introverted (2), shy (2)
See also: friendly

outlaw
noun

a person who often breaks the law
The outlaw is being hunted by a posse.
criminal, bandit, crook, desperado, brigand

verb

to make illegal
Hunting is outlawed in the city.
ban, bar, forbid, prohibit, proscribe

Antonym: permit

outline ❷ *See* design, figure, mark, plan, shape

output *See* production

outside
noun

the outer side or surface
Please write your name on the outside of your notebook.
exterior, surface, shell

Antonyms: inside, interior
adjective

1 of or relating to the outer side or surface
Clean the pot's outside surface, too.
outer, exterior, external, outward, surface

2 not likely
He has only an outside chance of winning.
distant, faint, remote, slender, slight, slim, small

Antonyms: inner (1), internal (1), strong (2)

outsider
noun

a person who does not belong to a particular group
She feels like an outsider in her new school.
alien, foreigner, outcast, stranger

Antonyms: insider, member

outstanding *See* excellent, great, major

outward *See* outer, outside

over *See* down

overall *See* generally, totally

overcome *See* beat, conquer, defeat, swamp, top, win

own
adjective

belonging to oneself alone
I bought this hat with my own money.
individual, particular, personal, private

A B C D E F G H I J K L M N O P Q R S T U V W X Y Z

 Living World Physical World Natural Environment Economy Government and Law

a
b
c
d
e
f
g
h
i
j
k
l
m
n

o

p
q
r
s
t
u
v
w
x
y
z

verb

1 to have possession of
We own our house.
have, hold, keep, possess, retain

2 to take responsibility for (often **own up to**)
He owned up to his mistake.
acknowledge, admit, concede, confess, disclose

Antonyms: conceal (2), hide (2)
See also: have, admit

oxygen  *See* **air**

Human Body   Human Mind   Everyday Life   History and Culture   Communication

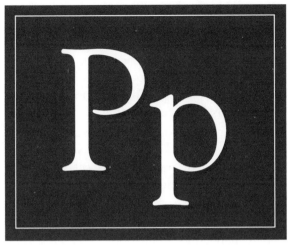

pace *See* **step, walk**

pack *See* **band, crowd, fill, load, package, squeeze, animal**

package
noun
an object or bundle that is packed
I bought a package of socks at the store.
box, bundle, pack, carton, packet, parcel
verb
to place in a container or in wrapping
She packaged the gift in a red box.
box, bundle, pack, wrap

Antonyms: unpack, unwrap

packed *See* full

pad ○
noun
1 a piece of soft material used as cushioning
for protection or comfort
I need a pad for this hard seat.
cushion, padding
2 a block of paper sheets glued together at one
edge
She bought a supply of writing pads.
tablet, notebook

page *See* leaf

pain ○ ○
noun
1 hurt feelings; emotional suffering
Our friend's death caused us great pain.
agony, anguish, discomfort, distress, grief,
heartache, hurt, sorrow, torment, woe

Agony, discomfort, distress, hurt, and **torment** can also be used for physical pain. *Did you hurt yourself when you fell off the bike?*

2 (plural) great care or effort
*She took pains to make
the party perfect.*
care, effort, trouble

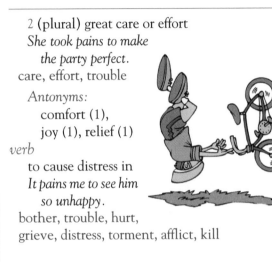

Antonyms:
comfort (1),
joy (1), relief (1)
verb
to cause distress in
*It pains me to see him
so unhappy.*
bother, trouble, hurt,
grieve, distress, torment, afflict, kill

Kill is informal in this sense. That means it is used in everyday speech and writing but is probably not suitable for a formal report or presentation.

Antonyms: comfort, gladden, relieve
See also: hurt, care

painful *See* **injury**

paint ○ *See* **coat, color, picture, art, home**

painting ○ *See* **picture, art**

palace *See* **home**

pale
adjective
1 light in color
*I spotted an airplane in the
pale blue sky.*

A B C D E F G H I J K L M N O **P** Q R S T U V W X Y Z

dull, faded, light, pastel, soft

2 light in color because of illness or emotion
Her pale form lay still on the hospital bed.
wan, pallid, pasty, ashen, anemic, ghastly

Antonyms: dark (1), deep (1), intense (1), ruddy (2)

verb

to become pale
He paled when he saw the blood.
blanch, blench, whiten

Antonym: brighten

palm *See* **tree**

panic

noun

a sudden feeling of dread or anxiety
The fire caused panic in the building.
alarm, fear, fright, horror, scare, terror

Antonyms: calm, relief, tranquility
See also: fear

paper ○ ● *See* **report**

parade ○

noun

a public procession of people, bands, or vehicles
Our town has a parade every Fourth of July.
procession *The wedding procession made its way down the aisle.*
march *We joined the protest march on its way to the capitol.*
cavalcade *The colorful cavalcade delighted the spectators.*
cortege *The cortege of mourners arrived at the cemetery.*
motorcade *The mayor's limousine was escorted by police motorcycles in the motorcade.*

See also: march

parallel *See* **equal, match**

parliament ○ *See* **assembly**

part

noun

1 a separate piece of a whole
That store sells car and truck parts.
I live in an old part of town.
component, piece, section, portion, member, segment, branch, constituent

2 an important basic characteristic
Hard work was a large part of her success.
feature, element, ingredient, aspect, characteristic, component

3 share; duty
Did you have a part in making this mess?
share, hand, duty, obligation

Antonym: whole (1)

verb

to separate one from another
They shook hands and parted as friends.
depart, leave, separate, go, split

See also: piece

particle *See* **bit, grain**

particular

adjective

1 being distinct and apart from others
This particular house is the one I live in.
specific, definite, distinct, individual, unique

2 worth noting because unusual
Renee has a particular talent for cooking.
distinctive, special, peculiar, singular, remarkable, unusual

3 concerned too much with details
Mr. Pickett is very particular about his garden.
exacting, finicky, fussy, picky, persnickety, fastidious, selective, dainty

Antonyms: adaptable (3), flexible (3), unconcerned (3)
See also: special

party ○ ○

noun

1 a gathering of people to celebrate or have fun
I was invited to a graduation party.

 Human Body Human Mind Everyday Life History and Culture Communication

affair, blast, celebration, ball, festivity, fete, function, gathering, reception, social

> 2 a group brought together for a particular purpose
> *The search party found the missing child.*

crew, team, squad, band, company, corps, gang, troop

> *See also:* group

pass
verb

> 1 to move to someone else
> *Please pass this note to Tiffany.*

give, hand, carry, convey, deliver, send, transfer, transmit

> *Please hand me an apple.*

> 2 to make into law
> *Congress passed a law against drunk driving.*

approve, adopt, enact, authorize, ratify

> 3 to move ahead
> *The week is passing slowly.*

advance, drift, go, move, proceed, progress, roll, elapse, flow, slip

> 4 to stop living
> *He passed during the night.*

depart, die, expire, perish

> 5 to be over or done with
> *The storm finally passed.*

cease, disappear, end, fade, recede, terminate, vanish, blow over

> *Antonyms:* reject (2), repeal (2), veto (2)

passage
noun

> a way through which something can pass
> *This cave has an underground passage.*

channel, corridor, pass, passageway, alley, hall, hallway, opening, path

> *See also:* trip

passing
adjective

> lasting a short time
> *She had only a passing interest in tennis.*

brief, fleeting, casual, momentary, temporary, fugitive

> *Antonyms:* lasting, long-term, permanent

past ○ *See* old

paste
noun

> 1 a mixture used to stick paper or other light materials together. Paste is usually made of water and flour

adhesive, cement, glue

> 2 any soft, thick, moist substance or mixture
> *One of the ingredients in this recipe is tomato paste.*

mash, mush, plaster, spread, goo

verb

> 1 to cause to stick by means of paste
> *She pasted the photos into an album.*

affix, bond, cement, glue, stick

> 2 to cover with paste or some material that has paste on it
> *He pasted the walls of his room with posters of his favorite singers.*

daub, plaster, smear

pat *See* pet, love

patch
noun

> 1 a part that is different from a larger area
> *There is a sore patch of skin on my arm.*
> *There is a rough patch of road ahead.*

spot, area, section, stretch, zone, place

> *She has a dark spot on her shirt.*

> 2 a small piece of land used for growing

A B C D E F G H I J K L M N O P Q R S T U V W X Y Z

There is a vegetable patch behind the house.
plot, bed, garden

verb

to put together or repair in a quick way
He patched the broken ski with duct tape.
The kids patched together a swing with a board
and some rope.
cobble, doctor, improvise, piece, slap, throw

path See **passage, way**

patient See **understanding**

pattern See **example, model**

pause

noun

a short stop
The game will resume after a brief pause.
break, halt, intermission, interval

verb

to stop or cause to stop for a short time
We paused to think before diving into the pond.
She paused the videotape when the phone rang.
delay, halt, recess, suspend, wait, stop

pay ◍

verb

1 to settle by giving money
He paid his bill at the restaurant.
settle, discharge, satisfy, repay

2 to experience revenge or punishment
The robber paid for his crime by doing community
service.
atone, make amends, answer

peace ◍

noun

the absence of disturbance or hostility
There is an air of peace about this town.
calm, quiet, serenity, still, tranquility

Antonyms: conflict, hostility, tension, war

peaceful See **calm, still, leisure**

peak

noun

1 the highest point or degree
This new job is the peak of her career.
crest, apex, pinnacle, summit, acme, zenith

The view from the
summit of the
mountain was
spectacular.

2 the projecting
front part of a
cap
The team logo is on
the peak of her cap.
bill, visor, brim

peculiar See **curious, funny, particular,**
strange, weird

peer See **equal, look, match, stare**

pen ◍ ◍ See **write**

peninsula See **point**

people

noun

1 all persons who belong to the same community, country, religion, or race
The people of this country come from all over the
world.
folk, community, clan, kindred, kith and kin,
nation, race, tribe

2 family; relatives
My people came from Scotland.
family, folks, kin, kindred, kinfolk, relations,
relatives

3 the mass of ordinary persons
The president looked to the people for support.
the public, the masses, the populace, the
multitude, commoners, the herd

verb

to come to live in or settle
Native Americans were the first to people the
country we now call the United States.
colonize *The ancient Scots colonized the Shetland*
Islands.

 Human Body ? Human Mind Everyday Life History and Culture Communication

inhabit *Inhabiting the land along the river, they hunted and fished for their food.*

populate *The king decided to populate the island with prisoners, who could build houses and work the soil.*

settle *Pioneers settled the Ohio River valley.*

perception
noun

understanding that is based on the senses
My perception of what he said is different from yours.

sense, awareness, cognizance, attention, consciousness, feeling, heed, notice

perfect *See* **accurate, complete, develop, ideal, polish, total**

perform ● *See* **achieve, do, play, stage, theater**

performance *See* **act, play, practice, program, show**

perhaps
adverb

maybe; possibly
Perhaps I will see you tomorrow.

conceivably *It could conceivably rain tomorrow.*

maybe *Maybe the sun will come out today.*

possibly *She is possibly the tallest girl in the fourth grade.*

potentially *Jeremy could potentially win the class election.*

Antonyms: absolutely, certainly, definitely

period ●● *See* **season, spell, stretch, time, history**

permanent
adjective

lasting or meant to last for a very long time

The accident caused permanent damage to her legs.

People have always hoped for permanent peace.

enduring, persistent, unchangeable, constant, endless, eternal, everlasting, perpetual, indelible, timeless, indestructible

Antonyms: short-term, temporary

permission
noun

consent from an authority to do something
I asked the teacher for permission to hand in my homework late.

approval *After getting the teacher's approval, the student went ahead with his project.*

authorization *The rally required formal authorization by the mayor's office.*

consent *Pat had his parents' consent to drive their car.*

leave *When he asked if he could stay up late, his mother gave him leave.*

license *I have license to tell you her secret.*

sanction *The principal gave her sanction for our field trip.*

Antonyms: ban, disapproval, prohibition

permit
verb

1 to allow; let
Will you permit me to go to the dance?

allow, let, authorize, concede, grant, sanction, tolerate

2 to give the opportunity for or to
An extra traffic lane would permit the faster drivers to pass.

The rules don't permit smoking in this building.

allow, enable, authorize, concede, empower, entitle, grant, sanction

noun

a written statement that officially allows someone to do something; license
He got a building permit for the new porch.

The officer asked to see his fishing permit.

commission *The author received a commission to write a biography of a film star.*

license *My brother got his driver's license today.*

A B C D E F G H I J K L M N O P Q R S T U V W X Y Z

warrant *The judge issued a warrant so the police could arrest a fugitive.*

permitted *See* **welcome**

person
noun

a human being
Each person who lives in this country should obey its laws.

human, human being, individual, mortal, personage, someone, soul

personal
adjective

1 of or relating to a person; private
He writes personal thoughts and feelings in his diary.

individual, intimate, own, private

2 of or relating to the body
My personal health habits include eating right and exercising every day.

bodily *Parents want to keep their children from bodily harm.*

physical *He did hard physical training to prepare for the race.*

Antonyms: impersonal (1), open (1), public (1)

See also: intimate

personality
noun

1 all of the qualities of a person that make that person different from others
One twin has a cheerful personality, while the other is more serious.

character, disposition, individuality, nature

words that describe personalities
adventurous, affable, aggressive, agreeable, artificial, belligerent, bold, charming, colorful, conservative, dreadful, dull, enthusiastic, fake, generous, genial, good-natured, gullible, happy-go-lucky, imaginative, impulsive, insincere, likable, lousy, magnetic, mischievous, moody, nervous, nosy, obnoxious, plastic, playful, pleasant, polite, reckless, reserved, rotten, serious, shy, silly, sincere, somber, stiff, stubborn, sweet, timid, unnatural, unpleasant, warm, witty

people who have a specific kind of personality
angel, brat, bully, conservative, crank, devil, extrovert, follower, fool, grouch, introvert, jerk, leader, monster, rascal, rat, rogue, snake, villain

2 a famous person
There were many personalities in the audience at the movie awards event.

celebrity, star, notable, luminary, big shot, somebody, VIP

personally *See* **well**

persuade ⓘ
verb

1 to cause to do something by using reason or argument
The lawyer persuaded the judge that I was not the thief.

convince, get, influence, sway, induce, coax, move, prompt, talk into

2 to cause to believe something
She persuaded her mother that singing lessons are a good idea.

convert *The salesman tried to convert us into thinking his product was the best.*

convince *She convinced the judge of her innocence.*

inspire *She inspired him to confidence.*

proselytize *The missionaries proselytized the people in their jungle villages.*

Human Body   Human Mind   Everyday Life   History and Culture   Communication

pet ○ ◐
noun
> a person who is treated better than others or with special kindness; favorite
> *She is her father's pet.*
darling, favorite, pride and joy

verb
> to pat or stroke; touch or treat as a pet
> *My sister was petting all the cats at the animal shelter.*
caress, fondle, pat, stroke

phase *See* point, stage

phenomenon *See* fact, wonder

phone *See* call

photograph ○ ◑ *See* picture, advertisement

photography
noun
> the art or practice of taking and making photographs

> *some words related to photography*
> copy, crop, develop, distort, enlarge, expose, film, filter, focus, mount, pose, print, project, sit
> *some words that describe photographs*
> action, aerial, close-up, digital, landscape, panoramic, remote, satellite, still, underwater

phrase ◑ *See* put, word

physical ◐ ◔
adjective
> 1 of the body
> *He did hard physical training to prepare for the race.*
bodily, anatomical
> 2 of the material world
> *My physical surroundings consist of a small room with a bed, chair, and desk.*
> *Two physical features of this area are hills and lakes.*
material, concrete, earthly, solid

noun
> an examination of the body given by a doctor
> *I get a yearly physical to make sure I stay healthy.*
checkup *It's a good idea to get an annual checkup.*
exam *You must pass a health exam before you can play football.*
examination *The doctor conducted a complete examination to be certain the student was healthy enough to return to school.*

physics ◔
plural noun
> (used with a singular verb) the science that deals with matter and energy, their qualities, and the relationships between them

> *some kinds of physics*
> advanced, atmospheric, basic, fundamental, nuclear, optical
> *some aspects of physics*
> atoms, electricity, energy, force, friction, gravity, heat, inertia, light, magnetism, matter, motion, nuclear energy, sound, space, time, work

pick
verb
> 1 to choose from a group
> *From five flavors of ice cream, I picked chocolate.*
choose, pick out, select, single out, settle on, elect
> 2 to gather by pulling off or out
> *She picked cat hair off her sweater.*
pluck, gather, pull, collect, remove, withdraw
> 3 to cause an argument to happen
> *He picked a quarrel with his father.*
incite, prompt, provoke, start, cause, initiate

noun
> 1 the best part
> *That bright yellow banana is the pick of the bunch.*
best, choice, cream
> 2 an act of choosing
> *Take your pick of these tomatoes.*
choice, selection, preference
> *Please make a selection from*

the menu.

3 something or someone chosen
What is your pick for the best movie of the year?
choice, selection, preference

picnic *See* **leisure**

picture ○ ○
noun

1 a painting, drawing, or photograph
The hall was lined with pictures of the Presidents.
depiction, drawing, likeness, illustration, image, painting, photo, photograph, portrayal, representation, sketch, snapshot

2 a description or mental image
My grandparents try to give us a picture of what life was like when they were young.
description, idea, image, vision, visualization

3 a motion picture; movie; film
The local theater is showing a really good picture.
film, motion picture, movie, show

verb

1 to create an image of in one's mind; imagine
It's hard to picture your parents as children.
conceive of, dream of, envision, fancy, imagine, think of, visualize
He visualized climbing the mountain.

2 to make a drawing, painting, or photograph of
The artist pictured a young boy holding a puppy.
depict, draw, illustrate, image, paint, photograph, portray, represent, sketch

3 to describe
My uncle's letter colorfully pictured the cities he was visiting in Europe.
depict, describe, detail, illustrate, portray

piece
noun

1 a section or part separated from the whole
Only three pieces of pie were sold at the bake sale.
bit *The dog chewed off a bit of the chair leg.*

chunk *She gave him a chunk of chocolate to nibble on.*
division *We each received a division of the money.*
fraction *I found only a fraction of the lost money.*
fragment *She remembered only a fragment of the song.*
hunk *We ate the whole hunk of cheese at lunch.*
parcel *That section of his land was divided into parcels.*
part *We couldn't finish the puzzle because it was missing two parts.*
portion *He read a portion of the book.*
section *He cut the pie into equal sections.*
segment *She divided the orange into segments.*

2 an item that belongs to a group of such items
There are so many pieces to this puzzle.
part, component, element, section, segment, item, member, constituent, unit

3 a work of art, literature, or music
The pianist practiced the piano piece until he could play it perfectly.
composition, work

verb

to join in order to mend or make a whole (usually **piece together**)
He pieced together the broken vase.
assemble, join, combine, connect, conjoin, unite, relate, aggregate

pile *See* **load, lot, store**

pilot ○
verb

to steer or operate
He piloted the ship through dangerous waters.
captain *He captained the ship.*
drive *She learned to drive a truck.*
fly *My father has flown several types of aircraft.*
navigate *The astronauts navigated the space shuttle to and from the space station.*
sail *The helmsman sailed the ship through the narrow strait.*
steer *I steered the car toward the exit.*

Human Body Human Mind Everyday Life History and Culture Communication

pin
noun

a wooden or metal peg used for connecting or holding parts together

On older bicycles, the pedal is held to the crank by a steel pin.

cotter, dowel, peg, rivet

verb

1 to hold together with pins

She pinned together the pieces of the dress before she actually sewed them.

attach, peg, rivet

2 to hold firmly, so as to prevent motion

He pinned his brother to the ground.

fix, secure, jam, rivet, stick

pipe ○ ○ ○ *See* tube

pit ○ *See* hole, fruit

pitch
verb

1 to throw or toss

He pitched a curve ball in hopes of a strike.

toss, throw, fling, hurl, chuck, lob, sling, cast, heave

2 to set up or anchor

The campers pitched their tent on level ground.

anchor, establish, fix, rig, set

3 to throw toward the batter in baseball or softball

He pitched three strikes in a row.

hurl, lob, throw

4 to rock or move suddenly from one side or end to the other

The ship pitched hard in the storm.

lurch, heave, rock, roll, toss, yaw

Antonym: catch (1)

noun

1 the rise or slope

The pitch of the road makes speeding dangerous.

angle, slope, incline, slant, grade, cant, tilt, rise

2 the highest degree or pace

The children were in a pitch of excitement before the party.

fever, peak, height

See also: slope, throw

place
noun

1 a certain area of space that is taken up by something

She cleared a space on the shelf for her books.

location, space, area, position, room, spot, scene, setting, whereabouts

2 a space used for a specific purpose

Here is a place to work on your art projects.

position, space, spot, station

3 a duty or job

It's the photographer's place to take pictures of the wedding.

duty, function, job, post, role, station

She was happy with her role as a mother.

4 situation or position

Wouldn't you hate to be in her place?

circumstance, position, shoes, situation

5 one's home

Let's meet at your place tomorrow.

house, home, residence, abode, dwelling, domicile, pad

6 a point in a series

He finished in third place in the race.

position, rank, spot

verb

1 to put in a certain spot or position

He placed a spider in my shoe.

put, deposit, lay, locate, stand, position, install, set, stick

The ocean waves deposit shells on the beach.

2 to finish a contest in a particular position

The magician placed second in the talent contest.
finish, rank

See also: duty

plain 🔘
adjective

1 easily seen or heard
The tower on the hill is in plain view of everyone in town.

apparent, clear, conspicuous, evident, noticeable, obvious, unobstructed, unconcealed, visible

2 clear and understood; obvious
Our principal is known for his plain speaking.
It was plain to everyone that she was angry.

apparent, clear, clear-cut, obvious, distinct, blatant, explicit, overt, unmistakable

It's apparent that you care for your dog very much.

3 not complicated or fancy
The manager wore a plain suit today.

simple, ordinary, commonplace, unadorned, uncomplicated, homespun, austere, bare

4 not outstanding; common looking
He is tall and rather plain.

commonplace, homely, ordinary

Antonyms:
elaborate (3),
exotic (4),
fancy (3),
obscure (1)

adverb
without question or doubt
The belief that the earth is flat was just plain wrong.

> Little I ask; my wants are few,
> I only want a hut of stone,
> (A very **plain** brownstone will do,)
> That I may call my own.
> —From "CONTENTMENT," a poem by Oliver Wendell Holmes (1809-1894), American author

certainly, clearly, doubtlessly, flatly, plainly, simply, surely

noun
(sometimes **plains**) a large, flat area of land without trees
Many years ago, thousands of buffalo lived on the western plains.

grassland, prairie, savanna, steppe

plains 🔘 See range

plan ❓
noun

1 an action one intends to take; aim
Her plan is to travel in Europe after she graduates.

aim, design, goal, idea, intent, intention, plot, purpose, scheme

2 a way something is to be done that is thought out ahead of time
If you want the surprise party to be a success, you must have a good plan.

agenda, design, game plan, program, scheme, strategy, tack, tactics

3 a drawing that shows how something is to be built
The architect showed the builders her plans for the new planetarium.

blueprint, design, diagram

verb
to develop or design a plan for
The children planned the best way to ask their mother if they could have a puppy.

arrange, chart, design, develop, devise, draft, draw up, map out, outline, plot, scheme

plane See even, side

planet ⬆ See world

planned ❓ See deliberate

plant 🔘🔘🔘 See farm, garden, grass

plaster See paste, spread

plastic See artificial, personality

 Human Body   ❓ Human Mind   Everyday Life   History and Culture   Communication

platform *See* **program, stage**

play 🔊 🔄

noun

1 activity that is meant to relax or amuse
The parents watched their children at play.
amusement, diversion, entertainment, frolic, fun, merrymaking, recreation, revelry

2 a story written to be acted on a stage; drama
Our class put on a play for the whole school.
drama, performance, production, show

move

Antonyms: work (1)

verb

1 to act the part of in a drama
She will play Cinderella in the school production.
act *She acted in the school play.*
perform *He performed the role of the king.*
portray *He portrays the bad guy in the new film.*

2 to be in a game or contest
Let's play soccer.
compete, contest, vie

3 to have fun
The children played all day in the yard.
fool around, frolic, gambol, lark, rollick, romp

Antonym: work (3)

player

noun

1 someone who takes part in a game or sport
My brother is the best player on our baseball team.
competitor, contestant, participant

2 someone who plays a musical instrument
She is the piano player for the choir.
musician, performer, virtuoso

3 an actor in a drama
All of the players took a bow at the end of the play.
actor, actress, performer, Thespian

Antonym: observer (1)

pleasant *See* **friendly, good, nice, sweet, face, personality**

please

verb

to make content or give pleasure to; make happy
His thoughtful answers pleased the teacher.
cheer up *The good news cheered them up.*
delight *He delighted us with his wild stories.*
gladden *The burst of sunshine gladdened our spirits after many days of rain.*
gratify *Her good behavior gratified her parents.*
satisfy *She was satisfied with her performance.*
tickle *The funny story tickled the children.*

Antonyms: disappoint, displease, distress, grieve, pain, sadden, upset

pleased *See* **happy**

pleasure

noun

1 a feeling of happiness, delight, or joy
Walking the dog gives her pleasure.
delight, glee, joy, bliss, happiness, enjoyment, elation, satisfaction, contentment

2 something that gives a feeling of joy or happiness
Curling up with an interesting book is always a pleasure.
delight *That child is such a delight!*
fun *Flying the kite was a lot of fun.*
joy *The baby is a joy to its parents.*
treat *Chocolate is his favorite treat.*

3 a desire or preference
Which of these two flowers is your pleasure?
desire, wish, preference, fancy, liking, inclination

Antonyms: displeasure (1), pain (1), suffering (1)

A B C D E F G H I J K L M N O P Q R S T U V W X Y Z

plenty
noun

a full amount or supply
There was plenty of food in the kitchen for a picnic lunch.
abundance, store, lot, wealth, quantity, hoard, bounty, cornucopia

> Use the article "an" before **abundance**, **store**, **lot**, **wealth**, **quantity**, **hoard**, **bounty**, and **cornucopia**. *There was an abundance of food at the Thanksgiving dinner.*

Antonyms: lack, scarcity, shortage

plot ☉ See **chart, patch, plan, property, literature**

plow See **farm, garden**

plus See **advantage, extra, positive**

pocket See **hole, clothes**

poet See **writer, art**

poetry ☉ ☉ See **art, literature**

point
noun

1 the sharp end of something
The pencil point broke when he pressed on it.
prong, spike, tip
> *We couldn't climb over the fence spikes.*

2 a piece of land that stretches out into the water
We had a picnic on the point.
cape, headland, peninsula, promontory, spit

3 a position or degree on a scale
Do you know the freezing point of water?
level, stage, step

4 a particular moment in time

She was at the point of eating dinner when the phone rang.
moment *The moment he got home, the phone rang.*
instant *The instant they left home, she arrived.*
brink *That country is on the brink of war.*
juncture *The statue's disappearance was still a mystery at that juncture.*
stage *Adolescence is the stage between childhood and adulthood.*
phase *The "terrible twos" are a phase when children say "No" a lot.*
threshold *The researchers felt they were at the threshold of a major discovery.*
verge *The scientists are on the verge of a major discovery.*

5 the meaning or purpose of a statement or action
What's the point of that joke?
importance, meaning, significance, gist, import, object, purpose, thrust, substance, tenor, meat

6 a special quality
This horse has many good points.
attribute, quality, characteristic, trait, property, detail, specific

verb

1 to aim or direct at something
The captain pointed the sailboat into the wind.
aim, direct, home in, focus, level, train, shine, sight

> *He directed the beam of light at the back of the closet.*

2 to call attention to by signalling
The guide pointed out many interesting buildings.
designate, indicate, note, show

See also: moment, instant

Human Body   Human Mind   Everyday Life   History and Culture   Communication

poison
noun

1 a substance that can kill or seriously harm living beings if it is swallowed, breathed, or otherwise taken in
Parents should keep bug sprays and other poisons where children cannot reach them.
toxin, bane, biocide, venom

2 something that destroys or injures pleasure, happiness, or other good things
His frequent rages were poison for the family.
blight, cancer, plague, scourge, infection, disease, bane

verb

1 to give poison to
The jealous queen hated Snow White and tried to poison her.
dope, drug, intoxicate

2 to add poison to
The queen poisoned an apple and gave it to Snow White.
contaminate, pollute, dope, corrupt, drug

3 to harm or pollute; corrupt
Some people think that watching violent shows on TV poisons children's minds.
corrupt, pollute, contaminate, taint

poisonous ○
adjective

1 filled with or containing poison
The scorpion has a poisonous sting.
toxic *The factory spilled toxic waste into the lake.*
venomous *Only a few snakes are venomous.*

2 likely to cause serious harm or death
Some berries are poisonous to humans but not to birds.
baneful, deadly, injurious, lethal, noxious, pernicious, toxic

3 full of ill will or evil feelings
She wrote a poisonous letter but decided not to send it.
vicious, malicious, malevolent, malignant, black-hearted, baleful, wicked

Antonym: beneficial (2)

policy See **program**

polish
verb

1 to give a shiny surface to
She polished the furniture before the guests arrived.
buff *My dad buffs his shoes every Sunday to make them look nice for the week.*
burnish *Grandfather burnished the brass door knocker.*
gloss *Aunt Betty glosses her nails every morning.*
shine *He shines his shoes whenever they get dusty.*
wax *My father waxes his car every Sunday.*

2 to cause to become finished or more perfect
She is polishing her acting skills in a summer theater.
hone, perfect, refine, cultivate, smooth

noun

a substance used to make something smooth or shiny
The furniture polish made the woodwork shine.
finish, glaze, gloss, lacquer, shellac, varnish, wax

polite
adjective

showing good manners or being thoughtful of others
She didn't like the food, but she ate it to be polite.
courteous, gracious, nice, cordial, thoughtful, well-behaved, well-mannered

Antonyms: discourteous, impolite, rude

political See **belief, culture, theater**

pool ○ See **river**

poor
adjective

1 without money, possessions, or other basic needs
The community center serves free meals to poor people.
destitute, impoverished, needy, indigent, broke, penniless, bankrupt

2 wanting; lacking
The land was so poor that nothing could grow there.

A
B
C
D
E
F
G
H
I
J
K
L
M
N
O
P
Q
R
S
T
U
V
W
X
Y
Z

barren, deficient, inadequate, inferior, lacking, insufficient, meager, wanting, feeble

> 3 having bad fortune or bad luck
> *The poor woman's husband died.*

unfortunate, hapless, ill-fated, unlucky, luckless, wretched, star-crossed, miserable, pathetic, pitiful, sorry

> *Antonyms:* affluent (1), rich (1), wealthy (1)

noun

> poor people considered as a group
> *There are many community programs to help the poor.*

homeless, paupers, unfortunates, indigents

pop ⟳ *See* **burst, crack, run, spring**

popular *See* **common, dance**

population ◯ *See* **country**

porch *See* **home**

portion *See* **amount, divide, length, part, piece, section**

position *See* **arrange, belief, business, condition, grade, job, judgment, lay, level, location, office, opinion, place, rank, set, space, spot, stand, station, view, work**

positive
adjective

> 1 certain; sure
> *I am positive that she lives on this street.*

certain, sure, confident, convinced, definite

> 2 favorable or helpful
> *The coach said positive things about how the team was playing.*

favorable, beneficial, constructive, good, profitable

noun

> something that is good or helpful
> *Having a college education is a big positive in life.*

advantage, asset, boon, benefit, plus

possess *See* **have, own**

possession
noun

> 1 the act or condition of having or owning something
> *The soccer players struggled for possession of the ball.*

grasp *She held her employees in a firm grasp.*

custody *After the divorce, the parents went to court to determine who would get custody of the children.*

occupation *Germany's occupation of France took place in 1940.*

control *England had control of the American colonies until the Revolutionary War.*

hold *The homeless man had few things in his hold.*

> 2 something that is owned
> *I have many possessions besides my car.*

belongings, property, goods, things

> 3 an area ruled by a state or country
> *Guam became a possession of the United States after the Spanish-American War.*

colony, territory, domain

possibility *See* **chance**

possible
adjective

> 1 capable of being, happening, being done, or being used
> *Riding a bike is one possible way to get to school.*

potential, probable, feasible

> 2 capable of being true
> *If he didn't answer, it's possible that he didn't hear you.*

believable, conveivable, likely, probable

> *Antonyms:* impossible (1,2), improbable (1,2), unlikely (2)

possibly *See* **perhaps**

post *See* **office, place, record, station, stick**

potential *See* **ability, possible, power**

pound *See* **beat, hit, thump**

a b c d e f g h i j k l m n o p q r s t u v w x y z

 Human Body Human Mind Everyday Life History and Culture Communication

pour *See* **dump, flood, flow, rain, storm, stream, wash**

pouring *See* **weather**

poverty *See* **misery, need**

power 🌍 📖

noun

1 the ability to act, cause, or function

That comedienne has the power to make people laugh.

ability, capability, capacity, faculty, force, might, strength, potential

Atlas used all his might to hold up the world.

Most birds have the ability to fly.

2 the ability to control others

The peasants feared the king's power.

authority, control, command, strength, influence, sway

some kinds of power
economic, military, national, personal, physical, psychological
some words used to describe power
absolute, almighty, sovereign

3 a person, group, or nation that has control or influence over others

The United States is one of the world's great powers.

authority, government, force, influence, ruler, establishment

4 the right of a government or other organization to do something

The government has the power to tax its citizens.

authority, privilege, right

5 energy that can do work

This car has more power than any car in its class.

energy, force, steam, vigor, horsepower

verb

to supply with energy or force

Gasoline powers most car engines.

drive, fuel, propel

The golfer drove the ball three hundred yards.

powerful

adjective

having or able to use power or force

The race car has a powerful engine.

The principal is in a powerful position.

forceful *Sojourner Truth was a forceful speaker.*

strong *A strong wind blew the old barn down.*

mighty *The lion gave a mighty roar.*

influential *She is a very influential person in this town.*

authoritative *If you speak in an authoritative voice, people will listen.*

Antonyms: helpless, powerless, weak

practical

adjective

1 having to do with real life and experience

We are looking for an applicant with practical experience.

worldly, realistic, common-sense, down-to-earth

2 able to be used or put into practice

They needed a practical solution to the problem of how to get the kite out of the tree.

usable, useful, effective, handy, functional

Antonyms: impractical (2), ineffective (2), useless (2)

practically *See* **almost, mainly, much**

practice

noun

1 the doing of some activity many times to become skilled at it

Leila spends a few hours every day on violin practice.

🌲 Living World 🔬 Physical World 🏭 Natural Environment 〰️ Economy 📖 Government and Law

A B C D E F G H I J K L M N O P Q R S T U V W X Y Z

drill, exercise, repetition, rehearsal

2 an activity that is the usual way of doing something

It is our family's practice to have dinner together every night.

custom, habit, rule, way, convention, routine

3 the act or process of doing a thing

The best way to test your woodworking skills is to put them into practice.

action, exercise, performance, activity, procedure

4 the work of an occupation or profession

Her goal is to have a medical practice.

career, profession, occupation, pursuit, work, employment

verb

1 to do many times in order to become skilled

I practiced the poem until I could recite it from memory.

rehearse, repeat, train

practices *See* **tradition**

prairie *See* **plain, range**

praise

noun

words that show admiration or respect

The dog received praise for doing a trick.

compliment, acclaim, approval, honor, recognition, applause, flattery, reverence

> We refuse **praise** in order to be praised twice.
> —*François, Duc de la Rochefoucauld (1613-1680), French author*

verb

1 to speak well of

The coach praised the players for their hard work.

commend, compliment, cite, acclaim, congratulate, salute, celebrate, hail, applaud, flatter

2 to honor with words or song

The poet praises human nature in this poem.

glorify, exalt, worship, hymn

prayer ○ *See* **appeal**

precious *See* **dear, love**

precise *See* **accurate, careful, definite, exact, very, communication**

precisely *See* **just**

predict

verb

to tell in advance that something will happen

The general predicted an easy victory.

foretell, foresee, forecast, divine

prediction

noun

a statement that something might happen or is expected to happen

Jean's prediction was that her favorite team would win.

foretelling, prophecy, forecast

A **prophecy** is usually a prediction made far in advance, often dealing with religion. A **forecast** is a shorter-term prediction, usually of weather.

---

prefer *See* **choose, like**

preferred *See* **favorite**

prehistoric ○ *See* **history**

preparation *See* **drug, medicine**

prepare *See* **arrange, fix, guard, make, set, drug**

prepared *See* **instant, ready**

present

adjective

existing at this time

The present head of the company has been in charge for two years.

current, actual, immediate

Human Body   Human Mind   Everyday Life   History and Culture   Communication

presently *See* **now, soon**

presents *See* **celebration**

preserve *See* **hold, protect, save**

press *See* **force, pressure, push, rush, squeeze, thrust, clothes**

pressure
noun
  1 a steady force upon a surface
  Put pressure on a cut to make it stop bleeding.
  force *He applied force to the orange to squeeze the juice out.*
  stress *The weight of the books put a lot of stress on the shelf.*
  2 a strong influence or burden on the mind or emotions
  I'm under a lot of pressure at school.
  strain, stress, tension, heat
    Antonym: relief (2)
verb
  to force into an action by strong influence or urging
  My friend pressured me to try out for the soccer team.
  compel, force, press, twist someone's arm, crowd
    See also: press

pretty ⓘ *See* **attractive, beautiful, nice, very, face**

previous *See* **old**

prey ❶ ⑥ *See* **victim**

price *See* **charge, cost, worth**

pride
noun
  1 an inborn feeling of self-worth
  Although she had a poor finish in the race, she carried herself with pride.
  dignity, honor, assurance, self-respect, confidence, self-esteem

  2 a sense of personal value that comes from what one has or can do
  He takes pride in his work.
  satisfaction, pleasure, gratification
  Building the model airplane gave me great satisfaction.

  3 a sense of one's own value that is too high
  Roger's pride made him hard to like.
  arrogance, haughtiness, smugness, loftiness, vanity
    Antonyms: embarrassment (2), guilt (2), humility (3), modesty (3), shame (1)

primary *See* **basic, first, lead, main**

prime *See* **first, lead, main**

primitive
adjective
  1 having to do with an early stage or a condition that is not developed
  Primitive humans learned how to use fire.
  I have only a primitive understanding of how computers work.
  undeveloped, barbarian, early, beginning

  2 simple or not developed
  The holy man lived in a primitive house made of mud and grass.
  plain, crude, rude, simple, undeveloped, austere
    Antonyms: advanced (1), developed (1), high-tech (2), modern (2), up-to-date (2)

principal *See* **first, lead, main, major**

principle *See* **honor**

principles *See* **character, moral, value**

print ◑ *See* **photography**

A B C D E F G H I J K L M N O P Q R S T U V W X Y Z

prison 🔊
noun
a building for holding and punishing people who have broken the law
People who sell drugs will be sent to prison.
jail, penitentiary, stockade, dungeon, brig, can, jug, tank

> Stone walls do not a
> **prison** make,
> Nor iron bars a cage;
> Minds innocent and
> quiet take
> That for an hermitage;
> —From "TO
> ALTHEA FROM
> PRISON," a poem
> by Richard Lovelace
> (1618-1657?)

Except for **prison** and **jail,** all these words should be used with "the": *Throw him in the dungeon!* The last four are only used informally.

private
adjective
1 personal and not to be shared
I write my private thoughts in a diary.
intimate, personal, confidential, secret

2 owned by a person or group rather than by the government
There is no swimming on Mr. Jones's private beach.
personal, exclusive, nonpublic

3 tending not to talk about personal things or feelings
My father is a very private person.
reserved, restrained, aloof, remote
Antonyms: open (2), public (2)
See also: secret

prize
noun
1 a reward given to the winner of a contest or game
Mrs. Higgins won a prize for her roses at the state fair.
award, honor, purse, stake, booty

2 anything worked or aimed for; something that is worth a great effort
Freedom is a prize many have fought and died for.
goal, treasure, reward, desire
verb
to hold in high honor
The cowboy prized his palomino horse.
value, treasure, esteem, cherish, adore, appreciate, worship
We treasured our mother on Mother's Day.

probe See **examine, explore, research, test**

problem
noun
1 a question or condition that is difficult to understand or to deal with
Poverty is still a problem that faces our nation.
difficulty, knot, question, challenge, matter, dilemma, trouble, issue, complication

2 a question, puzzle, or statement that is to be discussed or solved
He racked his brain trying to solve the problem.
question, puzzle, riddle
Antonyms: answer (1), remedy (1), solution (1)
adjective
difficult to manage
His boss thinks he is a problem worker.
difficult, obstinate, stubborn, unruly

procedure See **practice, process, step, way**

proceed See **continue, move, pass**

process
noun
1 a series of actions used to produce something or reach a goal
The process for making butter involves churning.
procedure, operation, method, practice, routine, system, strategy, machinery, mechanism

2 a series of changes or acts that happen one after another
The process of growing up takes many years.

Human Body   Human Mind   Everyday Life   History and Culture   Communication

course, procedure, act, business

verb

  to handle, treat, or change something by following a procedure

  The new computer processes data at very high speeds.

handle, treat, deal with

procession *See* **flow, march, parade, train**

produce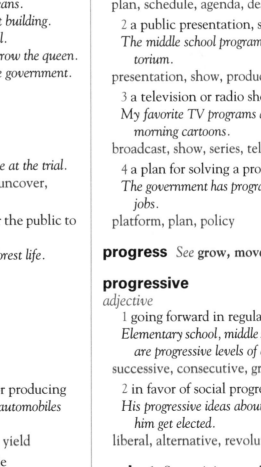

verb

  1 to bring into being

  Our chickens produce eggs for market.

generate *The human body generates heat.*

give *Cows give milk.*

yield *Our garden yielded lots of vegetables this year.*

create *Poor planning creates problems.*

grow *The farmer grows corn and beans.*

author *She authored a book on boat building.*

bear *Apple trees bear fruit in the fall.*

hatch *They hatched a plot to overthrow the queen.*

do *She does public sculptures for the government.*

  2 to make or manufacture

  This factory produces towels.

make, manufacture, issue

  3 to bring forward into view

  The lawyer produced new evidence at the trial.

disclose, present, expose, reveal, uncover, show, display

  4 to put together and present for the public to enjoy

  The class produced a play about forest life.

stage, present, put on, organize

  Antonym: destroy (1)

product 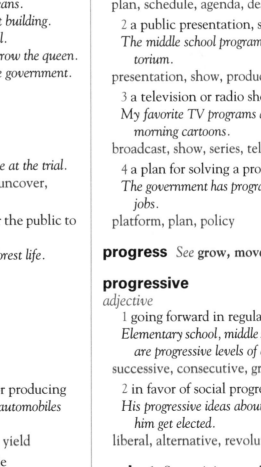 *See* **work**

production

noun

  1 the act or process of making or producing

  That factory began production of automobiles eighty years ago.

generation, manufacture, output, yield

  2 a thing or amount that is made

A new kind of seed has increased the farm's production of corn.

output, yield, turnout, volume

productive *See* **busy**

profession *See* **business, career, claim, living, practice, work**

professional *See* **theater**

professor *See* **teacher**

profit *See* **advantage, gain, use**

program

noun

  1 a plan of what will be done

  The library has a weekly program for young readers.

plan, schedule, agenda, design, scheme

  2 a public presentation, such as a play

  The middle school program was held in the auditorium.

presentation, show, production, performance

  3 a television or radio show

  My favorite TV programs are the Saturday morning cartoons.

broadcast, show, series, telecast

  4 a plan for solving a problem

  The government has programs to help people find jobs.

platform, plan, policy

progress *See* **grow, move, pass**

progressive

adjective

  1 going forward in regular or ordered steps

  Elementary school, middle school, and high school are progressive levels of education.

successive, consecutive, gradual

  2 in favor of social progress or change

  His progressive ideas about the economy helped him get elected.

liberal, alternative, revolutionary, radical

project *See* **activity, work, photography**

a
b
c
d
e
f
g
h
i
j
k
l
m
n
o
p
q
r
s
t
u
v
w
x
y
z

prominent *See* **famous, great, important, major**

promise *See* **guarantee, oath, word**

promote *See* **develop, recommend, communication**

prompt
adjective

1 done immediately and without pause
This snack bar is known for its prompt service.
immediate, instant, punctual, quick, rapid, swift

2 swift to answer
The fire department was prompt in getting to the burning building.
punctual, quick, swift

Antonyms: delayed (1), slow (1,2)

verb

1 to cause to act
He prompted the dog to jump through the hoop.
cause, egg on, incite, prod, provoke, push, spur, move, stir, urge, encourage, get

2 to assist by providing forgotten words in theater, radio, and television
The stage manager prompted the actress when she forgot her line.
remind, cue, aid, assist

promptly *See* **immediately, quickly**

pronounce
verb

1 to make the sound of or express with the voice in a specific way
He pronounced the long words very slowly.
articulate, enunciate, say, sound, voice, utter

2 to state something officially
I now pronounce you husband and wife.
declare, proclaim, ordain, decree, announce

proof *See* **evidence**

proper
adjective

1 correct for a certain purpose
Shorts and a T-shirt are not proper clothing for a wedding.
appropriate, apt, fitting, suitable, suited, right

2 following accepted methods or rules
Pat showed Tom the proper way to address a letter.
Is it proper for children to call adults by their first name?
correct, conventional, right, decent, respectable, legitimate, formal, orthodox

Antonyms: improper (1,2), out of place (1), unacceptable (2), wrong (1)

properly *See* **well**

property
noun

1 anything that is owned; all of one's possessions taken as a whole
The poor man's property included some clothing and little else.
belongings, estate, possessions, goods, things, assets, stuff

2 a piece of land or real estate
We plan to build a summer house on our property by the lake.
lot, plot, ground, estate

3 a quality that something is known by
A tour of the plant showed us the useful properties of steel.
attribute, characteristic, quality, trait, feature, aspect

proportion *See* **size**

propose
verb

to present or suggest as an idea to be considered
The council proposed a new bike path around the lake.

Human Body   Human Mind   Everyday Life   History and Culture   Communication

advance, offer, present, recommend, submit, suggest, pose, introduce
I recommend that we not disturb the hornets' nest.

prosperity *See* **success**

protect
verb
to defend or keep safe
A fence protects us from our neighbor's vicious dog.
defend, guard, safeguard, shield, secure, shelter, preserve
The dog guarded the sheep.

protected
See **safe**

protection
noun
1 the act of keeping something safe from harm or the condition of being protected
We lock the doors at night for protection.
care, defense, safeguarding, guarding, security, preservation, safety

2 a person or thing that protects
Use sunscreen as protection against sunburn.
defense, guard, safeguard, shield, guardian

protest
noun
an objection or complaint
The teacher ignored his protests about having too much homework.
objection, dissent, resistance, challenge
verb
1 to make a protest
People will protest if the law gets passed.
The town protested against the plan to pave over the ball fields.
argue *Will you argue for or against the plan for developing the city?*
dissent *He dissented to the judge's decision.*
object *The lawyer objected to the harassment of his witness.*

contend *The police chief contended with the mayor's new policy.*

2 to express objection to or disagreement with, in a planned, organized way
Thousands of citizens protested the Vietnam war during the 1960s.
oppose, resist, dispute

Antonyms: accept (2), concede (1), embrace (2), give in (1), relent (1)

proud
adjective
having too high an opinion of one self
The millionaire was too proud to ride the bus.
cocky, complacent, conceited, smug, vain, haughty, arrogant, lofty

Antonyms: discreet, humble, modest, reserved
See also: pride

prove
verb
to show to be true or correct
The lawyer failed to prove the guilt of the prisoner.
demonstrate, establish, verify, confirm, attest

Antonyms: debunk, discredit, disprove

provide
verb
to give what is needed
The math teacher provided books, rulers, and paper.
furnish, serve, supply, give, afford, provision

province *See* **area, country**

psychological *See* **mental, power**

psychology *See* **science**

public *See* **common, country, open, society**

pull
verb
1 to bring closer by using force upon
She pulled the door shut.

draw *She drew her son near.*

haul *The fisherman hauled a big fish out of the water.*

tug *The girl tugged her mother's skirt.*

> 2 to draw after oneself or itself by attaching and moving forward
> *The tow truck pulled the car.*

drag *We dragged the logs up the hill.*

tow *We use our truck to tow our horse trailer.*

tug *The child tugged her toy with a rope.*

draw *We drew the sleeping dog across the floor on a blanket.*

snake *The farmer snaked a row of wagons behind his tractor.*

> 3 to remove with force from a fixed position
> *The carpenter pulled the nail from the board.*

extract, pick, pluck, yank, tear, wrest, wrench

Antonyms: press (1), push (1)

See also: carry

punishment
noun

> a penalty for doing something wrong
> *The punishment for littering is a fine.*

penalty, discipline, fine, sentence, rap

Except for **rap**, these synonyms can also be used as verbs: *The club fined me for not doing my duties.*

Antonym: reward

purchase ☻ *See* **buy, money**

pure
adjective

> 1 Not mixed with anything else
> *This watch is made of pure gold.*

unmixed, unadulterated, uncontaminated

> 2 without evil
> *The hero had a pure heart.*

clean, immaculate, innocent, good, unstained, moral

> 3 nothing but
> *It was pure good fortune to win the lottery.*

mere, sheer, absolute, utter

Antonyms: evil (2), immoral (2), impure (2)

purpose
noun

> 1 a reason or plan that guides an action
> *My father says the purpose of cats is to clear the world of mice.*

reason, aim, design, end, goal, motive, objective, point, object, sense, intent, intention, plan

> 2 determination or will
> *He practices violin with a great sense of purpose.*

determination, resolution, resolve, will, single-mindedness, steadfastness, intentness

Antonyms: ambivalence (2), apathy (2), indifference (2)

See also: use, point

push
verb

> 1 to use pressure against in order to move
> *I pushed my bed under the window.*

move, press, shove, propel, drive, jostle, propel

> 2 to move ahead by shoving
> *They pushed their way through the crowd.*

press, shoulder, shove, elbow, jostle, ram, thrust, bull

> 3 to urge strongly toward a particular action or way of thinking
> *Jeff pushed his friends to elect him team captain.*

prod, urge, compel, press, pressure, persuade

Antonym: pull (1)

noun

> a shove
> *She gave the door a push.*

shove, thrust, jostle, nudge, butt

Human Body · Human Mind · Everyday Life · History and Culture · Communication

put
verb

1 to move to a particular position or place
The cashier put the groceries in a bag.
place, set, deposit, lay

2 to express
Put it in your own words.
express, phrase, say, state, word, frame, couch

Antonym: remove (1)

puzzle
verb

to confuse
The book's ending puzzled me.
baffle, confuse, mystify, stump, bewilder

See also: mystery

pyramid *See* shape

A
B
C
D
E
F
G
H
I
J
K
L
M
N
O
P
Q
R
S
T
U
V
W
X
Y
Z

Living World Physical World Natural Environment Economy Government and Law

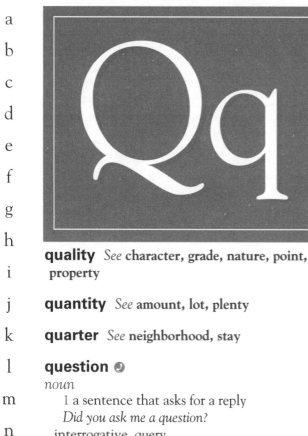

quality *See* **character, grade, nature, point, property**

quantity *See* **amount, lot, plenty**

quarter *See* **neighborhood, stay**

question 🔵
noun
1 a sentence that asks for a reply
Did you ask me a question?
interrogative, query

2 a matter to be discussed
Our town is looking at the question of whether to build a new school.
issue, matter, topic, subject, proposal

3 a matter that is in doubt or not certain
Many scientists study the question of how the dinosaurs died out.
problem, puzzle, riddle, enigma, mystery
verb
to ask a question or questions of
Dad questioned me about my new baseball team.
ask, query, quiz, examine, interrogate, grill

Use **interrogate** and **grill** when the questioner is asking several questions of a person who does not want to answer: *The police officer interrogated the suspect about her whereabouts last Monday night. The principal grilled the kids about the fight on the playground.*

---

quick
adjective
1 done in a short time
I received a quick response to my letter.
prompt, fast, hasty, rapid, swift

2 moving with speed
She is a very quick runner.
fast, speedy, rapid, swift, brisk, fleet

3 thinking, acting, or learning with speed
She has a quick mind.
alert, keen, sharp, agile, nimble, smart
Antonyms: slow (1), sluggish (2)
See also: fast

quickly
adverb
in a short time; rapidly
Get ready quickly so that we'll get to the movie on time.
fast, on the double, promptly, rapidly, soon, speedily, swiftly
Antonym: slowly

quiet
noun
freedom from noise
We vacation at the lake because of the peace and quiet.
silence, peace, calm, still, stillness

Antonyms: clamor, noise, racket

Human Body Human Mind Everyday Life History and Culture Communication

adjective

making little or no sound
That car has a quiet engine.
That quiet baby hardly ever cries.
soft *The soft music lulled us to sleep.*
hushed *Our parents spoke in* hushed tones so as not to disturb us.
low *We heard a low rumble in the distance.*
silent *The house was silent after midnight.*
still *The yowling cats finally became still.*
noiseless *Everyone was asleep in the noiseless house.*

Antonyms: loud, noisy

verb

to make or cause to make quiet or quieter
Will you please quiet your dog?
hush, shush, silence, muffle, mute, shut up

> What are the wild waves saying,
> Sister, the whole day long,
> That ever amid our playing
> I hear but their **low**, lone song?
> —From *"WHAT ARE THE WILD WAVES SAYING?"* a poem by Joseph Edwards Carpenter (1813-1885)

Writing Tip: Let Adverbs Tell the Story

Adverbs are words that tell how things happen. They answer the questions "how" "when" and "where." They describe verbs, adjectives, phrases, or sentences. Most adverbs are easy to spot: they are the words that end with "-ly." Think of adverbs as "stage directions" for your writing.

"Lulu!" shouted Bobo.
"Lulu!" shouted Bobo desperately.
"Lulu!" shouted Bobo cheerfully.

I did not see what was behind the door.
Fortunately, I did not see what was behind the door.
Sadly, I did not see what was behind the door.

The soup was hot.
The soup was exceedingly hot.
The soup was barely hot.

You see how an adverb can change the entire meaning of a sentence: Is Lulu in trouble, or does Bobo have some happy news to share? What or who was on the other side of the door? Did the soup burn your mouth, or did you have to reheat it? When you let adverbs help tell the story, you will find that you can get across more information with fewer words. Using adverbs will improve your writing, and make it more enjoyable for others to read.

A B C D E F G H I J K L M N O P Q R S T U V W X Y Z

a
b
c
d
e
f
g
h
i
j
k
l
m
n
o
p
q
r
s
t
u
v
w
x
y
z

Shut up is an informal, mildly rude phrase that refers to making a person become quiet. It is not appropriate for formal presentations or polite conversation, even if preceded by "please."

See also: calm

quit
verb

1 to refuse to take further part in
She quit her job as a teacher to become a truck driver.

resign, leave, abdicate, abandon, forsake, back out of, withdraw from

2 to do no longer
He quit soccer when he was twelve.

stop, cease, halt, drop, discontinue

Antonyms: begin (2), continue (1), persevere (1), start (2)

See also: stop

quite
adverb

1 to the greatest degree
Bart is not quite finished with his book report.

absolutely, altogether, completely, entirely, fully, thoroughly, totally, wholly

2 to a large degree
I thought that I did quite well cleaning my room.

fairly, rather, highly, largely, very, really

See also: really, very

quotation ⊘
noun

words quoted from a book or other writing
Rob's report included a quotation from a poem by Emily Dickinson.

quote, excerpt, citation

 Human Body ? Human Mind Everyday Life History and Culture Communication

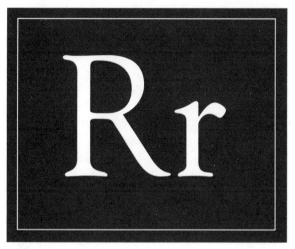

race ○ *See* **contest, fly, people, run, rush, dog, sport**

racket
noun
loud, confusing noise
The racket in the street kept me awake all night.
clamor, noise, din, commotion, hubbub, tumult, uproar, ruckus, pandemonium
See also: noise

radiant *See* **bright**

radical *See* **extreme, progressive**

raft *See* **boat**

rage ○ *See* **anger, storm, emotion**

rain ○
noun
1 drops of water that form in the clouds and fall from the sky to the earth
Rain soaked the parched fields.
rainfall, raindrops, shower, precipitation
2 a fast and steady fall of anything
The soldier tried to protect himself from the rain of arrows.
downpour, shower, deluge, torrent
verb
to come down as water from the clouds
It started to rain as we were walking home.
drizzle, mist, shower, sprinkle, pour, precipitate

rainfall *See* **rain, weather**

rainy *See* **weather**

raise
verb
1 to move to a higher position
I raised my hand to signal Ms. Marvel.
boost *He boosted the child up so that she could see over the counter.*
lift *He lifted his hand to salute.*
elevate *Members of the team elevated their star player onto their shoulders.*
heft *The stock clerk hefted the box onto the top shelf.*
hoist *He hoisted the flag to the top of the pole.*
hike up *He hiked up his slacks.*
2 to build
The farmer raised a barn on his property.
build, construct, erect, put up
3 to cause to grow
My parents raised four children.
The farmers down the road raise beans and corn.
grow, cultivate, rear, nurture, foster
Antonyms: demolish (2), lower (1), raze (2)

ranch *See* **farm**

range
noun
1 the amount or extent by which something can vary
This shirt comes in a wide range of sizes and colors.
scale, spectrum, extent, gamut
2 a large, open area where animals live
Cattle wander on the open range.
grassland, plains, prairie, savanna
verb
1 to vary within certain limits
The ticket prices range from twenty to fifty dollars.
extend, span, stretch, vary
2 to move freely across an area
He ranged all over Kentucky before settling down.

Living World   Physical World   Natural Environment   Economy   Government and Law   205

wander, roam, ramble, rove, meander

> Great herds of buffalo once roamed the plains.

See also: wander

rank

noun

1 a position in society
The mayor is a person of high rank in the city.
position, standing, station, status

2 an office or position
She achieved the rank of general.
degree, grade, level, position

verb

to place in order
The magazine ranked snack foods from most to least nutritious.
rate, sort, order, organize, categorize, classify

rapid *See* **fast, instant, prompt, quick, sharp, sudden, communication, river**

rapidly *See* **fast, quickly**

rare *See* **unusual**

rat *See* **personality, rodent**

rate

verb

1 to look at and form an opinion of
He rated the book excellent.
regard, consider, deem, gauge, judge, reckon

2 to put in a certain rank or order
The judges rated the skaters.
rank, categorize, classify, grade, order, organize, sort

See also: cost, rank

rather *See* **quite**

rattle

verb

1 to make a series of knocking sounds

The windows rattled during the storm.
clatter, chatter, clack, vibrate

2 to speak quickly, without thought or purpose
He rattled on about the game long after it was over.
babble, blabber, chatter, jabber, prate, prattle

3 to cause to rattle by shaking
The prisoner rattled the bars on the window.
rock, shake, vibrate, flutter, jiggle

4 to confuse or upset
The lawyer's rapid questions rattled the witness.
upset, fluster, ruffle, shake, unsettle, perturb

See also: shake

raw

adjective

not cooked or changed by any process
Raw carrots make a great snack.
crude *That pile of crude fiber will be made into yarn.*
uncooked *I prefer uncooked peas to cooked peas.*
unrefined *Unrefined oil will be shipped to the refinery.*
unprocessed *Bobo only eats unprocessed, whole foods.*

Antonyms: cooked, processed, refined

reach

verb

1 to extend as far as
Her hair reaches her shoulders.
touch, come, extend, run, span, stretch

It is sometimes necessary to use "to" after **come, extend, run,** and **stretch**: *The streamers stretched to the other side of the room; This road runs to the next town.*

2 to arrive at
We reached the lake after a three-hour drive.
Have you reached your goal?
make *We made it to the movie on time.*
gain *They finally gained the entrance to the cave.*
attain *She attained her goal of becoming a doctor.*
achieve *Who will achieve victory?*

Human Body   ? Human Mind   Everyday Life   History and Culture   Communication

end up *Lulu could not remember how she ended up at the zoo.*

noun

the limit of a person's under-standing

That physics problem is beyond the reach of most middle-school students.

grasp, ken, capacity, command

> Ah, but a man's reach
> should exceed his
> **grasp**,
> Or what's a heaven for?
> —From
> *ANDREA DEL
> SARTO, by Robert
> Browning (1812-1889),
> British poet*

read

verb

1 to examine and understand the meaning of something written
Have you read this book yet?
peruse, scan

2 to understand the nature or meaning of
I could read the disappointment on her face.
He read my mind.
understand, see, know, fathom, sense, grasp, comprehend

See also: understand

ready

adjective

mentally or physically prepared
I am ready to go home.
Our school is ready for any emergency.
equipped, prepared, primed, set

Antonym: unprepared

real *See* **natural, original**

reality *See* **fact, truth**

realize *See* **achieve, effect, get, know, understand**

really

adverb

in fact; actually
We may not look alike, but we really are brothers.

I'm really sure about my decision.
actually, certainly, definitely, indeed, surely, genuinely, truly, in fact

rear *See* **raise, stand**

reason

noun

a cause or explanation for an action, opinion, or event
He had a good reason for being late.
What's the reason for the party?
case *Is there a case for not paying the taxes you owe?*
cause *There is no cause for worry.*
explanation *Jeremy had an explanation for his absence.*
foundation *Your ideas about her are completely without foundation.*
grounds *What are the grounds for your argument?*
motive *His motive for robbing the bank was not clear.*
rationale *Is there a rationale for this law?*

reasonable

adjective

using good sense and clear thinking
The judge made a reasonable decision.
wise, sound, rational, prudent, sage, sensible, logical, thoughtful

Antonyms: irrational, rash, unreasonable, unwise

reasoning *See* **mental**

rebellion

noun

the act of disobeying rules or fighting against authority
The student rebellion took the form of refusing to wear school uniforms.
revolt, uprising, insurgency, insurrection, mutiny

Antonym: obedience

recall *See* **know, memory, remember, think, mind**

A B C D E F G H I J K L M N O P Q R S T U V W X Y Z

receive
verb

1 to get or take
He received many gifts while he was in the hospital.
get, accept, earn, acquire, gain, obtain, reap

2 to welcome or greet
They receive guests often.
We received him as a member of our club.
greet, welcome, accept, accommodate, admit, embrace

3 to experience
She received a serious injury in the accident.
undergo, endure, experience, suffer

recent *See* late, new

recognition *See* praise

recognize *See* acknowledge, honor, know, observe

recognized *See* standard

recommend
verb

1 to speak or write of in a favorable way
She recommends him highly for the job.
advocate *He advocates buying fruits and vegetables grown on local farms.*
back *The governor hopes the president will back him in the next election.*
champion *The senator championed higher pay for teachers.*
endorse *He endorsed her for governor.*
promote *The supermarket is promoting Italian foods this week.*

2 to present as worth doing
I recommend that we not disturb the hornets' nest.
advocate, counsel, propose, suggest, urge
Antonyms: condemn (1), denounce (1), discourage (2), disparage (1)

record
verb

to put in writing

The nurse recorded my height and weight in my health chart.
document, jot, log, note, post, put down
Antonyms: delete, erase

noun

a written account or other collection of information
The historical record shows that Native Americans once owned this land.
A record of our tax payments is kept at city hall.
chronicle, log, history, diary, journal, register, document, statement

recover
verb

1 to get back
She recovered her lost wallet.
reclaim, recoup, regain, retrieve

2 to make up for
Mike recovered lost hours of sleep by taking a nap.
compensate, make up, offset

Compensate and **make up** are followed by **for**: *Joe compensated for not eating breakfast by having a large lunch; Jane made up for being late to school by staying in at recess.*

---

3 to return to a normal or healthy condition
It took two weeks for Tom to recover from surgery.
recuperate, heal, mend, rally, revive, bounce back
Antonyms: lose (1), mislay (1), relapse (3)

recreation *See* play

red *See* hair

reduce
verb

to make less in amount or size
The new roads reduced traffic jams.
Ms. Krabbe reduced the amount of homework she assigns.
decrease, diminish, lessen, lighten, lower, pare

Human Body   Human Mind   Everyday Life   History and Culture   Communication

Antonyms: expand, extend, increase

reduced *See* low

reduction *See* cut, decrease, loss

refer
verb
  1 to pass or hand over for advice or help
  We referred the problem to an expert.
entrust, submit, consign, hand over
  2 to speak of
  She referred to his work in her speech.
mention, cite, reference, allude to

reference
noun
  a source of information
  This dictionary is an excellent reference for writers.
authority, resource, source

reflect ⓘ *See* consider, express, think

reform *See* behavior

refuse
verb
  to not accept or agree to; turn down
  I refused the stranger's offer of a ride.
  The bank refused his request for a loan.
decline, deny, reject, scorn, spurn, veto
  Antonyms: accept, consent to

regard *See* consider, favor, rate, see, stare, watch, way, mind

regardless *See* anyway

region ⓖ *See* area, territory

register
noun
  a book used to record names, events, or other information
  The hotel kept a register of its guests.
log, journal, catalogue, ledger

verb
  1 to write down or enter in a record book or register
  The clerk asked me to register my license number.
book, enter, log, record
  2 to sign up for something by having one's name put on an official list
  Have you registered to vote yet?
  He registered for the draft.
enlist, enroll, sign up
  3 to show on a measuring device or scale
  The butcher piled bacon on the scale until it registered three pounds.
indicate *The scale indicated the hog's weight.*
measure *The temperature measured ten degrees below zero.*
read *The clock reads eight o'clock.*
show *The tape measure showed the sidewalk as three feet wide.*
  See also: show

regular
adjective
  1 normal or usual
  We'll meet at the regular place.
everyday, normal, ordinary, routine, standard, usual, typical
  2 following the same or standard way of doing something
  He is very creative and doesn't do things in the regular way.
conventional, customary, general, normal, regulation, standard, usual
  3 even or steady
  She tapped a regular beat with her foot.
consistent, constant, even, steady, uniform
  Antonyms: atypical (1), unconventional (2), uneven (3)

regulate *See* adjust, control, scale, set

regulations ⊗ ⓞ *See* law

relate *See* describe, piece, repeat, report, say, speak, tell, literature

A
B
C
D
E
F
G
H
I
J
K
L
M
N
O
P
Q
R
S
T
U
V
W
X
Y
Z

a
b
c
d
e
f
g
h
i
j
k
l
m
n
o
p
q
r
s
t
u
v
w
x
y
z

related
adjective

1 having some connection
The two robberies were related.
tied, linked, connected, associated, affiliated

2 connected by family ties
I am related to a famous actor.
akin, kin, kindred

> *Antonyms:* unconnected (1), unrelated (1,2)

relation See **connection, relationship, relative**

relations See **people**

relationship ○
noun

1 the condition or fact of being related or connected
There is a relationship between exercise and good health.
connection, association, correlation, relation

2 a connection between people

> *some words used to describe relationships*
> loving, mutual, romantic, long-term, casual, understanding, hostile, unfriendly

relative
noun

a person who belongs to the same family as someone else
All our relatives, including my mother's aunt Gertrude, are coming to visit.
family member, kin, kinfolk, kindred, relation

> **Kin, kinfolk,** and **kindred** refer to relatives as a group: *All our kin gathered for a reunion last summer.*

relatives See **people**

relax
verb

1 to make looser or less stiff
Relax your leg so the doctor can test your reflexes.
ease, loosen, release, slack

2 to become less tense or more at ease
She relaxed by the lake after class.
unwind, rest, calm down, loosen up

> *Antonyms:*
> stiffen (1,2),
> tense (1),
> tense up (2),
> tighten (1)

relaxed See **easy**

> **Rest** is not quitting
> The busy career,
> Rest is the fitting
> Of self to one's sphere.
> —*From "REST," a poem by John Sullivan Dwight (1813-1893)*

release
verb

1 to set free
We released the tadpoles into the pond.
The court released the prisoner.
emancipate, free, liberate, loose, discharge

2 to let go of or loosen
He released the handle.
detach, drop, loosen, undo

> *Antonyms:* cage (1), capture (2), enslave (1), trap (2)

reliable
adjective

capable of being trusted or relied on
Her boss knows that she is an honest and reliable employee.
dependable, faithful, steadfast, steady, sure

> *Antonym:* unreliable

relief
noun

1 help given to those in need
Relief was promised to the victims of the flood.
aid, assistance, comfort, help, succor

2 a person or persons taking over the work of others for a time
After several hours of work, our relief finally arrived.
alternate, replacement, substitute, stand-in

 Human Body   Human Mind   Everyday Life   History and Culture   Communication

religion 🔵 ⚫
noun

a set of beliefs about the origin and purpose of the universe and that usually involves worship of a god or gods

creed, faith, theology, persuasion, church

> *some words associated with religion*
> anoint, atone, believe, bless, celebrate, confess, fast, meditate, ordain, practice, praise, pray, preach, profess, sanctify, worship
>
> *some words used to describe religions*
> divine, holy, moral, ethical, orthodox, sacred, spiritual, supreme
>
> *feeling religious*
> devout, holy, moral, pious, spiritual

religious
adjective

having to do with religion
The cross is a religious symbol.
holy, pious, sacred, spiritual

Antonyms: secular, worldly

rely *See* depend

remain *See* keep, last, live, stand, stay

remaining *See* other

remains *See* rest, wreck

remarkable *See* great, particular, special, unusual

remember 🔵
verb

to bring back into the mind from memory
I could not remember his name.
recall *Do you recall the day we went to the zoo together?*
recollect *I can't recollect when I last saw him.*
reminisce *We reminisced about our vacation in Tahiti.*
remind *Jill reminded herself that she had to fetch water from the well.*

Antonym: forget

remind *See* prompt, remember

remote
adjective

1 at a far distance in space or time
The moon is remote from the earth.
In the remote past, dinosaurs walked the earth.
distant, far, faraway, removed

2 far from towns or human settlement
The lake is in a remote area.
desolate, isolated, lonely, secluded

3 small in degree
He has a remote chance of surviving the accident.
slight, faint, meager, negligible, slim

Antonyms: close (1), great (3), near (1)

remove *See* draw, move, pick, take

removed *See* remote

rent *See* hire

repair
verb

1 to put in good condition again after damage has been done
I took my broken bicycle to the shop to be repaired.
fix, mend, patch up, restore

2 to make right; correct
I will repair these mistakes.
correct *She needs glasses to correct her eyesight.*
cure *She cured the oversight by inviting her aunt to the wedding.*
fix *Do you think you can fix my bike chain?*
mend *Mend your ways or you will be in trouble.*
remedy *Whenever she makes a mistake, she tries to remedy it.*
straighten out *The manager promised to straighten out the bill.*

Antonyms: break (1), ruin (2)

A B C D E F G H I J K L M N O P Q R S T U V W X Y Z

a
b
c
d
e
f
g
h
i
j
k
l
m
n
o
p
q
r
s
t
u
v
w
x
y
z

repeat
verb

1 to do, say, or make again
I repeated a joke that I heard from my sister.
Bobo had to repeat second grade.
echo, redo, duplicate, reiterate,

2 to tell to another
You must promise never to repeat this secret.
tell, relate, divulge, reveal

replace
verb

1 to take the place of
A new girl replaced the lead singer in the band.
The CD has replaced the phonograph record.
supplant, displace, substitute, fill in for

2 to put back in the same place as before
I replaced the mower in the shed after I finished mowing the lawn.
put back, restore, return

reply   *See* answer

report
noun

1 a statement or account of something
Lulu read the report on tropical tree frogs.
paper, study, account, statement

2 a loud noise made by a gun or explosive device
I was startled by the gun's loud report.
verb

to tell publicly
I reported the good news to my friends.
tell, state, relate, disclose, reveal

reporter   *See* writer

represent
verb

to stand for or be a sign of
A skull and crossbones represents danger.
mean, indicate, designate, denote, signify, symbolize, stand for

representative ◯ *See* example, typical

reproduce
verb

1 to make a copy of
The furniture maker reproduced an antique chair.
copy, duplicate, imitate, mirror, replicate, simulate

2 to make or produce again
Can you reproduce that sound you just made?
duplicate, re-create, replicate

3 to have young or offspring
Many animals reproduce once a year.
bear, breed, increase, multiply, procreate, spawn

reproduction ◯ ◯ *See* copy

republic ◯ *See* government

request   *See* appeal, ask, beg

require   *See* claim, demand, make, need, take

required   *See* necessary

rescue   *See* save

research ◯
noun

careful study of something
Scientists are doing research on the effects of pollution.
analysis, examination, inquiry, investigation, study
verb

to do research into
I researched the U.S. Civil War for my history class.
study, analyze, investigate, probe

resemblance
noun

the condition of being or looking alike
The twins have a strong resemblance to each other.
likeness, similarity, sameness, conformity

 Human Body   ? Human Mind   Everyday Life   History and Culture   Communication

Antonyms: contrast, difference

reserve *See* **hire, hold, save, store**

reserved *See* **private, shy, personality**

resist
verb
  1 to fight against or oppose
  The workers are resisting the new rules.
  defy, oppose, fight, combat, strive against
  2 to keep away or not be affected by
  The raincoat is made out of fabric that resists water.
  The milk is treated with chemicals to resist spoiling.
  fend off, repel, withstand, ward off, stave off
    Antonyms: attract (2), encourage (2), support (1)

resistance
noun
  1 the act or process of resisting
  The proposal to tear down the library was met with resistance.
  defiance, opposition, protest
  2 the opposing power of one force against another
  Vitamins help your body build resistance to disease.
  strength, resilience, immunity, durability, hardiness
    Antonyms: consent (1), support (1), weakness (2)

resource *See* **reference**

resources *See* **ability**

respect ❓ *See* **favor, honor, observe, way**

respected ❓ *See* **special**

respond ❓ *See* **answer**

response *See* **answer**

responsibility
noun
  something for which a person is responsible
  The puppy is your responsibility.
  duty, charge, job, obligation, burden, onus

responsible
adjective
  1 expected to take care of particular duties
  He is responsible for keeping track of our money.
  bound, charged, liable, accountable, obligated
  2 able to make the right decisions
  She is very responsible and can be trusted.
  conscientious, prudent, sensible, mature
    Antonyms: irresponsible (2), untrustworthy (2)

rest
noun
  a piece or part that is left
  Do you want the rest of the cake?
  remainder, remains, scraps, remnant, leftover, residue

restrict
verb
  to keep within limits
  They restricted their dog to the yard.
  Can we restrict our discussion to one topic?
  confine, contain, restrain, limit, control, hem in
    Antonyms: free, liberate

restriction
noun
  something that limits or restricts
  There are restrictions on making campfires in the park.
  limit, check, regulation, constraint, limitation, control

result
noun

something that happens because of something else
We were surprised by the results of the contest.
conclusion *The conclusion of the book was a surprise.*
outcome *I'm pleased with the outcome of your work.*
consequence *Her stomach ache was a consequence of eating too much.*
effect *The effect of the blizzard was a day off from school.*

Antonym: cause

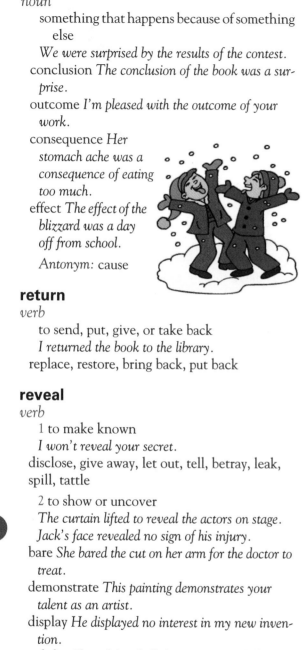

return
verb

to send, put, give, or take back
I returned the book to the library.
replace, restore, bring back, put back

reveal
verb

1 to make known
I won't reveal your secret.
disclose, give away, let out, tell, betray, leak, spill, tattle

2 to show or uncover
The curtain lifted to reveal the actors on stage.
Jack's face revealed no sign of his injury.
bare *She bared the cut on her arm for the doctor to treat.*
demonstrate *This painting demonstrates your talent as an artist.*
display *He displayed no interest in my new invention.*
exhibit *She exhibited all the symptoms of plague.*
expose *The newspaper exposed the criminals in city hall.*
show *His yawn showed that he was tired.*
uncover *The student uncovered a plot to steal the test questions.*

Antonyms: conceal (1), cover (2), hide (2),
secret (1)
See also: display, show

revenge
noun

harm or punishment desired or done as payment for something
Lulu locked me out of the house as revenge for eating her candy.
reprisal, repayment, retribution, retaliation, vengeance

review ➋ See discuss, study

revolt
noun

the act of rising up against the government or other authority
The army put an end to the revolt.
revolution, rebellion, mutiny, uprising

A **mutiny** is usually a **revolt** against the captain of a naval ship, but it may also be used when describing a revolt by a group against its leader: *The mutiny of the players against the cruel coach led to the formation of a new team.*

---

verb

to cause to feel disgust or shock
Horror movies revolt me.
appall, disgust, horrify, repel, shock, sicken
See also: disgust

revolution See revolt

revolutionary See progressive, technology

reward
verb

to give something to as a reward
Mom rewarded us for our good grades by letting us stay up late.
repay, compensate, honor

Antonyms: fine, penalize
See also: prize

 Human Body   ? Human Mind   Everyday Life   History and Culture   Communication

rice *See* **grain**

rich 🌐
adjective
> having a great amount of money or valuable
> property
> *He is rich enough to own three houses.*
affluent, prosperous, wealthy, well-off, flush
> *Antonyms:* poor, broke, destitute, penniless

riches *See* **success**

ride ○ *See* **depend, drive, trip**

ridge *See* **fold, wrinkle, mountain**

right
adjective
> 1 in keeping with what is fair and good
> *Telling the truth was the right thing to do.*
good, fair, honest, upright, proper, virtuous,
righteous
> 2 in keeping with fact
> *All your answers were right.*
correct, true, sound, accurate, valid, logical
> 3 appropriate
> *Is Fluffy the right name for such a mean cat?*
proper, appropriate, suitable, fitting, ideal
noun
> 1 something due to a person by nature or law.
> *Free speech is a right enjoyed by Americans.*
freedom, privilege, birthright, entitlement
> *See also:* accurate, adjust, honest, normal,
> proper

rigid *See* **firm, hard, narrow, set, steady, stiff**

rim *See* **circle, edge**

ring ○ *See* **band, circle,
jingle, surround, jewelry**

rise
verb
> to move upward
> *The hot-air balloons rose
> above the trees.*

arise *Steam arose from the boiling water.*
ascend *The climbers ascended the cliff.*
climb *The airplane climbed sharply after it took
off.*
lift *The fog lifted.*
mount *Smoke from the forest fire mounted in the
sky.*
surface *The submarine surfaced from the ocean
floor.*
> *Antonyms:* descend, fall, sink
noun
> an area of ground that slopes upward
> *I'll meet you at the top of the rise.*
slope, incline, ascent, hill

risk *See* **adventure, chance, danger**

river 🌐
noun
> a large natural stream of water flowing in a
> particular course toward a lake, ocean, or
> other body of water

> *some parts of rivers*
> curve, eddy, estuary, everglade, ford, fork,
> headwaters, mouth, pool, rapid, shoal,
> waterfall, whirlpool
> *some terms for land associated with rivers*
> bank, basin, divide, sandbar, shore,
> watershed

road ○ *See* **street, way**

roar
verb
> to make a deep, loud cry as in anger, or excite-
> ment
> *The angry crowd roared at the referee.*
bellow, growl, yowl, holler, howl, shout, yell,
explode
noun
> a loud, steady noise
> *The roar of the machines could be heard outside
> the building.*
boom, clamor, rumble, din, blare, thunder, roll
> *See also:* noise, laugh

A B C D E F G H I J K L M N O P Q R S T U V W X Y Z

a
b
c
d
e
f
g
h
i
j
k
l
m
n
o
p
q
r
s
t
u
v
w
x
y
z

rob *See* **steal**

rock¹
noun
a piece of solid mineral matter as found in the earth's outer layer
We cleared the soil of rocks before planting a garden.
boulder, pebble, stone

A **stone** is a **rock** of any size. A **boulder** is a rock of great size, too large and heavy to be lifted by a person. A **pebble** is a rock of very small size.

rock²
verb
to move strongly back and forth
The ship rocked in the storm.
lurch, pitch, quake, roll, shake, sway, wobble

rodent
noun
a small mammal with long front teeth used for gnawing.

some examples of rodents
beaver, chinchilla, chipmunk, dormouse, gerbil, gopher, groundhog, guinea pig, hamster, hedgehog, lemming, mouse, muskrat, nutria, porcupine, prairie dog, rat, squirrel, vole, woodchuck
some behaviors of rodents
build, burrow, chew, collect, dig, gnaw, hibernate, scamper, scurry, store, swim

role *See* **place**

roll
verb
to move by turning over and over
Jill and Jack rolled down the hill.
turn, rotate, spin, twirl, whirl, tumble
The dancers twirled around the floor.

noun
a cylinder around which certain material is wound; roller
Please hand me the roll of tape.
bobbin, reel, roller, spool

romantic
adjective
1 daring and heroic
He loved to read the romantic tales of knights and dragons.
adventurous, bold, daring, gallant, heroic

2 expressing strong emotions but little thought
She wrote a romantic letter to her boyfriend.
sentimental, mushy, sappy, gushy

roof *See* **home**

room
noun
1 space that is used or available for use
There is room for dancing in the gym.
place, space, area

2 an area of a building separated from similar areas by walls or doors
Our house has ten rooms.
chamber *The mysterious man never left his tiny chamber.*
compartment *Passengers may not enter the baggage compartment on an airplane.*
cubicle *She works in a cubicle in a large office.*
ward *There are beds for ten patients on this hospital ward.*

root
noun
1 the origin or cause of something
The root of his problem is that he does not believe in himself.
bottom, core, heart, origin, seed, source, essence, substance

2 family or ethnic background
I traveled to Vietnam to learn more about my roots.
background, culture, heritage, origins

 Human Body   Human Mind   Everyday Life   History and Culture   Communication

verb
> to grow a new root or roots
> *These plants will root if placed in water.*
> germinate, sprout

roots ● *See* **country**

rope
noun
> a strong cord of twisted or woven fiber
> line, cable, band
> *See also:* tie

rope *See* **mark**

rough
adjective
> having an uneven surface
> *Our car shook as we drove over the rough road.*
> ragged, jagged, rugged, bumpy, coarse, uneven,
> irregular
> *Antonyms:* even, flat, smooth

round
adjective
> having a curved surface or outline
> *You can't put a square peg in a round hole.*
> curved, rounded, circular
> *Antonyms:* angular, straight

rounded *See* **round**

route *See* **beat, direction, way**

routine *See* **ordinary, practice, process,**
regular, standard, usual

row *See* **fight, line, boat**

rub *See* **shine**

rugged *See* **harsh, muscular, rough, solid,**
sturdy, face

ruin *See* **break, damage, decay, defeat,**
destroy, destruction, doom, spoil, wreck

ruined *See* **lost**

ruins *See* **wreck**

rule ○ ●
noun
> a law or direction
> *Baseball has many rules of play.*
> code *The dress code at school does not allow us to*
> *wear shorts or jeans.*
> law *According to the law, you must be eighteen*
> *years of age to vote.*
> regulation *City regulations require buildings to*
> *have fire escapes.*
> dictate *I followed the dictates of my heart and mar-*
> *ried Leslie instead of Laura.*
> requirement *Gym class is a requirement at many*
> *schools.*

A **code** is a set of **rules** or laws, not just one
rule or one law. For example, a school dress
code might have four rules: no shorts, no
torn jeans, no skirts above the knee, and no
long earrings.

---

verb
> to have authority over
> *The queen rules the country.*
> govern, head, lead, command, control
> *See also:* lead, law

ruler ○ *See* **power**

rules ○ ● *See* **law**

ruling ○ ● *See* **judgment**

run ○
verb
> 1 to propel oneself forward by moving the legs
>   very quickly
> *She ran for miles across the open fields.*
> race, sprint, dash, course, lope
>
> 2 to move quickly; make a fast trip
> *Run over to the barn and get my toolbox.*
> hurry, rush, hasten, fly, pop, hustle
>
> 3 to escape by moving away quickly
> *If you don't keep the dog on a leash he will run*
>   *away.*

escape, flee, bolt, split

Use **bolt** and **split** in informal, everyday speaking and writing. Use **escape** or **flee** in formal reports and presentations.

See also: work

rural *See* community

rush
verb
1 to act or go quickly; hurry
We rushed to catch the bus.
dash *He dashed across the street before the light changed.*
fly *She flew from the room when she heard her mother calling.*
hasten *She hastened to catch the bus.*
hurry *If we don't hurry up we'll miss the train.*
hustle *They hustled to finish the assignment on time.*
race *I raced to school to get there before the last bell.*
scurry *Mice scurried about in the walls.*
speed *She sped across the street.*
tear *He tore around the house looking for his keys.*

2 to cause to hurry or act too quickly
Don't rush me; I'm coming.
hasten, hurry, hustle, press, speed

Antonyms: delay (2), hinder (2), lag (1), mosey (1), slow (2)

noun
1 a quick and sudden forward movement
There was a rush of water over the falls.

> Take time for all things. Great **haste** makes great waste.
> —Benjamin Franklin (1706-1790), American author

surge, wave, stampede, scramble, torrent
2 a state of hurry
I'm in a rush, so don't bother me.
haste, hurry, scramble
3 a quick movement by many people to a place
There was a rush to the doors when the movie ended.
surge, wave, stampede, scramble

 Human Body
Human Mind
 Everyday Life
History and Culture
Communication

sack *See* **fire, load**

sacred ○ *See* **holy, religious, religion**

sad
adjective
> unhappy or without joy
> *Steve was feeling so sad when his dog died.*

> *feeling sad*
> black, bleak, blue, dark, depressed, dismal, down, downcast, dreary, gloomy, glum, heartbroken, heavy, lonely, lonesome, low, miserable, somber, sorry, sullen, unhappy

> *Antonyms:* glad, happy, joyful
> *See also:* unhappy

saddle *See* **burden**

sadness ○
noun
> the state or quality of being unhappy
> *I felt terrible sadness over my parents' divorce.*
> sorrow, unhappiness, depression, gloom, melancholy, blues, woe, grief

> *some things people do out of sadness*
> bawl, blubber, complain, cry, grieve, groan, howl, mope, mourn, pout, sigh, sniffle, sob, wail, weep, whimper, yowl

> *Antonyms:* glee, happiness, joy, mirth
> *See also:* sorrow

safe
adjective
> 1 not in danger; free from harm
> *We were safe at home when the storm hit.*
> protected, secure, all right, sheltered

> 2 careful
> *Nico is a safe driver.*
> careful, cautious, prudent, unadventurous, wary, conservative

> *Antonyms:* careless (2), dangerous (1,2), reckless (2)
> *See also:* careful, cautious

safety *See* **protection**

sag
verb
> to sink, hang, or bend in the middle
> *The shelf sagged from the weight of the TV.*
> bend, bow, dip, droop, sink, slump, wilt

> *Antonym:* rise

sail ○
verb
> to travel on a sailboat
> *We will sail down the coast this summer.*
> boat, cruise, yacht
> *See also:* boat

sake *See* **good**

sale *See* **special**

salt ○ ● *See* **season**

same *See* **alike**

sample *See* **example, taste, try**

satellite ● ● *See* **photography**

satisfaction *See* **pleasure, pride, emotion**

satisfactory
adjective
> good enough to meet a need or desire

satisfy – saying

My grade in English is *satisfactory, but I had hoped to do better.*

acceptable, adequate, all right, enough, OK, sufficient, suitable

Antonyms: inadequate, insufficient, unacceptable, unsatisfactory, unsuitable

satisfy
verb

to give what is wanted or needed
The small snack didn't satisfy her.

content *The hungry child was contented with an apple.*

fulfill *He has fulfilled the physical education requirement.*

appease *He appeased his sweet tooth with a piece of cake.*

gratify *The actor was gratified by the applause.*

please *His thoughtful answers pleased the teacher.*

Antonyms: deprive, frustrate
See also: please

savage
adjective

1 fierce or cruel
The wolf rushed at the man in a savage attack.
The critic wrote a savage review of the new play.

brutal, cruel, ferocious, hostile, vicious, fierce, violent, harsh, malicious, ruthless

2 not tamed
Savage beasts live in the jungle.

wild, untamed, undomesticated

3 not civilized
Those children who live next door are savage, always running around naked, dirty, and out of control!

barbarian, wild, crude, vulgar, uncultivated, primitive

Antonyms: civilized (3), cultured (3), domesticated (2), gentle (1), tame (2)

noun

a cruel or vicious person

animal, monster, barbarian, ogre, maniac

Antonyms: angel, benefactor
See also: cruel, fierce, monster

save ◆
verb

1 to rescue from harm or danger
The lifeguard saved the girl who fell out of the boat.

rescue *Firefighters rescued the family from their burning house.*

help *We helped the accident victim by calling 911.*

deliver *Sir Gallante delivered the maiden from the dragon's lair.*

salvage *We managed to salvage only a few belongings from the flood.*

Use **salvage** when referring to things, not people.

2 to keep or store for future use
Jerome saved the rims from his car before he took it to the junkyard.
They are saving money for college.

keep, store, preserve, reserve, put aside, salvage

Antonyms: discard (2), junk (2), trash (2)
See also: store

saw *See* **cut, saying**

say
verb

1 to speak in words
Did you say something just now?

speak, utter, voice, articulate, pronounce

2 to express in speech or written words
I said how glad I was to see them.
In my letter, I said what was bothering me.

express, speak, tell, communicate, relate, convey, state

3 to report
Everyone says that the story is true.

declare, maintain, relate, report, allege, assert, claim

See also: speak, state, report, pronounce

saying
noun

a familiar statement that often contains advice or wisdom

a b c d e f g h i j k l m n o p q r s t u v w x y z

Human Body   Human Mind   Everyday Life   History and Culture   Communication

"Don't cry over spilled milk" is a saying.
expression, proverb, adage, byword, saw, cliché

The words saw and cliché refer to old sayings that have been repeated so often they have lost their impact.

scale
noun
degree, extent, or level
The movie director does things on a large scale.
degree, grade, order

verb
to change or adjust
Phil scaled down his hopes of what was possible.
adjust, adapt, regulate
See also: climb

scan   *See* **examine, leaf, read**

scarce   *See* **low**

scarcely   *See* **just**

scare
verb
to frighten
Your screaming scared me.
frighten, spook, startle, alarm, terrify
Antonyms: calm, quiet, reassure, settle, soothe, still
See also: frighten

scared   *See* **afraid, nervous**

scatter
verb
1 to toss here and there
The farmer scattered grain for the chickens.
spread, sprinkle, shower, strew, disperse, broadcast, distribute

2 to separate and move quickly apart
The crowd scattered at the sound of thunder.
flee, disband, dispel, disperse
Antonyms: assemble (2), collect (2), gather (1,2), pile up (1), reap (1)

scene   *See* **place, view**

scent
noun
a smell
Roses have a lovely scent.
aroma, fragrance, odor, perfume, smell, stink, stench, reek

Aroma, fragrance, and perfume are used only of pleasant scents, while stink, stench, and reek are used only of unpleasant scents.

See also: smell

schedule   *See* **program**

school
noun
a place for teaching and learning

some kinds of schools
academy, boarding school, college, elementary school, grade school, grammar school, high school, institute, institution, junior high school, kindergarten, middle school, nursery school, primary school, private school, public school, seminary, trade school, university, vocational school

See also: teach

science
noun
a system of studying, testing, and experimenting to search for knowledge about the world

some examples of the sciences
anatomy, archaeology, astronomy, biology, botany, chemistry, ecology, genetics, geography, geology, medicine, meteorology, paleontology, physics, psychology, physiology, zoology

scold
verb
to speak in a sharp or angry way

Mom scolded me for being mean to my brother.
berate, chide, reprimand, lecture, bawl out, chew out, take to task, tell off

Antonym: praise

score ○ ◑ *See* **arrange, cut, grade, mark, music, sport**

scorn
noun
a feeling of hatred for someone or something thought of as worthless or evil
She looks upon liars with scorn.
contempt, derision, disdain

verb
to treat as hateful or not proper
They scorned the idea of dressing in silly costumes.
ridicule, deride, mock, sneer at, scoff at

The other kids mocked him when he fell down.

See also: mock

scramble
verb
to mix or throw together in a quick or random way
She scrambled the pieces of the puzzle.
confuse, jumble, mix, muddle, tangle

Antonyms: organize, sort, unscramble
See also: confuse, mix

scrap
noun
a small bit, such as a piece left over or thrown away
I picked up a scrap of paper.
They tossed scraps of bread to the ducks.
bit, crumb, fragment, shred

verb
to throw away because useless or without value

He scrapped his old computer.
chuck, discard, jettison, junk, throw away

Antonyms: reclaim, salvage
See also: bit, junk

scrape
noun
an injury or damage caused by rubbing
She has a scrape on her elbow.
abrasion, graze, scratch, scuff

See also: scratch

scratch
verb
to scrape or damage with something sharp
I scratched the side of my car while I was trying to park.
cut, mark, nick, rasp, scuff, scrape, gouge

noun
damage or injury caused by something sharp
The scratch on his arm started to bleed.
graze, nick, scrape, cut, mark, scuff

See also: cut

scream ⑦
verb
1 to make a shrill, loud cry or sound
The girl screamed in terror.
howl, screech, shriek, squeal
The parrots shrieked at us from the trees.
2 to speak in a lound, harsh, or angry tone
Ms. Pickett screamed at her employee.
holler, screech, shout, shriek, squawk, yell

noun
a shrill, loud cry or sound
I let out a scream when I saw the lion.
holler, screech, shout, shriek, squeal, yell

See also: shout

🏃 Human Body   ❓ Human Mind   👕 Everyday Life   🚩 History and Culture   📞 Communication

screen

noun

anything that shields, hides, or protects
The tall hedge acted as a screen around the yard.
cover, curtain, mask, protection, shield

verb

to hide from view
The trees screened us from his view.
conceal, hide, mask, shield, veil, cloak

See also: cover, mask

sea

noun

1 the salt water covering most of Earth
The schooner sailed the stormy sea.
ocean, waves, deep, main

> *some words that mean "having to do with the sea"*
> marine, maritime, nautical, oceanic

2 a vast area or a great number
The field was a sea of wheat.
A sea of people gathered at the stadium.
expanse, mass, multitude

See also: ocean

seal

noun

a stamped design that shows a document is authentic
The letter carried the seal of the president.
emblem, insignia, stamp

verb

to close using a seal
Seal the box with tape.
close, fasten, secure

Antonym: open
See also: close

search

verb

to look through in order to find
I searched my room for the missing book.

comb, drag, examine, hunt, rummage, scour

Use drag when searching for something lying on the bottom of a body of water: *The police dragged the river for the missing person.*

noun

an act of
searching
*The pirates went
on a search
for hidden
treasure.*
hunt, look,
pursuit, quest

See also: look

season

noun

a certain part of the year that is marked by a
particular condition or activity
*Our family will get together for the holiday
season.*
period, span, stretch, term, time

verb

to improve the flavor of by adding salt, herbs,
spices, or other flavorings
*The cook seasoned the dish with garlic and
pepper.*
flavor, accent, salt, pepper, spice

See also: flavor

seat ○ See bottom, clothes

second See bit, flash, instant, moment, spell

secondary

adjective

less important
*For my sister, playing the piano is secondary to
playing the violin.*
*The secondary roads were not plowed after the
snowstorm.*
lesser, lower, minor, subordinate

Antonyms: major, primary

 Living World Physical World ⊙ Natural Environment ⋀⋁⋀ Economy ▢ Government and Law 223

a
b
c
d
e
f
g
h
i
j
k
l
m
n
o
p
q
r
s
t
u
v
w
x
y
z

secret
adjective

1 kept from being seen or known by others
The spy went on a secret mission to Alaska.
hidden, confidential, private, covert,
clandestine

2 known only to those involved
We voted to let David into our secret club.
confidential *The information in this letter is confidential.*
inside *He has inside information about the crime.*
intimate *The magazine revealed intimate details of the actor's life.*
private *They held a private meeting to discuss how the money should be spent.*

Antonyms: open (2), public (2)

section
noun

a part separated from the whole
I like living in this section of town.
I found that book in the mystery section.
division *We each received a division of the money.*
district *The store is located in the commercial district.*
part *Joe assembled all the parts of his model.*
fraction *Do you understand even a fraction of what the teacher said?*
fragment *Kiki remembered only fragments of the poem.*
length *Please cut me a two-foot length of rope.*
portion *He read a portion of the book.*
segment *She divided the orange into segments.*
piece *Only three pieces of pie were sold at the bake sale.*

Antonyms: entirety, total, whole
See also: part, piece

secure See **confident, fasten, fix, gain, get, lock, pin, protect, safe, seal, steady, sure, tight, fear**

security *See* **defense, guard, protection**

see
verb

1 to look at
Let's go and see the animals at the zoo.
eye *She eyed him with suspicion.*
notice *I noticed a black cat slinking across the lawn.*
observe *We went to the pond to observe the rare ducks*
sight *After six weeks at sea, the bosun sighted land.*
look at *Let's go look at the stars.*
view *I haven't had a chance to view the new koala video.*
behold *The princess beheld the prancing unicorn with awe.*
witness *Cal called the police after he witnessed the accident.*
gaze at *Ms. Hart gazed lovingly at her newborn baby.*
glimpse *Jack glimpsed Jill through the crowded room.*
regard *I regarded my rival with contempt.*
spot *We spotted out friends near the mall entrance.*
stare at *It's impolite to stare at people.*
watch *I watched two birds build a nest outside my window.*

2 to know the meaning of
I don't see the point of this assignment.
Do you see what I mean?
apprehend, catch, comprehend, fathom, get, grasp, perceive, understand

3 to visit for a specific reason
I must see my lawyer.

224

 Human Body   ? Human Mind   Everyday Life   History and Culture    Communication

call on, visit, confer with, consult, meet with

   4 to learn the cause of
   Would you please see what the trouble is?

discover, find out, determine, ascertain

   See also: watch, understand, visit

seed ❶ *See* **root, source, fruit, grass**

seeing *See* **sight**

seek
verb
   1 to try to find
   I am seeking a pair of shoes for my costume.
look for *She looked for the lost keys.*
search for *I searched everywhere in my room for the book.*
hunt for *He hunted for the lost gloves.*

   2 to try
   Juan sought to find the answer.
attempt *He attempted to balance a ball on his nose.*
try *She tried fixing the car herself to save money.*
strive *My brother strives to be a better piano player.*
endeavor *We should endeavor to finish painting the house before dark.*

seem *See* **appear, look**

select *See* **choose, favorite, pick**

selection *See* **choice, pick**

sell
verb
   1 to exchange with another for money
   Robert sold his baseball cards.
exchange, trade

   2 to offer for sale
   Which store sells balloons?
carry *Monster Mart carries party supplies.*
offer *Burger Mart is offering two for the price of one.*
market *That company markets camping goods on line.*
vend *This machine vends sandwiches.*

auction *They auctioned off their furniture before they moved to South Africa.*
traffic *The gangsters trafficked in stolen cars.*
hawk *The artist hawked his paintings on the sidewalks of New York.*
peddle *She peddles steaks from the back of her pick-up truck.*

Peddle means to sell by traveling from place to place. **Hawk** means to sell by crying out or traveling from place to place.

   3 to have a particular price
   That T-shirt sells for twelve dollars.
cost, retail, go for

   Antonym: buy (1)
   See also: deal

senate *See* **assembly**

send
verb
   1 to cause to be carried to another place
   I will send you a letter.
   He sent her flowers.
dispatch *He was dispatched to the gym to get a soccer ball.*
transmit *Please transmit this message to the commander.*
mail *She mailed a birthday card to her cousin.*
convey *I hope I have managed to convey my gratitude.*
relay *Dave relayed my message to Mr. Meanie.*

   2 to direct or cause to move to a certain place or point
   He sent the ball over the fence.
direct *He directed the beam of light at the back of the closet.*
propel *The paddle propelled the canoe through the water.*
launch *A rocket launched the shuttle into orbit.*

sense ⊕ *See* **feel, get, knowledge, perception, purpose, read, take, mind**

sensitive *See* **delicate, irritable, injury**

sentence ⊘ ⊙
noun
a punishment for a particular crime decided in a court of law
He received a sentence of thirty days in jail for stealing a purse.
conviction, judgment, punishment, rap
verb
to pass a sentence on
The judge sentenced him to thirty days in jail.
condemn, convict, judge
See also: judgment, punishment

separate *See* **alone, branch, different, divide, independent, part, single, split**

separation *See* **distance, split**

sequence *See* **order, series, train**

series
noun
a group of related things that come one after another
She read a series of articles in the newspaper.
He had a series of back injuries.
chain, sequence, string, succession, battery

serious ⊙
adjective
1 not smiling or laughing
The policeman had a serious look on his face.
grave, earnest, sober, solemn
2 needing careful thought
Air pollution is a serious matter.
grave, heavy, important, crucial, vital
3 requiring attention right away
He has a serious heart problem.
A serious storm is heading toward Buffalo.
acute, severe, critical, grave, dangerous, hazardous, menacing, bad
Antonyms: insignificant (2,3), minor (3),

trivial (2), unimportant (2)

serve
verb
1 to have a particular use
This table serves as a desk.
function, act, work
2 to provide with something
The diner serves breakfast and lunch.
furnish, provide, supply, present, give
See also: provide

service ⊛ ⊙
noun
1 the act or an instance of helping
He provides many services as a nurse.
aid, assistance, help
2 any work done for another
We offered our services to the neighborhood clean-up team.
labor, work, assistance
3 the armed forces
He was in the service after high school.
armed forces, military
verb
to repair and to keep in working order
My father was able to service our washing machine.
fix, repair, restore
Antonym: break
See also: aid, help, fix, army

services ⊛ ⊙ *See* **economy**

set
verb
1 to put in a particular position or location
Rebecca set the glass on the table.
lay, place, put, position
2 to arrange so as to make ready for use
Please set the table for lunch.
arrange, lay, prepare, spread, furnish
3 to position for proper operation
Francis set the hands on the clock.
adjust, align, regulate, fix
Antonym: remove (1)

  Human Body   Human Mind   Everyday Life   History and Culture   Communication

noun

a group of related objects that are used together
I bought a new set of tools.
kit, suite, battery, collection
They performed a suite of lovely dances.

adjective

not willing to change
She is set in her ideas.
firm, iron, rigid, steadfast, inflexible, obstinate, stubborn

Antonyms: flexible, open
See also: place, arrange, adjust

setting See environment, place, literature

settle
verb

1 to finally agree upon or decide
We settled our argument.
conclude, decide, determine, resolve, square

2 to come to a decision
We settled on the green car instead of the red one.
agree, decide, resolve

3 to make calm
The music settled the crying baby.
calm, quiet, soothe, steady, pacify, relax

Antonyms: disturb (3), unsettle (3), upset (3)
See also: decide, agree, calm

settlement See agreement, deal, decision

severe
adjective

1 very strict
The prison had severe rules.
harsh, stern, strict, hard

2 very strong or intense
A broken bone can cause severe pain.
The news reporter warned us of severe weather.
acute, fierce, harsh, intense, violent, terrible, extreme

Our teacher was having acute pains in his head.
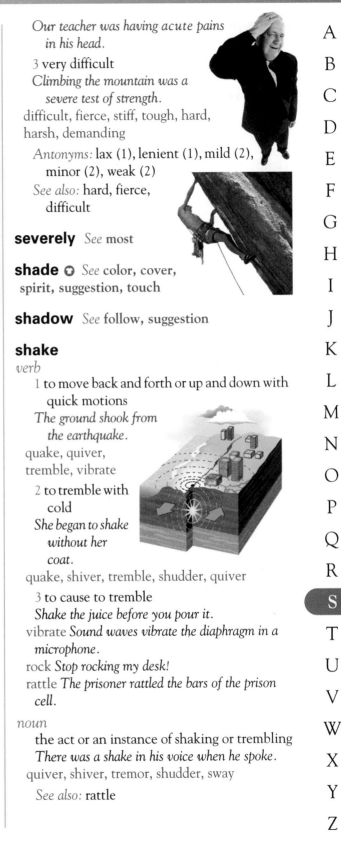

3 very difficult
Climbing the mountain was a severe test of strength.
difficult, fierce, stiff, tough, hard, harsh, demanding

Antonyms: lax (1), lenient (1), mild (2), minor (2), weak (2)
See also: hard, fierce, difficult

severely See most

shade See color, cover, spirit, suggestion, touch

shadow See follow, suggestion

shake
verb

1 to move back and forth or up and down with quick motions
The ground shook from the earthquake.
quake, quiver, tremble, vibrate

2 to tremble with cold
She began to shake without her coat.
quake, shiver, tremble, shudder, quiver

3 to cause to tremble
Shake the juice before you pour it.
vibrate *Sound waves vibrate the diaphragm in a microphone.*
rock *Stop rocking my desk!*
rattle *The prisoner rattled the bars of the prison cell.*

noun

the act or an instance of shaking or trembling
There was a shake in his voice when he spoke.
quiver, shiver, tremor, shudder, sway

See also: rattle

a
b
c
d
e
f
g
h
i
j
k
l
m
n
o
p
q
r
s
t
u
v
w
x
y
z

shallow
adjective

without deep thought or feeling
I can only have shallow conversations with Peter.
light, idle, empty, superficial, frivolous

Antonyms: deep, profound
See also: light, empty

shame
noun

a painful feeling caused by knowing that one
has done something wrong
She felt shame after failing the test.
guilt, remorse, regret

Antonym: pride
verb

to make someone feel ashamed
She shamed her family by lying.
disgrace, embarrass, humiliate

Antonyms: exalt, honor
See also: guilt, embarrass

shape ⚫
noun

1 the appearance of an object as defined by its
outer surface or outline
This car has a beautiful shape.
contour, figure, form, outline

> *some shapes*
> circle, cone, cube, decagon, hexagon,
> octagon, oval, pentagon, pyramid,
> quadrilateral, rectangle, rhombus, sphere,
> square, trapezoid, triangle
> *some parts of shapes*
> angle, edge, face, side
> *some measurements of shapes*
> area, circumference, depth, diameter,
> height, length, perimeter, radius,
> thickness, volume, width
> *some descriptions of shapes*
> circular, congruent, cubic, geometric,
> irregular, oblong, oval, regular, round,
> similar, square

2 physical condition
The professional athlete is in top shape.

condition, form,
trim
verb

to give a certain
form or shape
to
*We shaped the
clay into a pot.*
fashion, model,
mold, form, mold

See also: figure,
condition

share
verb

to divide and give out in shares
I shared the money with her.
divide, split, allot,
partition, ration,
distribute

Let's split up the pie.

Antonyms: hoard,
hog
See also: divide

shared *See* common

sharp
adjective

1 quick and sudden
Try not to take the sharp turn too fast.
abrupt, quick, sudden, rapid, drastic

2 harsh and causing hurt
Her sharp words hurt her friends.
harsh, cutting, cruel, tart, unkind

3 intelligent
The sharp student knew the answers right away.
alert, bright, clever, keen, quick, smart, apt,
brilliant, intelligent, shrewd

Antonyms: dim (3), dull (3), gentle (1,2),
gradual (1), mild (2)
See also: quick, sudden, smart

sheet *See* leaf

shelf ⚪ *See* stand

 Human Body   ? Human Mind   👕 Everyday Life   🏳 History and Culture   📞 Communication

shell ❶ *See* outside, war

shelter ⑥

noun

a place or structure that gives protection against weather or danger

A tent was our shelter during the storm.

cover, harbor, haven, refuge

verb

to give cover, protection, or shelter to

We sheltered the lost dog in our home.

harbor, haven, house, protect, lodge, safeguard, guard

Antonyms: expose, imperil

See also: cover, house

shield *See* cover, defense, guard, protect, protection, screen

shift

verb

1 change the position of

He shifted books from the top shelf to the bottom shelf.

move, switch, transfer

2 to change from one position to another

She shifted seats so that she could see better.

change, switch

noun

a change from one person, place, condition, or thing to another

There was a shift in the wind.

The woman felt a shift in her health.

change, switch, turn

See also: move

shine

verb

1 to give off or reflect light

The moon shone on our house.

beam, glow, gleam, glisten, glare, radiate, sparkle, glitter, twinkle

The water sparkled magically.

The freshly painted planes gleamed in the sunlight.

> How far that little candle throws his beams!
> So **shines** a good deed in a naughty world.
> —From THE MER- CHANT OF VENICE, by William Shakespeare (1564-1616), British dramatist and poet

2 to cause to shine

He shined the car.

buff, polish, gloss, rub

noun

reflected light

I admired the shine of the polished floors.

gloss, luster, glow

See also: beam, glow

shining *See* light

shiny *See* bright, sleek, hair, light

shock ❀❶❷

noun

1 a sudden and powerful scare; an upset of the mind or feelings

News of the disaster came as a shock.

blow, jar, jolt

2 a sudden, powerful blow or jar

The shock of the explosion knocked down trees and buildings.

concussion, jar, blow, crash, impact, collision, jolt

verb

to disturb suddenly, in a way that causes intense surprise, upset, or disgust

She shocked us with her rude comments.

dismay, jolt, stagger, stun, surprise, astound, startle, astonish, rock, bowl over

Antonyms: calm, lull

See also: jolt

a
b
c
d
e
f
g
h
i
j
k
l
m
n
o
p
q
r
s
t
u
v
w
x
y
z

shoes ⊙ *See* place

shoot
verb
1 to cause to fly forth
He shot three bullets from his rifle.
fire, discharge, issue
2 to move with great speed
The speeding car shot by us.
flash, fly, jet, streak, whiz

shop *See* business, store

shore ⊙ *See* river

short *See* low, body, grass, hair, measurement

shorten
verb
to make shorter
I shortened the dress by three inches.
cut *He cut his speech to ten minutes.*
abridge *Do not be surprised if the magazine abridges your story before publishing it.*
abbreviate *John abbreviated his speech.*
pare *He pared his nails.*
crop *He cropped the photo to fit in the frame.*
trim *She trimmed his hair.*
Antonyms: extend, grow, lengthen, stretch
See also: cut

shorter *See* less

shortly *See* soon

shoulder ⊙ *See* bear, push, support

shout
verb
to call out loudly
He shouted to his friend across the street.
call, cry, holler, yell, bellow
Antonym: whisper
noun
a loud cry or call
The sailor gave a shout of warning when he saw the huge wave.
call, cry, holler, whoop, yell, hail

Antonym: whisper
See also: call, cry

show ⊙
verb
to make clear by example
The teacher showed the answers on the blackboard.
clarify, demonstrate, explain, illustrate
By using a prism, she illustrated how rainbows are formed.
noun
a public performance or demonstration
We won first prize in the talent show.
display, exhibition, presentation, program, performance, exhibit
See also: explain, display

shower ⊙ *See* rain, scatter, spray, hygiene, weather

shriek *See* cry, scream

shut *See* close

shy
adjective
not comfortable with other people
The shy child did not talk to anyone in class.
bashful, reserved, timid, meek, ill at ease
Antonyms: bold, brazen, outgoing

> The birch, most **shy** and ladylike of trees.
> —*From AN INDIAN-SUMMER REVERIE, by James Russell Lowell (1819-1891), American poet*

sick ⊙
adjective
suffering from an illness
Phoebe was sick with a cold.
ill, unwell, under the weather, out of sorts
Antonyms: healthy, well

sickness *See* illness

 Human Body   Human Mind   Everyday Life   History and Culture   Communication

side
noun

1 an outer surface of an object
I bumped the right side of your car while I was parking.
surface, plane

2 one of the ways a thing appears or is understood
They each told a different side of the story.
angle, aspect, facet

See also: plane

sight ◔
noun

1 the ability to see
Pilots must have good sight.
eyesight, vision, seeing

2 the act or an instance of seeing
Do you believe in love at first sight?
glance, glimpse, look, view

Antonym:
blindness (1)
See also: glance, look

sign ◕
noun

1 something that shows that a fact, event, or quality exists
Her smile was a sign that she agreed.
There was no sign of John anywhere.
indication *Lance's sigh was an indication that he wanted to leave.*
mark *The certificate on the wall was a mark of his success.*
symptom *Pain can be a symptom of disease.*
token *The gift was a token of our respect for him.*
evidence *We searched the attic for evidence of mice.*
trace *The detective examined the traces left by the robber.*

2 a symbol that stands for a word or thing
The sign "+" stands for addition.
symbol, emblem, insignia, signal

A raised flag was the signal to begin the race.
See also: mark

signal *See* **alarm, sign, wave**

significance *See* **importance, point, weight, worth**

signs ◕ *See* **appearance**

silence *See* **quiet, still**

silent *See* **quiet, still, communication**

silently *See* **still**

silk *See* **clothes**

silly *See* **crazy, foolish, personality**

similar *See* **alike, shape**

simple *See* **bare, easy, informal, modest, neat, plain, primitive**

simply *See* **only, plain**

sing ◔ ◕ *See* **art, theater**

single
adjective

1 only one
A single act of kindness can make a big difference.
one *She is the one person who can help us.*
only *You are the only student who answered every question correctly.*
sole *He is the sole remaining blacksmith in the town.*
solitary *One solitary dime is all I have left.*
lone *The lone grocery store in that area was always busy.*
odd *The bottom drawer is for odd socks.*

2 considered as a separate or individual thing
Every single person had a good time at the party.

A B C D E F G H I J K L M N O P Q R S T U V W X Y Z

independent, individual, particular, separate, singular,
specific, distinct
This particular house is the one I would like to live in.
See also: only, particular

singular *See*
particular, single, special, strange, unusual

sink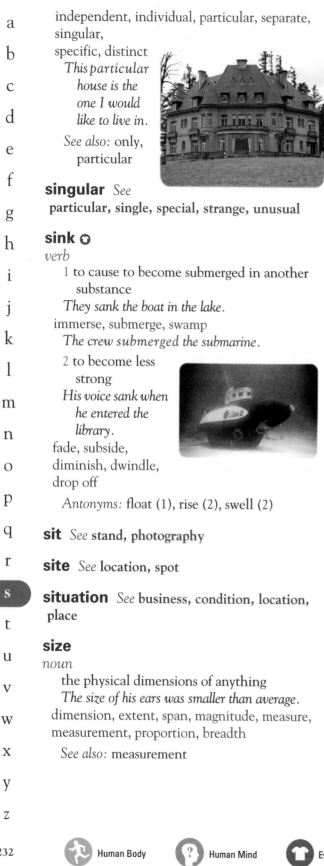
verb

1 to cause to become submerged in another substance
They sank the boat in the lake.
immerse, submerge, swamp
The crew submerged the submarine.

2 to become less strong
His voice sank when he entered the library.
fade, subside, diminish, dwindle, drop off

Antonyms: float (1), rise (2), swell (2)

sit *See* **stand, photography**

site *See* **location, spot**

situation *See* **business, condition, location, place**

size
noun

the physical dimensions of anything
The size of his ears was smaller than average.
dimension, extent, span, magnitude, measure, measurement, proportion, breadth

See also: measurement

skill
noun

1 the power or ability to perform a task well, especially because of training or practice
She embroiders with great skill.
art, craft, deftness, dexterity, facility

2 a kind of work or craft that requires special care and training
Photography is a skill that painters and sculptors often learn to help them with their work.
craft *Sue has learned the carpenter's craft.*
handicraft *Weaving, pottery, and carving are all handicrafts.*
trade *He is a mason by trade.*

skilled *See* **able, expert**

skin
noun

1 the thin tissue covering the body of a person or animal
Snakes shed their skin many times during their lives.
hide *Leather is made from cow hides.*
pelt *He hunted beaver for their pelts.*

2 the outer covering of some fruits and vegetables
The skin of an apple can be red, green, or yellow.
cuticle, peel, rind

skinny
adjective

very thin and bony
He became quite skinny while he was ill.
thin, scrawny, lean, lanky, gaunt, meager, spare

Antonyms: corpulent, fat, obese
See also: thin

skirt *See* **border**

sky *See* **air**

slave *See* **labor**

Human Body Human Mind Everyday Life History and Culture Communication

sleek
adjective

1 smooth or shiny
*Muskrats have sleek fur
    that repels water.*
shiny, slick,
smooth,
satiny, silky

2 healthy and well fed
The basketball players all looked sleek.
fit, healthy, trim

Antonyms: coarse (1), ragged (1)
See also: fit

sleep
verb

to be in a state of rest
I will sleep when I get tired.
slumber, doze,
nap, rest,
snooze
    *The cat dozed
    in the sun-
    light.*

sleepy
adjective

in need of or
    starting to sleep
Reading a boring book makes me sleepy.
drowsy, fatigued, weary, tired

Antonyms: alert, lively, wakeful

slender See **outside, thin, measurement**

slide
verb

1 to move easily along a surface
The children were sliding on the ice.
skim, coast, glide, slip, skid

2 to move without being noticed
No one saw her slide into the car.
slip *She slipped away when no one was looking.*
sneak *The burglar was sneaking through the house.*
steal *The cat stole into the kitchen.*

slight
adjective

not important
*He made a slight error on the test but still got a
    good grade.*
insignificant, petty, trivial, unimportant, light,
small, minor

Antonyms: huge, important, major

slim See **narrow, outside, remote, thin,
measurement**

slip See **fault, mistake, pass, slide, steal, bank**

slope
verb

to slant up or down
The trail slopes down to the pond.
incline, lean, slant, tilt
    *The road up to the fortress
    inclines sharply.*

Antonyms: flatten, level

noun

the amount that
    something slants
    or slopes
The road has a steep slope here.
gradient *The engineers measured the gradient of
the road.*
grade *The locomotive chugged up the steep grade.*
pitch *This roof has a steep pitch.*

See also: pitch

slouch
verb

to sit, stand, or move with a bent, careless pos-
    ture
He slouches instead of standing straight.
slump, stoop, hunch

slow
adjective

not moving or not able to move quickly
We sat and watched the slow river roll along.
sluggish, unhurried, lazy, slack

a
b
c
d
e
f
g
h
i
j
k
l
m
n
o
p
q
r
s
t
u
v
w
x
y
z

sly
adjective
devious or not to be trusted
The guard had to be extra careful with the sly criminal.
crafty, cunning, tricky, devious, slick

small *See* little, low, miniature, minor, modest, outside, slight, tiny, measurement

smart
adjective
intelligent
The smart boy taught himself how to read.
bright, clever, intelligent, apt, sharp, brilliant

smear
verb
1 to spread or apply on or over a surface
They smeared jelly on the bread.
spread, apply, daub, slap on

2 to be or become spread or smudged on or over a surface
Her makeup smeared in the rain.
smudge, run, spread, stain

noun
a mark or spot made by smearing
I wiped off the smear with a rag.
smudge, stain, mark, spot

See also: spread

smell
verb
to have or give off a bad odor
The rotten vegetables started to smell.
stink, reek

noun
an odor or scent
She likes the smell of coffee.
odor, scent, whiff, aroma, fragrance, stink, stench, reek

Aroma and **fragrance** are used for pleasant smells, while **stink**, **stench**, and **reek** are used for unpleasant smells.

See also: scent

smile
verb
to have an expression on the face that shows a person is happy, amused, or friendly
She smiled when she saw me.
beam, grin, smirk

To **smirk** is to smile in an unfriendly way: *Ross smirked when I tripped over his outstretched foot.*

Antonyms: frown, grimace

smoke *See* cook

smooth *See* even, graceful, polish, sleek, soft

snake *See* pull, personality

snatch *See* capture, get, grab, spell, steal

snow *See* water

so *See* very

social
adjective
enjoying the company of others
He enjoys parties because he is very social.
friendly, outgoing, extroverted, amiable, affable

See also: friendly, outgoing

society
noun
1 the members of a community or group considered together
It is important for every society to agree on certain laws.
community, public, people

3 a group of persons who get together for a particular purpose or activity
He is a member of the local art society.
association *You can join the association if you pay the dues.*
circle *Our sewing circle meets every Saturday.*

234

Human Body   Human Mind   Everyday Life   History and Culture   Communication

club *My friend belongs to a book club.*
fraternity *The fraternity held a membership meeting.*
guild *The hospital guild is looking for donations from the public.*
league *The women's league is holding a barbecue to raise money for the homeless.*
order *My grandfather belongs to a men's order that takes on community projects.*
organization *That organization helps people during emergencies.*
sorority *My mother joined a sorority when she attended college.*
union *Several English teachers formed a poetry-reading union.*

See also: community

soft
adjective

1 easy to bend or to shape; not firm or hard
I like to sleep on a soft bed.
The metal became soft when we heated it.
flexible, mushy, pliant, spongy, supple

2 smooth; not rough
She has soft skin from the special lotion she uses.
satiny, silky, smooth, velvety

3 not loud
There was soft music playing as we ate dinner.
low, hushed, mellow, muted, quiet, whispered

Antonyms: coarse (2), firm (1), hard (1), loud (3), rough (2), solid (1)

soften
verb

to make or become soft or softer
The warm sauce will soften the ice cream.
The grass softened his fall.
cushion *The air bag helped to cushion the impact of the crash.*
break *The bushes broke her fall.*
dim *Could you please dim the lights?*
melt *The piecrust melts in your mouth.*
lower *He lowered the music.*

Antonym: harden

soil *See* **country, dirt, dirty, ground, stain**

solar *See* **energy, light**

solid
adjective

1 without a break
A no-passing zone is marked by a solid line down the center of the road.
constant, continuous, endless, steady, straight, uninterrupted

2 sturdy
The masons built a solid wall of brick.
durable, robust, rugged, stable, strong, sturdy

Antonyms: flimsy (2), sporadic (1), spotty (1), unstable (2), weak (2)
See also: strong

solution *See* **answer, mixture**

solve
verb

to find an answer to
She solved all of the math problems.
He solved the crime.
crack, explain, figure out, unlock, unravel

See also: explain

somebody *See* **figure, personality**

someone *See* **person**

song
noun

a short musical composition for singing
He sang us a song about true love.
ballad, ditty, jingle, melody, tune

See also: tune

soon
adverb

in a short time
Dinner will be ready soon.
anon, by and by, directly, presently, shortly

Antonyms: eventually, later

a
b
c
d
e
f
g
h
i
j
k
l
m
n
o
p
q
r
s
t
u
v
w
x
y
z

sore *See* **angry, mad, wound, injury**

sorrow
noun
> 1 the suffering or distress that results from a loss, misfortune, or injury
> *He felt a lot of sorrow when his grandmother died.*
anguish, gloom, grief, melancholy, misery, pain, sadness, unhappiness, woe
> 2 the cause of such suffering and distress
> *It was a great sorrow when our cat ran away.*
hurt, misfortune, tragedy, woe
> *Antonyms:* fortune (2), gladness (1), glee (2), happiness (1,2), joy (1,2)
> *See also:* grief

sorry *See* **bad, miserable, poor, unfortunate, sad**

sort *See* **class, grade, group, kind, model, nature, order, rank, rate**

soul *See* **person, spirit**

sound *See* **blow, fit, healthy, normal, pronounce, reasonable, well, economy, health, mind, physics**

source
noun
> the start or cause of something
> *Knowing Latin was the source of his knack for scientific terms.*
root, origin, germ, inception, inspiration, mother, father, seed, fountainhead, wellspring
> *See also:* root

space
noun
> 1 an empty area or place
> *There is a space in the back row of the room.*
clearing, expanse, gap, opening, void
> 2 an area set aside for a particular use
> *Your car is in my parking space.*
place, position, slot, spot
> *See also:* clearing, place

span *See* **distance, length, range, reach, season, size, time**

spare *See* **skinny, thin**

sparkle *See* **flash, shine**

speak
verb
> 1 to utter words in one's usual voice
> *Can you speak louder?*
talk, utter, vocalize
> 2 to say in one's usual voice
> *She spoke my name.*
articulate, say, state, talk, utter, voice
> 3 to express
> *They spoke the truth.*
express, relate, say, state, tell, voice
> 4 to take part in conversation
> *He interrupted as we were speaking.*
chat, converse, gossip, rap, talk, chew the fat
> *See also:* talk

special
adjective
> 1 different from others
> *His father designed him a special kind of knee brace.*
distinctive, individual, novel, particular, singular, unique
> 2 better or more important than the usual
> *Your birthday is a special occasion.*
> *We're going to a special restaurant to celebrate.*
distinctive *The actor, John Wayne, had a distinctive way of walking.*
exceptional *Mark has an exceptional singing voice.*
extraordinary *We marveled at the extraordinary paintings in the museum.*
particular *Mothers have a particular talent for guessing what their children are thinking.*
remarkable *The summer was remarkable because of its lack of rain.*
singular *He does singular work.*
uncommon *His work received uncommon praise.*
> 3 valued and respected

Human Body   Human Mind   Everyday Life   History and Culture   Communication

He is a special friend of mine.
dear, esteemed, respected, true

   Antonyms: common (2), ordinary (2), standard (1), typical (2), usual (2)

noun

a sale of certain things for lower prices
The supermarket has a special on picnic supplies this week.
clearance *The car dealership holds a year-end clearance.*
markdown *There was a big markdown on socks.*
sale *The store is having a big sale on winter coats.*

   See also: particular

species ❶ *See* kind

specific *See* definite, particular, point, single

spectrum *See* range

speech ❷

noun

a talk given in front of an audience
The mayor gave a speech at city hall.
address *Many people watched the president's address on TV.*
lecture *The professor gave a lecture to his class.*
monologue *Most comedians deliver jokes as part of a monologue.*
oration *His oration at the assembly was long and boring.*
soliloquy *Shakespeare's plays are famous for their soliloquies.*
talk *The visitor gave a talk on how to stay fit and healthy.*

   See also: talk

speed *See* fly, rush

spell

noun

1 a short period of time
Let's rest a spell.
bit, minute, moment, sec, second, snatch, space, stretch, while

2 a period that stands out because of one kind of event or experience

The river was low after the dry spell.
interval, period, run, stretch, term

3 a period of work or other activity
He did a spell in the factory.
hitch, shift, stint

   Antonym: eternity (1)

verb

to take the place of for a time
The children spelled each other during the soccer game.
fill in for *Can you fill in for me at work?*
relieve *At noon, a new crew will relieve the morning workers.*
sub *Ms. Smith was sick, so Mr. Jones subbed for her.*
substitute *He substituted for our usual teacher.*

spend *See* use, money

sphere *See* area, world, shape

spike *See* point

spin *See* drive, roll, trip, turn, sport

spiral *See* twist

spirit

noun

1 a force that is thought to be a part of human beings
Some people believe that when you die, your spirit lives on.
essence, ghost, soul

2 a being that is not of this world
That old house is haunted by evil spirits.
apparition, ghost, phantasm, phantom, shade, spectre, wraith

3 feeling marked by qualities such as courage and energy
He led the team with his courageous spirit.
grit, heart, mettle, morale, pluck, vigor

4 a feeling or mood
He was in low spirits from the bad news.
humor, mood

5 the meaning or intent of a thing
The judge tried to stay true to the spirit of the law.

essence, intent, intention, purpose, substance

Antonym: body (1)

spirits *See* mood

spite

noun

the wish to hurt, bother, or embarrass a person

He told my secret out of spite.

animosity *It is true that dogs and cats show animosity toward each other.*

hostility *He felt hostility toward her after she hit him.*

ill will *There has been ill will between the two brothers for many years.*

malice *Gossip is sometimes an act of malice.*

Antonyms: benevolence, generosity, good will

verb

to act with spite toward

To spite them, she did not show up at their party.

humiliate, hurt, malign, mortify, shame, wound

Antonyms: benefit, gratify

splash

verb

to dash or spray

The car splashed mud all over me.

dash, slosh, spatter, splatter, spray

noun

the act or sound of splashing

At night I could hear the splash of waves.

lap, patter, slap, slosh, splat, spatter

See also: spray

splendid *See* **excellent, fine, great, noble**

split

verb

1 to divide along the length or in layers

We split the wood for the fireplace.

cut, part, rip, slit, cleave, wedge

2 to divide, break up or off, or separate

The road splits here.

The rock split into small pieces.

break, divide, fork, part, separate, sever

The river divides into two smaller streams.

3 to break up or separate by force or as though by force

Physicists split atoms.

He split a seam in his pants.

break, burst, cleave, fracture, rend, rupture

4 to break or fall apart, from pressure or disagreement

The package split open.

The couple split in a very sad divorce.

break *His favorite cup broke into pieces.*

burst *The balloon burst.*

crack *The window pane cracked from the sudden gust.*

rupture *The dam ruptured and let loose a flood.*

5 to divide into parts

Let's split up the pie.

divide, share, distribute, parcel

6 to divide or separate into different groups or directions

The class was split at lunch time.

divide, segment, separate

Antonyms: combine (2,4,6), fuse (3,4), join (4), link (4), merge (2,6), splice (2), wed (4)

noun

1 the act or result of splitting

There was a split in my shirt.

breach, break, cleft, crack, divide, fissure, rift, rupture

2 a division between two or more people

There was a split over who would be president of the club.

division, schism, separation, divorce

See also: divide, break

split *See* burst

Human Body   Human Mind   Everyday Life   History and Culture   Communication

Sports

a
b
c
d
e
f
g
h
i
j
k
l
m
n
o
p
q
r
s
t
u
v
w
x
y
z

spoil
verb

1 to make unable to be used or enjoyed
She spoiled her new dress.
The rain spoiled our camping trip.
ruin, wreck, blight, damage, foul

2 to harm the character of by giving too much freedom, too much money, or not enough punishment
They spoiled their daughter.
baby, pamper, dote on, overindulge

3 to go rotten
Meat spoils rapidly in hot weather.
decay, decompose, rot, sour, turn

noun

material goods or other things gained by winning a victory
The pirates laughed as they divided up the spoils.
booty *The army carried off a lot of booty during the campaign.*
loot *Before sinking the enemy ship, they took all the loot they could carry.*
plunder *The robbers grabbed their plunder and ran off.*
See also: wreck

spoken ● *See* communication, language

sport ● ○
noun

an athletic event or game played according to rules, and involving two people or teams on opposite sides

> *actions related to sports*
> assist, bench, block, bunt, defend, foul, fumble, hit, jump, kick, miss, pass, race, run, save, score, serve, slice, spin, sprint, swing, tee off, trail, try out, volley

spot
noun

1 a mark, such as a stain, different in color from the area around it
She has a dark spot on her shirt.
blot, blotch, dot, mark, patch, speck, stain

2 place

His name was written in the first spot on the list.
location, place, position, space

3 an uncomfortable position
If we don't finish on time, we'll be in a spot.
bind *By not showing up, you put us in a real bind.*
fix *I'm in a fix because I lost my lunch money.*
jam *Peter was in a jam at work.*
predicament *Cornered by an angry bear, the campers found themselves in a bad predicament.*

4 an area or location
We found a good vacation spot by the lake.
area, location, site

verb

1 to cause to be marked with spots
The street is spotted with oil.
dot, mark, speckle, freckle, dapple, blotch

2 to notice or catch sight of
He spotted his sister in the crowd.
glimpse, notice, discern, perceive, sight, detect
See also: stain, place

spray
noun

1 water or another liquid flying or falling in fine drops
mist, shower, sprinkle

2 a device used to send out liquid in a mist of tiny drops
I am using a spray to paint the house.
fogger, mister, shower, sprinkler, atomizer

verb

1 to send out in a spray
He sprayed poison on the windows to kill the flies.
fog, mist, shower, sprinkle

2 to use a spray on or cover with a spray
She sprayed her throat with medicine.
It's quicker to spray walls with paint than to use a brush.
fog *He fogged the backyard prior to the picnic in order to keep the bugs down.*
mist *She misted the windows before wiping them clean.*
shower *We showered the driveway until it was drenched.*
sprinkle *She sprinkled the salad with dressing.*

 Human Body   Human Mind   Everyday Life   History and Culture   Communication

3 to come out in a spray
Water sprayed from a hole in the hose.
mist, shower, sprinkle

See also: shower

spread

verb

1 to open or stretch out
He spread the map on the table.
She spread her arms to catch the ball.
expand, extend, open, stretch, unfold

2 to put on in a layer
She spread some jam on her bread.
apply, coat, plaster, smear

3 to scatter or send forth
Please spread the news that there will be a meeting tonight.
broadcast, circulate, disperse, distribute, scatter

Antonyms: close (1), contract (1), shrink (1)

noun

1 the act of spreading
We stopped the spread of the smoke by sealing the door.
dispersal, distribution, diffusion

2 a stretch of open space
This spread of land has been plowed.
expanse *The oceans are great expanses of water.*
field *From the plane, he looked down on a field of ice.*
reach *We drove through an enormous reach of desert.*
stretch *We drove over a long stretch of desert land.*

sweep *The farmer looked out across the sweep of farmland.*

3 a cloth covering that is put over furniture such as a bed or table
bedcovering, bedspread, blanket, coverlet, quilt, tablecloth

4 food that can be spread on crackers, bread, vegetables, or other foods

butter, jam, jelly, paste

See also: expand

spring

verb

1 to move upward quickly or suddenly
The dog sprang to catch the ball.
bound, hop, jump, leap, vault

These words can also be used as nouns:
With a single bound, the deer cleared the wall.

---

2 to change position suddenly
He sprang into action when he went into the game.
bound, dart, dash, jump, leap, shoot

The lizard darted out of sight.

3 to come into being quickly
Flowers are springing up in the garden.
burgeon, burst, pop, shoot up, sprout

noun

a flow of water from the earth
We stopped in the woods to drink water from a spring.
well, wellspring, fountainhead

See also: jump

square ⬤

noun

an outdoor space or plaza within a town or city
We sat by a fountain in the town square.
mall, common, plaza, agora

verb

1 to put straight or even
He squared the blankets on the bed.

align, even up, right, straighten

  2 to fit or match with
Her answer on the test squared with mine.
correspond, match, balance

  3 to agree
Mike's story does not square with the facts.
accord, agree, coincide, conform, correspond, tally

adjective

  1 making a right angle
The carpenter made sure the corners of the frame were square.
perpendicular, rectangular, right

  2 old-fashioned
I have some really square neighbors.
uncool, conservative, old-fashioned, out-dated

Square and **uncool** are informal words that mean old-fashioned in a bad way.

squeeze

verb

  1 to press firmly together
He squeezed my hand as he said goodbye.
clamp, compress, pinch, press

  2 to put pressure on or crush so as to pull something from
She squeezed oranges for juice.
crush, press, wring

  3 to hug
My mom squeezes me every morning before I leave for school.
cuddle *I cuddled my puppy in my arms.*
embrace *I embraced my father before I got on the bus.*
hug *I hugged my sister when she graduated from college.*

  4 to press into a small or crowded space
He squeezed two more people into the elevator.
cram, crowd, jam, pack, press, ram, wedge

  5 to force one's way through a crowd or small space
We squeezed through the people to get to the front of the line.

jam, muscle, press, push, wedge

noun

  1 the act of squeezing
A squeeze of lemon will add flavor to the food.
pinch, twist, wring

  2 a hug
My teacher gave me a big squeeze when the school year ended.
embrace, hug, cuddle

squirrel *See* **store, rodent**

stable *See* **firm, solid, steady, economy**

staff *See* **office, team**

stage ○ ●

noun

  1 a raised platform used for concerts, plays, talks, and other performances
dais, platform

  2 the job of acting in the theater
He started his career on the stage after finishing school.
acting, theater

  3 a separate period or step in a process of growth or development
Adolescence is a stage between childhood and adulthood.
level, phase, step, chapter

verb

  to perform or present on a stage
The theater club is going to stage a play by Shakespeare this year.
enact *They will enact a scene from a famous play.*
present *The theater presented a play by Shaw.*
perform *The theater club performed three plays last semester.*
put on *We put on a play we had written ourselves.*

stain

noun

  1 a spot or colored mark
Dirt stains on the carpet are hard to remove.
blotch, smear, smudge, soil, speck, spot

  2 something that causes shame

Human Body   Human Mind   Everyday Life   History and Culture   Communication

The lies he told at school left a stain on his character.

blot, brand, smear, spot

verb

1 to spot
The grape soda stained my pants.

blot, blotch, spot, smear, smudge, soil

2 to mark with shame or dishonor
Cheating on the exam stained his reputation.

blacken, brand, soil, tarnish, smear

See also: smear, soil

stammer

verb

to speak in an anxious or uncertain way
He stammered as he read the poem to the class.

stutter, stumble, falter, hesitate, sputter

noun

a stammering manner of speech
I speak with a stammer if I'm upset.

stutter, impediment, hesitation

stamp *See* **character, seal, step, anger, dance**

stand ◐ ○

verb

1 to get in or be in a position on one's feet
The teacher told the class to stand.

rise, arise, get up, rear

Rear is usually used of animals standing up on their hind legs: *The frightened horse reared and whinnied.*

2 to put or put upright
She stood the doll on the shelf.
He stood the vase back up.

put, place, raise, upright

3 to remain in effect
Our offer will stand for another week.

hold, remain, continue, last, persist, endure

4 to be located somewhere
The church stands in the valley.

be, lie, sit, rest

5 to put up with
Pip could not stand being poor.

bear, endure, take, tolerate, stomach, withstand

Antonym: sit (1)

noun

1 a determined attitude or position
We must take a stand on this issue.

point of view, position, stance, standpoint

2 a table or rack for holding a certain thing
He looked over the magazine stand in the waiting room.
Her clock is on a stand by her bed.

rack, table, holder, shelf

See also: rise, stop

standard

noun

1 something that is used as a guide or authority
This bike helmet meets the government safety standard.

model *Mr. Magnus, the millionaire, is my model of success.*

yardstick *Grades are the yardstick of success in school.*

example *His big brother set a good example by helping around the house.*

ideal *A community without violence is an ideal worth working for.*

precedent *Amelia Earhart's flight across the Atlantic Ocean set a precedent for other female pilots.*

2 a flag or banner

banner, ensign, flag, pennant

adjective

1 widely accepted as an authority
Many schools have standard science books that teachers must use.

recognized, authoritative, approved

2 normal; routine; usual
It is standard for me to go to bed at nine o'clock every night.

A
B
C
D
E
F
G
H
I
J
K
L
M
N
O
P
Q
R
S
T
U
V
W
X
Y
Z

a

conventional, normal, ordinary, regular, routine, usual, everyday, common, commonplace, customary

Antonym: unusual (2)
See also: usual

b

c

d

standards *See* **character, moral, value**

e

standing 🧠 👕 *See* **rank**

f

star 🧠 👤 *See* **personality, theater**

g

stare
verb
to look in a steady, fixed way
Everyone stared at the boy with the ripped shirt.
peer, goggle, look, regard, watch, gaze

h

i

Antonym: glance
See also: look

j

k

stars 🧠 👤 *See* **heaven**

l

start *See* **establish, found, jolt, jump, open, pick, fear**

m

n

state
verb
to say or write
He stated his opinion.
assert *He asserted his innocence.*
declare *She declared she would never speak to him again.*
say *He said what was on his mind.*
affirm *I affirmed that I had washed my hands before sitting down to eat.*
put *Put it in your own words.*
announce *She announced that she was getting married.*
express *He expressed his anger.*
present *He presented his case to the judge.*
allege *The police alleged that he had robbed the bank.*
claim *She claimed that he took her money.*
proclaim *He proclaimed that all citizens should be treated fairly.*

o

p

q

r

s

t

u

v

w

x

See also: condition

y

z

statement *See* **message, notice, record, report, word, bank**

station
noun
1 the place where a person or thing is normally found
The soldier went to his station.
post, place, position, stand, location

2 a regular stopping place on a route or road
The railroad station was crowded with people waiting for the next train.

depot, terminal, stop
verb
to assign to a particular place
The soldier was stationed in England.
post, assign, locate, install, place

See also: post

statistics *See* **material**

status *See* **grade, level, rank**

stay
verb
1 to spend time in a place
She stayed in London for five years.
live, remain, reside, settle

2 to continue spending time in a place or with a group
Stay with us for another ten minutes.
remain, linger, continue, loiter

Loiter means to stand around without doing anything or in a suspicious way.

3 to live for a short time
We stayed with cousins for six months.
live, lodge, quarter, room, camp, visit, run

4 to remain in a particular condition or state

🏃 Human Body   ❓ Human Mind   👕 Everyday Life   🏴 History and Culture   📞 Communication

She stayed healthy.
remain, keep, continue, hold

steady
adjective

1 firmly fixed in position
The craftsman built a steady table.
firm, solid, stable, rigid, secure, sturdy

2 having a regular movement or course of action
We took a slow but steady pace to get the job done.
constant, continuous, even, regular, continual, persistent, unvarying

3 not easily upset
We remained steady when the fire alarm rang.
calm, even, sober, level, stable, cool, poised, sensible

4 one who can be trusted
He is a steady player on our team.
dependable, reliable, secure, sure, solid, steadfast

5 not shaking
He has a steady hand with the hammer.
firm, unshaking, steadfast, stable, solid

Antonyms: jittery (5), shaky (1,5), uneven (2), unstable (1), unsteady (5), wobbly (1)

verb

1 to make or keep steady or stable
We steadied ourselves in the canoe.
fix, settle, poise, brace, balance, secure

2 to become steady
The rocking chair steadied when he got up.
settle, calm, balance

adverb

in a steady manner
Hold the board steady while I cut it.
firm, securely, fast, solidly, stably

See also: firm, solid, constant, calm

steal ⊙
verb

1 to take from another without permission or right
Someone stole my bicycle.

take, rob, lift, walk off with, rip off, spirit away or off, abscond with

2 to get in a clever or secret way
She stole a glance at the comic book.
sneak, snatch, grab, catch

3 to move secretly or without being noticed
He stole away from the party and went home.
sneak, slide, slip

Antonym: give (1)

noun

something bought at a very low price
At this low price the car is a steal.
bargain, deal

See also: take

steam ⊙ ⊚ *See* anger, energy, power, cook, hygiene, water

steep
adjective

having a sharp slope or slant
The goat scampered easily down the steep, rocky slope.
abrupt, sheer, sharp

step
noun

1 the motion used in walking
He took a step toward the door.
footstep, pace, stride, move

2 the sound made when walking
She heard steps on the front porch.
footstep, tread, stomp

3 an act or stage in a series
Follow the steps carefully in putting together the bicycle.
procedure, stage

verb

1 to move by taking one or a few steps
I stepped to the other side of the room.
tread, walk, stride, stroll, pace, shuffle, pad, trudge, tramp, march

2 to place the foot down
He stepped on an ant.
tread, stomp, tramp, trample, stamp

A
B
C
D
E
F
G
H
I
J
K
L
M
N
O
P
Q
R
S
T
U
V
W
X
Y
Z

● Living World ● Physical World ● Natural Environment ● Economy ● Government and Law   245

a
b
c
d
e
f
g
h
i
j
k
l
m
n
o
p
q
r
s
t
u
v
w
x
y
z

stick
verb

1 to pierce or poke with a pointed object
She stuck her finger with a piece of glass.
pierce, stab, poke, puncture, prick, stab

2 to fix into place by pushing the pointed end of an object into something
She stuck a poster to the wall.
pin, tack, post, affix

3 to put in a particular place or position
Stick your coat in the closet.
lay, place, set, put

4 to remain or become fixed in place
The tape stuck to the wall.
adhere, hold, bind, cling

5 to be or become set or caught and unable to move
My boots stuck in the mud.
catch *Her hair caught on a branch.*
lodge *A stone lodged in the tread of her boot.*
hook *His sweater hooked on a nail.*
lock *The steering wheel locked, and she could not turn it.*

sticky
adjective

1 tending to stick to or hold on to something when touched
Glue is sticky.
adhesive, tacky

2 hot or warm and very humid
Let's go swimming on this sticky day.
humid, muggy

stiff
adjective

1 not easy to bend
This thick cardboard is really stiff.
firm, inflexible, rigid, hard

2 not moving or operating easily
I could hardly open the stiff door.
She complained about her stiff ankles.
stubborn, rigid, tense, arthritic

Arthritic applies only to parts of the body.

3 not easy in expression or movement
I felt uneasy because of her stiff manner.
aloof, formal, wooden, cold, stuffy

4 difficult
It was a stiff climb up the mountain.
There's some stiff competition for the job.
difficult, hard, tough, heavy

5 severe
He endured some stiff punishment for stealing.
harsh, severe, strict, exacting, hard

6 very high; above normal
Stiff prices make it hard for poor families to get by.
excessive, steep, high

Antonyms: bland (5), easy (3,4), flexible (1), gentle (5), light (5), limber (2), loose (3), low (6), mild (5), pleasant (3), pliant (1), relaxed (3), simple (4)

adverb

completely
I was bored stiff during the meeting.
She was scared stiff by the monster.
totally, absolutely, thoroughly, completely

See also: firm

still
adjective

1 not moving
We were told to be still.
static, stationary, motionless, unmoving, calm

2 making or having no sound
The room was still after everyone left.
silent, quiet, mute

3 calm
They sat by the still lake and watched the sun set.
calm, placid, tranquil, serene, quiet, peaceful, untroubled

Antonyms: animated (1), loud (2), mobile (1), moving (1), noisy (2), raging (3), turbulent (3), wild (3)

noun

calm
In the still of the night, she walked in the moonlight.

 Human Body   Human Mind   Everyday Life   History and Culture   Communication

calm, quiet, silence

Antonyms: commotion, turbulence, turmoil

adverb

1 neither moving nor making sound
He sat still and waited for her call.
motionless, silently

2 at a particular time
They still live with their parents.
yet, as yet

3 despite that
He may be sick, but he still needs to exercise.
nevertheless, all the same, however

verb

1 to cause to be quiet
She stilled the class by raising her hand.
hush, quiet, calm, silence, moderate

2 to cause to stop moving
He stilled his bicycle at the corner.
stop, idle, check, damp

3 to become still
The lake stilled after the storm.
calm, hush, quiet

Antonyms: disturb (1), propel (2), rouse (1,3),
stir (1,3), unsettle (1), whip up (3)
See also: calm, quiet

stimulus *See* cause

stir

verb

1 to mix or move in a circle with a hand or
object
She stirred her coffee with a spoon.
mix *The chef mixed the cookie dough.*
swirl *She swirled some milk into her tea.*
blend *He blended the cake mix.*
beat *Beat the eggs.*

2 to put into
motion
*The alarm stirred
me from my
sleep.*
move, agitate,
hasten, upset

3 to make excited or full of energy (usually **stir
up**)
*Please don't stir up the children right before
dinner.*
rouse, excite, stimulate, agitate

4 to cause excitement or feelings in
The music stirred her.
touch, move, rouse, excite, inspire, exhilarate,
agitate

Antonyms: brake (2), calm (3), dampen (3,4),
deaden (4), halt (2), hush (3), mute (4),
pacify (3), quell (3), quiet (3), still (2),
stop (2), subdue (3,4)

noun

1 act of stirring; stirring motion
He gave the batter a stir.
mix, swirl

2 state of excitement
The speech caused a great stir.
commotion, excitement, sensation, fuss

Antonyms: calm (2), hush (2), lull (2),
quiet (2), stillness (2)
See also: mix, excite

stock ◯ ☢ *See* **carry, goods, store**

stomach ☢ *See* **stand, take**

stone ☢ *See* **rock, fruit, jewelry**

stop

verb

1 to halt or cause to halt
The sudden cloudburst stopped our picnic.
*My mother stopped the videotape when it was
time to eat dinner.*
halt *The crossing guard halted the cars so the children could cross.*
cease *Cease that noise now!*
interrupt *Loud banging on the door interrupted the
conversation.*
brake *I braked my bicycle when I saw the stop sign.*
discontinue *The newspaper has discontinued my
favorite comic strip.*
kill *The driver killed the engine.*

a
b
c
d
e
f
g
h
i
j
k
l
m
n
o
p
q
r
s
t
u
v
w
x
y
z

2 to cease moving, acting, or proceeding
The car stopped at the red light.
He stopped in the middle of the story.
cease, halt, quit, discontinue, leave off

3 to do no longer
Will you stop yelling?
quit, cease, discontinue, leave off, refrain from

4 to reach an end
The fun stopped when someone got hurt.
conclude, end, close, finish, discontinue

5 to close or plug
He stopped the bottle with a cork.
close, plug, cork, stopper, seal

6 to block (often **stop up**)
Grease stopped up the drain.
choke, clog, close, plug, block

7 to prevent from moving or traveling
The accident stopped traffic.
arrest, interrupt, prohibit, block, halt, obstruct

Antonyms: carry forward (2), carry on (2), continue (2,3,4), go on (4), impel (1), linger (4), open (5,6), persist (3), press on (2), promote (7), run on (2), start (1), unclog (6), unstop (5,6)

noun
the act of stopping or state of being stopped
The car came to a stop in front of our house.
stand, stay, halt, stoppage

store 🔘 🌐

noun
1 a place where things are sold
Please pick up some bread at the grocery store.
shop, business, outlet, market

2 a supply kept or saved for future use
The best mothers keep a store of cookies in the cupboard.
stock, supply, reserve

3 a large amount
There is a store of talent in this classroom.
abundance, plenty, wealth, pile

Antonyms: lack (3), need (3)

verb
to gather and keep for future use
The squirrel forgot where he stored his nuts.

accumulate, collect, keep, save, hoard, gather, stock up, reserve, squirrel

Antonyms: consume, squander, waste

storm ❓ 🌐

noun
1 a violent disturbance in the atmosphere that brings rain, snow, wind, thunder, or lightning
squall, tempest, downpour, hurricane, tornado, blizzard

A downpour, hurricane, or tornado can occur only in warm weather, and a blizzard can occur only in cold weather.

---

2 an outburst of strong feeling
On hearing the bad news, the crowd broke into a storm of anger.
eruption, outburst, hail

verb
1 to blow with heavy rain or snow, and sometimes with thunder and lightening
It stormed all night.
bluster, rage, squall, blow, pour, howl

2 to move or rush angrily
We stormed out of the house.
charge, rush, rage, tear, stomp

3 to attack
The army stormed the enemy position last night.
charge, rush, attack, strike, besiege, beset, descend upon, raid, assault, siege, invade

story 🔘 🎵

noun
1 an account of something that happened, either true or made up
Did I ever tell you the story of when I saw the wolf?
account, narrative, tale, anecdote, fable

A fable is always a made-up story.

---

2 a lie
Don't tell stories about where you were.

 Human Body   Human Mind   Everyday Life   History and Culture   Communication

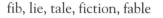

fib, lie, tale, fiction, fable

straight
adjective
1 without a curve or bend
He drew a straight line.
uncurving, unbending, linear, direct

2 direct
I appreciate your straight talk on this sensitive subject.
direct, frank, open, square, plain

Antonyms: circuitous (2), curvy (1), elusive (2), evasive (2), meandering (1)

adverb
in a straight line or course
He went straight to the baseball game after dinner.
direct, directly, right

strain See **burden, labor, pressure, stress, tune, wear, injury**

strange
adjective
1 unusual
The strange behavior of the fox led us to believe that it had rabies.
odd, peculiar, curious, eccentric, funny, queer, singular, unusual, weird, abnormal
She had never seen such an unusual bird before.

2 not known or familiar
He likes to visit strange countries.
foreign, unfamiliar, alien, exotic

Antonyms: familiar (2),

Once upon a midnight dreary, while I pondered, weak and weary
Over many a quaint and **curious** volume of forgotten lore,
While I nodded, nearly napping, suddenly there came a tapping,
As of some one gently rapping.
--From "THE RAVEN," a poem by Edgar Allan Poe (1809-1849), American author

normal (1), ordinary (2), typical (1), usual (1), well-known (2)
See also: unusual

stranger See outsider

stream
noun
1 a small, flowing body of water
We went fishing in the stream.
brook, creek

2 a steady flow of a liquid, people, or some other thing
A stream of lava poured down the volcano.
A stream of fans came up to the stage.
flow, river, issue

verb
1 to flow, as in a current or stream
Sweat streamed down his face as he worked in the sun.
flow, run, course, roll, pour, wash

2 to give forth
His wound was streaming with blood.
gush, flow, pour, spout, well, overflow

3 to float or wave
The flag streamed in the wind.
wave, flap, flutter, float

4 to pour forth beams of light
Sunshine streamed in through my window.
beam, flood, pour, shine

See also: river

street
noun
a public road in a town or city along which vehicles travel
road, thoroughfare, drive, highway, avenue, boulevard

strength See **ability, energy, force, power, resistance, weight**

strengthen
verb
to make or grow strong or stronger
I strengthen my mind by reading lots of books.

fortify, heighten, nourish, reinforce, develop

Antonyms: cripple, debilitate, impair, weaken

See also: develop

stress 🏃 ❓

noun

1 special attention given to something
My teacher puts a lot of stress on reading.
emphasis, accentuation, importance

2 a condition of strain or tension
I could feel the stress in the exam room.
tension, pressure, strain

verb

1 to place importance on or give special attention to
He stressed the need for more food for people hurt by the war.
accentuate *His white T-shirt accentuated his suntan.*
emphasize *Your essay emphasizes only the bad side of having a little brother.*
underline *The governor underlined the importance of creating jobs.*
weight *He weighted his speech toward public healthcare.*
punctuate *I want to punctuate my commitment to fair wages.*
focus on *The talk focused on space exploration.*

2 to say with a stronger tone
Stress the first syllable when you say the word "favorite."
accent, accentuate, emphasize

Antonym: downplay (1)

See also: importance

stretch

verb

1 to spread out or reach out to the full length in order to make loose and flexible
He always stretches his legs before playing soccer.
expand, extend

2 to cause to extend or reach from one point to another
He stretched a wire from the pole to the house.
extend, string, connect

3 to reach out or extend

He stretched his hand to help me.
extend, offer, put out, reach out

4 to cause to become longer or wider
He stretched his chewing gum into long strings.
lengthen, widen, broaden, pull, expand

5 to extend over an area or in a certain direction
The storm will stretch across the state.
extend, reach, spread, run, go, carry

6 to lie down (often **stretch out**)
He stretched out on the couch for a nap.
lie down, recline, lie, sprawl, lounge

Antonyms: recoil (3), retract (3), withdraw (3)

noun

1 the act of stretching
The team sat down for a well-deserved stretch of the arms and legs.
expansion, reach, extension

2 a continuous area or distance
We drove over a long stretch of desert land.
expanse, reach, sweep, extent, spread

The farmer looked out across the sweep of plains.

3 a continuous period of time
He left town for a long stretch.
period, while, run, space

See also: expand, extend

stretched *See* **long**

strict *See* **accurate, exact, hard, harsh, severe, stiff**

strike *See* **attack, hit, storm, thrust, touch**

striking *See* **bold, lively**

string ⊙ *See* **line, series, stretch**

strip *See* **band, clothes**

stroke *See* **brush, hit, pet, art, body, first aid**

 Human Body   Human Mind Everyday Life History and Culture   Communication

strong

adjective

1 having or showing great physical power or strength

The strong man lifted the heavy log.

forceful, mighty, powerful, sturdy, robust, muscular

2 having power of mind or character

He gave a strong objection to the ruling of the court.

He has a strong belief that life is sacred.

determined, firm, tough, steadfast, stern

3 showing great movement, force, or energy

A strong wind blew the old barn down.

forceful, powerful, intense, mighty

4 having a bad or powerful taste or smell

I hate the strong smell of your feet.

Just put a thin slice of cheese on your cracker, because it's very strong.

pungent, robust, sharp

Antonyms: bland (4), feeble (1), hollow (2), lame (2), mild (4), powerless (1), shallow (2), weak (1,2,3)

See also: powerful

structure

noun

1 a thing made up of a number of parts joined together in a certain way

A human cell is a sophisticated structure of organic material.

construction, complex, arrangement, formation

2 the way in which such a thing is joined together

A craftsman knows about the structure of furniture.

composition, construction, form, makeup, organization

struggle *See* **battle, contest, effort, fight, try, war**

stubborn

adjective

not willing to accept change, help, or control

She is very stubborn and won't do what they tell her.

obstinate, willful, headstrong, inflexible, contrary

Antonyms: compliant, obedient, willing

study

noun

a close look at something

She did a study of insects.

examination, investigation, observation

verb

1 to try to gain knowledge or skill

He studies at college.

educate oneself, school oneself, learn

2 to examine in detail

She studied her next move in the game.

analyze, examine, scrutinize, survey, inspect, pore over, review, investigate

We examined an insect with a magnifying glass.

3 to commit to memory

She studied her lines for the next scene.

learn, memorize, cram

Cram is used to speak of studying that is done very intensely to meet a deadline.

Antonym: forget (3)

See also: education, learn

stuff *See* **crowd, fill, goods, load, property, cook**

stuffed *See* **full**

stupid *See* **foolish, learn**

A
B
C
D
E
F
G
H
I
J
K
L
M
N
O
P
Q
R
S
T
U
V
W
X
Y
Z

Living World   Physical World   Natural Environment   Economy   Government and Law

a b c d e f g h i j k l m n o p q r s t u v w x y z

sturdy
adjective

strong
Your sturdy shelves will hold the weight of these heavy books.
hardy, rugged, solid, strong, durable, tough, robust, mighty, hearty

Antonyms: decrepit, flimsy, rickety
See also: solid, strong

style
noun

1 the manner in which something is said or done
I like the style of her writing.
manner, mode, way, fashion

2 the special quality or manner in which something is said, done, or made
I enjoy watching this dancer because he has style.
grace, pizzaz, dash, flair, zing

3 a state of being in fashion
Short skirts are back in style.
vogue, trend, fashion

verb

to give a style to; design or fashion in a certain manner
How would you like me to style your hair?
design, fashion, arrange, dress

subject
noun

the topic of what is said, written, or studied
The subject of the book was Native Americans.
theme, topic, issue, concern

adjective

likely to have or to get
He is subject to sore throats.
disposed, liable, prone, vulnerable

submerge *See* dive, flood, sink, swamp

substance *See* point, root, spirit, weight

substitute *See* relief, replace, spell

succeed
verb

1 to have a good or favorable result
No one thought his new business would succeed.
flourish, prosper, thrive, take, work, triumph

2 to get what is wanted
He succeeded in getting her to quit smoking.
triumph, win, click

3 to follow or come after
Who will succeed the president if he dies while in office?
follow, replace, displace

Antonyms: fail (1,2), fizzle (1), flop (1), precede (3)
See also: win

success
noun

1 a person or thing that does or goes well
Her book was a huge success, selling millions of copies.
smash, hit

Smash and **hit** are informal words that can be used in everyday speech and writing. Notice that their original meaning of a damaging blow or crash has been reversed to mean something favorable.

2 the reaching of something desired or intended
After years of trying to find a good job, he finally had success.
accomplishment, achievement, triumph, victory

3 having become rich or famous
Her success made her a snob.
prosperity, riches, wealth, fortune
The sultan has great riches.

Human Body   Human Mind   Everyday Life   History and Culture   Communication

successful
adjective

1 ending or doing well

The successful coffee shop had people waiting in line to get in.

flourishing, prospering, thriving, prosperous

2 having reached a wanted goal

The firemen were successful in putting out the fire.

victorious, effective, efficacious, effectual

3 having gained a lot of money or a high social position

The successful doctor drove an expensive car.

affluent, flourishing, prosperous, rich, thriving, wealthy, well-off

Antonyms: failing (1), poor (3), struggling (1)
See also: effective

successfully *See* well

succession *See* order, series, train

sudden
adjective

1 happening without notice or warning

A sudden noise frightened us.

abrupt, unexpected, unforeseen, unanticipated

2 sharp, quick or abrupt

I made a sudden turn into the traffic.
There was a sudden change in her mood.

abrupt, precipitate, rapid, sharp, hasty, quick

Antonyms: gradual (1,2), steady (1,2)

suffer *See* bear, brave, experience, receive, take

sufficient *See* decent, enough, satisfactory

sufficiently *See* enough

suggest
verb

1 to put forth for thinking about

We suggested several ways to raise money.

advance, offer, propose, pose, submit

2 to bring to mind in a way that is not direct

The story suggests a deeper meaning.

imply, hint

Use the preposition "at" after hint.

Antonym: retract (1)
See also: offer, propose

suggestion
noun

1 the act of suggesting or state of being suggested

He made a suggestion that we go to the new restaurant for dinner.

proposal, offer

2 something that is suggested

The teachers did not like my suggestion that they allow students to chew gum in class.

offer, pointer, proposal, proposition, idea

3 a small amount

The delicious soup had a lot of cream with a suggestion of garlic.

glimmer, hint, shade, touch, shadow, trace, whisper, note

Antonyms: mandate (2), order (2)
See also: offer

suit *See* adjust, become, fit

suitable *See* appropriate, decent, fit, proper, satisfactory

suite *See* set

suited *See* appropriate, proper

sum *See* amount, whole

summit *See* height, peak, top

summon *See* call

sunlight *See* light

sunny *See* bright, light, merry, light, weather

sunshine *See* light

a
b
c
d
e
f
g
h
i
j
k
l
m
n
o
p
q
r

s

t
u
v
w
x
y
z

superior *See* **best, better, excellent, fine, great**

supernatural
adjective
having to do with forces separate from or higher than natural laws
Last night my dreams were full of super-natural crea-tures, such as ghosts and vampires.

miraculous, spiritual, uncanny

Antonyms: natural, real, worldly

supply *See* **carry, provide, serve, store, economy**

support
verb
1 to bear
I can't support your weight, so you will have to walk.
bear, carry, shoulder

2 to hold up
The table is supported by four legs.
uphold, bear, brace, buttress, prop, bolster

3 to help during a time of trouble or stress
She supported me when I was ill.
bolster, comfort, uphold, encourage, reassure, help, cheer, buoy up

4 to provide enough for
Parents support their families by working.
maintain, provide for, take care of, foster

5 to provide proof or evidence for
What other people say supports his story.
back up, evidence, fortify, confirm, verify, vouch for

Antonyms: afflict (3), beat down (3), contradict (5), discredit (5), oppress (3)

noun
1 the act of supporting, or the condition of being supported
Where can he get support?
encouragement, aid, assistance

2 someone or something that gives support
He has been such a support to me during this time of trouble.
brace, buttress, prop, stay

Antonyms: hindrance (2), pest (2)

See also: bear, carry

suppose
verb
1 to assume to be true in order to make clear or to explain
I suppose she loves him, because she married him.
assume, imagine, presume, fancy

2 to consider to be possible
I suppose we might stay until next week.
imagine, conceive

Conceive is often preceded by "could" and followed by "of" or "that."

3 to believe
I suppose that his plan will work.
believe, fancy, guess, think, suspect, expect, reckon

See also: imagine, guess, believe

supreme *See* **extreme, grand, main, religion**

sure
adjective
1 free of doubt as to the truth of something
I am sure that this water is safe to drink.
certain, definite, doubtless, positive, confident, secure

2 certain to be; not possible to avoid
They are sure winners.
bound, certain, destined, doomed

Doomed is used to speak only of things cer-tain to end in an awful way.

Human Body   Human Mind   Everyday Life   History and Culture   Communication

3 steady and without fail
Is he a sure friend?
The baby took a few sure steps on her own.
dependable, reliable, secure, steady, faithful, good, steadfast

> *Antonyms:* improbable (2), shaky (3), uncertain (1), unlikely (2), unsteady (3), unsure (1), wobbly (3)

adverb
(informal) certainly
It sure is cold today.
surely, certainly

> *See also:* certain, definite

surely *See* plain, really, sure

surface *See* face, outside, rise, side

surprise
verb
1 to catch off guard; come upon or occur to suddenly
He surprised her with a kiss.
catch, startle, shock, stun

2 to cause a feeling of wonder in
Vicky's ability in chess surprised us.
amaze, astonish, astound, bowl over, floor, stun

> *Antonym:* bore (2)

noun
1 the state of being surprised, astonished, or struck with wonder
He could not hide his surprise at seeing his old enemy after so many years.
amazement, astonishment

2 that which brings about such a state
Winning the lottery was a surprise.
shock, jolt

> *See also:* shock

surround
verb
1 to close off all sides of
The wall surrounds the town.
compass, enclose, encompass, encircle, ring

2 to form in a circle around
Fans surrounded the singer after the concert.
circle, encircle, encompass, ring

> **Ring** is often followed by "around."

surroundings *See* environment

survey *See* study, view

survive *See* brave, live

suspect ⚫ ⬤ *See* believe, doubt, imagine, suppose

swallow ⚫
verb
1 to cause food to go from the mouth to the stomach
The baby swallowed a mouthful of cereal.
consume, eat, gulp, take

2 to take in and cover completely; make disappear (usually **swallow up**)
Darkness swallowed up the village.
engulf, envelop, absorb, gulf

3 (informal) to believe or to accept without questioning
The principal swallowed Al's story about why he was late.
buy, take, accept, believe

4 to hold or keep back
She swallowed her anger.
choke back, hold, restrain, withhold, contain

noun
the amount that is or can be swallowed at one time
Take a swallow of water.
gulp, sip, mouthful

a
b
c
d
e
f
g
h
i
j
k
l
m
n
o
p
q
r
s
t
u
v
w
x
y
z

swamp ○ 🜂

noun

a wet, low area of land that is usually covered with water

bog, marsh, swamplands, bottoms, mire

My brother and I hunted for frogs in the marsh.

verb

1 to weigh down
We were swamped with junk mail.
avalanche, deluge, flood, overwhelm, overcome, burden

2 to become flooded with water or sink, as a boat
The ship swamped in the storm.
flood, sink, submerge

See also: flood

sweat 🜂 *See* **fear**

sweep *See* **brush, spread, stretch**

sweet

adjective

1 having a taste like that of sugar or honey; not bitter, salty, or sour
I love this sweet chocolate.
saccharine, sweetened, sugary

2 not spoiled
The milk will stay sweet in the refrigerator.
fresh, good, unspoiled

3 gentle or pleasant
She is such a sweet girl that she brings her mother flowers every day.
lovable, nice, gentle, good-natured, kind, pleasant, dear

4 pleasant to the mind or senses
There are sweet smells in the flower garden.
pleasant, lovely, wonderful

Antonyms: bitter (1), foul (4), rank (4), sour (1,2), spiteful (3), turned (2)

swell

verb

1 to become larger by growth or pressure
My hand swelled when I slammed it in the door.
expand, grow, increase, balloon, enlarge, puff

2 to cause to be greater or larger in amount, force, or loudness
The constant rain swelled the river.
augment, enlarge, increase, intensify, magnify

3 to become greater in amount, force, or loudness
The sound swelled louder and louder.
increase, rise, build, grow, enlarge

Antonyms: decrease (2,3), die (3), dwindle (2), fall (3), shrink (1,2)

adjective

fine
He is a swell friend.
What a swell day!
cool, dandy, great, super, fine, excellent, nice

See also: expand

swift *See* **fast, instant, prompt, quick**

swiftly *See* **fast, quickly**

swim ○ *See* **animal, rodent**

swing *See* **dance, sport**

switch

noun

a shift
We made a switch in our lives when we moved to the country.
change, shift

verb

1 to change
Let's switch the discussion to another topic.
change, shift, move, turn

2 to change or shift course
The tone of the speech switched from being very cheerful to very sad.
change, deviate, shift

3 to exchange
They switched their old car for a new one.

 Human Body   ❓ Human Mind   👕 Everyday Life   🏳 History and Culture   Communication

exchange, swap, trade, change
See also: change

symbol

noun

an object or picture that represents something else

The rose is a symbol of love.

emblem, figure, mark, synonym, token

sympathy

noun

the ability to share another's feelings

Her sympathy for others makes her a good listener.

compassion, heart, humanity, pity

Antonyms: coldness, detachment, inhumanity

See also: heart

system   *See* process

A
B
C
D
E
F
G
H
I
J
K
L
M
N
O
P
Q
R
S
T
U
V
W
X
Y
Z

a
b
c
d
e
f
g
h
i
j
k
l
m
n
o
p
q
r
s
t
u
v
w
x
y
z

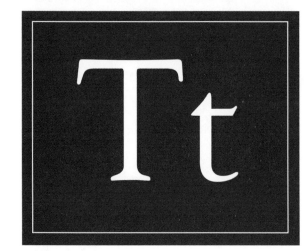

table ⊙ *See* **stand**

tail ➊ *See* **follow, airplane, animal**

take
verb

1 to cause to be in one's hands
Take these flowers and put them in some water.
grab *The man grabbed his hat and rushed out.*
grasp *He grasped the suitcase by its handle.*
nab *The thief nabbed her purse.*
seize *He seized a cookie from the plate.*
hold *I picked up a cricket and held it gently.*
draw *She drew his hand into hers.*

2 to carry away
Please take some brownies home with you.
carry, bring, bear, move, convey, transfer, transport, remove

3 to get through force, skill, or trick
The army took the city at dawn.
gain, obtain, seize, appropriate, confiscate, capture

4 to accept; follow
Don't take orders from him.
accept, follow, heed, observe, submit to

5 to experience
I take pleasure in helping you.
experience *He experienced defeat for the first time.*
feel *She felt a headache starting.*
have *We always have a good time at recess.*

sense *Susan sensed the cold as soon as Rick opened the window.*

6 to put up with
I can't take the cold weather.
bear, stand, tolerate, endure, stomach, suffer, withstand, abide

7 to require
This job takes a lot of time and effort.
call for, claim, demand, require, need, consume, use up

Antonyms: give (3), return (3)
See also: hold, steal, get, catch

tale ⊙ ⊚ *See* **lie, story**

talent *See* **ability, gift**

talk
verb

1 to use spoken words
Can the baby talk yet?
speak, articulate, enunciate

2 to discuss
They talked business at the meeting.
address, debate, discuss, converse, chat about, bat around

3 to bring to or convince
The salesman talked her into buying new shoes.
cajole, persuade, sweet-talk, wheedle

noun

1 the act of talking
They had a long talk about school.
conversation, dialogue, discourse, discussion

2 a speech
The visitor gave a talk on how to stay fit and healthy.
address, lecture, speech, oration

> They never taste who always drink;
> They always **talk** who never think.
> —From UPON A PASSAGE IN THE SCALIGERANA, by Matthew Prior (1664-1721), British poet

tall *See* **high, body, grass, measurement**

 Human Body   Human Mind   Everyday Life   History and Culture   Communication

tank ○ ▣ *See* **prison**

tap *See* **dance**

target *See* **design, goal, object, objective, victim**

task
noun
a piece of work to be done
He gives me a different task to complete every day.
duty, chore, assignment, charge, job, mission

taste ●
verb
to eat a little bit of
I would like to taste the chocolate cake.
nibble, sample, try

noun
a personal liking
I have a taste for flying.
liking, inclination, preference, weakness, zest
Antonyms: aversion, dislike

tax ● *See* **wear**

teach ●
verb
to give lessons
She teaches in a public school.
coach, educate, instruct, train, tutor

teacher
noun
a person whose job is teaching
coach, instructor, master, mentor, professor, tutor

teaching ● *See* **knowledge**

team ○
noun
1 a group of people on one of the sides in a sports event
Our hometown team won the state tournament.
crew, squad, side
2 a group formed to work together

A team of scientists worked on the problem.
squad, crew, army, brigade, company, corps, party, staff, shift

Army, **brigade**, **company**, and **corps** all have their origins in the military, but may be used for any large group of people working together to accomplish the same task. A **staff** is used when speaking and writing about a group that is employed, or working for money, in the same place.

---

tear
verb
to pull apart or into pieces
She tore the old clothes into rags.
pull, rip, shred, rend
Antonyms: mend, patch

tease
verb
to make fun of or annoy in a playful way
He teases his little sister.
josh, kid, needle, rib, poke fun at

technique *See* **way**

technology ◉
noun
the results of using science for the concerns of everyday life

> *some kinds of technology*
> agricultural, chemical, electronic, environmental, industrial, medical, military, nuclear
> *some words used to describe technology*
> advanced, appropriate, complicated, convenient, current, dangerous, efficient, impractical, modern, new, obsolete, revolutionary, up-to-date, useful

telephone ○ ● *See* **call**

tell
verb
to express in spoken or written words

A B C D E F G H I J K L M N O P Q R S **T** U V W X Y Z

a
b
c
d
e
f
g
h
i
j
k
l
m
n
o
p
q
r
s
t
u
v
w
x
y
z

Tell me about your summer plans.
express, relate, report, speak, articulate

The synonyms for **tell** are often followed by "to": *She expressed to her parents a wish to play hockey.*

See also: **speak**

temper ⊙
noun
1 a usual state of mind of manner of feeling
She has a sunny temper.
attitude, disposition, nature, temperament
2 sense of calm or patience
She lost her temper when I broke her vase.
composure *Her composure helped to end the fight.*
poise *The speaker faced the audience with poise.*
calm *He maintained his calm in the face of danger.*
self-control *It's hard to maintain self-control when someone teases you.*

temporary *See* **passing**

tempt
verb
to be attractive or very appealing to
The idea of a swim tempts me.
attract, beckon, charm, enchant, appeal to

tend *See* **keep, watch, care**

tense ⊛ ⊙ *See* **nervous, stiff**

tension *See* **pressure, stress**

term *See* **call, length, name, season, spell**

terminal *See* **end, last, station**

terrible
adjective
1 causing fear, terror, or horror
A terrible wave almost swallowed the ship.

awful, dire, dread, fearful, frightening, frightful, ghastly, horrible, terrifying
2 very bad; not acceptable
That's a terrible drawing of a frog.
awful, rotten, atrocious, dreadful, hideous, horrid, lousy

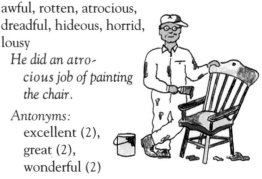

He did an atrocious job of painting the chair.

Antonyms:
excellent (2),
great (2),
wonderful (2)

territory ❶ ⊕
noun
an area or region of land
This is rattlesnake territory, so be careful where you step!
area, district, region, sector, tract, zone

terror ⊙ *See* **fear, panic**

test ⊛ ❶ ⊖
noun
1 a set of questions or tasks to find out about a person's ability or knowledge
She gives us a test at the end of every math lesson.
exam, examination, quiz, assessment
2 a trial to find out what something is, what it is made up of, or how good it is
A blood test is part of a complete physical exam.
Tests showed that the water was safe for drinking.
examination, inspection, analysis, check, study, trial
verb
to give a test to or do a test of
The doctor tested my hearing.
The teacher tested us on two chapters of the math book.
analyze, assess, check, evaluate, examine, inspect, investigate, probe, quiz

thanks
plural noun
an expression of gratitude

 Human Body   Human Mind   Everyday Life   History and Culture   Communication

Please accept our thanks for all you have done.
appreciation, gratitude, gratefulness

theater

noun

the art or business of writing or performing plays

Randy wants a career in theater or ballet.

acting, drama, the stage, stagecraft

> *some kinds of theater*
> comedy, drama, mystery, tragedy
> *some actions associated with theater*
> act, audition, bow, cast, cue, dance, direct, enact, enter, exit, express, improvise, interpret, memorize, perform, portray, produce, prompt, put on, rehearse, sing, stage, star, take a bow, try out
> *some words used to describe theater*
> amateur, classical, contemporary, dramatic, epic, experimental, modern, musical, political, professional

theme *See* **subject, tune, literature**

theory *See* **belief, idea, view**

therapy *See* **treatment**

thick

adjective

large in measurement from one side of a surface to the opposite side

We placed a thick book on the chair so that Sarah could reach her dinner plate.

broad, deep, fat, wide

Antonyms: narrow, thin

thief

noun

a person who steals

A thief took all our money.

robber, burglar, cat burglar, housebreaker, embezzler, bandit, highwayman, pickpocket, shoplifter

Thief and **robber** are general terms that can describe any criminal who steals. A **cat burglar** uses stealth to break into places where valuables are kept, usually under cover of darkness. A **housebreaker** breaks into houses for the purpose of stealing. An **embezzler**, sometimes called a "white-collar criminal," steals from his or her own workplace, often a bank, without violence. **Bandit** and **highwayman** are old-fashioned terms for thieves who rode on horseback, holding up travelers in coaches and making a quick getaway. A **pickpocket** is a a person who steals by deftly reaching into a victim's pocket and removing a wallet or loose money. A **shoplifter** takes small things from stores without paying.

thin

adjective

1 having little width
The young tree has a thin trunk.
narrow, slender, slight, slim

Most jockeys have a slight build.

2 having little flesh
The dog is so thin that its ribs are showing.
underweight, skinny, lean, slender, scrawny, gaunt, rawboned, slight, spare, emaciated

Antonyms: fat (2), hefty (2), thick (1), wide (1)

thing

noun

1 any nonliving object that has shape and form and can be touched
Please pick those things up off the floor.
object, article, item, entity

2 an event
A bad thing happened yesterday.
incident, event, happening, occurrence, occasion, episode

a
b
c
d
e
f
g
h
i
j
k
l
m
n
o
p
q
r
s
t
u
v
w
x
y
z

things *See* **goods, possession, property**

think 🔵
verb
1 to use the power of the mind
A philosopher once said, "I think, therefore I am."
reason, reflect, imagine, cogitate, ratiocinate
2 to judge or reason about a matter
I thought about the question for a long time.
consider, deliberate, ponder, weigh, contemplate, meditate, ruminate, muse, mull over
3 to remember or have in mind
She was thinking how happy she had been.
recall, recollect, remember, reminisce

I could not remember his name.

What was his name...?
Mr. Parks
Mr. Weiss
Mr. Tavares
Mr. Dudla
Mr. Wheeler

4 to have an opinion
I think he is a good man.
believe, imagine, feel, suppose, deem
See also: remember

thinking 🔵 *See* **understanding**

thoroughly *See* **quite, stiff, well**

thought 🔵
noun
1 the result of thinking
I just had a thought.
idea, notion, concept, perception

> *some words used to describe thoughts*
> abstract, clever, conscious, deep, deliberate, eccentric, illogical, incoherent, ingenious, logical, original, profound, reasonable, serious, sobering

2 serious or careful attention
He gave thought to the problem.
attention, consideration, heed
Antonym: neglect (2)

thoughtful
adjective
1 having or showing careful thought
She wrote a thoughtful book about the causes of war.
serious, sober, reflective, considered, reasoned
2 giving careful attention to the needs of others
The thoughtful child always remembered her mother's birthday.
attentive, considerate, conscientious
Antonyms: inconsiderate (2), thoughtless (2)

threads *See* **clothes**

threat *See* **danger**

threaten
verb
to say that one will harm or punish
The mugger threatened him with a knife.
intimidate, menace, bully

throw
verb
to send through the air with force by using the arm and wrist
She threw the baseball to the shortstop.
cast, chuck, fling, heave, hurl, launch, pitch, toss
noun
the act or result of throwing
He made a strong throw from the outfield.
cast, fling, heave, hurl, pitch, toss
See also: pitch

thrust
verb
to push or drive with force
He thrust his fist through the door in anger.
drive, force, jam, poke, press, propel, push, ram, shove
Antonyms: pull, yank
noun
1 the act of pushing forward with force
The knight finished his enemy with one last thrust of his sword.

 Human Body

? Human Mind   👕 Everyday Life   🏳 History and Culture   📞 Communication

drive, push, shove, poke, jab

   2 an attack by the army, navy, or other force
   The officers planned a thrust into enemy lands.
assault, attack, charge, onslaught, strike

   Antonyms: pull (1), retreat (2), yank (1)

thumb *See* **leaf**

thump

noun
   a heavy, dull sound of one thing hitting
      another
   I heard the thump of elephant feet in the distance.
clump, clunk, pound, thud, wham

verb
   to beat or strike with a heavy, dull sound
   Miss McLoud thumped the desk with her fist.
beat, bump, club, pound, slam, wham
   Our car bumped the car parked in front of it.

thunder *See* **roar**

ticklish *See* **delicate**

tie

verb
   to fasten, secure,
      or bind with a
      cord or string
   *He tied the boat to
      the dock.*
bind, lace, lash,
moor, rope, tether
   *He will bind the
      newspapers
      with string.*

   Antonyms: undo, untie
   See also: rope

tied *See* **related**

tiger *See* **cat**

tight

adjective
   1 fastened in a secure way; fixed in place
   I made a tight knot so my shoes would stay tied.
fast, firm, secure, solid

   2 close in fit
   I need new shoes because these are too tight.
close, constricted, narrow, snug

   3 made so that nothing can pass through
   *This window has a tight seal so that heat cannot
      escape.*
impermeable, solid, impenetrable, impervious,
airtight

   Antonyms: loose (1,2), roomy (2), slack (1)

till *See* **farm**

time 🌐 🔬

noun
   1 the measured period between the beginning
      and the end of an event
   We waited in line a long time.
   *She napped for a short time before returning to
      work.*
duration, interval, period, span, spell, stretch,
while

   2 (often **times**) a period marked by particular
      events
   Socrates lived in ancient times.
age, period, era, epoch

   3 a particular instance or event
   I remember the time you broke your leg.
   She called me two times.
moment, occasion, point, instance

   See also: moment, stage

tiny

adjective
   very small
   This kitten is tiny.
diminutive, minuscule, miniature, minute, itty-
bitty, small, teeny, wee, microscopic

   Antonyms: enormous, huge, immense
   See also: small

tip *See* **end, point, top, boat, mountain**

A
B
C
D
E
F
G
H
I
J
K
L
M
N
O
P
Q
R
S
T
U
V
W
X
Y
Z

a
b
c
d
e
f
g
h
i
j
k
l
m
n
o
p
q
r
s
t
u
v
w
x
y
z

tire
verb

1 to make tired
The long hike tired us.
fatigue, weary, exhaust, drain, sap, weaken

2 to become tired
She tires quickly because she never exercises.
droop, flag, weaken, weary, poop out, burn out

Antonyms: energize (1), invigorate (1), refresh (1)

tired *See* exercise

title *See* call, literature

title *See* name

today *See* now

toe *See* foot

tomorrow *See* future

tone *See* air, color, literature

tongue *See* language

tons *See* many, much

tool *See* device, instrument

tooth
noun
one of the hard, bony objects that grow in rows in the jaws of animals with backbones

some kinds of teeth
bicuspid, bucktooth, canine, eyetooth, fang, incisor, molar, tusk, wisdom tooth
some things done with the teeth
bite, chatter, chew, click, crush, cut, grind, rip, tear

top
noun
the highest area, point, or surface
We climbed to the top of the mountain.
summit, crest, peak, apex, crown, tip, pinnacle, vertex, zenith

Antonym: bottom
verb
to go beyond
He topped his brother in the swimming race.
better *She bettered the school record in that race.*
best *This team bested last year's state champion.*
break *She may break the world record.*
exceed *This student has exceeded our expectations.*
overcome *I overcame his lead on the last turn of the race.*
surpass *This year's rainfall surpasses last year's.*

topic *See* question, subject

total
adjective

1 making up or including the whole
I paid the total amount that I owed.
complete, entire, full, whole

2 complete
He made a total fool of himself by wearing pajamas to work.
absolute, complete, downright, outright, perfect, thorough, utter
verb
to add up
She totaled each team's points.
tally, count, calculate, compute, add up

totally
adverb
completely; entirely
The new computer was totally useless after it fell into the bathtub.
absolutely, altogether, downright, entirely, fully, outright, overall, plumb, wholly
Antonyms: barely, hardly, scantly, scarcely

touch
verb

1 to make contact with
Don't let your feet touch the grass.
brush, bump, contact, feel, graze, strike

2 to be next to
Their yard touches ours.
border, adjoin, neighbor, abut

Human Body   Human Mind   Everyday Life   History and Culture   Communication

3 to have an effect on
Her story touched the lives of many people.
affect, move, stir, influence

noun

1 the act or an instance of touching
He felt a touch on his arm and turned to find an old friend.
brush, bump, contact, graze

2 the state of communicating closely
Please keep in touch with the office while you are out of town.
contact, communication, association, connection

> The spider's **touch**, how exquisitely fine!
> Feels at each thread, and lives along the line.
> —From "ESSAY ON MAN," a poem by Alexander Pope (1688-1744), British poet

3 a small amount
This recipe calls for a touch of garlic.
He felt a touch of guilt for saying those mean things.
trace, hint, bit, shade, tinge, suggestion

There was a trace of snow, but not enough to play in.
See also: feel

touching See moving

touchy See delicate, irritable

tough See difficult, hard, harsh, severe, stiff, strong, sturdy

tour See travel, trip

tower See excel, building

town See community, country

toy See miniature

trace See bit, copy, draw, find, mark, sign, suggestion, touch

track See hunt, way, dog

trade See business, deal, give, sell, skill, switch, economy

tradition

noun

a culture's beliefs and customs as passed from parents to children over many years
customs, practices, folkways, heritage, legacy

In Jewish tradition, the groom smashes a glass with his foot at his wedding.

> *some adjectives used to describe traditions*
> ancient, cultural, established, ethnic, family, formal, national, oral, religious, social, written

traffic See deal, sell

trail See drift, follow, sport

train

noun

1 a long, moving line of persons, animals, or vehicles
The train of horses climbed the hill.
column, parade, convoy, file, procession
The procession made its way down the street.

2 a series of things or ideas
He lost his train of thought.
order, chain, sequence, succession

 Living World  Physical World Natural Environment Economy Government and Law

a
b
c

verb
to teach skills or actions
He trained his dog to heel.
teach, coach, drill, instruct, school, groom, condition

d **training** 🧠 👕 *See* **knowledge**

e **trait** *See* **point, property**

f **transfer** *See* **move, pass, shift, take**

g **transport** *See* **carry, move, take, airplane**

h **trap** *See* **catch**

i **trash** 👕 🏳️ *See* **destroy, junk**

j **travel**
verb

k
1 to journey from place to place
My father traveled to many countries.

l
journey, tour, trek, voyage

m
She journeyed to the Arctic in search of adventure.

n
o
p
q
r
s
t

To **trek** means to travel a great distance on foot. To **voyage** means to travel by sea.

u
2 to journey over
We traveled the country on our vacation.
cover, cross, traverse, range

v
noun

w
(usually **travels**) a journey
Our travels took us through Europe and the Middle East.

x
journey, tour, trip, voyage, excursion, expedition

y
z

See also: trip

treasure *See* **favorite, prize, value, love**

treat
verb
to attempt to relieve or cure
She treated the child's illness with antibiotics.
aid, doctor, nurse, tend to

treatment
noun
the means used to cure a disease or heal an injury
Chicken soup is a good treatment for a cold.
cure *Scientists are searching for a cure for cancer.*
remedy *Aspirin is a good headache remedy.*
therapy *Eric needed months of physical therapy after the accident.*

treaty *See* **agreement**

tree 👕 💧 🏳️
noun
a woody plant that has a long main trunk and leaves

some kinds of trees
citrus, coniferous, deciduous, evergreen, flowering, fruit, palm

tremendous *See* **excellent, giant, great, huge, incredible, vast**

trend *See* **style**

trial 🧠 💬 *See* **check, test**

tribal *See* **culture**

tribe *See* **band, people**

trick
noun
1 a mischievous act
Gigi is up to her old tricks again.
Lulu loves to play tricks on her little brother.
prank, practical joke, antic, caper, gag, shenanigans, monkeyshines

🤸 Human Body   ❓ Human Mind   👕 Everyday Life   🏳️ History and Culture   📞 Communication

Trees

acacia

weeping willow

Japanese maple

orange

pine cones

cherry

crabapple

bonsai

birch

banyan

sequoia

birch

bark

a
b
c
d
e
f
g
h
i
j
k
l
m
n
o
p
q
r
s
t
u
v
w
x
y
z

As a gag, they gave him a rubber chicken for his birthday.

2 an act of skill or magic
He taught his monkey a new trick.
The gymnast did tricks on the high bar.
feat, stunt, illusion, sleight of hand

Use **illusion** and **sleight of hand** when speaking or writing about magic tricks.

verb
   to cheat or fool someone
   He tricked me into paying for his vacation in Tahiti.
cheat, deceive, fool, dupe, mislead, hoodwink, sucker, swindle

tricks *See* **magic**

trip
noun
   1 the act of traveling
   They took a trip to Bali.
journey, excursion, junket, tour, ride, voyage, expedition
   2 a short journey from one point to another
   I made two trips to the store today.
hop *It's just a short hop to my grandmother's house.*
jaunt *We took a jaunt to the beach yesterday.*
run *Brian made a run to the store for milk and bread.*
spin *Rocky took me for a spin in his new car.*
   See also: travel

triumph *See* **succeed, success, win**

troops ○ ⬤ *See* **army**

trouble
noun
   1 a state of being disturbed or in need
   The drowning man was in serious trouble.

difficulty, distress, hardship, bind, fix, hot water, jam, predicament

Use the indefinite article "a" before **bind, fix, jam,** and **predicament**: *Mimi found herself in a bind; Jojo was in quite a predicament.*

2 a source of difficulty or distress
The werewolf's approach meant trouble for the villagers.
misfortune, ordeal, annoyance, grief, nuisance, burden, curse, hassle, problem, worry

true *See* **accurate, honest, loyal, natural, special, love**

trust ⊙
noun
   1 a belief in the strength or truth of a person or thing
   You have earned my trust because of your honesty.
confidence, faith, reliance
   2 the charge or care of a person or thing
   They left the child in the trust of his grandmother.
care, custody, charge, protection, guardianship, safekeeping
   Antonyms: doubt (1), mistrust (1)
verb
   1 to rely upon (usually **trust in** or **trust to**)
   We trusted in the old bridge to get us safely across the creek.

count on *Can I count on you to keep a secret?*
depend on *We're depending on your help.*
lean on *I lean on her for good advice.*
rely on *May I rely on your help to finish this job?*
   2 to believe
   I trust his word.
accept, believe, put stock in, swear by
   See also: care, hope, believe

🏃 Human Body   ❓ Human Mind   👕 Everyday Life   🏳 History and Culture   📞 Communication

truth
noun

1 agreement with the facts or what is real
There is no truth to what he said.
accuracy, credibility, reality, veracity

2 the state or condition of being true
We are relying on the truth of your statement.
accuracy, correctness, validity, truthfulness

3 a fact or principle that has been proved
It is a truth that this world is round and not flat.
fact *It is a fact that water covers most of the earth's surface.*
law *"What goes up must come down" is a law of nature.*
certainty *It is a certainty that she will win the prize.*
given *It is a given that he will always be late.*

Antonyms: fallacy (3), falsehood (3), lie (3)

try
verb

1 make an effort
Ringo tried to push the goat away.
attempt, endeavor, strive, struggle, aim, bother, take a crack at

Bother means "make an effort" when used in a negative statement: *Billy did not even bother to keep his room clean.*

2 to test the quality or take a taste of
She tried our apple pie.
sample, taste, test

Antonym: refuse (2)

noun

an effort or attempt
It was a good try, but he did not win the race.
attempt, effort, bid, endeavor

Antonym: give up

tube
noun

a long, hollow piece of glass, metal, or rubber used to hold or carry liquids or gases
There's a tube that carries fuel to the engine.
pipe, duct, hose, line, main, conduit

tune ⊘
noun

a series of pleasing musical tones; melody
He played a tune on the piano.
melody, song, strain, theme

See also: song

tunnel *See* **dig, hole, animal**

turn
verb

1 to cause to move around a center point
Turn the key in the lock to open the door.
crank *Tim cranked the lid open.*
wind *He wound the crank.*
pivot *I pivoted my chair to get a better view.*
roll *We rolled the tire into the garage.*
rotate *I rotated the globe to find South America.*
spin *Tim spun a basketball on his finger.*
swirl *The washing machine swirled the clothes.*
twirl *She twirled a baton in the air.*
whirl *She whirled her partner across the dance floor.*
swivel *Mina swiveled her desk chair.*
twist *Tina twisted the door handle and entered the room.*

2 to change the nature, character, or color of
The change of season turned the leaves many colors.
change, alter, modify, transform, convert, metamorphose

noun

an angle, bend, or curve
There are many turns in the path.
bend, corner, curve, arc, crook, twist, zigzag

twin *See* **match**

twirl *See* **roll, turn, twist**

a
b
c
d
e
f
g
h
i
j
k
l
m
n
o
p
q
r
s
t
u
v
w
x
y
z

twist
verb

to wind or coil around something else

I twisted my hair around my finger.

coil, wind, loop, roll, twirl, spiral, twine, wrap

The snake wound around the tree branch.

The staircase spiraled from the top floor to the floor below.

Antonyms: untwist, unwind

twisted *See* bent

type *See* class, grade, kind, model, nature

typical
adjective

having the expected qualities of a particular type of person or thing

A typical baby walks at about one year old.

normal, usual, ordinary, characteristic, classic, representative

Antonyms: abnormal, atypical, unusual

See also: normal, usual

 Human Body   Human Mind   Everyday Life   History and Culture   Communication

ugly
adjective

1 unpleasant to look at; not attractive
He has an ugly scar on his face.
unattractive, unsightly, hideous

2 causing offense; mean in a repulsive way
That was an ugly thing to say.
disgusting, hideous, offensive, objectionable, obnoxious, nasty, abominable, loathsome, rotten

Antonyms: attractive (1), beautiful (1), considerate

unbelievable *See* incredible

uncertain
adjective

1 not known for sure
It is uncertain whether eating too much salt causes health problems for everyone.
ambiguous, indefinite, unclear, unsettled

2 not knowing with certainty
Lottie is uncertain about what to do next.
doubtful, undecided, unsure, hesitant

3 likely to change
You shouldn't go sailing in uncertain weather.
undecided *I said I would go, but I'm really undecided.*
variable *Weather conditions in the mountains are variable.*
unpredictable *The time the bus will arrive is sometimes unpredictable.*

Antonyms: certain (1), convinced (2), stable (3), sure (1,2)

uncommon *See* special, unusual

under *See* subject

underside *See* bottom

understand
verb

to get the meaning, nature, or importance of
Do you understand what you're reading?
comprehend *Do you comprehend what the teacher said?*
grasp *The detective suddenly grasped the importance of the clue.*
see *I don't see the point.*
get *Do you get the meaning this story?*
follow *Did you follow the story he told?*
fathom *I'll never fathom how to use this kind of computer.*
perceive *She read the paragraph over and over until she perceived what it meant.*
realize *Do you realize how big a redwood tree is?*

understanding
noun

1 the ability to understand
Her clear understanding makes her a fine leader.
intellect, intelligence, reason, wit, mind, perception, thinking

2 knowledge or skill in a particular area
She has a good understanding of math.
grasp, knowledge, command, grip

Grip is usually followed by the preposition "on" when it means **understanding**: *I finally got a grip on playing the piano after a great deal of practice.*

---

adjective
feeling or having sympathy

I'm glad to have such an understanding friend.
sympathetic, tolerant, accepting, kind, patient, thoughtful

underwater *See* **photography**

unfamiliar *See* **new, strange**

unfortunate
adjective
1 having bad luck
Those unfortunate people lost everything they owned in the fire.
poor, unlucky, wretched, sorry
2 causing a difficult or harmful condition
An unfortunate event left us stranded without transportation.
unlucky, sorry, unhappy, ill, adverse
Some say it is unlucky for a black cat to cross your path.

Antonyms: auspicious (2), blessed (2), fortunate (1,2), lucky (1)
See also: poor

unhappy
adjective
1 not glad or cheerful
My nephew is unhappy about having to change schools.
blue, down, gloomy, glum, sad, dejected, downcast, melancholy, low
2 causing results that are not wanted
He made an unhappy choice of job.
unfortunate, unlucky, regrettable
Antonyms: cheerful (1), glad (1), happy (1)

unhealthy
adjective
1 in bad health
The unhealthy child missed a lot of school.
ill, sick, unwell, sickly
2 causing poor health or disease

Smoking is an unhealthy habit.
bad, harmful, detrimental, toxic
Antonyms: healthful (2), healthy (1), sound (1), well (1), wholesome (2)

uniform ○ *See* **regular**

union
noun
1 the condition of being united
The union of the two companies was what kept their business successful.
unity, merging, alliance, marriage, confederation
2 a group of states or countries united under a single government
The U.S. Civil War began when the northern states refused to allow the southern states to leave the Union.
alliance, confederation, federation, league, confederacy
Antonyms: division (1), divorce (1), partition (1)

unique *See* **original, particular, special**

unit ● *See* **piece**

unite
verb
to join together into a whole
The prime minister united the members of her party.
combine, join, unify, ally
Antonyms: divide, separate, split
See also: join

unity *See* **union**

universal
adjective
of, having to do with, or characteristic of the whole world or the world's population
Universal peace seems like an impossible dream.
global, worldwide, international
Antonyms: local, regional

 Human Body   Human Mind   Everyday Life   History and Culture   Communication

universe 🌐 *See* world

university 🎓 🏫 *See* school

unlike *See* different

unlucky *See* poor, unfortunate, unhappy

unnecessary
adjective
not needed or required
*It is unnecessary to carry an umbrella on such a
fine day.*
needless, unneeded, excessive
Antonyms: essential, necessary

unpleasant
adjective
not pleasant or agreeable
*The unpleasant odor comes from the fish that was
left out all night.*
disagreeable, distasteful, offensive, foul,
displeasing, obnoxious, objectionable
Antonyms: agreeable, nice, pleasant
See also: foul

unusual
adjective
not usual or ordinary; remarkable
She had never seen such an unusual bird before.
*It is unusual for workers in the
United States to take an afternoon nap.*
exceptional, remarkable,
strange, uncommon,
extraordinary,
abnormal, rare,
singular, odd
*Aunt Martha found an
uncommon beetle in her garden.*
Antonyms: commonplace, typical, usual
See also: strange

unusually *See* extra

up *See* forward

upright *See* good, honest, just, stand, moral

uproar
noun
a loud, confused disturbance
*When stock prices fell, there was an uproar on the
floor of the stock exchange.*
commotion, hubbub, clamor, pandemonium

upset 🌐 ⚖️
verb
to bother or to make uncomfortable
Their complaints upset her.
Milk upsets his stomach.
agitate, distress, disturb, fluster, discomfort,
trouble
Antonyms: calm, comfort, ease
adjective
bothered
I have an upset stomach.
Be kind to an upset friend.
agitated, flustered, bothered, disturbed
Antonyms: composed, relaxed, untroubled
See also: disturb, trouble

urban *See* community, culture

usage *See* use

use
verb
to spend
He used his last dollar to buy some bread.
consume *That old car consumes a lot of fuel.*
spend *He spent his energy on the tasks that interested him.*
apply *Jane applied her knowledge of math in solving
the problem.*
noun
1 the act or practice of using
We made use of wood for heating this year.
application, employment, usage
2 benefit
There is no use in fighting.
advantage, benefit, profit, usefulness, value,
worth, gain, point

A
B
C
D
E
F
G
H
I
J
K
L
M
N
O
P
Q
R
S
T
U
V
W
X
Y
Z

3 purpose
This machine has many uses.
function, purpose, application

useful
adjective
able to be used in a helpful, practical, or effective way
We have a useful book that tells which mushrooms are safe to eat.
handy *This hammer is a handy tool.*
practical *We need a practical solution to the traffic problem.*
usable *This sponge is so dirty it's not usable.*
convenient *Everything in this office is in a convenient place.*

Antonyms: useless, worthless
See also: helpful

useless
adjective
having no good or practical purpose
It is useless to try to move all this furniture when we're so tired.
aimless, worthless, impractical, vain

This sense of **vain** may be applied only to situations or attempts, not to things or people.

Antonyms: practical, useful, worthwhile

usual
adjective
most common or expected
My backpack was in its usual place.
customary, habitual, normal, routine, standard, typical, regular, conventional, accustomed, common

Antonyms: atypical, uncommon, unusual
noun
that which is usual
He comes into this diner every morning and orders the usual.
ordinary, routine, standard, commonplace

Antonyms: extraordinary, uncommon, unusual
See also: normal, ordinary

usually *See* **generally**

Human Body Human Mind Everyday Life History and Culture Communication

valley
noun
a long area of low land between mountains or hills
dale, basin, canyon, chasm, glen, gorge, gulch, gully, hollow, ravine

valuable *See* **helpful**

value
noun
1 the worth, importance, or usefulness of something
She places great value on education.
merit, usefulness, worth, meaning, importance
2 (usually **values**) principles considered most important
Protecting the natural environment is one of his values.
ideals, morals, principles, standards, beliefs
verb
to think of as important or valuable
He valued her help.
appreciate *We appreciate spring after the cold winter.*
esteem *He esteems friendship more than money.*
prize *The cowboy prized his palomino horse.*
treasure *I treasure her faith in me.*

cherish *She cherishes those old photographs.*

values *See* **character, moral, culture**

vapor *See* **fog, water**

variable *See* **irregular, uncertain**

variety *See* **kind, model, nature**

various
adjective
of many different kinds
I have various reasons for wanting to quit the team.
assorted, different, diverse, miscellaneous
Antonyms: identical, like, one
See also: different

vary *See* **change, range**

vast
adjective
1 very large in size or area
They drove past vast fields of corn.
extensive, immense, enormous, spacious, huge, tremendous, wide, monstrous, great, large, massive
2 very large in number or amount
A vast crowd attended the concert.
tremendous, enormous, great, large, huge, extensive
Antonyms: compact (1), few (2), limited (2), minuscule (1), minute (1), small (1)
See also: great

very
adverb
to a great extent; in a high degree
He is very sad.
It is very cold tonight.
awfully *That was an awfully nice thing to do.*
especially *The chicken is especially good at this restaurant.*
exceedingly *Gordon talks exceedingly fast.*
extremely *I did extremely well on that last quiz.*

a
b
c
d
e
f
g
h
i
j
k
l
m
n
o
p
q
r
s
t
u
v
w
x
y
z

quite *I thought that I did quite well cleaning my room.*
so *I'm so happy the job is finished.*
terribly *She was terribly upset by what you said to her.*
pretty *It snowed pretty hard last night.*

Antonyms: barely, scarcely, slightly

adjective
exact; precise
Your help was the very thing we needed.
exact, precise, particular

Antonyms: not a bit, not at all

vessel *See* boat

vice *See* evil, fault

victim
noun
someone who is hurt, injured, or killed by a person, group, or event
The murderer stabbed his victim.
The orphan was a victim of war.
butt *I hate when I am the butt of my big sister's jokes.*
prey *The crooks chose him as their prey.*
target *They made him a target because he wears unusual clothes.*
casualty *There was a train accident, but there were no casualties.*

Antonyms: perpetrator, survivor

victory *See* success, win

view ⊙
noun
1 the area that can be seen from a particular point
There is a beautiful view from the top of Pike's Peak.
landscape, scene, scenery, vista, outlook, panorama
2 (usually **views**) a way of thinking about something; opinion; perception
She told us her views on education.

attitude, idea, judgment, notion, opinion, perception, outlook, position, viewpoint, conception, conviction, feeling, theory, thought

verb
to look at with great care; survey
The police will view the evidence.
examine, inspect, look at, scrutinize, survey

See also: see

village ⊙ ⊚ *See* community, country

villain
noun
an evil person or character
The wolf is the villain in the story of Little Red Riding Hood.
scoundrel, rogue, antagonist, evildoer

violence
noun
an act that causes injury or harm
The criminal uses violence to try to get what he wants.
bloodshed, force, assault, attack

violent
adjective
1 acting with great force or ill will
The violent criminal was sent to prison for twenty-five years.
brutal *The brutal attack on the woman was reported in the newspapers the next morning.*
ferocious *Mother bears can become ferocious if their cubs are hurt.*
savage *The wolf rushed at the man in a savage attack.*
vicious *Stay away from the vicious dog.*
2 very strong; harsh
The violent storm tore off the roof of our house.
ferocious, harsh, mighty, overpowering, raging, severe, brutal, fierce, rough, wild
3 having strong emotional force
He has a violent temper.

🏃 Human Body   ❓ Human Mind   👕 Everyday Life   🚩 History and Culture   📞 Communication

furious, passionate, hot, wild, ardent, fiery, intense, raging

> Antonyms: gentle (1,2), nonviolent (1), peaceful (1), placid (2)

visible
adjective

1 able to be seen
The skyscraper is visible from across the river.
apparent *It is apparent that you didn't make the bed.*
external *He's a sad person, but he gives the external impression of being happy.*
plain *The tower on the hill is in plain view of everyone in town.*

2 easily seen; obvious
There has been a visible change in the patient's condition.
noticeable, obvious, conspicuous, plain

> Antonyms: concealed (1), hidden (1), invisible (1)

See also: plain

vision ⊙ See picture, sight

visit
verb

1 to go or come to see
We visit our cousins every year.
I visited the zoo last week.
call on, drop by, see

2 to stay with for a short time as a guest
Our friends visited us in February.
sojourn, stay, stopover, stop by, stop in

> Antonyms: avoid (1), bypass (1), sidestep (1)

noun

the act of staying somewhere as a guest
I go to my grandparents' house for a visit every year.
stay, sojourn, stop, stopover

visualize See imagine, picture

vital See important, lively, living, serious

voice ⊘ See express, pronounce, say, speak

volume See amount, production

voyage See travel, trip

A
B
C
D
E
F
G
H
I
J
K
L
M
N
O
P
Q
R
S
T
U
V
W
X
Y
Z

a
b
c
d
e
f
g
h
i
j
k
l
m
n
o
p
q
r
s
t
u
v
w
x
y
z

waist *See* **clothes**

wait
noun
>the act, instance, or period of waiting
>*There was a long wait before the movie started.*
>delay, holdup, postponement, pause

walk
verb
>1 to move at a steady pace by steps
>*She walked about the neighborhood.*
>step, tread, pace, stride, march, amble, stroll, saunter, mosey, plod, trudge, slog, perambulate

>2 to lead or go with on foot
>*He walked her home after the party.*
>accompany, escort, lead, guide, usher

noun
>an act or instance of walking
>*Let's take a walk after dinner.*
>hike, stroll, constitutional

wall ○ *See* **barrier**

wander
verb
>to move about with no purpose or plan
>*We wandered through the halls of the ancient castle.*
>ramble, roam, rove, range, meander, traipse

want
verb
>to desire or wish for
>*Do you want to dance?*
>*Kristen wants a new bicycle.*
>wish *Do you wish to leave now?*
>desire *I do not desire to go with you.*
>care *Would you care to dance?*
>like *We can dance, if you'd like.*
>long *He longed to visit Texas again.*
>covet *Kristen coveted Pat's bicycle.*

Wish, **desire**, **care**, and **like** are more formal and polite ways of saying **want**, when used in sentences like the ones above. Saying "Would you care to...?" is an elegant way of asking whether someone wants to do something. Among your friends, you probably use the more informal "want."

See also: desire

wanting *See* **poor**

war ○
noun
>a state or time of armed fighting between countries, states, or other groups of people
>*Many lives were lost in the war.*
>conflict, hostilities, warfare, clash

> Sometime they'll give a **war** and nobody will come.
> —*Carl Sandburg (1878-1967), American poet*

>*some words associated with war*
>assault, attack, battle, besiege, blockade, bomb, bombard, charge, combat, conquer, defend, destroy, devastate, fight, invade, kill, retreat, rebel, revolt, shell, struggle

Antonym: peace

Human Body   Human Mind   Everyday Life   History and Culture   Communication

warm
adjective
1 having or giving off heat
The fire in the fire-place made the room feel warm.
hot, toasty, cozy

2 lively; enthusiastic
The musicians received a warm round of applause.
hearty, enthusiastic, lively

3 full of kindness
She took him in a warm embrace.
You have a warm heart to do such kind things.
affectionate, friendly, sincere, kind, cheerful
Antonyms: cold (1,2,3), cool (1), frosty (3), unenthusiastic (2)
verb
to increase the temperature of
He warmed the soup for dinner.
heat, thaw, cook, melt
Antonyms: chill, freeze, refrigerate
See also: hot, friendly

warmth   *See* affection, cheer

warn
verb
to tell of a possible danger
They warned us about the snowstorm.
alert, caution, forewarn, notify, admonish
The police alerted the town that a tiger had escaped from the zoo.

warning   *See* alarm, notice

wash
verb
1 to make clean by using water or soap
He washed all the dinner plates.
clean, launder, cleanse, rinse, scrub, mop

2 to flow over
The waves washed over the dock.
flow, pour, rush, stream, lap, splash
Antonyms: dirty (1), soil (1)

washed   *See* clean

waste   *See* decay, junk, loss

watch
verb
1 to look closely or carefully
He watched as the bug crawled across the table.
look, regard, gaze, see, stare, observe, view

2 to guard or tend attentively
Grandmother is watching the children.
guard, tend, mind, supervise, baby-sit, look after, take care of
Antonyms: ignore (2), neglect (2)
See also: look

water
noun
a clear liquid that has no taste or odor. Water takes the form of rain, rivers, oceans, and lakes and is a requirement for most forms of life

some words associated with moving water
deluge, dribble, drift, drip, drizzle, ebb, flow, flush, gush, leak, trickle, wave
some forms of water
fog, hail, ice, liquid, rain, sleet, snow, steam, vapor

wave
noun
a sudden increase of a feeling, activity, or condition
She felt a wave of happiness.

A B C D E F G H I J K L M N O P Q R S T U V W X Y Z

Water

mist

icicle

dew

falls

fog

rainbow

snow

clouds

wavelets

There was a wave of cold weather.

surge *She felt a surge of anger when she saw the broken window.*

gush *The plumber knew how to stop the gush of water from the pipe.*

rush *There was a rush to the doors when the movie ended.*

outburst *There was an outburst of laughter in the audience when a barking dog ran across the stage.*

verb

1 to move up and down or back and forth with ease

The flags waved in the breeze.

flap, flutter, fly

2

to give a sign or direct by moving one's hand up and down or back and forth

I waved hello.

He waved them off the stage.

motion, sign, signal, beckon

waves 🌀 *See* **sea**

wax *See* **grow, polish**

way

noun

1 a road or path leading from one place to another

Which is the fastest way home?

path, route, course, track, road, approach

2 an opening that is a passage

The front window is the only way in.

🏃 Human Body ❓ Human Mind 👕 Everyday Life 🚩 History and Culture 📞 Communication

passage, access, approach, opening, entrance, exit

An **approach** is a way toward, an **entrance** is a way in, and an **exit** is a way out.

---

3 a particular manner of acting or means of doing
He wants everything to be done his way.
I'll show you the way to solve that problem.
manner, mode, style, fashion, technique, method, procedure, process

4 method of thinking or acting
In some ways, she's right.
aspect *From this aspect, the tree looks easy to climb.*
respect *She is like her father in many respects.*
facet *You must consider all the facets of that problem.*
regard *I agree with you in that regard only.*

weak
adjective
1 having little physical strength or power
I was too weak to walk after the accident.
feeble, frail, infirm, limp, faint, faltering

2 likely to break or fail under strain or pressure; not sturdy
The weak branches on the tree broke off during the storm.
flimsy, fragile, shaky, delicate, rickety, brittle
Antonyms: hardy (2), mighty (1), powerful (1), robust (1), strong (1), sturdy (2)

weakness *See* **fault, flaw, taste**

wealth *See* **plenty, store, success**

wealthy *See* **rich, successful, money**

wear
verb
1 to cause to become damaged through long use, friction, or exposure
Constant kneeling wore the knees of his jeans.
erode *Pounding waves eroded the beach.*

batter *Fear battered his confidence.*
eat *Rust ate away at the metal fence.*
fray *Frequent use frays a shirt collar.*
wash *Rain washed the topsoil away.*

2 to make weak
This child is wearing my patience.
exhaust, drain, weaken, fatigue, strain, tax, weary

noun
clothing of a particular kind
She stocks women's wear at the department store.
clothing, dress, attire, apparel, garments

weather
noun
the conditions outside at a particular place and time. Sunshine, clouds, temperature, and rain are some of the changing conditions that make up the weather

some kinds of weather
blizzard, downpour, drizzle, drought, flurry, hail, hurricane, mist, precipitation, rain, rainfall, shower, sleet, snowstorm
some words used to describe weather
arctic, arid, bleak, clear, cloudy, cold, fair, foul, hot, humid, pouring, rainy, sunny, temperate, warm, windy

weigh *See* **consider, judge, think**

weighed *See* **deliberate**

weight
noun
1 the quality of being heavy
There's a lot of weight to this bowling ball.
mass, heft, size, heaviness

2 importance or influence
My father's advice had a lot of weight in my decision.
importance, influence, significance, emphasis, gravity, strength, value, substance

See also: importance

a b c d e f g h i j k l m n o p q r s t u v w x y z

weird
adjective

   1 puzzlingly unusual
   His weird behavior has his parents worried.
odd, strange, peculiar, queer

   2 having a strange and unnatural character
   A weird laugh came from the attic.
eerie, uncanny, ghostly, mysterious, supernatural, unnatural, unearthly

   Antonyms: normal (2), routine (1), typical (1)

welcome
verb

   1 to receive with pleasure and friendliness
   We welcomed them into our home.
greet *The Porters greeted their dinner guests at the door.*
receive *We received him as a member of our club.*
include *They would be happy to include you in their plans.*

   2 to be glad to receive or accept
   I would welcome some help with the vacuuming.
embrace *I embraced the chance to go to Europe.*
invite *The physicist invited questions about his latest findings.*
encourage *The performers encouraged the audience's participation.*
appreciate *Mrs. Lund appreciated the neighbors' help.*
accept *I'll gladly accept your suggestions.*

   Antonyms: bemoan (2), regret (2), reject (1), rue (2), snub (1)

adjective

   freely allowed
   You are welcome to share this food.
invited, encouraged, free, permitted

   Antonyms: prevented, unwelcome

welfare *See* good

well
adverb

   1 in a good, proper, or acceptable way
   Her work is going well.
properly, successfully, satisfactorily, adequately, nicely

   2 in a careful, thorough way
   He did his job very well.
carefully, completely, thoroughly, fully, conscientiously

   3 with skill
   She sings well.
excellently, superbly, splendidly, skillfully, commendably

   4 in a close or familiar way
   I knew her well.
closely, personally, familiarly, intimately

   Antonyms: badly (1,2), ineptly (3), poorly (1), scarcely (4), unskillfully (3), vaguely (4)

adjective

   healthy; sound
   She is not well today.
fit, fine, healthy, sound, all right

   Antonyms: ill, sick, unhealthy

   See also: good

well-known *See* famous

western *See* culture, film

wet
adjective

   soaked or covered with a liquid
   Hang those wet clothes out to dry.
damp, moist, soggy, sodden, soaked, drenched, sopping, waterlogged

   Antonym: dry

noun

   water; moisture
   There was wet all through the rotted wood.
dampness, moisture, water, damp

   Antonym: dryness

wheat *See* grain

wheel *See* airplane

while *See* spell, stretch, time

whip *See* beat

whispered *See* soft

Human Body   Human Mind   Everyday Life   History and Culture   Communication

whistle 🔊 *See* alarm, blow, bird

white *See* light, hair

whole
adjective
1 having all the parts
I put together the whole puzzle.
complete, entire, total, full

2 all in one piece; not divided
The snake swallowed the whole frog.
entire, intact, complete

Antonyms: apart (2), incomplete (1), partial (1), separated (2)

noun
the entire amount of a thing
I gave him the whole of my coin collection.
total, gross, sum, entirety, aggregate
He settled for half of the bone but would have rather had the whole.

Antonyms: fraction, fragment, part, piece

wicked 🔊 *See* bad, dark, evil, mean, naughty, poisonous, wrong, behavior, hate, moral

wide
adjective
reaching across a large area
The three of us walked through the wide doorway together.
broad, vast, extensive, large, spacious

Antonym: narrow
adverb
as fully as possible
The window was wide open.
fully, completely, totally, entirely, wholly

Antonyms: barely, scarcely

widespread *See* common

width *See* shape

wild 🔊 🌍
adjective
1 living in a natural state; not tamed
There are wild animals in the jungle.
untamed, savage, undomesticated

2 without discipline
The teacher could not control the wild students.
unruly, disobedient, undisciplined, disorderly

The **wild** sea roars and lashes the granite cliffs below,
And round the misty islets the loud strong tempests blow.
—From THE SEA-FOWLER, by Mary Howitt (1799-1888)

3 out of control
He was wild with grief at the awful news.
frenzied, frantic, crazy, hysterical, insane, beside oneself

Antonyms: calm (3), collected (3), composed (3), cool (3), disciplined (2), domesticated (1), orderly (2), tame (1)

wilderness *See* forest, nature

will 🔊 *See* determination, leave, purpose

win
verb
1 to gain a victory
Our team won in the state basketball championship.
triumph, prevail, conquer, beat, overcome

2 to get through great effort
The slaves won their freedom after years of pain and struggle.

You can no more **win** a war than you can win an earthquake.
—Jeanette Rankin (1880-1973), U.S. Congresswoman

a
b
c
d
e
f
g
h
i
j
k
l
m
n
o
p
q
r
s
t
u
v
w
x
y
z

achieve, acquire, attain, earn, gain, obtain

Antonyms: fall (1), lose (1,2), relinquish (2), surrender (2)

noun

a victory in a competition

After losing several games, our team finally had a win.

triumph, victory, success

Antonyms: defeat, loss

wind

noun

air as it moves naturally over the surface of the earth

The wind blew papers across the park.

air *The cool air blew across the desert.*

breeze *The cool breeze refreshed us.*

draft *Dede closed the window because of the draft.*

gust *A sudden gust turned my umbrella inside out.*

zephyr *A gentle zephyr rustled the leaves.*

wing ◐ ◑ *See* fly, airplane, building, insect

wings ◐ ◑ *See* bird

winner

noun

a person who wins or succeeds

She was the winner of several races.

champion, champ, master, victor

Antonym: loser

winning *See* attractive

wire *See* line, electricity

wisdom *See* knowledge

wise ?

adjective

having good understanding and judgment

Years of experience have made her wise.

sage, prudent, shrewd, sensible

Antonyms: empty-headed, foolish

wish *See* desire, hope, like, pleasure, want

wither

verb

to dry up or wilt

The flowers in the garden withered from lack of rain.

shrivel, wilt, dry, parch, dehydrate

Antonyms: bloat, swell

wolf *See* eat

wonder

noun

1 a thing or event that causes admiration or amazement

The mountains in Oregon are natural wonders.

marvel, miracle, phenomenon

The plural of phenomenon is phenomena.

2 the feeling caused by something amazing

I gazed in wonder at the vast ocean.

awe, amazement, surprise, astonishment, admiration, wonderment

wonderful

adjective

causing feelings of wonder

She has made wonderful progress in school this year.

admirable, amazing, extraordinary, marvelous, sensational, awesome, fabulous, fantastic, incredible, spectacular, terrific

 Human Body ? Human Mind Everyday Life History and Culture Communication

The space shuttle launch was a marvelous sight.

wooden *See* stiff

woods *See* forest

wool *See* clothes

word

noun

1 a short remark or statement
I'd like to say a word about the recent election.
comment, remark, line, phrase, statement

2 a message; news
Lady Luella sent word of her arrival to the king.
news, message, notice, bulletin, report, tidings

3 a promise
He gave his word that he would be there for us.
assurance, pledge, promise, oath, guarantee, vow

verb

to choose words to express
She worded her thoughts carefully.
phrase *How should I phrase this introduction?*
articulate *Rosalie articulated her feelings clearly.*
put *Put it in your own words.*
express *I need help expressing this idea.*
craft *The senator crafted a statement for the press conference.*

word *See* message

work

noun

1 the use of energy or effort to achieve a result
It takes a lot of hard work to build a house.
labor, effort, toil, exertion

> The happiness of men consists in life. And life is in **labor**.
> —From
> *WHAT IS TO BE DONE?* by Leo, Count Tolstoy (1828-1910), Russian author

2 a task or project that uses such effort
He finished his work at the office.
job, project, task, assignment, chore, duty

3 something made or done as the result of an effort
His painting was a work of art.
creation, product, accomplishment, achievement, feat, deed

4 a job
She is seeking interesting work.
occupation, position, job, career, profession, vocation
Does your job require you to wear a suit every day?

verb

to run or act properly
This old car still works well.
function, operate, run, go

workers *See* office

working *See* busy

world

noun

1 the universe; everything that exists
creation *We looked all over creation for you!*
universe *Do you think Earth is the only planet in the universe with intelligent life?*
cosmos *Our solar system is a tiny part of the cosmos.*

2 the earth and all those who live on it
I would like to travel around the world someday.
Earth *For now, people live only on Earth.*
globe *My sister lives on the other side of the globe.*
planet *Will you help preserve the planet's resources?*

Do not capitalize **earth** when you write the word "the" before it: *Trees grow on the earth.* Do use a capital letter when referring to our planet without "the" before it: *The astronauts left Earth.*

3 all humans

 Living World   Physical World Natural Environment  Economy Government and Law

a
b
c
d
e
f
g
h
i
j
k
l
m
n
o
p
q
r
s
t
u
v
w
x
y
z

The world was amazed when men landed on the moon.

Earth *Earth hopes for peace.*

humanity *He devoted his life to the betterment of humanity.*

humankind *We must have respect for all of humankind.*

man *Man cannot live without air and water.*

mankind *It is up to mankind to make the world a safe place to live.*

society *Society will benefit from our efforts.*

4 a particular area or field, along with all the people and things having to do with it
Mexico is part of the western world.
The business world is competitive.
realm, sphere, arena, area, domain, field

worm ❶ *See* edge

worn ❷ *See* dull

worried ❓ *See* afraid

worry ❓
verb
1 to feel anxious, troubled, or uneasy
Don't worry, I'll take care of the problem.
fret, despair, brood, trouble

> These are the times that **try** men's souls.
> —From THE AMERICAN CRISIS, by Thomas Paine (1737-1809), British-American author

2 to cause to feel troubled or anxious
He worried his mother by staying out so late.
concern, distress, disturb, trouble, bother, dismay, upset, try
Her careless attitude concerns me.

Antonyms: calm (2), ease (1), relax (1), soothe (2)
noun
a cause of troubled or anxious feelings
Please try to forget your worries for a while.
anxiety, trouble, care, concern, woe, fear, problem

worship ❓
verb
to give devotion, honor, and love to
Many ancient people worshiped Mother Earth.
adore, glorify, honor, praise, pray to
He adores his grandmother and often brings her flowers.

worth
noun
1 the value of a thing or person
His mother's necklace is of great worth to him.
value *She places great value on education.*
merit *Fifi's actions have some merit to us.*
use *There is no use in fighting.*
usefulness *I can easily see the usefulness of this book.*
account *Riches are of little account to her.*
benefit *Your help will be a great benefit to us.*
importance *Lola's happiness is of great importance to me.*
significance *Don't waste time on matters of no significance.*

2 value in money or material
The necklace's worth is about one thousand dollars.
value, market, cost, price

worthy *See* acceptable

wound ❸
noun
a cut or other injury to a part of the body
injury, cut, sore, trauma, bruise

 Human Body   Human Mind   Everyday Life   History and Culture   Communication

verb

to injure or harm by cutting, piercing, or tearing the skin

He wounded his knee by falling on a rock.

hurt, injure, bruise, cut, damage, harm

See also: injury

wow *See* goodness

wreck
verb

1 to cause the destruction of

The fire wrecked two buildings.

His mean words wrecked their friendship.

demolish, destroy, ruin, total, devastate

2 to tear down or apart

The town wrecked two old houses to build a new library.

demolish, raze, level, tear down

Antonyms: build (2), construct (2), erect (2), rebuild (1), repair (1)

noun

what is left of something that has been destroyed

The once beautiful ship is now just an old wreck on the bottom of the lake.

ruins, wreckage, debris, remains

See also: destroy

wrinkle
noun

a fold or ridge on an otherwise flat surface

Please iron the wrinkles out of my gown.

People get wrinkles as they grow old.

crease, crumple, pucker, crinkle, fold, pleat, ridge

verb

to make or cause folds or ridges in

The baby wrinkled her nose at the smell of the fish.

The kitten sat on my lap and wrinkled my skirt.

crease, crinkle, crumple, pucker, furrow

Antonyms: flatten, iron, level, smooth

write
verb

1 to form on a surface with a pen, pencil, typewriter, or other instrument

Write your name on the paper.

jot, scrawl, scribble, inscribe

2 to express or record by writing

She wrote her ideas in a notebook.

draft, pen, draw up, put down

3 to be the author or composer of

Jack wrote the melody, and Jill wrote the lyrics.

pen, author, compose, draft

writer
noun

one whose job is to write books, articles, poems, or other materials

some kinds of writers
author, poet, novelist, essayist, journalist, reporter, correspondent, columnist, critic, dramatist, playwright, screenwriter

written *See* communication, language, tradition

wrong
adjective

1 not true or correct

Your answer is wrong.

false, inaccurate, incorrect, mistaken, untrue, off base

2 not moral or good

Murder is wrong.

bad, immoral, evil, wicked

3 not proper or suited

We added the wrong ingredients.

He chose the wrong moment to speak.

improper, inappropriate, unsuitable, incorrect

> He lies like a hedgehog rolled up the **wrong** way, Tormenting himself with his prickles.
> --From HER DREAM, by Thomas Hood (1799-1845), British poet.

a
b
c
d
e
f
g
h
i
j
k
l
m
n
o
p
q
r
s
t
u
v
w
x
y
z

4 **not working or operating properly**
*There is something
wrong with my car.*
amiss, on the blink, out
of whack

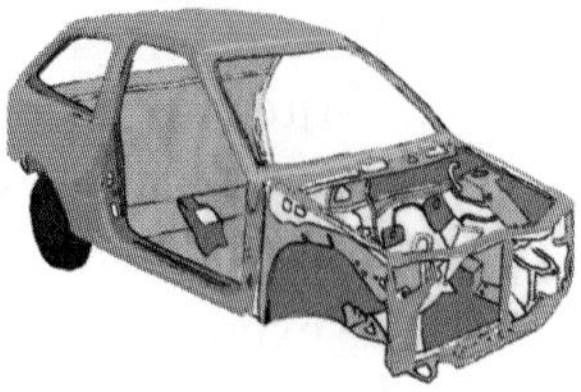

Antonyms:
accurate (1),
appropriate (3),
correct (1), good (2), proper (3), true (1)

verb
to treat badly
He was wronged by his friend.
abuse, mistreat, misuse, persecute

Human Body   Human Mind   Everyday Life   History and Culture   Communication

X

verb

    1 to indicate with a mark shaped like the letter "x"

Xavier x'ed the box that said "boy".

cross, mark, check, tick

    2 to cross out, often with a mark shaped like the letter "x"

Maxie x'ed out the misspelled word on her paper.

cross, scratch, cancel

 Living World
 Physical World
Natural Environment
 Economy
Government and Law

yard
noun

an open area next to a house or other building
We have trees and flowers in our yard.
Students play in the school yard.
lawn, grounds, courtyard, field

yet *See* **still**

yield *See* **bear, lose, produce, production**

young ⓘ
adjective

at an early stage of life or growth
My sister is still a young child.
juvenile *The juvenile elephants played in the mud.*
immature *Immature apples taste sour.*
infant *He puts a lot of time into his infant business.*

Antonym: old

noun

offspring that have been recently born
The mother gorilla takes care of her young.
offspring, litter, brood, baby, child

See also: youngster

youngster
noun

a young person; child
The playground is full of youngsters every Saturday morning.
child, youth, adolescent, baby, infant, juvenile, teen-ager, toddler, kid, tot

Antonyms: adult, elder, oldster

youth *See* **child, kid, youngster, life**

A B C D E F G H I J K L M N O P Q R S T U V W X Y Z

 Living World Physical World Natural Environment Economy Government and Law

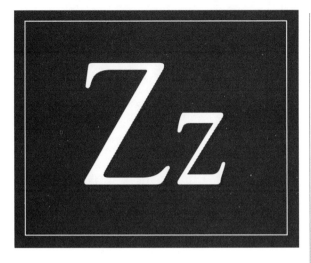

zeal

noun

> great enthusiasm for a person or cause
> *The leader's followers were filled with zeal.*
> *Her zeal for helping the poor was known by everyone in the community.*

ardor *The crowd showed their ardor for the candidate.*

enthusiasm *He has more enthusiasm for playing sports than for anything else.*

fervor *His fervor to get ahead seemed boundless.*

fever *The kids were in a fever about the latest action movie.*

fire *There was fire in his eyes when he talked about sailing.*

passion *Swimming is his passion.*

> *Antonyms:* apathy, indifference, reluctance
> *See also:* passion

zero

noun

> nothing
> *With her family safe and happy, her worries were zero.*

none, nothing, nil, naught, nada, zip, zilch, zot

Nil and **naught** are in common use in Britain, and **nada** is a Spanish word. **Nada, zip, zilch,** and **zot** are informal. They are used in everyday speech and writing but are not suitable for a formal paper or presentation.

> *Antonyms:* everything, infinity, totality

Writing Tip: Emphasis

To emphasize something means to draw attention to its importance. Knowing how to use emphasis in your writing can help you get your message across. One way to emphasize a word is to use very or really before it: *Those ants are really, really small. Bobo was very angry at Lulu.* But using words like *very, really, quite, rather,* and so on can, in fact, draw attention away from the word you are trying to emphasize. They slow the reader down and keep her from getting to your meaning.

An effective way to show emphasis is to use an unusual, uncommon word. Uncommon words are great attention-getters, and your thesaurus will help you find the right one. Look up **small** to find a word that emphasizes the smallness of those ants—perhaps **tiny** or **minuscule**. Look up **angry** to find a word that conveys how angry Bobo was—perhaps **furious** or **raging**. Learning new words and using them for emphasis will make you a better writer.

A B C D E F G H I J K L M N O P Q R S T U V W X Y **Z**

a
b
c
d
e
f
g
h
i
j
k
l
m
n
o
p
q
r
s
t
u
v
w
x
y
z

adjective

being none or nothing in number or quantity

The store's new owners promised zero change in prices.

no, null, nonexistent

Antonyms: countless, infinite

zest

noun

a sense of great pleasure or enjoyment

The old woman's zest for living made her seem much younger.

appetite, gusto, passion, relish, zeal

Antonyms: apathy, displeasure, distaste

See also: passion

zip

noun

(**informal**) energy or pep

At eighty years old, she is still full of zip.

bounce *There was a bounce in her step as she left for home.*

energy *He spoke with energy on the subject of boat building.*

go *The old horse still has a lot of go in her.*

life *He is full of life.*

liveliness *The puppies were full of liveliness.*

pep *He has a lot of pep for his age.*

spirit *The colt showed a lot of spirit as it raced across the pasture.*

vigor *He is full of vigor, even at eighty years of age.*

Antonyms: lethargy, lifelessness, sluggishness

See also: energy

zone *See* area, patch, territory

 Human Body

? Human Mind

Everyday Life

History and Culture

Communication

Acknowledgments

Many talented people and organizations contributed to this project. Wordsmyth would like to acknowledge the photography of Douglas J. Davenport and the illustrations by Keren Cohen, Jim Houghton, J.M. Barringer, Robert (Mac) Myers, Chris Jung and Brian Dudla. These images make this reference book a unique work of art. Other images are from the collections of NASA, Getty Photo Collection, U.S. Department of Defense, Hemera Photo Collection, ClickArt Collection, Art Explosion, and The McGraw-Hill Companies.